FOR WOMEN AND GIRLS ONLY

For Women and Girls Only

*Reshaping Jewish Orthodoxy Through
the Arts in the Digital Age*

Jessica Roda

NEW YORK UNIVERSITY PRESS
New York

NEW YORK UNIVERSITY PRESS
New York
www.nyupress.org

Library of Congress Cataloging-in-Publication Data
Names: Roda, Jessica, author.
Title: For women and girls only : reshaping Jewish Orthodoxy
through the arts in the digital age / Jessica Roda.
Description: New York : New York University Press, 2024. |
Includes bibliographical references and index.
Identifiers: LCCN 2023020454 | ISBN 9781479809752 (hardback) | ISBN 9781479809820
(ebook) | ISBN 9781479809790 (ebook other)
Subjects: LCSH: Ultra-Orthodox Jewish women—Intellectual life. | Jewish women artists—
New York (State)—21st century | Jewish women artists—Canada—Montreal—21st century. |
Media literacy—Social aspects—Judaism. | Mass media—Religious aspects—Judaism. |
Orthodox Judaism.
Classification: LCC HQ1172 .R63 2024 | DDC 305.48/8924—dc23/eng/20230515
LC record available at https://lccn.loc.gov/2023020454

This book is printed on acid-free paper, and its binding materials are chosen for strength and durability. We strive to use environmentally responsible suppliers and materials to the greatest extent possible in publishing our books.

Manufactured in the United States of America

10 9 8 7 6 5 4 3 2 1

Also available as an ebook

To my son, Matteo,
for teaching me about
resilience, patience, and love!

CONTENTS

NOTE ON TRANSLITERATION AND TRANSLATION

For the transliteration of Yiddish and Loshn Koydesh I used the Yivo Institute for Jewish Research system and occasionally modified it to make it easier for English readers. The transliteration may differ from the Hasidic or Litvish ones, but this is of minimal concern, as the pronunciation may also differ from one community to another. For instance, "צניעות" has been transliterated as "*tsnius*" and "שבת" as "*shabbes*." The terms are italicized, transliterated, and translated as they appear for the first time in the text.

ACKNOWLEDGMENTS

Writing is driven by a profound paradox. Often lived as an experience of solitude, it is also the result of exchange and collaboration with many actors and organizations, without which the process would be impossible. Because I am a mother navigating between multiple countries and spaces, doing ethnography and writing this second book took a village. I am thankful to all the people and institutions who made this project possible. The lines below are attempts to express my gratitude, but the words will never do full justice . . .

This book is the result of an ethnography built on generosity, collaborations, and friendships with dozens of girls and women, as well as men, who trusted me to share their life stories and to open the doors of their homes, institutions, schools, and private circles. This project started in Montreal and ended in Washington, DC, with constant stops in New York City and many visits to Europe, Brazil, and Israel/Palestine. First, I would like to thank all the individuals who gave me access to their worlds, some of whom became my closest friends and family by choice. It has been a privilege to work all these years alongside you.

Special thanks are owed to Malky Goldman, whose expertise, experience, and critical thoughts about the making of the arts, both inside and outside Orthodoxy, were an inimitable resource. Beyond her brilliant, nuanced, and refined analysis of the multiple social and cultural universes she lives in, Malky became one of my closest friends and kin, constantly reminding me of the distorted and blurred boundaries between the personal and professional life of the anthropologist. Malky and Shmuly created an irreplaceable home in New York City, and I am indebted for being part of it.

From the moment I entered the home of Rivka, Hasidic life grew into a place of sound, color, and taste, full of complexities. The relationship we were able to build thanks to our common interest in and passion for music confirmed the power of the arts to defeat boundaries and cultivate closeness and familiarity. I am also thankful to her children, her husband, and her extended family, for always being curious about my work and for giving me space in their lives.

Malky Weingarten has been a tremendous supporter and endless respondent to this project. She included me on sets and introduced me to many other women artists and her closest friends. It has been a treat to have you discuss your position as an artist in your community with my students at Georgetown University, with great passion and humility. I express my deepest gratitude for everything you have done to facilitate this research.

Melissa Weisz was one of the first artists I encountered who left the community. I saw her transforming her artistic life as well as her discourse about Orthodoxy, now engaged in activism against antisemitism. Melissa always responded with generosity to my requests and opened many doors. I am deeply thankful to her for agreeing to meet me that afternoon in 2016. Our meeting changed the trajectory of my research.

I would like to also thank Rifka Wein Harris for sharing her experience as a mother of a talented girl navigating the music world within and outside Orthodoxy. It has been an honor to follow your journey with Abby and to count yourself as my friend.

I am also grateful to Franciska Kosman for her countless insights into the *frum* artistic world, and for the attention she gave to my work. It has been a privilege to communicate with you on your podcast and to learn about your journey.

To Devorah Schwartz and Dobby Baum for responding to my requests from day one. Their generosity and enthusiasm have been priceless. Collaborating with both of them and following their respective rise has been a treat.

Many other women and girls were central to this project, helpful, cooperative, generous, and patient. I want to give much-deserved credit to all of them as they enable me to understand the worlds of Orthodoxy in ways I could have never imagined. To respect their privacy, I cannot thank all of them by their full names. Deborah Ratti introduced me to Mrs. Glustein in Montreal, and I started my adventure teaching women in the community. During this year, these women offered a unique understanding of the Orthodox world, specifically the Hasidic. Among them, Malky Oberlander became a friend. Our rich phone or in-person exchanges nourish several parts of this book. Chaya Libby, Faigy Zelcer, Hudy Herzog, Michal Hartman, Mindy Pollak, Miri, Miriam Leah Gamliel, Nechi, Ruchele, Ruchy, Suri, Tzortele, and Ylana were tremendous support. In New York, Adina Miles-Sash, Beatrice Weber, Bracha Jaffe, Chany Rosengarten, Chava Rosenbaum, Chaya Sara Schlussel, Chayala Neuhaus, Dalia Shusterman, Emily Cheeger, Leah, Leah Forster, Libby Pollak, Mimi Friedman, Nechama Cohen, Rikki Rose, Rochelle Miller, Shaindy Antelis-Schorr, Shaindy Plotzer, Toby, and Tzivia Kay. On the other side of the country, Robin Garbose gave me a unique glimpse into her creative world.

I also had the privilege to exchange with men and learn about Orthodoxy from their gendered point of view. They gave me tremendous assistance in refining and nuancing my understanding of their communities and lifestyle. Some of them read my work, commented, and criticized it. They gave me access to knowledge that complemented what I have learned alongside women. Avi Fishoff, Chaim Miller, Gershy Schwarcz Isaac Schoenfeld, Lipa Schmeltzer, Meyer Labin, Moshe Wigder, Pinny Segal Landau, Simcha Weinstein, Yakov Horowitz, Yanky Lemmer, Yossi Krausz, and Ysoscher Katz are some of them. There are many others I can't name for privacy reasons, but I know they will recognize themselves.

At the beginning of my research, I encountered many people who left the community. In Montreal, the filmmaker Eric Scott was my entry door. He introduced me to Joey Tanny, Levi Riven, and Mendy Pape, with whom I participated in the adventure of building a community of support for people leaving Orthodoxy, an adventure that led me to encounter many audacious and courageous people and to connect with founders and members of organizations such as Footsteps, OTD-Meetups, Unchained at Last, and Makom from Jews in the City. I am grateful to all of them for their time and dedication to this research.

This book is also the product of various institutional supports, exchanges, debates, care, and mentorships. I am indebted to terrific scholars who inspired me to think differently and pushed my writing in new directions. From the moment I first worked with Erica Lehrer as a postdoctoral fellow in 2015, she has served as a constant source of inspiration, a tremendous mentor, and a connector of people. She became a friend I continuously admire, not only for her work but for her

generosity and honesty. She is a role model as a woman and as an anthropologist. Ayala Fader has served as an inspiration for scholarship
and academic generosity since I first reached out to her many years ago.
I am grateful to her for her constant guidance and invaluable expertise.
Jonathan Boyarin, whose work I had long praised, graciously agreed to
meet at the very beginning of my research. I am thankful for his time,
for the stimulating and engaging debate, and for guiding me throughout
the years. He provided an example of blurring boundaries, of love for
fieldwork and the people we are writing about, and of discussing and
exploring the intricate emotions traversed by the ethnographers. Naomi
Seidman inspired me with her writing but also her brilliant performance
and provocative sense of humor. As a great enthusiast of my research,
she inspired the title of this book at the end of a long day discussing my
manuscript. I will always be thankful. I also have had the great honor to
count ethnomusicologists Kay Kaufman Shelemay and Anne Rasmussen
as irreplaceable interlocutors. I became an ethnomusicologist by reading their absorbing work and having both discuss my work has been
an exceptional gift. Marcin Wodzinski for transmitting his passion and
dedication to Hasidic life. To Edwin Seroussi for his long-term friendship and mentorship. My masters who brought me where I am today,
Francois Picard, Monique Desroches, and Gilles Bibeau—I thank them
for initiating me to fieldwork with passion, love, and humility, and for
transmitting to me the centrality of doubt to better growth. For sharing materials, works in progress, valuable feedback, and interest, I am
thankful to Beatrice De Gasquet, Christopher Silver, Gaby Abramac,
Gordon Dale, Henry Bial, Hervé Roten, Jeremiah Lockwood, Julien
Mallet, Laura Yares, Lea Taragin-Zeller, Mark Kligman, Martine Cohen,
Michal Kravel-Tovi, Michal Raucher, Nadia Malinovich, Naomi Cohn
Zentner, Orit Avishai, Sam Shuman, Sasha Goldstein-Sabbah, Talia
Bachir-Loopuyt, and Tanya Zion-Waldoks.

From the book proposal to the final version of the manuscript, I have
derived benefits from trying out writing and thinking at a series of research groups and workshops. At the New York Working Group on Jewish Orthodoxy, the exchanges on various works-in-progress enriched
my thoughts. At Georgetown University, members and affiliates of the
Americas Initiatives, the Department of Anthropology, the Center for
Jewish Civilization, and the Music Working Group offered vital support.

I owe a special thanks to the Mortara Center, to Abraham Newman and Jenna Zabarah for organizing my manuscript workshop; this book would not have been the same without this exceptional opportunity. Among colleagues and staff, I would like to thank Benjamin Harbert, Brittany Fried, Carole Sargent, Denise Brennan, Elizabeth Saunders, Emily Mendenhall, Fida Adely, Fred Hosken, Jay Hammond, Jenny Laguardo, Jocelyn Flores, Kate Chandler, Katherine Benton-Cohen, Katrin Sieg, Ken Opalo, Robynn Stilwell, and Shiloh Krupar for engaging with my work in a thought-provoking way. The online working group Ethnographic Disruptions in Jewish Studies, the Collectif Judaité in Canada, the Groupes Genre, Religions, Laicité (CNRS, France), the Oxford Summer Institute on Modern & Contemporary Judaism, the Unité de recherche migrations et société of Université de Paris, Université de Tours (Unité de Recherche Interactions Culturelles et Discursives), the American Studies Colloquium Series at the University of Warsaw, the Tadeusz Taube Department of Jewish Studies at the University of Wroclaw, the Department of Jewish Studies at the Séminaire d'études ethnomusicologique of Sorbonne University, the Jewish American Music Working Group, the Institute for Gender, Sexuality, and Feminist Studies at McGill University, the Heyman Center and the Institute for Religion, Culture, and Public Life at Columbia University—thank you to the organizers of and participants in these working groups and centers for offering insightful suggestions on my work.

I started this research as a postdoctoral fellow, and this book was made possible with the support of many institutions. I extend my thanks to the readers of my work on all these committees I applied for to support the ethnography and the writing process: the Canadian Social Sciences and Humanities Research Council, the Department of Jewish Studies at McGill University, the Department of Jewish Studies at Fordham University, the McGill Institute for the Study of Canada, the Heyman Center at Columbia University, Georgetown University, the Mortara Center for International Studies, and the Association for Jewish Studies. Portions of the Georgetown University funding, including a grant from the Mortara Center, have enabled me to work with several outstanding graduate and undergraduate research assistants. I thank Aashia Bose, Charlotte Rosenblaum, Celine Park, Joshua Bernard-Pearl, Nate Rowe, and Rohan Somji for their great work. For her hard labor, patience, curiosity, and dedication to this book until the end, I am ever so appreciative of Sofia Doroshenko—the best research assistant anyone could ever ask for. To Alexandra Stankovich, my thanks are extended for being the most engaged, dedicated, and perfectionist PhD student any professor could hope for.

At NYU Press, I want to thank the entire editorial team, especially Jennifer Hammer, for taking this project at its very early stage, for believing in the amplification of these women's voices, and for bringing it to the world. Jennifer has been constantly present and offered me unmatched support throughout the writing process. My gratitude also extends to the anonymous reviewers.

This project has also been steered into a safe harbor thanks to new and long-standing friendships in the continent and across the globe. In Washington, DC, I am indebted to the ones who made my transition easy and supported me throughout my ethnography and the writing process. To Anna Sommer, who became not only a wonderful teammate and colleague but a cherished friend—I cannot wait to see the development of joint projects from both sides of the Atlantic, and our boys growing up together and making fun of us. For his provocative thoughts, constant support, and warm welcome at the Center for Jewish Civilization, Jacques Berlinerblau. To Bethania Michael for her good spirits, friendship, and assistance from the beginning to the end of the project. Sarah Newman for the meaningful exchanges and for making DC a fun place to live—I am grateful that our paths crossed that night in May 2019. Nawar Shahar for her constant support, presence, and creating a home for me and my family. Some people touch you for intellectual and emotional reasons, and understand you beyond words; Marta Barcelos is one of them. Our closeness and amity grant me the ability to finalize this project; thank you for always pushing me, for reminding me to take breaks, and for always being present, even in the most difficult times.

Thanks to Soraya Batmanghelichi for constantly being ready to read my work, and for becoming a true friend. Despite the ocean and time zones separating us, our connection remains intact, and your support has been priceless. For accompanying me from the first to the last lines of this manuscript, Karolina Krasuska and Ronnie Olesker, my writing partners. Karolina, what a great idea you had to reach out to both of us that summer of 2020; that email changed everything! My book would not have been written without you and our safe intellectual and emotional virtual space; ladies, you simply rock! We succeeded in finding something beautiful, powerful, and meaningful during one of the most challenging times of the pandemic! For her friendship and curiosity, and for never doubting the interest in my work, Nadine Blumer. While writing some of the chapters of the book, Nadine, Julien, and Munia made my Montreal winter fun, something I could not have imagined myself saying. To Daniela Moisa, my ally and longtime friend—our last decade has been particularly enlivened and tumultuous; I can't wait to see the next one! My French comrade-in-arms with whom I reunited after almost ten years after we lost touch, Geraldine Gudefin—our bond transcends all the possible boundaries. Laura Jordan Gonzalez, her long-term amity is ever so sustaining. Let us always find a way to meet somewhere around the globe. The Silvers for their friendship and great advice regarding my transition to the United States. To Valentina Gaddi, who became not only a great partner in the Montreal fieldwork but also a friend. I am happy that you have changed your mind about friendship and ethnography! Raphaelle Bouix and Pauline Ouin, my childhood friends that I miss too often, for keeping our ties intact over the years.

For bringing me where I am today, my parents. They taught me curiosity, audacity, and hard work. I know I would have had wonderful exchanges with my father about the book and that he would have read it with great passion. There is not a day that I do not think about him. My mother has been an example and model of perseverance and determination, always allowing and inspiring me to search for the person I wanted to be. To my brother and sister-in-law for their encouragement and for having all the cousins together during some of my field trips. To Teresa, for coming so many times to Paris, Berlin, Montreal, and Washington, DC, looking after her grandson while I was in the field, at conferences, teaching, or writing, but also for her care, advice, time, generosity, patience, and for the long hours spent discussing her passion for life, for the world, and for family. The love and support of Andre. I will always be thankful for everything he has done for our family, for the copious amount of time he spent reading my work, for calling me out on my broken written and spoken English, and for always encouraging me to follow my passions. This book would not have existed without him.

My last words are for my son, Matteo. For his humor, intelligence, curiosity, and patience. Throughout the years, we crossed oceans, spaces, and universes so many times together; I hope to have transmitted to you the thirst for knowledge, for learning about differences, and for finding joy in everyday life. This book is for you, for the man you will become, to be able to comprehend the intricacies of the worlds around you, and of all the women and girls that you will encounter . . .

Prelude

Departure: A Story of Origins

This book tells the story of ultra-Orthodox and former ultra-Orthodox Jewish women in New York City and Montreal who defy expectations about their roles in liberal and religious societies. It explores and challenges beliefs that they serve solely as mothers, wives, and, in the case of those who have left their communities, pariahs. With their use of the arts and technology, these women are reshaping the face of Orthodoxy and Jewishness more broadly—some from within their communities, others from outside. As ultra-Orthodoxy continues to grow exponentially, these women will play a vital part in their diasporic community's future, influencing perceptions of Jewishness in North America and beyond.

This book emerged at the intersection of several academic and personal interests as well as experiences, including my search for a ritualized practice of Judaism, an interest in the public image of marginal and visible Jews, and a critical reflection on the meaning of secularism and religiosity spurred once I moved from French Guiana to Paris in 2001, and then to Montreal in 2010. Most importantly, it began as a voyage whose terminus was not quite known—unlike my previous work, where I knew what I wanted to investigate, understand, and write about. Inspired by Brazilian anthropologist Mariza Peirano's analysis of the exploration of alterity in the context of anthropology at home, I offer this scene of departure as a prefatory note to situate myself within this ethnographic study of women and the arts. I hope that it serves to lay bare the continuing process of my conflicted journey navigating alterity so close to home, and how the process of writing about the arts unfolds in an unpredictable trajectory. Someone may wonder why I label this prelude "departure" instead of "arrival," which has been the convention in anthropology since the birth of the discipline. Encountering "radical otherness" at home, to echo Peirano, was not an arrival but instead a departure from my former understandings of religiosity, women, and the arts.

The story of my encounter with ultra-Orthodoxy began in 2015 as part of a personal search for "traditional Judaism" after the sudden death of two loved ones. After investigating the making of Jewish heritage by people very much like myself—those seeking a "lost" Jewishness through explorations of history, culture, and the arts—I now aspired to explore alterity, to engage in an ethnography that would take me away from home, away from the comfort of my belief systems. After five years of living in Montreal and discovering the ethnic, racial, and linguistic diversity that the metropolis offered, I became quite curious about the insular world of Hasidism, a movement within ultra-Orthodox Judaism. Hasidic Jews lived a few blocks from my home. Nevertheless, I knew very little about them apart from how they were portrayed and described in academic literature, media, popular culture, and liberal Jewish circles. I imagined their culture as a deeply ritualized version of Judaism, one in which I would encounter individuals whose ancestors, unlike my own, had not abandoned their Jewish identity to fit into secular society. I wanted to access this local community that was so strongly Orientalized, to borrow from Edward Said's critique of Western constructions of the "East" as backward, inferior, and in need of saving due to its self-seclusion and eschewal of modernity and Western secularism.

This personal search intersected with an interest in the political role of Jewishness—and more specifically, of Jews marginal to mainstream North American Jewish structures and establishment—when represented in public. My previous work examined the representation of Jewishness among Jews who migrated from the Ottoman Empire to France, as well as from Morocco to Canada, wherein the promotion of their heritage reinforced community cohesion and created dialogues with other minorities as well as the majority. Now, I was drawn toward another mode of representation of Jewishness, one rooted in conservative religiosity, communitarianism, gender segregation, and mysticism. I wanted to work with a Jewish minority that challenged the public image of Jewishness in relation to liberalism and Western secularism. As a secular Jewish woman who decides when and to whom I express my Jewishness, I had to reexamine my assumptions about the impact of Jewishness in public, and my baseline belief that minorities participate in their public representation and engage in dialogue with the majority. The ultra-Orthodox Jewish community does not traditionally participate in or respond to its representation in mainstream media. Instead of working with those who are invested in their public image, I wished to explore the Jewish universe from a different vantage point, one that secludes itself even from other Jews and yet has a tremendous impact on the collective imagination of Jewishness in twenty-first-century North American society, as the increased media coverage of ultra-Orthodox Jews underlines.

In the process of questioning the public representations of Jewishness through the experience of ultra-Orthodox Jews, I witnessed how local politics drastically impacted the way Hasidic Jews, and especially Hasidic women, were exposed to public criticism. When the nationalist Parti Québécois took power in 2012 and introduced the Quebec Charter of Values—also known as the Charter of Secularism (*Charte de la laïcité*)—I became increasingly captivated by Quebec political life and, more importantly, the public image and social life of religious minorities in North America, all of which echoed the more publicized controversies over *laïcité* unfolding on the other side of the Atlantic. The charter targeted visible religious minorities, prohibiting those who worked in the public sector from wearing or displaying religious symbols. This was often described as an anti-Muslim act, but Jews and Sikhs also protested the controversial bill. Debates about the charter resembled those concerning the long-standing issue of reasonable accommodation, focusing on modifying or adjusting bylaws to accommodate individuals or groups facing discrimination based on religion. The charter died in March 2014, but it created an enduring political tumult over the role of religiosity in Quebec society.

In September of that same year, the Toronto International Film Festival designated *Félix and Meira*, a film written by Maxime Giroux and Alexandre Laferrière about the struggles of a Hasidic woman in her community, the best Canadian film of the year, and selected it as the Canadian entry for Best Foreign Language Film at the eighty-eighth Academy Awards. *Félix and Meira* tells the story of a woman, oppressed in her Montreal Hasidic community, encountering a secular Quebecois man who introduces her to modernity, secular music, jeans, dance parties, bars, and Manhattan night life. The film reinforced the message of the Quebec Charter of Values and its supporters, advocating a society in which religion and the state were completely separated. While the writers were outsiders to the

Hasidic community, they hired two former Hasidic Jews as consultants and actors in an effort to guarantee an insider take on the representation.

I had been puzzled by the tension between secularism and religiosity that animated Quebec society, by the politicization of religious women's bodies—notably of Muslim women—and the repetitive discourse that "Muslim women needed to be saved" regularly available in the media at that time. I wanted to encounter Jewish men and women who embodied what I perceived as a traditional ritualized version of Judaism in order to understand their point of view on such public representations of religiosity. My access started with *former* ultra-Orthodox Jews in Montreal (also known as exiters or OTD, "off the *derekh*") who sought to share their experience and use it to engender professional and economic opportunities outside of their community. I became a board member of an organization supporting people in transition to secular society and advocated for their cause. Some individuals still resided in the ultra-Orthodox community, hiding their secret interactions with the secular world, while others had cut their ties. Many remained connected to their friends and family without really knowing how to tell them about their new lives, or simply did not want to discuss their new selves. Many were originally from New York City or had family there, and I followed them on trips across the border. Over time, I was able to participate in the world in which they had grown up, in Montreal and New York City, thanks to various connections.

In 2017, while I was at a congress in Jerusalem, I met Rebecca, a French sociologist who was teaching a group of women from various Orthodox and ultra-Orthodox communities in Montreal as part of a program in social work and was now moving to New York City. She gave my name to the director of the program as someone who might replace her. Following an interview with the director, I began spending my Sunday mornings and Wednesday evenings teaching socio-anthropology to these women. For one year, the class—which served as a real laboratory for all of us—constantly challenged me on the way we as anthropologists interact with our fieldwork, and how we should translate our knowledge and our responsibility for doing it. I chose topics I thought might challenge their assumptions and my own assumptions about them and their response to such topics: LGBTQ rights, the difference between gender and sex, the history of the Enlightenment, and the concept of social construction. I grew there as a person, a pedagogue, a woman, an ethnographer, and a scholar. I also taught piano and French to several girls, enjoying rich exchanges with talented and curious teenagers. Throughout the years 2015–2021, I met many other women in Montreal and New York, some of whom I became very close with and count as my friends.

During this period, I noticed the increased mediatization of ultra-Orthodox life in streaming film platforms as well as the secular mainstream press through the voices of exiters—in reality shows, television series, documentaries, and novels. In this representation of ultra-Orthodoxy through fiction and nonfiction, women were often central, perpetuating a stereotype of the "oppressed woman," a representation that applied even to those women who had left their communities. These media present the women as lacking autonomy, agency, and creativity while they remain in their community, using hair covering such as a *sheytl* (wig) or *shpitzel* (headscarf worn in most conservative Hasidic families)—which Orthodox women wear after their marriage for modesty purposes—as a symbol of oppression, similar to the way many people often view the Muslim *hijab*. In these representations, the ultra-Orthodox women always depend on their husbands and are never entrepreneurs, celebrities, or creators, while those who have left Orthodoxy embody only rejection of family and community. These images were not evocative of the complex realities I had observed since 2015 in my interactions with both groups of women. I have met ultra-Orthodox women and former ultra-Orthodox women in fortuitous places and in roles unexpected by both societies, the strictly religious and the secular. I wanted to investigate further their positionalities and the impact of these on their individual and collective lives, to complicate mainstream secular narratives. As an ethnomusicologist, former pianist, flutist, and dancer, I was particularly intrigued by ultra-Orthodox women's unpredicted roles as celebrities in the arts on stage, on screen, and online, for audiences of women and girls only. I felt the need to examine these new role models, which appeared neither in the academic literature nor in public debate and which contradict the established boundaries between public and private space that religious norms imposed on the exhibition of ultra-Orthodox Jewish women and the ones who left.

I engaged with two types of lived artistic experiences. The first was produced by women who had left ultra-Orthodoxy, and included their struggles in navigating the public space, reinventing themselves as artists in the secular entertainment industry, and trying to reshape the public image of

Orthodoxy. I then immersed myself in the technological art worlds created by ultra-Orthodox women inside their community. I met women and girls dancing in amateur and professional private productions of all sizes, building home recording studios and art schools, and producing movies, music videos, and social media content. In addition to exploring this *private* world, I traced the connections between it and the *public* art worlds. These intertwined feminine spaces do include men, but men are not central to the story I am writing here. The men whom I met were husbands, brothers, collaborators, advisers, clients, and friends of the women I decided to write about. They are peripheral to what I have been observing, even though they appear as inspirational to, supportive of, or opposed to the decisions these women made for their careers in the arts.

My collaboration with ultra-Orthodox and formerly ultra-Orthodox women put me in the company of many other secular and liberal individuals, both Jews and non-Jews, from Montreal, New York, and beyond, who were similarly intrigued by this secluded world that defines itself as an alternative to modernity. My examination of the making of today's ultra-Orthodoxy, not through textual or rabbinical regulations but through the bodies and voices of these arts-involved women, led me to reflect on the broader role of the arts as a form of agency and social change in the digital age. Approaching this culture through artistic performances enabled me not only to capture a dynamic present but to imagine the future and rethink authority, norms, agency, and autonomy in North American society. While the arts are not the only realm in which women participate in the making and reshaping of Orthodoxy, these spaces illuminate the tumultuous changes affected by the 2.0 digital age that implements a global participative online culture.

Such reflections encouraged me to keep returning to women's circles I have participated in with an openness to our relatedness and affinity, expanding my sense of belonging. I approached ultra-Orthodoxy in search of ritual and tradition, to find a counterbalance to modernity, but I found women engaged in searches of their own. Today, when both women who remain in the ultra-Orthodox world and those who have left call me family, I know that the intricacies of these feminine worlds—of my own worlds and the way I share them with these women, of the messiness and paradoxes that pervade our lives—are at the center of the story I wanted to write.

1

The Translocal Ethnographer

Encountering Ultra-Orthodox Women in the Arts

The ethnographer, like the artist, is engaged in a special kind of vision quest through which a specific interpretation of the human condition, an entire sensibility, is forged. Our medium, our canvas, is "the field," a place both proximate and intimate as well as forever distant and unknowably "other." In the act of "writing culture," what emerges is always a highly subjective, partial, and fragmentary—but also deeply felt and personal—record of human lives based on eyewitness and testimony.
—Nancy Scheper-Hughes, "Death without Weeping: The Violence of Everyday Life in Brazil"

It feels like only yesterday when I met Goldie for the first time in Montreal. I was Goldie's piano teacher from 2016 to 2017, and since then, a shared love of music has sustained our friendship. I witnessed Goldie growing up, as she developed from a shy, talented, and artistic child to a confident woman, full of grace and elegance, working full-time as an administrative assistant, enrolled in college, singing, acting, and playing the piano informally, as well as recording her music in a home studio owned by a Montreal Hasidic woman, Rochel. Rochel advertises her music business in the local Hasidic press—without depicting any female faces, as is the norm in ultra-Orthodox media.[1] Like all the girls and women in their Hasidic communities, Goldie and Rochel are guided by a diverse range of norms of *tsnius*, translated as "modesty," which prevent them from publicizing their artistic activity in front of men except their siblings and parents.

From the first time we met, at her parents' home for a *shabbes* in May 2016, Goldie set herself apart. After she lit the candle with her mother,

Rivka, I started a conversation about my childhood in French Guiana, my background in the arts, and my appreciation of Yiddish and Hasidic music. While Goldie's siblings were moving in and out of the living room, she herself was very attentive to the conversation, looking at me with a mix of curiosity, suspicion, and interest, certainly puzzled by my presence as a Jewish artist who was different from her. Rivka talked to me about her women's singing group, her love for painting, her desire to dedicate more time to her hobbies once the kids grew older, and her three girls' wish to learn the piano. She also gave me a tour of the house, exhibiting with pride the still-life paintings by her husband's talented grandmother, who had decorated their apartment. She then asked me about my research, and I told her that I wanted to explore the Hasidic women's artistic space, since many people present Hasidic women as unable to express themselves artistically and as subjugated to men. Rivka objected:

> People look at us, *frum* [observant or pious] women,[2] as oppressed, uneducated, and uncreative, but they are wrong. There are plenty of talented and artistic women in our communities; we just do not expose it publicly to prevent men from accessing it. It is also a different way to look at the arts, but we also have our own female dancers, singers, composers, and filmmakers collaborating in the US, Canada, Israel, and Europe. They just create differently because they are guided by the law of the Torah.

Rivka's comments brought a different perspective on the Hasidic feminine art world, reflecting on ways to define and express artistic creativity without exposing names, faces, and bodies.

Once Rivka's husband arrived from *shul* (synagogue) and we started the meal, the sounds of the family's *shabbes* illustrated Rivka's comment on female talent and expression. The couple's sons and daughters alternated between singing in unison and singing in harmony. Goldie and her sisters displayed no timidity; their bright and colorful voices rose above those of their brothers. I sensed cohesion and complementarity, but I could also perceive the rivalry among the children in their performance for the *shabbes* and for me, the guest. Besides this vivid musical experience at the *shabbes* table, Goldie frequented the home recording studio to make recordings and share them via email with her cousins and friends in North America and Israel. Over the years, I witnessed several Hasidic women besides Goldie using the home studio to transform their artistic talents and productions into an informal market that has been legitimized by advertisements for women's art-related businesses, produced and disseminated in the ultra-Orthodox press without images of their faces.

Alongside Goldie's artistic production, I uncovered another alternative art scene exclusive to women and girls within ultra-Orthodoxy where women labeled themselves as *frum* female artists.[3] This art scene, instead of being an informal market hiding women's faces and voices, took the stage as a formal market that exists online on social media and is advertised as being "for women and girls only." Contrary to Goldie's closely controlled personal dissemination of her music to close family and friends, the women and girls invested in this new art scene available online considered "for women and girls only" advertisements to be a sufficient marker to underline the privacy of the content, an indication that boys and men should not access it.[4] In taking this approach, they suggest new avenues for negotiating between the public aspect of the arts and modesty.

I discovered this online art scene during the COVID-19 pandemic, in March 2020. While the world was on lockdown, I, like many other anthropologists, started a virtual ethnography. I was connected over the phone and WhatsApp with women I had met in person in Montreal and New York City. Some of them told me to connect myself to Instagram, since many women in the arts were shifting their artistic production online. I logged into this online world every day during the first weeks of the pandemic, meticulously took notes, and participated in this digital *frum* art scene, envisaging it as a new site where I was a participant observer. I analyzed the online performances of women artists who were already on social media and observed some of them becoming celebrities and creating online personas during this unprecedented time of digital connectedness.

Among these emerging celebrities, I followed Bracha Jaffe and Shaindy Plotzker, two ultra-Orthodox Jewish singers from Brooklyn with, respectively, a public and a private Instagram account. Together they were producing and financing their first music video. After witnessing the growing interest and participation of women and girls in online concerts and podcasts by pioneers such as Franciska Kosman (*Franciska Show*) and Dobby Baum (*Dobby Show*), Bracha Jaffe saw an opportunity to connect with her audience virtually and aspired to produce a music video by collaborating with other *frum* female artists. She developed a friendship with Shaindy Plotzker, who was finding her footing regarding the proper way to put her music out. Shaindy was in a unique situation after losing her voice due to vocal nodules and having to undergo medical treatment to regain her ability to sing. She had promised herself that if she were to regain her vocal ability, she would go out and use it to spread "good to the world." As a single ultra-Orthodox woman, Shaindy Plotzker was unsure if there was a place or a need for her music. When she was a young child, she hardly imagined herself being able to publicize her performances on social media and still be celebrated in ultra-Orthodox circles. Prior to the COVID-19 pandemic, the art world for and by ultra-Orthodox women was almost invisible on social media, and notably on YouTube, due to a ban on the publication of women's images and faces in the ultra-Orthodox presses and media. The pioneers who broke the ceiling, such as Shaindel Antelis, Nechama Cohen, and Franciska Kosman, were rare and timid, sometimes even posting unlisted videos.

Shaindy Plotzker had promised herself that she would sing for others if she regained her voice, which she did a few weeks prior to the pandemic. When Bracha contacted her about participating in the collaborative music video she envisioned, the time was right for them to gauge how they would be received by a female-only audience online.[5] They decided to cover and remix one of the official 2014 FIFA World Cup songs, "This Is the Time of Our Lives," interpreted by the famous Moroccan singer Chawki. Bracha and Shaindy told me that they valued this catchy song as a global hit that stimulates joy, echoing the idea of "connectivity and unity" that they wanted to disseminate. But instead of a simple cover, they wanted to involve their audience. They posted a message and a video on their respective private Instagram accounts, inviting their female audience to participate. With specific instructions, they advised learning the flash-mob dance prepared by *frum* choreographer Maáyan Davis, then recording their video and sending it by email. The music video was edited by Michal Hartman, a *frum* female filmmaker who founded the company Vision & Hart,[6] which works within and outside ultra-Orthodox circles.

After forty-eight hours, they had received over three hundred videos and were encouraged by the receptiveness of their audience. They had created a buzz. Although the positive words of the refrain of the song "This Is the Time of Our Lives" may have appeared inappropriate, as they were singing it during the pandemic, this collaborative music video suggests reinventing the art scene for women and girls as a tool to unite, connect, dance, sing, and be empowered virtually. When the video was posted on their respective YouTube channels on May 17, 2020, under the label "for women and girls only," they did not initially realize how these videos would transform their careers.[7] Growing up in ultra-Orthodox Jewish communities, they were both used to performing alongside their girl classmates in summer camps and schools, as did Goldie, although they never imagined singing as soloists online to publicize their artistic work for thousands of women and girls globally.

After two years, the total number of views on both women's YouTube channels exceeded five hundred thousand, a very high number for this niche YouTube market that, until the pandemic, was very marginal. This premiere propelled Bracha's and Shaindy's careers as ultra-Orthodox female singers beyond what they expected. Following their joint music video, they recorded a few other music videos on their own and together. After their rise to fame, the main difference was that Jewish charity organizations such as Bonei Olam, Chesed 24/7, and Thank You Hashem—invested in connecting the global community of Orthodox Jewish women—financed their music videos. More broadly, Thank You Hashem, which does not seem to have any ties with a specific religious authority, produced and promoted several music videos by *frum* female singers on their platform alongside ultra-Orthodox male singers during the pandemic. One of their most meaningful and transformative music videos was released in April 2022 with Bracha Jaffe as the star. Keeping the label "for women and girls," this music video captures an unprecedented moment in publicizing ultra-Orthodox women's names, images, and voices. The idea of "women's Orthodox publicity" refers to a new way of making visible women in the arts, as well as their products and services, by exposing their names, faces, and bodies on social media.

The music video is a cover and remix of the 2021 song "A Yid" (A Jew), written by Hasidic woman composer Chayala Neuhaus, which became a hit among a broad range of ultra-Orthodox communities in

North America, Europe, and Israel, even being translated into Yiddish, a first in the publicizing of a song composed by a woman.[8] The music video is a high-quality professional production involving leading male videographers, producers, and composers in the Jewish music industry, featuring Bracha Jaffe as the star of the song. Jaffe is dancing throughout a cartoon city accompanied by her "mini-me's," young girls dressed in the same black sequined "YID" sweatshirt, long black skirts, black converse sneakers, and colorful socks. They are singing and dancing a sort of TikTok or flash-mob dance in the streets of a colorful and animated metropolis. Prior to the refrain, and on several other occasions throughout the song, Bracha sings "tililala lalalala," echoing the Hasidic masculine traditional singing of *nigunim* in a pop version with vocal fry and growling voice, two techniques emblematic of North American vocal popular music. With this music video, Thank You Hashem institutionalized and professionalized artistic productions by and for women and girls only, transforming the norms in ultra-Orthodox circles regarding the publicizing of women's faces and voices. The music video reached over one hundred thousand views within one month, a record number of views for an ultra-Orthodox female singer in such a short period of time.

* * * * *

Goldie, Bracha, and Shaindy are some of many ultra-Orthodox Jewish women I have collaborated with who are using technology and the digital for their artistic productions in music, film, and dance. Goldie uses the studios of Hasidic women who have home recording studios as a business to create music and then share it via email with her female audience. Alongside other women from her community, she consumes and observes *frum* female artists such as Bracha and Shaindy. I remember Yocheved, an instrumentalist I met in Kiryas Joel, sharing with me how her daughter describes Bracha Jaffe as the most talented of the Jewish women singers today. Bracha and Shaindy recently disseminated their productions on YouTube, advertising them "for women and girls" and publicizing their work on social media to create a kosher music industry, putting the responsibility on men to not listen rather than, as has been the norm, restricting their own activities so that men would not encounter their voices and faces.

The "kosher music industry" is a term largely used in Orthodox and ultra-Orthodox circles. It is part of the broader ecology of kosher art and entertainment and refers to an art form or expression aligned to Orthodox Jewish laws, including the norms of *tsnius*, which aim to inspire the Jewish audience and bring them closer to God. Because of the restriction on boys and men listening to women's singing voices, the kosher music industry traditionally has included only Orthodox Jewish male musicians and singers. *Frum* female artists such as Bracha, Shaindy, and many others are challenging the "traditional" shape of this industry by advocating for a distinct branch within it. While they are working with women and men from inside and outside their communities, Bracha and Shaindy perform for various ultra-Orthodox female audiences, from conservative to liberal ones, online in summer camps and schools, as well as at private events. They are also collaborating with women artists who have decided to break away from Orthodoxy, as did some of the *frum* female filmmakers I collaborated with, or who are not Jewish Orthodox or not Jewish.

Throughout my ethnography, I observed the constant contact and exchange between ultra-Orthodox women artists from these various backgrounds, from the most conservative to the ones who have left. The latter are known as OTD, meaning "off the *derekh*" in Hebrew, translated as "off the path," referring to their departure from the path of Orthodoxy. I realized how the women are connected by the circulation of their artistic productions, as well as knowledge and savoir faire, forming what I call "*frum* female art worlds," to borrow sociologist Howard Becker's concept of art worlds, which he developed to examine secular and liberal art as a collective action.[9] Throughout the years, I have met not only singers, filmmakers, dancers, and actors but also promoters, agents, technicians, media producers, podcasters, and influencers, as well as members of these individuals' audiences, all functioning within a cooperative network where everyone is guided by the ultra-Orthodox conventions pertaining to *tsnius* existing through a spectrum of practices.

Thanks to digital, media, and technology changes, broader and deeper transformations are occurring within Orthodoxy itself, manifesting in new forms of relationships with religious authority, with informal leaders emerging online, a process that anthropologist Ayala Fader has defined as a crisis of authority.[10] Even though religious leaders have engaged in a war to control their communities' access to the Internet, they could not prevent its use by so many of their members, nor escape the economic need for the community to use the Internet for professional purposes. These transformations manifest differently according to the norms in place in their respective religious environments, but they are all reshaping the binary distinction between privacy/publicity, local/global, informal and formal leadership—complicating the line between inside and outside the community. As noted earlier, by the time I witnessed women and girls embracing technology for their creative projects, an emphasis on ultra-Orthodox Jewish women as backward, noncreative, and repressed had taken hold in the mainstream public media in North America, mobilizing the women who have left the Orthodox community to prove this narrative simplistic and inaccurate. While this media portrayal was not surprising, as it follows the logic of public discourse about and mediatization of religious women (who, according to this narrative, must be rescued with the help of Western liberal feminism), I wanted to understand what was behind the stereotypes and fallacies about the women I have met, including the ones who left their communities, as they often participated in the making of these narratives by acting and/or being interviewed on secular media. Throughout my years of ethnographic research, I heard many comments from friends, colleagues, and others about the oppression of Hasidic women, a category used to refer to ultra-Orthodox women at large. These comments reflect the politicization of women's bodies as a way to critique religion, instead of reflecting a broader contextualization of women's roles, status, and power in society at large.

I felt compelled to tie my ethnography to the discrepancies between the depictions I encountered and the reality I observed, to encourage a rethinking of the intricate relation between, on the one hand, accepting the guidance of religious authority and, on the other, abandoning it. I wanted to write a book that delves beyond the politicization of women's bodies, images, voices, and names to offer a story that pushes us to reconsider the role of the digital and the arts in our everyday lives, positionalities, and ways of defining publicity and privacy.

This book is a study of ultra-Orthodox womanhood in twenty-first-century North America and the role of the arts, technology, and media in reshaping religion. Shedding light on a new market and industry created by ultra-Orthodox and former ultra-Orthodox women, the book offers a theoretical framework for rethinking Orthodoxy through an ethnography of women's lives in these fortuitous artistic spaces. As a key catalyst of the recent crisis of religious authority manifested by the democratization of the digital, the *frum* female worlds have become a case for understanding daily life changes in ultra-Orthodox communities, punctuating not only social and cultural life but also economic life. Contrary to most research on religious women in conservative communities, which focuses on their predictable positions as wives and mothers, I collaborated with women in rare roles, including as singers, musicians, producers, studio owners, dancers, filmmakers, and actresses who are using the arts as an economy. While the arts might be considered a liminal practice existing in peripheral spaces, and therefore unrepresentative of broader societies, in these *frum* communities they nevertheless reveal important changes in the making of publicity in conservative religious circles. The *frum* female art worlds encapsulate the contradictions between the need for privacy of ultra-Orthodox women and the publicity of the arts. They offer alternative ways to understand religious norms that insist on privacy and artistic norms, whose raison d'être dwells in publicity. By producing music, plays, films, and dance on stage, on screen, online, and in the studio, these women have created two vibrant artistic scenes that both challenge and reinforce Orthodoxy. Former ultra-Orthodox women accomplish this work by diversifying women's narratives in theater and film for general audiences, reframing cultural appropriation of Hasidic identities on North American stages and screens. Ultra-Orthodox women do it by negotiating religious norms to create a market and industry in the arts for those within their communities, redefining the standards for publicity that dictate the Orthodox public space.

Updating Theories of Orthodoxy, Gender, and the Arts

Ultra-Orthodox Jews are known for their religious stringency, which increased after the Holocaust with the communities established in North America.[11] They created enclaves with distinctive educational, economic, social, and cultural systems as well as institutions and forms of leadership. Nevertheless, the maintenance and growth of these communities were only possible thanks to the interaction with and support of the secular and liberal world, which accepts religious differences and allows conservative religious communities to maintain their secluded way of life.[12] Indeed, the emergence, development, and transformation of Orthodoxy throughout time and space reflect the broader impact modernity has had on societies, communities, and individuals. All the same, the stringency of ultra-Orthodox groups hinges on adherence to religious authority, which tightly controls the education, bodies, and public behaviors of boys and girls, from whom secular topics and knowledge are largely excluded. Despite the restrictions imposed by these norms, women generally act as mediators between the ultra-Orthodox and the secular or modern worlds since they must interact with the latter for pragmatic reasons due to their care of children (encountering doctors, social workers, etc.) while men and boys are supposed to study in religious schools, *yeshivot* for unmarried boys and *kollel* for married men. Girls are prepared to enter the job market as well as to maintain their households, especially at the beginning of their marriages when their husbands are still studying in *kollel*. Thus, women are often the primary providers of income, also known as *parnasse*, for their families while their partners study in religious schools and get a small allowance. This work-life balance used to shift once women had more children, but today the economic burden of sustaining large families in expensive metropolises has altered this dynamic, particularly in New York City, and to a lesser extent in Montreal, where social support is much more present from the government of Quebec and Canada (free healthcare, more accessible childcare). Given the high cost of living, even as men may enter the workforce later in their marriages, women in New York are much more involved in the economic life of their families than in Montreal.

Strict religious norms, combined with their mediating role in relation to the "outside world," have led girls and women to adapt and create new forms of womanhood. If, on one hand, they perform womanhood in their everyday lives according to the norms dictated by religious authority, they have, on the other hand, also developed their own spaces, where they have autonomy and allow themselves to interpret religious authority according to their needs. Though women were initially largely banned from using the Internet, it has become somehow accepted and normalized in certain circles for professional and economic reasons; as a result, women's autonomous private spaces have expanded, allowing them to develop new career paths, connect across borders, and transmit new ways of being Orthodox online. The access to technology that can occur behind closed doors in the comfort of the home, with a second, non-kosher phone, or even with a filter, has transformed women's experiences, desires, and knowledge in a process often sheltered from the gaze of male religious authorities.

The ultra-Orthodox women presented in this book come from a variety of communities that differentiate themselves from the centrist modern Orthodox movement through the relationships they establish with modernity and what they call the "outside world." Modern Orthodoxy and ultra-Orthodoxy both follow an authoritative interpretation of rabbinical and ancient texts, including Jewish law (*halakha*), which represents the divine revelation to Moses on Mount Sinai. However, members of modern/centrist Orthodoxy do so while still overtly engaging with the secular world—attending universities or liberal arts colleges and participating in the culture and workforce of the broader society. Meanwhile, ultra-Orthodox Jews believe that the maintenance of Jewish *halakha* dictates severe limitations on engagement with this broader society and modernity. For this reason, they have established ideological, economic, social, cultural, and physical boundaries with the "outside world" to protect themselves from what they describe as a perverse, superficial, and purposeless society. Ultra-Orthodox Jewish communities define themselves by their strict opposition to modernity, as well as by their insularity and their commitment to religious authority and leadership, labeling themselves, depending on their specific community, as Hasidic, Litvish, Yeshivish, or simply Orthodox.

The lives of women in conservative circles are dictated by the concept of *tsnius*, laws of modesty that involve privacy and discretion. Yet once women transformed their arts into a commodity, issues of the public nature of their productions arose. To transform their arts into a market and an industry, they have renegotiated and redefined religious norms about modesty, modifying the strict demarcation between Orthodox and non-Orthodox public media.[13] Though ultra-Orthodox men are also making changes relating to the arts and technology due to expanding use of the Internet, their market and industry are not dictated by norms of privacy preventing them from becoming celebrities and artists. This book is not about men, as reevaluating the impact of technology on the definition of publicity and privacy in religious settings has been largely undertaken by women. This observation does not mean that men do not have an impact on women's experiences. They often support their wives, daughters, or sisters as well as influence women's artistic productions through their own performances as celebrities, but they are not at the core of the story when it comes to religious women's agency in the digital age.

The first of three arguments this book makes is that religious women, in the face of changes in the arts and technology, are redefining the act of being public and private and engendering social change.[14] This is an argument that lies at the intersection of the anthropology of religion, gender, and the arts and contributes to that anthropology. To be sure, anthropologists have extensively written about the diversity of mechanisms used by women in conservative religious communities to gain agency and autonomy, defying the oppositional mantra of religion versus feminism that occupies much feminist analytics and politics. The work of Saba Mahmood and her successors in the socio-anthropology of religion has been central to the development of new perspectives on women and religion.[15] These works have contributed significantly to challenge universalizing treatments of women's agency. They explore going beyond the subordination and resistance paradigms of feminist analysis and offer multiple avenues through which to discuss and describe women's lives, beings, and experiences in what Mahmood called "inhabiting the norms."[16] Nevertheless, this literature relegates women to their private roles, focusing essentially on women's positions as daughters, mothers, and wives or on the agency they express through their investment in religion, religious knowledge, and practice. This book is aligned with this anthropological tradition that defies the liberal universal feminist tropes and recognizes that women's agency should not be determined only by public expression and women's publicity,[17] but I approach the question of private and public space in a manner that goes beyond the public/private divide that has nourished the literature for decades. By investigating the making of an artistic market and industry that necessitates publicity, I argue for expanding our understanding of women's agency beyond the private/public divide as well as focusing on the *counterpublic* to describe alternative interpretations of this divide.[18] Throughout the book, I use "publicity" to refer to the process of making public, visible, audible, and accessible creators, their projects, their ideas, and their work. All the women creators I encountered were looking for publicity, but the process by which they accomplished it, as well as the visibility of their selves and their work, changed according to their willingness to lose control of the audience. The visible dimension of any publicity also has multiple shapes that do not necessarily imply the exposure of faces, bodies, or names.

Second, this book makes the case for the significance of technology and the arts in the making of new senses of belonging, arguing for a redefinition of conservative religious communities beyond the local. I observed how technology transformed women's sense of belonging beyond blood and traditional kinship ties, expanding it to a global scale through a strengthening of the sense of relatedness. Because conservative religious communities dictate strict gender segregation, this developing sense of global belonging within the arts, media, and technology is gendered, affecting Orthodox womanhood. Of course, ultra-Orthodox Jewish women are no strangers to performance,[19] but their access to technology at home and beyond the home has completely transformed it. This access has facilitated the creation of a transnational market and industry where the concepts of copyright, intellectual property, and celebrity are redefining the various expressions of modesty in Orthodoxies. I show how the products of this transnational network of artists mold, consolidate, and transmit new forms of Orthodox womanhood. Inspired by the current focus on new media and technology in the anthropology of religion,[20] I mobilize an array of previously unexplored sources and connect them to the literature about performance, celebrity, and creativity as a framework within which to explore the transformation of womanhood. Women artists are now connecting to each other online far beyond their local communities, encouraging us to think about kinship ties that are not necessarily limited to descent.[21] Focusing on the creative ways in which Jewish women express their Orthodoxies, my research captures the fervent desire of religious women to engage with the twenty-first-century digital era and create a market and industry outside of the public, male-dominated one, within and outside Orthodoxy. With this second main argument, this book posits that the arts are useful in understanding the social, cultural, and economic promises and gauges posed by our digital era.

The third argument builds on scholarship that rethinks religion as a social category connected to secularism and belief,[22] as well as recent studies of exit among ultra-Orthodox Jews.[23] By revealing the common experiences among ultra-Orthodox and formerly ultra-Orthodox women of using artistic performances to gain social, cultural, and economic agency and autonomy, this book complicates the boundaries between Orthodoxy's defectors and its followers. Many anthropologists and social scientists of religion have taught us that the social categories of the secular and the religious are sociohistorical products of European modernity and Christianity that therefore must always be considered, or even deconstructed.[24] Inspired by my experience of moving my body and my mind between Montreal and New York, among defectors, doubters, and observers of Orthodoxies, this book shows how these categories are better thought of as a single, shifting spectrum, with individuals in constant contact along it. Former ultra-Orthodox Jewish women artists serve as central agents of change in ultra-Orthodox public culture, and their performance of Orthodoxies, I argue, creates new bridges between religiosity and secularism, challenging the "in-or-out" assumption that goes along with the "enclave" or "ghetto" model. Relying on a substantial number of theatrical and cinematic productions written by former ultra-Orthodox women, the book reveals how these women capitalize on their constant interaction with *Yiddishkeit* to renew Yiddish theater, create a new genre of cinema, and become artists.

Ultra-Orthodoxy has grown exponentially in the last forty years, and while stringency has been the norm in many ultra-Orthodox circles, internal diversity has emerged in parallel with such growth. Many women have taken the opportunity provided by the privacy they were required to maintain to experiment with new ways of being Orthodox women, creating what I call a modest public, and a counterpublic to the Orthodox public sphere.

Toward a Translocal Study of Orthodoxies

Even though the category "ultra-Orthodox" can seem derogatory in its decentering of the very groups it describes, it is a term that encapsulates the internal diversity and interconnectivity I witnessed among the women described here. Anchored in an understanding of religion as a tradition that exists alongside secularism,[25] ultra-Orthodoxy should be thought of in the plural. As suggested by Talal Asad, these tensions underline the creative role of institutional power as well as the diachronic and synchronic changes, reforms, debates, and dialogues occurring within ultra-Orthodoxy in both men's and women's circles. In light of the internal diversity of ultra-Orthodoxy, this book offers a sampling of multiple realities that exist within and without Orthodoxy. "Within Orthodoxy" invokes women invested in the arts for their ultra-Orthodox communities; "without Orthodoxy" refers to women who left their communities and do not regulate their lives around ultra-Orthodox institutions. Moreover, though in this book I sometimes use "Orthodoxy" and "ultra-Orthodoxy" interchangeably, I am always referring to the stringent branch of Orthodoxy. I did not work with modern and centrist Orthodox women, as they share a different vision of women's role in society and Judaism because of their participation in secular society beyond women-only private spaces. Additionally, when modern or centrist Orthodox women call for change, the focus is generally on the liturgical and ritualistic aspects of their Jewish life. Lastly, even though I encountered many Jewish artists who grew up liberal and joined ultra-Orthodoxy, known as *baalei tshuva*, this book is not about their experiences but instead about those of women born and raised in ultra-Orthodox communities that are not involved in outreach among the non-Orthodox, as the Hasidic communities of Chabad-Lubavitch are.

My use of the term "ultra-Orthodoxy" thus describes Jewish women who grew up and live within Hasidic and Litvish/Yeshivish circles, both of which emerged from traditionalist movements in eighteenth-century Eastern Europe in response to crises of modernity. The term "Orthodox" was used by German Enlighteners for Jews and Christians who opposed the Enlightenment, and only in the nineteenth century, with the birth of Reform Judaism, did it become a Jewish religious denomination.[26] Hasidic Jews are governed by a *rebbe*, or spiritual leader divinely appointed, a status that is now inherited and disputed through kinship, while Litvish or Yeshivish Jews follow prominent rabbis affiliated with institutions of Jewish academic learning, such as *yeshivot* and *kollel*.[27] Both groups originally opposed each other but became less adversarial after the Holocaust, during the rebuilding of their communities across the globe. Today, both communities have distinct religious practices, educational systems, languages, and rules for exposure to the secular world and to secular media, but still interact with each other. Within these social categories—Hasidim and Litvish/Yeshivish—distinctions also exist between localities, families, and individuals, as well as according to social and economic status. The sheer demographic growth of these communities has certainly influenced one of the most recent crises of religious authority that started at the turn of the twenty-first century, with the passing of a generation of important *rebbes* and rabbis, the fight over their succession, various economic challenges, sexual abuse scandals, and the democratization of the Internet.[28] Even though these matters were primarily debated in male circles, some women also began to distrust religious authority, though they did so in a less vocal manner.

Over the course of my ethnographic research, I saw many women disregard religious authority in making decisions about their creative projects, or search for an "open-minded," "liberal" rabbi to validate their choices. In the most conservative spaces, I met women wearing their conventional dark-colored clothing, covering their knees, elbows, and collarbone, as well as covering their hair with a wig (*sheytl*) with a hat or a band as required in their circles, often worn over shaved hair in Hasidic circles. However, these same women did not request rabbinical permission to initiate new practices such as founding a musical band, building a home studio for recording or teaching, making movies on controversial topics, producing music videos, or participating in social media campaigns to advocate for changes for the sake of "female empowerment." Some women did not expand on their decisions to ignore rabbinical authority; others mentioned that they find the right rabbi to validate their choices, and many expressed frustrations with their communities' restrictions on the use of social media, their invisibility in the press, or the lack of opportunities for professional training in the arts and technology. In many cases, husbands supported and defended the decisions of their wives. In fact, when these women had to cancel or alter their performances to conform to their communities' norms, it was often because not men, who generally ignore what is occurring or are not privy to the events, but other women voiced their opposition to these new practices and then reported them to rabbinical authorities.

One of the purposes of this book is to challenge localized ethnographies of Orthodoxy. This methodological intervention echoes major changes occurring in anthropology about the complex global assemblages and projects of fieldwork, changes that have nevertheless been timidly embraced by anthropologists working with conservative groups, notably in Jewish studies.[29] Most of the ethnography about Jewish life in Orthodoxy and ultra-Orthodoxy concentrates exclusively on the local and rarely integrates transnational dynamics in its analysis, neglecting that Hasidism and Litvish/Yeshivish Judaism have developed as transborder movements. The works of Asya Vaisman, Lea Taragin-Zeller, Ben Kasstan, and Sam Shuman are the exceptions,[30] but they are also not arguing for a rethinking of the movement beyond national borders. Besides conducting multi-sited ethnographies, ethnographers working at the intersection of media and religion and doing online ethnography have largely contributed to new ethnographic methods transcending geographic boundaries.[31] Nevertheless, the literature on conservative religion does not encompass multi-sited ethnography performed both on site and online and both inside and outside the community.

Even though local contexts are important, it is crucial to move beyond the supposed geographic boundaries of the ultra-Orthodox world and focus instead on its diasporic raison d'être. Rather than consider the neighborhoods inhabited by ultra-Orthodox Jews of Outremont, Kiryas Joel, or Williamsburg solely as self-contained *shtetlakh* (villages),[32] we must acknowledge that the *shtetl* exists in relation to other *shtetlakh* and to the broader local and global society, where people, sounds, movements, resources, practices, and ideas circulate. To be sure, many scholars in the social sciences have already deconstructed the idea of the enclave for secluded religious communities, underlining the porous boundaries between the inside and the outside of a community. However, the move toward translocalism, toward a pan-ultra-Orthodoxy, not only created thanks to traditional pilgrimages but consolidated by artistic productions, technology, and media, has not been proposed.

This ethnography is the result of examining these connectivities. Throughout the years, I have reflected on the meaning of my visits across these diverse physical and online spaces. Even though anthropologists have always moved from place to place for their research, leading to the birth of collaborative ethnography as a method to understand human society and behavior, the scale on which we are using this method today has changed, and indeed I conducted my research embracing this new scale. I was doing what anthropologist George E. Marcus labeled multi-sited ethnography during the spatial turn,[33] but I could not stop thinking about the disconnect between, on the one hand, the literature on Hasidism and, on the other, the interconnectedness my ethnography uncovered among these various spaces.

By discussing connectivity, I am advocating for a translocal approach in the ethnographic study of conservative religious groups such as Orthodox Jews. Here, I echo anthropologists Ulf Hannerz and Mark-Anthony Falzon,[34] who consider that the formulation "multi-sited ethnography" somewhat obscures that ethnography may have to be de-territorialized, as was the case with the virtual spaces I encountered. While the terms "multi-sited" and "translocal" are often interchangeable, I use "translocal" to specifically evoke the movement that occurs between spaces. In this context, the notion of translocality—which emerged from transnationalism but is not synonymous with it[35]—means looking at ultra-Orthodoxy in terms of fluidity and contact rather than structure and systems. It is about exchange and circulation beyond national borders, incorporating multiple mobilities while not losing sight of locality.[36] It is defined as the dynamic interconnectedness of localities linked by people and their actions, objects, productions, and ideas, resulting in the production and reproduction of spatial differences.[37]

I certainly do not wish to deny the usefulness of single-locality ethnography that has been and continues to be conducted with conservative religious groups, but I am calling for a new type of ethnography that is complementary to the traditional one. The classic focus on a locality is no longer sufficient for the ethnographic study of social life in the twenty-first century, even when it comes to self-secluded groups that have built a veritable "fortress" to protect themselves from the rest of society, to borrow from the title of a recent publication about the Satmar community of New York by historians Nathaniel Deutsch and Michael Casper.[38] Local spaces and communities are now intensively intersected by global movements of capital, labor relations, ideas, values, images, and sounds.

Globalization challenges the classical ethnography that involved meticulous attention to a single place. As anthropologist Sally Engle Merry explained over twenty years ago, the global does not simply frame the local, but constitutes it. In the case of ultra-Orthodox Jews, they define themselves as part of both a global and a local movement for Jews who respect the *halakha* in its strictest sense and eschew interaction with modernity. While ultra-Orthodox life has local specificities, notably when it comes to the application of secular and religious laws impacting everyday life, these variations share a common heritage, knowledge, sense of belonging, and history and participate in global debates on sensitive subjects such as sexual abuse, religious authority, technology, or health. Moreover, for Hasidim, these localities are able to grow thanks to the mobility of men joining their wives in their native countries and cities after their weddings. As anthropologist Sam Shuman noted, the arranged marriage network (*shiddukhim*) follows a matrilocal residence pattern whereby the husband lives in his wife's city after marriage. It is now essential to resituate ultra-Orthodoxy as a diaspora, moving beyond locality—beyond the *shtetl*.

The crossing and theorizing of boundaries had a great impact on my fieldwork and shaped the organization of this book. As Ayala Fader has written, many sociological and anthropological accounts of ultra-Orthodoxy have tended to portray discrete, bounded communities rather than messy movements and diversity. I pursue the path that Fader opened in the field, an ethnography of Orthodoxy beyond its geographic boundaries. But to write this book, I had to create new boundaries to make sense of what I observed. Because the performance of Orthodoxy by women artists varied according to the nature of the audience, I decided to re-create the boundaries of my fieldwork by writing about different spaces: the private space, strictly accessible to women; the modest public space, broadly accessible but from which men are warned away (with labels such as "*kol isha*," which means "a woman's voice"); the counter-public space, an online space where women contradict official discourse about their appearance and comportment in an effort to replace the official public Orthodox one; and, finally, the public space, where women reach out to non-Orthodox, and even non-Jewish audiences.

Following the Ethnographer Artist beyond the Religious Paradigm

Throughout my research, I let myself be guided by the women I met who were directing me toward new physical and virtual sites. I moved my body and mind according to my collaborators, beyond geographic, physical, and ideological borders. My research on women and the arts suited my methodology. My fieldwork consisted of various sojourns in two countries (Canada and the United States), two urban settings (Montreal and New York), multiple Orthodox and non-Orthodox neighborhoods (Tosh, Outremont, Cote des Neiges, Mile End, Plateau Mont-Royal, Borough Park, Williamsburg, Crown Heights, Flatbush, Manhattan, Kiryas Joel, Lakewood, and Toms River), and countless artistic spaces. I collaborated with women and girls ranging from sixteen to seventy years of age living in these various localities, who all chose different life and career paths by pursuing the arts while being raised in and/or operating according to ultra-Orthodox religious norms. The vast majority came from the working and middle classes, as deduced from their educational level and professional occupation, as well as those of their parents and husbands.

My exploration of this world began in 2016 when filmmaker Eric Scott, who had produced a film about individuals leaving Orthodoxy, opened various doors to me within the so-called OTD community of individuals who had left ultra-Orthodoxy in Montreal and New York City. Scott introduced me to a group of people engaged in supporting individuals transitioning out of ultra-Orthodoxy, and then invited me to participate in the institutionalization of this support community as a legal entity, which we named Forward. Members of the group nominated me as a member of the organization's advisory board. Believing fervently in its cause, I wanted to raise awareness about the issues faced by exiters of Orthodoxy. I organized fundraising events and contacted journalists as well as academic centers to bring their struggles to light.

Collaboration and friendship guided my approach toward a translocal experience.[39] As we built Forward, I imagined collaborating with the New York organization Footsteps, the first North American organization to help people in their transition out of the ultra-Orthodox community. For a year, I commuted between Montreal and New York so that I could build a transnational network. In January 2017, I left Montreal for six months of research in New York to investigate the ultra-Orthodox underground scene,[40] and progressively turned my attention to the public face of the community: theater and film actors who had left ultra-Orthodoxy.

After developing ties with Footsteps, I expanded my network to the governance of other organizations supporting OTD individuals and those at the fringes of the "system," to echo the language of my collaborators. In these circles, I met women and men from Hasidic and Litvish/Yeshivish backgrounds who performed for public audiences, but my attention rapidly turned to the women, both because they were often at the center of the public narratives and also because our interactions were easier and more direct. I followed them in theater productions, on film screens, and at film festivals, wrote letters for fellowships, participated in public discussions and animated Q&A sessions, put them in touch with journalists, and developed friendships. In the course of all this, I learned how they developed their passion for the arts while still within their communities, and how they maintained ties with ultra-Orthodox men and women, with whom they occasionally collaborated. Their descriptions of a private feminine creative space that they grew up in piqued my desire to know more about this world that they left behind, and the women invested in the arts who are still inside of it.

In 2018, I moved to Washington, DC, and began to expand my social network to include the women in the arts *still within* the ultra-Orthodox community. After the two years spent between Montreal and New York with OTD individuals as well as those who stood waveringly at the edge of the community, criticizing their leadership and doubting their system (also known as "doubters"), I had also connected with various ultra-Orthodox families thanks to my engagement as a piano and French teacher, as well as my position as a professor of socio-anthropology for the program mentioned earlier for women only in Montreal. Now that I had begun collaborating with people from within, my research began to take another shape. From 2018 to 2020, I traveled between DC, New York, and Montreal to meet professional, semiprofessional, and amateur singers,[41] music producers, studio owners, instrumentalists, dancers, painters, actresses, and filmmakers. I attended school plays, film screenings, charity events, and concerts, took dance classes, and participated in a film shoot where I briefly acted. My roles alternated between those of student, friend, professor, critic, advisor, mediator, spectator, and assistant. I took extensive notes after long days of activities, exchanges, and discussions, and organized interviews to solicit responses to specific

Figure 1.1: Photo of a film shoot on a street in Borough Park, January 2020, New York City (credit Jessica Roda).

Figure 1.2: Photo of a film shoot in an apartment in Flatbush, November 2021, New York City, Malky Weingarten and Chaya Sarah Schlussel (credit Jessica Roda).

questions and to allow all the women the opportunity to communicate their experience. I also often shared with them my observations and interpretations via phone calls, WhatsApp messages, and in-person visits.

In March 2020, when the pandemic hit, my ethnography transitioned from on site to online. Many of the women were already on social media, but their online presence drastically increased during this time. I was witness to an unprecedented moment, as girls and women from the UK, Israel, Canada, the United States, and Australia began attending Zoom concerts and having online discussions with women in the arts, sometimes reaching the maximum capacity of a thousand participants on Zoom with at least two or four girls on camera (mainly located in the United States). My online ethnography, even if at first continuous with my on-site work, soon became its own distinctive ethnographic space. This digital ethnography reoriented my corpus of analysis. I realized that the online, digitally transmitted images and sounds produced by these artists constituted a new aspect in making Orthodox womanhood. After surveying content published on YouTube, Instagram, and Zoom, I returned to the data I had collected on site with a new eye, reexamining the sounds and images I had captured, considering the influence of women's performances on social media. In the summer of 2020, I came back to Montreal to finalize my ethnography, verify the data collected, and start the writing process. I lived for ten months in Outremont, on a street inhabited primarily by Yiddish-speaking Hasidic families. During that period, I investigated the power of digital productions available on social media, on DVDs, and on MP3 files, and verified some of the arguments put forward in this book. Throughout the writing process, I shared sections of my writing with some of the women I extensively describe in these pages to get feedback and to test my arguments. Some were particularly attentive to the writing, while others did not care. Some of them asked me to add information or to be more specific about their relationship with religious authority, but none of these interactions affected my argument. Their eyes were often helpful in refining some information and complementing my analysis with new material. Most importantly, they often reinforced the purpose of my work by expressing how much more they were able to accomplish since the performance or video described in the piece that I submitted to them. By doing so, they confirmed the significance of what I was capturing in real time. This ethnography has thus been collaborative at every single step of the process.

While doing fieldwork and then writing about ultra-Orthodox Jewish women, I was constantly confronting my own biases. As a woman influenced by liberal feminist thought—especially second-wave French feminism—I did not grow up in the Orthodox feminine environment, even though I practiced Orthodox Judaism for a few years in my early twenties. During my childhood I backpacked with my parents across the globe and settled in a multiethnic, multiracial, working-class neighborhood in French Guiana. In French Guiana I grew up in a secular home, far from Jewish life. I attended the local public school, where my classmates included immigrants from Suriname, Brazil, Haiti, China, and Vietnam, as well as Bushinenges, Creoles, Indigenous people, and white Europeans. These early experiences stimulated my curiosity about and sensitivity to "difference," and influenced my development as a person, an anthropologist, and an ethnomusicologist.

In 2001, I left French Giuana for Paris to study piano, modern-jazz dance, and musicology at the Conservatory Erik Satie of the seventh arrondissement of Paris and the Sorbonne University. In these years I learned about the Sephardic Jewish heritage of my maternal grandmother and my father's family. I wanted to investigate the Jewishness of my family, originally from Spain and North Africa, and was searching for a sense of belonging. I started a journey into Jewish Orthodoxy, first in Paris and then in Montreal when I was an exchange student in 2003–2004. Becoming Orthodox was not animated by faith, nor by belief, but by a quest to reconnect with a lost identity and heritage. At the time, Orthodox Judaism in Paris was the dominant trend among Jews originally from North Africa (known as Sephardim), who now compose the majority of French Jewry. Throughout the years, my dedication to Jewishness transferred from a ritualized and religious experience to a cultural and intellectual one. When I joined the Fondation du Judaïsme Francais and the European Institute for Jewish Music in 2006 as a research assistant, the directors of both institutions, respectively Hervé Roten and Nelly Hanson, introduced me to another aspect of Jewish life, driven by traditions understood in a cultural way. During that period, I was immersed in a Jewish secular environment, abandoned Orthodoxy, and participated occasionally in services in a Conservative

Jewish congregation. While completing a joint PhD between France and Canada, I settled in Montreal in 2010, and I discovered another face of Jewishness tied to North American liberal Judaism. My journey into ultra-Orthodoxy was thus quite different from that of most men and women ethnographers on the subject. Most of them are coming from Ashkenazi backgrounds and have grandparents or parents from the Orthodox Eastern European tradition. They share names, food, music, and history with their collaborators and appear in the field as the perfect *baalei tshuva* candidates. As an atypical Sephardic woman who identifies as a liberal Jew and comes from a mixed background, my positionality could have limited my access to the field, but it never became a topic of conversation or obstacle to my research.

Unlike most Jewish women ethnographers in this field, who often describe the tensions between communal efforts at proselytization (*kiruv*) and the goals of ethnographic research,[42] I never struggled with such expectations regarding my commitment to Jewish law. Even with my mixed background, I was still Jewish according to Jewish law and could have been a great candidate to rejoin Orthodoxy for a second time in my life. While I was invited to *shabbes* meals or holiday celebrations, sometimes with my son, my hosts knew that my son was in secular school and never commented on his education or my lifestyle. I often felt embarrassed to respond to some of their questions, or even to see them on the street while I was wearing pants.

The arts facilitated our connection, and because of my position as a trained pianist, flutist, and dancer, our shared interests motivated their acceptance of me and their curiosity about my background. I had a genuine attentiveness to their creative spaces and highly valued their art even if it conformed to a different aesthetic from my own. My sense of aesthetics seemed to diverge the most from that of women and girls performing in private spaces. Yet my role was not to evaluate their professionalism nor to make any value judgment on their productions; it was to explain and interpret their creative process. I shared greater artistic and aesthetic commonalities with the professionally trained artists, whether *frum* or formerly ultra-Orthodox, because we had received comparable training and consumed similar media. They sought my comments on their creative works, emphasizing the growing significance of aesthetic judgment for all of them, from the conservative to the liberal. Over the years, I observed a change in their own judgments of musical and film productions. For many women and girls, it became essential to provide "professional" content, a concept associated with the work of experienced sound engineers, filmmakers, videographers, trained musicians, singers, and dancers. I remember an evening alongside Montreal Hasidic girls making fun of performances from a few years earlier regarding the lack of refinement of the costumes, the setting, and the out-of-tune live singing. All of them were searching for a kind of recognition of their "professionalism" in creating plays, concerts, and films, even though many did not receive "professional training." Women and girls did not want to be categorized as secondary to the male industry, but instead as complementary, responding to specifically feminine needs.

My experience of the artistic performances described in this book diverges from those of these women due to different constructions of gender, religion, and secularism. At the same time, however, they also converge. We found affinities based on our common interest in the arts, our curiosity toward otherness and the unfamiliar, and a strong desire to bond despite our differences. When I reflected on the writing process, I felt obligated to illustrate the diversity of women's experiences, the question of authority, and the politics of representation. The story I wrote does not give voice to ultra-Orthodox and former ultra-Orthodox women, nor does it advocate for them. Rather, it is my attempt to comprehend the intricacies of their lives as women invested in the arts, who sometimes claim the label "artists" and who exist at the margins of both the ultra-Orthodox and the liberal worlds. I use their performances in the arts as a testimony to their revelation of who they are, who they want to be, and the changes they are bringing about in their circles. Here I transcribe and translate my encounters with a world through the arts in a specific time. Almost like a photographer, I captured moments, images, sounds, and behaviors as social realities that I witnessed as they took place in a wide range of environments.

As a former pianist, I was not the potential *baal tshuva* woman they needed to rescue. They sought something else entirely from me and our relationship with the arts. The women who participated in my research had their own reasons for doing so and their own hopes for what the book might accomplish. Those performing in private spaces wanted the world to know about their talent, creativity, curiosity, and agency, to make even little changes in their circles by bringing in new ideas. Some of them are offended by the way Orthodox women are portrayed in the media. Meanwhile, women becoming celebrities and challenging norms aspired to display their professionalism and professional training, but also to share their struggles to get where they are now and their attempts to effect change by creating a community of *frum* female artists. Women on social media, however, wished to highlight their aspirations of transforming Orthodoxy from within (as well as the hardships they encounter while doing so), transformations that include the normalization of social media use that they in fact represent. Finally, the public artists wanted the chance to outline their difficulties in balancing the expectations of and the love they have for their families and communities, their professional desires and wishes, and their criticism of both ultra-Orthodox and liberal society.[43]

Reconsidering Feminist Anthropology

Feminist ethnography of ultra-Orthodox life is a contested field dominated by various feminist discourses—that is, by interpretations aligned with specific feminist ideologies.[44] It echoes the broader development occurring in feminist anthropology with a peculiar touch: most ethnographers are considered both as insiders because of their Jewishness and as outsiders because they are liberal Jews. Until recently, most women ethnographers working in this field were liberal and secular Jews. The power dynamic established when the white, educated, liberal Jewish woman observes the visibly Jewish Orthodox woman is central to feminist ethnographies of Orthodoxy. The first generation writing about ultra-Orthodoxy through the lens of Western universal feminism viewed it as a mode of patriarchal regulation, discipline, and oppression of women's bodies and sexuality, and as reinforcing this power relation.[45] Another generation of feminist Jewish ethnographers was influenced by postcolonial feminist scholars,[46] and was able to conceive of ultra-Orthodoxy as a locus where women find ways to gain agency and empowerment, as well as a dynamic space revealing the way religious authorities and texts are challenged and reinterpreted to construct new feminine ideals of modesty and beauty.[47] These scholars are also in

dialogue with religious feminists, who have deconstructed the antago-
nism between religion and feminism, something that is rarely addressed
by feminist anthropology.[48] By doing so, feminist ethnographers of conservative Jewish communities are contributing to the intersectional
approach, advocating for the inclusion of religion as a distinct category
through which to understand power relations, oppression, agency,
and autonomy. While feminist ethnographers working on Islam were
influenced by this intersectional approach as well, they nevertheless
have generally applied this approach from a postcolonial perspective
that rarely includes religion. Particularly influenced by these feminist
anthropologists, who noted and reflected upon their own positions
in relation to their research, I considered my position as a professor, a
trained pianist, and a dancer as a central parameter defining my access
to and analysis of women's being and doing.

As I navigated female-only spaces to which many feminist lenses
might be applied, my feminist politics often clashed with some of my
empirical findings. The feminist theoretical and methodological frameworks that have shaped me both constrained and enabled my interpretations of ultra-Orthodoxy. As detailed above, my entry point to the
ultra-Orthodox world was women who had left the community, and
I tackled the issue from an activist and liberal feminist point of view.
I aimed to bring public awareness to the struggles experienced by these
women, struggles that include a feeling of fondness for certain aspects of
their former life alongside firm rejection of others. When I encountered
frum women artists, I had to relearn gender roles and norms, to consider
forms of women's agency beyond public visibility and representation,
and, most importantly, to balance my subjective role as an anthropologist navigating multiple sites.

Feminist anthropology is a theoretical framework that influences the
research, either as a critical, feminist approach to the way knowledge
is produced or as an activist approach motivating a political research
agenda.[49] It can be all of this at the same time: a research agenda, a research method, an ideology that motivates research, a way of writing
about women, and an activist engagement. This book draws on this tradition of feminist anthropology that encompasses all these dimensions.
The research was motivated by a liberal feminist agenda, the ethnography was done with women, the data was analyzed through multiple

feminist lenses, and the writing involved a situational approach transcending feminism as one single category. In writing this book about ultra-Orthodox women and former ultra-Orthodox women, I have transcended my own feminist liberal agenda. Instead, I analyze and translate women's being, doing, and thinking as women and as artists. In this process, I have aimed to present these women as agents of change and influence in North American society, both within and outside Orthodoxy.

This research relies on the most recent era of feminist anthropology that correlated with the crisis of reflexivity and postmodernism in anthropology in the 1980s and 1990s. Building on the increased intersectionality of the second wave of feminism, third-wave feminists continued to investigate race, gender, sexuality, culture, nationality, and violence through the lenses of identity and power. New thinking emerged from this analysis of power regarding the lasting effects of colonialism and capitalism on women's oppression. Postcolonial feminists, inspired by Black feminists, acknowledge the past of feminism to be primarily white, Western, and colonialist, critiquing the idea of universal feminism.[50] This school of thought corresponds with the postmodernist movement in anthropology itself, in which the field shifted its focus towards questioning relationships between the ethnographer and the informant, challenging binaries such as us/them or the idea of the "other." In time, feminist anthropologists began to acknowledge the complex power relations between researchers and participants in ethnographies.[51] Some women anthropologists even questioned whether a feminist ethnography could exist, such as in Judith Stacey's 1988 article "Can There Be a Feminist Ethnography?" and Lila Abu-Lughod's 1988 speech of the same name. Stacey and Abu-Lughod posited that the shared identity of womanhood does not eliminate the hierarchy between researchers and their subjects. Women ethnographers also began to question their relationships with their communities of study, reflecting on their positionality as outsiders or insiders. Thus, more women began studying their communities of origin, leading to more engaged and in-depth analyses of their subjects and themselves.

I have long been troubled by the simplistic depictions in mainstream media of ultra-Orthodox Jews and of the ones who leave and the causal relationship drawn by the media between religious life and women's oppression, as if secularism necessarily precludes abuse. Nevertheless, an internal tension emerged in my understanding of the community's gender dynamics and the rules established for women in the arts: the tradition that men oversee the household economy even though women bring *parnasse* (income or livelihood), the prohibition against women driving, the requirement that women shave their hair, inequalities in their honoraria when performing, their struggles to be recognized as professional artists equivalent to their male counterparts, the restriction of not being able to sing at the *shabbes* table once their oldest sister gets married and brings her husband to the table—these were all phenomena with which I struggled. Many of these norms clashed with my upbringing, but instead of producing a liberal, secular, feminist critique, I needed to acknowledge that some of these women had different ambitions, desires, and perspectives; I also had to reconcile this idea with the notion that some of them could not meet the expectations of the ultra-Orthodox life and wanted a different one. In this book, I aim to illustrate their complex views, criticisms, frustrations, dilemmas, and satisfactions concerning both the ultra-Orthodox and the liberal worlds. This reflection on gender dynamics in a gender-segregated society also encouraged me to see the spectrum of possibilities and interpretations of both gender segregation and complementarianism.

Feminist anthropology is embedded in the research focusing on women. Studying and writing about women has implied and continues to imply a political and activist agenda achieved by women themselves. However, my experience collaborating with ultra-Orthodox women coming from a variety of backgrounds, and observing a multiplicity of experiences with and responses to the arts, encouraged me to think about feminist anthropology beyond the political and activist agenda— and to be humbler toward such an approach. My fieldwork guided my methodology, and my translocal ethnography led me to question the meaning of feminist anthropology in this context. As noted earlier, most of the ethnographies done by feminist anthropologists are embedded in one site and one community, guided by one political agenda, while my ethnography was not. This reflexive exercise encouraged me to think about a feminist ethnography transcending one specific ideology and goal, and most importantly to think about doing an ethnography of women's life that transcends the feminist label in order accurately to characterize what is at stake and to remember the modest attitude toward our field of research that we need to keep in mind as researchers.

With this research, I also draw on the work of anthropologists deconstructing the idea of the enclave to describe conservative religious groups and social changes, but expand on the role of the arts, technology, and women to understand these changes. In *Mitzvah Girls*, anthropologist Ayala Fader taught us how Hasidic girls embrace and adapt to North American society, though her analysis of this process ends when these girls become wives. Since the publication of her book (in 2009), the experiences of married Hasidic women, their ways of changing Orthodoxy and of being limited by it, and their adaptation to the digital turn, have remained unexplored in the North American context. In addition, documenting Montreal's ultra-Orthodox women's life alongside the one in New York has not been done. The arts and technology are rich fields for interpreting both the ongoing transformation of ultra-Orthodox Judaism as it adapts to the digital era and the translation of liberal ideas in such a way as to maintain and reinforce Orthodoxy. Women within Orthodoxy and those who have left it are forming a distinctive feature in North American Judaism as they renew perceptions and experiences of religious womanhood.

By tracking women's use of technology (the Internet, recording studios, mixing software, etc.) through the lens of their artistic productions, this book offers an exclusive window into new, alternative forms of economic agency that enable women to transform religious norms and the publicity of religion in twenty-first-century North American society. I demonstrate how women describe their changes through different discourses, decentering the debate on agency and feminism. Referring to famous Jewish female figures existing in recent Jewish histories (Sarah Schenirer, Vichna Kaplan, Rebbetzin Sara), or to biblical matriarchs, women are defining their actions in various terms such as "women's empowerment," "Jewish feminism as complementarianism," and "Jewish feminism as a need for gender equality in representation"— or they are simply acting without using any descriptive terms to characterize their action. By revealing the connection between *frum* and OTD artists, the circulation of sounds, movements, and images across borders thanks to technology, as well as the translocal connection beyond kin, this book proves the need for new ethnographic methods to study conservative religion in the twenty-first century, and to recontextualize it between and beyond boundaries.

Ultimately, this monograph is not about ultra-Orthodox women as they are imagined; it certainly does not describe a life that many outside the community might expect them to have. Rather, it offers an ethnography of feminist possibilities that encourage us woman ethnographers to reconsider feminist anthropology as an approach that can expose multiple voices and transcend our positionality and privilege.[52] As an ethnographer and analyst of these women's many narratives, I illuminate the possibilities of, and pockets of resistance to, alternative ways of being a woman in twenty-first-century North America.

Road Map of the Characters

What follows are five chapters and a postlude in which I analyze women's artistic spaces, illustrating ultra-Orthodox diversity in translating the concepts of privacy and publicity in such a way as to transform the arts into commodities. Beginning with an overview of the *frum* art worlds I have investigated, chapters progress from an assessment of the most conservative space in chapter 3 to an assessment of liberal ones in chapter 6. Through this trajectory, the book underlines the various strategies ultra-Orthodox women develop to negotiate the contradictions between the exposure of the art world and the privacy of the ultra-religious world.[53] Each chapter centers on a figure who embodies her specific space of performance and Orthodoxy. These figures uniquely exemplify the different trajectories of the women I discovered throughout my field research.

The following chapter, "The *Frum* Female Artist," offers an overview of the history and the current state of the art scenes I investigated. The figure of the *frum* female artist claimed by many women discussed in the book inspired me to view the multiple art scenes and characters I discovered and interacted with as "*frum* female art worlds." This chapter provides history and context to describe the birth, development, and changes of the art worlds presented in this book.

Chapter 3, "The Private Performer," investigates the emergence of an informal market for women's entertainment. This informal market contains a nested network of sounds, movements, melodies, and lyrics that are produced transnationally with the help of technology, and serve to fortify sisterhood, expand the concept of creativity, and contribute to *parnasse.*

Chapter 4, "The Celebrity," then sheds light on the birth of *frum* female artists and explores how they participate in the Americanization of ultra-Orthodoxy. These prominent women also transform collective performances that were once merely educational or spiritual into commodities that belong not anymore to an informal market but to the kosher music industry, creating a modest public space. This chapter theorizes Orthodoxy's integration of celebrity culture and encourages readers to imagine celebrities as products of something other than liberal individualism.

In chapter 5, "The Influencer," I focus on the way *frum* female celebrities have used social media as a subversive tool to defy Orthodoxy and to develop what I define as cyber*frum*enism (to play with the term "*frum*"). Despite mounting restrictions on social media use, some women artists have created a counterpublic space on Instagram, where they foster entrepreneurship and offer alternative ideas about womanhood within ultra-Orthodoxy that transcend the art worlds. I analyze their use of Instagram as a marketing tool to create the figure of the *frum* female artist and influencer. I also demonstrate that social media expands and strengthens their global and translocal network of followers and fans.

Next, a chapter on "The Public Artist" explores the participation of former Hasidic women in the making of public culture. Many of their theater and film performances of Hasidic Jewishness—a Jewish identity that I term "Hasidicness"—involve compromises vis-à-vis representations of Orthodoxy. In short, ultra-Orthodox performers must play the industry's game. By accepting the dilemmas that result and authenticating Hasidicness for the public, Hasidic women public artists are mediators between two worlds. This position allows them to reshape Hasidic public culture and representations of religious minorities.

Finally, in the postlude, "Arrival: Women Remaking Orthodoxy in the Digital Age," I continue to discuss gender and Orthodoxy by analyzing the interconnectivity of the women and artistic spaces presented in previous chapters. I revisit the concepts of privacy and publicity, as well as the economy of the *frum* female art worlds, and argue for an understanding of Orthodoxy as part of an ecology in which each space has a distinctive function while remaining connected to others. Through this constant interaction within and outside Orthodoxies, the social category of Orthodoxy is reinforced and transformed. Expanding beyond the case of ultra-Orthodox Jews, I argue for the integration of North American conservative religious women into debates on minorities, and for new ways to engage with publicity and privacy in the anthropology of religion. These concluding remarks serve as an entry point to reimagining the boundaries and the future of Orthodoxies in light of the broader changes guiding our world, now normalizing the digital, which is increasingly blurring the lines between the in-person and virtual worlds, privacy and publicity, the local and the global—all accelerated since the beginning of the COVID-19 pandemic.

This book is not an ethnography of religious life and Orthodoxy per se. It is a story of women embodying Orthodoxy with their arts, and of how Orthodoxy is presented, shaped, transformed, and rejected by these women in order to gain economic, cultural, and social agency. In this context, the idea of religion as the belief in and worship of a divine power is not relevant. This is a story about what today are defined as religious groups that exist within secular society, about women designated as religious but who live beyond this social category and are inspired by the broader world surrounding them. Most importantly, this is a book about women's autonomy, their power, and the limitations they face in challenging authority, and, on a personal level, about shared emotions and experiences with women who have changed my view on my own positionality and on the possibilities, as well as the limitations, I have as a woman and a working mother in a non-gender-segregated society.

2

The *Frum* Female Artist

Historicizing and Contextualizing Women's Art Worlds

In a society that relies on the contribution of women, you'd
do well to acquaint yourself with the tremendous power of
women. I think biases are not only outdated and limiting in
the extreme, but also fail to acknowledge what is true about
women. We are not LIKE men, we are way different, way
powerful, a force of proportion unknown to mere men.
—Chany Rosengarten, Instagram post, May 2018

During my ethnography in Montreal and New York City, I encountered
a diverse group of ultra-Orthodox women participating in the arts—
playing instruments, singing, recording in studios, making movies,
dancing, acting, and painting. Some of them embraced the label *"frum"*
to encompass the heterogeneous group of women from Hasidic and
Litvish communities across the globe, a term that I have adopted and
use throughout this book. They all performed exclusively for female
audiences, but developed different strategies to create boundaries to
establish artistic spaces distinct from those of their male counterparts.
While many of these women claim and adopt the label *"frum* female
artist"[1]—a novel concept that serves as a self-identifier and reshapes
the traditional interpretation of the feminine musical practice as a
collective space—others, coming from more conservative circles, prefer the description "being talented or creative." No matter how they
label themselves, the women I met feel bound by a sense of obligation
to contribute to a "better life" within Orthodoxy, but also to change
internal and external perceptions of it. They experience different types
of attachment and senses of belonging to Orthodoxy. Yet all of them
described a sense of relatedness that comes from their art and transcends their native communities.

Music, film, dance, and theater, as well as painting, are all contributions from these women that transform Orthodoxy in multiple ways. If they do not all explicitly express a desire to contribute to new ways of being Orthodox, their artistic projects do, often contradicting the way that Orthodoxy is defined. Part of their community might perceive their desire for creativity, novelty, and, most importantly, publicity as subversive. However, to exist and be recognized within this system, they all adopt a position that stresses the reinforcement of Orthodoxy. By advocating for a distinctive art scene for women and girls only, they align themselves with complementarianism, envisaging the paired roles and responsibilities of women and men in marriage, family life, and religious leadership. They tie their artistic projects to *parnasse*. Their actions are thus not perceived as heretical, even though the monetization of this market and industry by and for *haymish* Hasidic communities was not without backlash, and is still criticized in certain circles.[2] Because of their positionality in the arts, *frum* female artists are often perceived as residing on the fringes of society, recognized for their talent but holding no serious positions as problem solvers, witnesses, or leaders in their societies, so their subversive actions are often overlooked or viewed as not having a significant impact.

Of course, ultra-Orthodox girls have always engaged in the arts in gender-segregated spaces; that phenomenon is not new. What *is* new, however, is the transformation of the arts from educational, religious, and collective purposes to economic, social, and individual ones, including the birth of the "*frum* female artist." Most importantly, this shift touches various branches of Orthodoxy. Now, not only girls, *baalei tshuva*, or Lubavitcher women are the main players, but also women born in *haymish* Hasidic communities. In this chapter, the *frum* female artist serves as a central figure through which I illustrate the history of the art worlds surrounding her—borrowing the terminology of Howard Becker, as discussed in the previous chapter. These *frum* female art worlds have traditionally related to education, being spaces in which to strengthen one's connection with traditional Judaism, a practice exclusive to women and girls that has been endorsed by Orthodox rabbinical authority for decades. After marriage, women usually stop performing so that they can focus on their primary role as wives, mothers, and professionals in other domains than the arts. Indeed, with women now dominating the workforce, many have pursued new professional paths. They have emerged notably in the tech, social work, psychology, wellness, and marketing fields. Because the arts play an important role in education and, more recently, in wellness, entering this sector has also become an attractive path, especially for "talented" girls who aspire to continue their creative work beyond childhood.

The women I collaborated with recall their artistic journey beginning in childhood, usually in plays in school and at camps, where they acted, danced, sang, and/or painted. Often coming from creative, artistic, or musical families, they were said to have received a "gift from *Hashem*" (God) that must be cultivated. Private studios owned by women teaching dance, singing, music, painting, or acting are gaining popularity, signifying a growing demand for specialization in entertainment and educational arts, a phenomenon that is part of the increased demand for diverse opportunities in leisure within ultra-Orthodoxy. All of these players function within a cooperative network, guided by the ultra-Orthodox conventions pertaining to *tsnius*. This chapter offers an overview of the history, development, and current state of the art worlds made by ultra-Orthodox women, including the ones who decided to break away from Orthodoxy. Starting with the norms that established the *frum* female art worlds as a separate entity from the secular and liberal one, as well as from the male Orthodox one, this chapter acts as a preamble to the story narrated around the four ethnographic artistic scenes that occupy the core of this book.

The Conventions of *Tsnius* and *Kol Isha*

The concept of *tsnius*, often translated as "modesty" or "discretion," focuses on shaping bodies—both young and old—according to a ritualized and normative performance of the self and of gender that changes according to the privacy or publicity of the performance. The concept becomes increasingly important as children reach the age of twelve (for girls) or thirteen (for boys), when according to Jewish law they become responsible for fulfilling all the Jewish commandments.[3] Nevertheless, as many people have expressed to me, much less attention is paid to boys' modesty than to girls' since male bodies, unlike female bodies, are not perceived as sexual.

For the *frum* female art worlds, the conventions of *tsnius* resulted in a strictly gender-segregated and private artistic scene that should be invisible to men. Women and girls perform for female-only audiences or their immediate families.[4] The publicization of the arts, which is usually at the core of the raison d'être of the arts, is thus problematic. As we will see throughout this book, the concept of privacy (which is central to *tsnius* for girls and women) and the division of private events from publicly accessible ones, are constantly redefined and negotiated—not only according to community norms established by rabbinical authorities but also according to women's judgment and discursive actions. Women listen to and take inspiration from Orthodox male productions and are connected to the development of artistic creation, distribution, and performance in society at large. Nevertheless, their art worlds have their own function, form, and aesthetic due to the centrality of *tsnius* within the specific context of ultra-Orthodoxy.

Tsnius can be understood as an interpretation of the privacy and publicity of the gendered self, illustrating the discursive aspect of Orthodoxy.[5] It implies a spectrum of practices that religious authorities and individuals interpret, reinterpret, perform, and transmit, varying across space and time. *Tsnius* encompasses dress and hair coverings; appropriate thoughts, language, actions, and body language; and choice of literature, media, and entertainment. Different performative spaces produce variations in *tsnius* depending on the *hashkafic* norms of the community the women belong to[6]—often connected to their husband's affiliation[7]—as well as individual's opinions about *tsnius* and how it relates to their bodies, clothes, and gestures. There is indeed a contrast between the conventional norms within ultra-Orthodoxy and the way individual women decide to perform *tsnius*.

During my fieldwork, women described or defined *tsnius* in many ways, the concept serving as a central pillar on which to rest their Orthodox identities or—for those who left their communities—to chip away at in order to construct new identities wherein Orthodox and Hasidic identities are a cultural expression in which the observance of *halakha*, Jewish law, is irrelevant. Among the women who embrace *tsnius*, some harshly criticized religious authority and the way the concept is explained in school curricula. According to the Orthodox feminist activist

Rifka Wein Harris, *tsnius* is typically taught around two concepts: (1) the measuring tape with which the size of clothing and hair coverings is assessed; and (2) the effect of female attractiveness. Wein Harris criticizes this approach and suggests a new one, focusing not on the way teens present themselves to the world but on building up their sense of self. She writes about the three elements that, in her home, undergird the idea of *tsnius*: "privacy, humility, and *feinkeit* (refinement)."[8] Wein Harris comes from a mixed Hasidic and Litvish family. She is well connected to the *frum* female art worlds because of her daughter's musical dedication and talent in composition and piano. Her vision of *tsnius* largely conforms to the one espoused by women I encountered. Women like Rifka Wein Harris act subversively, defying established norms within the communities they grew up in and suggesting new ones, such as the exposure of women's faces in ultra-Orthodox public media.

Tsnius is transmitted and adapted through a nonverbal and verbal process of imitation across a diversity of spaces. Performances in music, dance, theater, and painting shape these conventions while offering the possibility to transform them.[9] Through an individual and collective creative process, these artistic performances reshape the way Orthodoxy itself is performed by adopting new expressions of *tsnius* that maintain continuity with the past. Inspired by the philosopher and gender theorist Judith Butler, I envisage Orthodoxy as a performative, gendered act, transcending the passing on of knowledge and rules.[10] Orthodoxy takes all of its meaning from the performance of the self, changing according to the age and the status of the gendered individual (married or unmarried). In other words, body performances sustain and reflect the identities of ultra-Orthodox women. Within the arts, women create and reinforce the group's narrative of these performances of Orthodoxy in an ongoing and systematic way. Throughout this book, the performance of Orthodoxy in the arts is understood not only by its bodily and audible expression but also by its reception by specific audiences.

An important part of *tsnius* is the concept of *kol isha*, or "a woman's voice," which prohibits women and girls from singing at events attended by men.[11] *Kol isha* has been at the center of *halakhic* debates because of its perceived erotic implications.[12] Debates over when and how men should hear women's voices have been crucial in the creation and consolidation of the *frum* female art worlds. The issue hinges on the Talmudic interpretation of a passage in the Tanakh (Hebrew Bible), Song of Songs 2:14:

> O my dove, in the cranny of the rocks,
> Hidden by the cliff,
> Let me see your face,
> Let me hear your voice;
> For your voice is sweet
> And your face is comely.[13]

Based on this passage, the sixth-century Talmudic scholar Samuel is cited as declaring "*Kol b'ishah ervah*" (Talmud, Berakhot 24a), which is typically translated as "the voice of a woman is a sexual incitement."[14] Rabbi Samuel's interpretation led other rabbinical scholars to deliberate whether the passage referred to a woman's voice in any context or if it applied specifically to women when singing, engaging in religious study, being in the presence of a male who is reciting prayers, or being nude.[15]

To avoid illicit relationships, restrictions were laid on men hearing the voices of "foreign" women (that is, not a wife or close family member) in the context of performance and, more specifically, of singing and entertainment. While the *halakhic* prohibitions primarily aim to prevent men from hearing women's voices, women and girls are not prohibited from singing or performing. Practices regarding this prohibition have taken different forms in different ultra-Orthodox communities at varying times.[16] Some women and girls sing and perform only in enclosed spaces (with curtains if there are windows), where they can be certain that no man will overhear them, as long as they do not project their voices. Others sing outdoors for a female-only audience, labeling their performance "for women and girls only" and shifting to men the responsibility for avoiding overhearing them. As a result of these restrictions, I have observed that girls and women in most conservative spaces rarely project their voices when singing individually, often singing with their chest voice and using breathy singing techniques. The distinction is particularly evident when one compares Hasidic male and female singing performances. Even though both genders now use microphones in many circumstances, the Hasidic male singer is recognizable by his strong and powerful vocal protuberance, using a forcing chest, head voice, and full belt, techniques and mobilization of the vocal apparatus that would not even require a microphone to be projected. Interestingly, at the *shabbes* table of Goldie, presented in the previous chapter, the girls imitated their male counterparts, singing with full belt for a powerful voice projection, while on stage, for their school performances, they mobilized a more timid chest voice to fit into the group. In other words, religious norms motivate the development of the *frum* female art worlds, and the ways these norms take shape is in the embodied and sounding practices of women and girls.

Origins: Education and Artistic Creation

I trace the genesis of the *frum* female art worlds to the combination of the Orthodox educational project for girls, which emerged in early twentieth-century Eastern Europe, and the way that modernity has affected older patterns of artistic creation, distribution, and performance. Indeed, the religious educational project for Orthodox girls emerged at a time when artistic creation, distribution, and exhibition were affected by drastic changes, starting in the mid-nineteenth century in Europe and in North America with the emergence of the music and film recording industry, the birth of the radio, and the popularization of theater and musicals.[17]

The project of expanding Orthodox education for girls to include performance can be traced to the vision of one woman born in Poland in the late nineteenth century: Sarah Schenirer. Schenirer came from a Polish rabbinic family with ties to Hasidic dynasties, and she is remembered now as a visionary in Jewish girls' education, having introduced performance as part of the curriculum in Krakow in the 1920s. She was not the first to provide formal Jewish education to girls in the region, but she was the first to do it in Krakow's Hasidic circles. Her movement continued to flourish throughout her lifetime, persisting even through the Holocaust and reaching a global scale after World War II.[18] Prior to Schenirer's project, Orthodox girls attended secular state or Christian schools and often ended up abandoning Orthodoxy. Jewish studies scholars Naomi Seidman and Rachel Manekin documented this phenomenon extensively, explaining that it resulted from the 1869

Compulsory Education Law issued by the Habsburg Empire, requiring all children in Austro-Hungary between the ages of six and fourteen to attend public school. Orthodox parents were often reluctant to send their sons to these schools because doing so would prevent them from studying Torah; they preferred to pay a fine rather than comply.[19] However, Aaron Marcus, a German Jewish intellectual who embraced Hasidism, encouraged parents to send their daughters instead; since space in the new public schools was limited, such a strategy would allow them to circumvent compulsory education for their sons. To echo Manekin, the education of Orthodox girls protected their brothers from exposure to the secular world but resulted in the "blossoming of a generation of Jewish young women from Orthodox homes who were fervent 'Poles' in their language, intellectual lives, and their appearance."[20]

Seeing these girls defect from Orthodoxy, Sarah Schenirer and others recognized the need to provide a systematic and uplifting religious education for girls to preserve *Yiddishkeit*. She sought to ensure the transmission and consolidation of religious life for girls through the establishment of a school curriculum that included plays featuring singing and dancing. The first school opened in Krakow in 1917 and became a model for the education of Hasidic girls in Eastern Europe.[21] The Bais Yaakov (House of Jacob) movement, as it was called, grew to encompass a network of schools and summer camps. The curriculum included both religious and secular subjects, but Schenirer's goal was to bring girls and women "back to Torah." Her unique vision was to inspire girls to remain Jewish and observant: "The main lesson was that Orthodox girls can have fun within the realm of Torah."[22] In addition to full-time schools, the movement included supplementary religious schools for girls who attended non-Jewish institutions during the day, teacher training seminaries, summer camps, youth clubs, publications, and international conferences.

The Bais Yaakov movement placed value on youth, women, innovation, and community performances with singing, acting, and dancing, which deepened shared Jewish identity, Ashkenazi ethnicity, and Orthodox/Hasidic religious ties. Collective performances that expressed and transmitted Orthodox femininity cultivated a sense of belonging to a community of shared affiliation, one that Schenirer expressed as sisterhood.[23] According to Naomi Seidman, Schenirer called all members of the school (spiritual) "sisters," and the bringing of girls "back to Torah" an act of "sisterhood." Metaphors of motherhood appeared too, to describe Schenirer's own role in the project.[24] In other words, Bais Yaakov mobilized the notions of motherhood and sisterhood to produce new forms of family and kinship, thus saving the traditional Jewish home.[25] Scholar Deborah Weissman explained the expansion of kinship beyond the nuclear family as a distinctive marker of modern social movements such as socialism, communism, and Zionism.[26] For Seidman, the Bais Yaakov movement—as a traditionalist phenomenon with few traditional precedents—"mobilized discursive tools such as those developed by other new social and political movements, selecting from a range of available options and creatively transforming them for its own purposes, which were ironically so distinct from theirs."[27]

Influenced by her love of theater,[28] Schenirer gave a central role in this project to plays, music, and dance, writing scripts for performances during the Jewish holidays.[29] One can imagine that performances came to serve as a recruitment tool for the movement. Schenirer also integrated a Hasidic spirit into the girls' education, often ending her speeches with circle dances and positioning herself at the center,[30] imitating the dance between Hasidim and their *rebbe*. In this case, the collective performance achieves the religious, moral, and ethical goals that the community sought to foster, and it reflects Hasidic perspectives on performance generally, particularly how it can constitute a form of communication with God.[31]

Beyond the centrality of performances for girls in the educational system, married women had, and continue to have, fewer opportunities to perform in conservative circles than younger girls because their social position as mothers and wives traditionally conflicts with the publicity and visibility of performing onstage. The early twentieth century—though not the origin of female creativity in traditional Ashkenazi Judaism—witnessed the institutionalization of female-only performance in educational circles, a project that was also influenced by the increased popularity of theater and musicals, and the transformations occurring in the domain of artistic production. As we will discover throughout the book, the changes occurring in the media and the entertainment industry in society at large continue to influence these *frum* female art worlds.

Sarah Schenirer's project flourished in Hasidic circles throughout Eastern Europe. After the Holocaust, the movement became more permanent in emerging centers of Orthodox life, notably in North America and Israel.[32] Vichna Eisen Kaplan, a student of Schenirer's, opened the first Bais Yaakov school in North America in Williamsburg, Brooklyn, in 1938, initially organizing it as an after-school supplementary program in her home, operating under the authority of the central office in Europe, then expanding into rented spaces and becoming an all-day school. As the movement spread, the tradition of plays and performances was also exported to North America, influencing the curricula of other ultra-Orthodox girls' schools.

The Development of the *Frum* Female Art Worlds in Postwar North America

While ultra-Orthodox schools vary in outlook and philosophy, especially in their interaction with secular culture and society, they share similar values, methodologies, and aims in developing a Torah-driven curriculum and valorizing the arts to strengthen the sense of community. Some Hasidic communities who have a strict interpretation of *tsnius*, such as Satmar, oppose Bais Yaakov, but they, too, have established their own school networks for girls and utilize school plays. Schenirer's model undoubtedly influenced other communities, in pursuit of the same goal that had motivated Bais Yaakov's founding: marrying girls to Orthodox boys. As with any tradition,[33] the custom of school plays has changed throughout the years, responding to new contexts and needs within and outside Orthodoxy. Many scholars have documented an increased Haredization of Jewish life—that is, amplified religious stringency—a phenomenon of which Bais Yaakov is part, in postwar North America.[34] Some Bais Yaakov schools produced Broadway shows in the 1960s, but this practice came under fire as time went on because Orthodox communities sought to prevent girls from accessing secular knowledge.[35] Instead, religious authorities and school leadership advocated for producing Jewish-themed plays, strengthening *halakhic* observance, and shutting out secular American culture, a process adopted in the Haredi world at large.[36]

This idea of artistic self-exclusion from North American culture has spread widely within the ultra-Orthodox world among both women and men, but the reality documented by scholars shows clear ties between this world and American popular culture, notably in music.[37] Ultra-Orthodox leadership disseminated secular plays adapted to a Jewish context, as well as original scripts and lyrics with Jewish themes and in Jewish languages (Yiddish and Hebrew), to give the impression of a creative space isolated from external influence. Nevertheless, artists who engaged with American popular culture brought new melodies, instrumental accompaniment, and choreographies from the secular world. Orthodox teachers and principals officially censor non-Jewish music, though the generation of women born before World War II openly listened to mainstream secular music in the 1950s and 1960s, in addition to Jewish secular music.[38] Despite such condemnations, non-Jewish melodies continued to enter the ultra-Orthodox musical space, as authorship in music is rarely credited, making it difficult to tell what is and is not Jewish music.[39] Secular musicals have been reintroduced through a process of disguise, where titles were changed, and some sections of the play erased or altered to fit Orthodox expectations. Composers, lyricists, and scriptwriters are not credited, as was the case with the N'shei Tzedakah Players in the 1990s and Rachel's Place Productions since 2011, two productions in New York directed by Miriam Handler. In 2012, Rachel's Place produced *The Song of the Hills*, a cover and remix of the 1959 Broadway original *The Sound of Music*—music composed by Richard Rodgers, lyrics by Oscar Hammerstein II, and script by Russel Crouse. As romance and reference to Christianity occur in the original, the producers of the kosher musicals—those framed to be in line with Orthodox norms—kept the music, most of the script, and the lyrics, but transformed certain references: the monastery where Maria is trained became a secular boarding school; the nuns "Sister Berthe, Margarette" and "Reverend Mother" were renamed "Fraulein Berthe and Margarette" and "headmistress"; and the romance between Liesl and Rolf became a friendship between two girls.[40]

A tradition of girls singing and performing has long existed in contexts beyond the school and the summer camp—namely, on *shabbes* with their families and at life-cycle events such as bat mitsvas, engagements, and weddings, at which women are separate from men. In contrast, during communal religious activities that occur at the synagogue, they remain silent. On rare occasions, they also perform at musical gatherings around Jewish music, known as *kumzits*.[41] The most talented girls from more liberal backgrounds also sing at *tsedakah* (charity) events alongside women, where they earn money for their performances. The repertoire performed in these spaces varies according to their specific ultra-Orthodox affiliation.

Hasidic girls (except for those who are Lubavitch) usually sing in Yiddish and in Loshn Koydesh—a mix of Hebrew and Aramaic found in religious texts and prayers, the term being used to differentiate from vernacular Hebrew—while Litvish and Lubavitcher girls sing in Loshn Koydesh as well as vernacular Hebrew or English.[42] The melodies come from a variety of sources, sometimes from *niggunim* (*nigun*, in the singular—refers to Jewish religious songs with repetitive sounds instead of formal lyrics) and *zmires* (Jewish hymns) but mostly from popular songs released by famous ultra-Orthodox male singers or composers (in Yiddish, Loshn Koydesh, Hebrew, or English) or from non-Jewish sources. Though girls often write lyrics, few compose melodies, so the common practice is to do a cover or a contrafactum (the act of using a melody from a song and changing the lyrics). Furthermore, the repertoire of songs used in schools and summer camps constantly evolves, featuring new popular songs from the male Orthodox music industry.

Historical information about these girls-only performances is extremely limited. While Hasidic singing by men was documented and recorded throughout the twentieth century,[43] I was not able to find official audio or video archives of girls' and women's performances within Orthodox circles. In the late 1990s and early 2000s, the democratization of video recording technology allowed schools to record their performances and create local archives of their annual plays. Apart from some of these informal videos, I was not able to illuminate the aesthetic transformations occurring in these collective creative female spaces. Moreover, very few historical and ethnographic studies exist on the subject. This dearth of literature might be explained by the lack of women scholars in the field and certainly by the disregard for women's performances. Until recently, men have dominated research on ultra-Orthodoxy and Hasidism, and performances and popular culture became the focus of attention only toward the end of the first decade of the twenty-first century, still largely centered on the male perspective.[44] This research focuses on sources and practices where women were invisible or silent, portraying women as peripheral to the masculine domain of ultra-Orthodox life.[45]

The first scholars who wrote about Hasidic women and performances in North America were Shifra Epstein and Ellen Koskoff in the 1970s and 1980s, respectively. Epstein wrote on the Bobov theater, and Koskoff exposed the causal relationship between the socioreligious status of women and their musical practices.[46] While pioneering in its scope, Koskoff's research was limited to the Lubavitch communities, and Epstein concentrated on one specific performance, the Purim play. Only later, in the 1990s and early 2000s, did some of the first publications on non-Lubavitcher women's performances emerge, with the works of Zelda Kahan-Newman on Satmar songs;[47] Asya Vaisman on various Hasidic dynasties across North America, Europe, and Israel;[48] and, more recently, Rose Waldman on Hasidic women's voices in North America,[49] and Jill Gellerman on the history of Hasidic dance.[50] All of these scholars highlight the communal experience of these performances, how *tsnius* requires discretion in the public display of individual talent, as well as the centrality of the educational, religious, and social nature of these performances.[51] However, none of them frame these communal performances as creative activities undertaken for economic and aesthetic purposes that are acting on Orthodoxy itself, even in the literature about ultra-Orthodoxy in Israel.[52]

The Early Twenty-First-Century Topography of the *Frum* Female Art Worlds

Today, all schools and summer camps serving ultra-Orthodox girls around the globe offer performing arts in their curricula—though some emphasize them more than others—providing a range of opportunities for dancing, singing, playing an instrument, or otherwise performing, as well as for observing and appreciating the performances of others. The nature and extent of arts-making often depend on the norms of *tsnius* and *kol isha* among the Hasidic or Litvish group the institution is affiliated with, the girls' ages (pre- or post–bat mitsva), and their marital status. The arts are considered beneficial for educational, social, and religious purposes, such as establishing gender roles or to strengthen faith and a sense of belonging.

A convergence of social, cultural, and economic changes in North American and ultra-Orthodox societies progressively transformed the role of ultra-Orthodox women in the arts, positioning not only girls but also married women at its center. The emergence of an ultra-Orthodox middle class with a taste for consumerism and entertainment,[53] a new emphasis on pedagogy for individual growth, the shift to the digital, and the increase in secular Jewish women artists joining ultra-Orthodoxy (notably, *baalei tshuva* among Chabad) all gave rise to a scene of professional performers and the birth of the *frum* female artist. Unmarried girls already performed in their communities, but now they continue to pursue these activities after marriage, often starting on the stages of *tsedakah* events. In time, they began to record, promote, and market their artistic work beyond these community events. Today, ultra-Orthodox women's performances appear not only live onstage but also as part of an industry and market for both commercial and noncommercial recordings online, on stage, and on screen.

The themes presented in these performances vary according to the audience and the women producing them, but they usually include historical events, faith, motherhood, Jewish holidays, redemption, self-sacrifice, *tsnius*, or the dangers of the outside world (sometimes ironically conveyed with a melody taken from the kosher male music industry adapted from that very world). Love songs and love stories are not traditionally performed in ultra-Orthodox circles, but more recently, larger companies such as Rachel's Place Productions have defied this tradition by, for example, adapting the Broadway show *Anastasia* and retaining those elements of the musical. Some *frum* female artists are also innovating in terms of genre and themes. For instance, Franciska Kosman tackled women's power, the refugee crisis, personal development, and painful loss, mobilizing religious references and texts for her inspiration and integrating hip-hop, Latino, and jazzy sounds; Dobby Baum introduced the topics of women's power and unity, mental health issues, and postpartum anxiety/depression. The women I encountered respond to and defy the Haredization of their lives and communities through various subversive mechanisms, as we will discover throughout this book. Their efforts to effect change in Orthodoxy from within take shape not only on stage (the traditional creative outlet for these women) but now also in films, online content, and studio recordings. They create material in women-owned recording studios, challenge the absence of women in ultra-Orthodox public media by posting songs and other performances online on YouTube and Instagram, create what I label a modest public space, and cultivate their own culture of celebrity to reinvent the *frum* female role model.

The Exodus from the *Frum* Female Art Worlds

Among the women participating in the *frum* female art worlds, some decided to break away from Orthodoxy. The reasons, motivations, and explanations for such exodus vary. For some of them, the norms of *tsnius, kol isha,* and strict gender segregation, and other aspects of ultra-Orthodox Jewry, were too restrictive. Some aspired to a different lifestyle and did not want to meet the expectations of their religious environment and families. The narratives around their exits were diverse, and tensions existed between the way exiters perceived their departure and the way they are perceived and described by their counterparts from within Orthodoxy. Indeed, the exit from Orthodoxy is often pathologized, and the journey of someone who decides to break away from this lifestyle and implicitly to exit the "tribe" is habitually interpreted as the result of trauma and/or abuse.[54] Throughout my ethnography, I had to navigate these systems of thought. I brought my knowledge of the experience and narratives of exiters to Orthodox circles to complicate their narratives and to connect the experience of exiters to Jewish history at large. Individuals have consistently exited and/or entered Orthodoxy since the reform movement,[55] but a new aspect of this phenomenon is the organization of the exodus into a collective experience that creates a community—as noted earlier, what is known as the "off the *derekh*" (or OTD) community—that uses media and technology to form and reinforce communal bonds.

Women from the *frum* art worlds who left Orthodoxy now reinvent themselves as public artists in music, cinema, theater, and dance. They perform for various audiences, including women and men still within ultra-Orthodoxy who lead double lives, others who left their communities, non-Orthodox people, and non-Jewish people. In fact, their knowledge of ultra-Orthodoxy, and more specifically of Yiddish as native speakers, often serves as a springboard from which to access the broader secular arts and entertainment industry. With their public performances, they both reinforce and defy stereotypes about conservative religious women.

Contrary to many assumptions, while women of the OTD community now perform in art worlds ruled by the norms of liberal society, they do not all cut ties with ultra-Orthodoxy. Rather, they maintain relationships with individuals still in the community, such as their families, and their artistic productions are sometimes consumed by ultra-Orthodox women and girls. They observe the artistic scene by and for ultra-Orthodox female artists in order to follow the internal changes and sometimes translate that scene for liberal circles. Women within and outside the community sometimes help each other, recommending technicians, teachers, and even other artists. The development of these art worlds both within and outside of Orthodoxy serves as a catalyst for the diversification of Orthodoxy as a discursive tradition.[56] It is this diversity within Orthodoxy that lies behind my use of the plural to speak of many Jewish Orthodoxies rather than one. Even when ultra-Orthodox women leave the religious lifestyle, they maintain cultural ties, which led me to consider them as culturally Orthodox or Hasidic.

Discovering the birth of the *frum* female artist, I went in search of her genealogy, trying to understand her emergence and her connections to the worlds of women's arts within ultra-Orthodoxy. In this chapter, the *frum* female artist has been mobilized as an ideal type to explain the raison d'être of the art worlds in which she participates as well as its origins and transformations, including ruptures. We discovered these links by looking at the transformations of the entertainment industry and the development of an educational system for Orthodox girls. In this context, these worlds of female art are defined by their private dimension vis-à-vis the Orthodox male public and the non-Orthodox public. However, the way in which this privacy manifests varies according to the audience and the community of belonging. Still, all of the women involved in these art worlds have developed subversive mechanisms to reconcile their need for privacy with the desire for advertising, even in the most conservative spaces that are invisible beyond their community.

3

The Private Performer

Expanding Creativity, Redefining Publicity

This is the most important thing we can give to the girls, to
be proud of who they are, and where they come from; the
play allows them to feel that way.
—Chaya, director of school performance, Montreal, 2019

Kiryas Joel, also known as KJ, is a village in Upstate New York known
for being the home of the most secluded Hasidic communities in North
America. On my way there in the summer of 2020, I met the female
Hasidic musician, singer, and educator Toby. Toby disseminates her creative work without her name, or her face, according to the norms of
tsnius in her community. Since that meeting, Toby and I have communi-
cated on a regular basis; she often sends me videos and announcements
about her musical endeavors, whether they are practice sessions, performances, or music lessons for girls. In mid-April of 2021, Toby sent
me a WhatsApp message to announce her published interview with
the Yiddish Hasidic women's magazine of her community of KJ. As
its title implies, *Balebusta* (a Yiddish term meaning "busy housewife")
covers issues of interest to Yiddish Hasidic women. It is distributed to
thousands of people throughout KJ. Emphasizing Toby's position as a
married woman, mother, performer, and educator, the interview nor-
malizes her musical project in KJ, which is teaching violin, piano, and
guitar to girls, highlighting how she serves her community by encouraging women and girls to develop their talent by learning an instrument.
The piece masks her first name behind her married name, referring to
her as Mrs. T. Chaimowitch, and includes no photos of her. Many in
feminist liberal circles would likely describe Toby as invisible, or at least
rendered unrecognizable to the many women who know her. Nevertheless, *Balebusta* promoted her individual and economic success by

publishing this interview and by discussing her music disconnected from any religious practice, creating an interesting paradox between *tsnius*, individuality, and self-promotion. Traditionally, musical talent is framed as given by God and, to respect the norms of *tsnius*, it should not be self-promoted. With this contradiction emerges an understanding of women's publicity and visibility that does not involve the exposure of faces, names, and bodies, defying Western liberal feminism and its view that cultural agency must be reflected by the visible exposure and celebration of women's images and their names.[1]

As a child, Toby never imagined she would perform on stage one day, even for a female-only audience. Watching the Orthodox Miami Boys' Choir growing up, she knew she would not be able to perform on stage—or sing or play an instrument at weddings, one of the most profitable activities for male ultra-Orthodox performers—as a Hasidic woman. The idea of making *parnasse* (income) by performing for and teaching music to a women-only audience did not exist in Kiryas Joel at the time. The integration of art programs for kids with special needs, subsidized by the government, made the art curriculum more accessible and extracurricular activities trendy. Productions for the entertainment of the ultra-Orthodox middle class—also known as kosher art, meaning that its practices can be trusted to satisfy the requirements of Jewish law—drastically grew, especially for women and girls. Moreover, broader access to the Internet and technology in general facilitated the emergence of print and online media, such as *Balebusta*, dedicated to women, easily disseminated, and made from the comfort of the home.[2] With these media, made within the community, people are able to gain new, easy access to knowledge and savoir-faire from outside their community without physically interacting with the outside world.

As a result of these technological and social developments, Toby's destiny proved different from what she expected. She started taking private keyboard lessons in eleventh grade with a woman from KJ. After her marriage in the mid-2000s, her husband encouraged her to pursue music as a way of making *parnasse*. He saw the potential of a career within his community. After visiting a musical instrument store in Monsey in Upstate New York, Toby immediately started researching teachers and instrument purchases online. She bought herself a violin and a saxophone, as well as a harp. Teaching herself the basics with help from

YouTube videos, she began performing as a hobby, singing at local organizations to entertain other women. After gaining some experience, she had a vision: to expand the creative prospects of Hasidic Satmar girls who lack opportunities to perform in their communities after the age of twelve (other than at gender-specific summer camps).[3] Inspired by the boys' choir that rocked her childhood and guided by the norms of *tsnius* in KJ—which reject the concept of the "soloist" to prevent artists from becoming consumed by fame—Toby formed a women's band. Alongside that new endeavor, she also launched an after-school program to teach keyboard, piano, and violin to girls who would ultimately perform in groups of their own. Despite emphasizing in her program that individual talent is a "natural" ability, Toby always presents creative expression as a collective experience. She offers individual lessons, but the girls perform only in groups. As she explained, "Their goal as Hasidic women and girls is not to become famous. Even if they learn and practice individually, they always think about the result of the performance as a collective. They are doing it for fun and for the community. It contributes to their self-esteem and confidence. They can shine during the performance, but I have to stay focused on *tsnius*, which values modesty and discretion."[4]

Ultra-Orthodox women developed various mechanisms to transform artistic performances into an informal market where musical aesthetic exploration is possible. Central among the strategies is the framing of creativity as a social and educational tool connected to *tsnius*, according to which individual talent is part of a collective experience designed to reinforce community and a connection to Orthodoxy. Casting the publicity of women's creativity in terms of the collective guides this expression of *tsnius*. For Toby—and many of the women I encountered who are private performers—creativity is dissociated from the culture of individual genius so often fostered in entertainment and the arts. Creativity is advertised and promoted through collectiveness, even though I could personally sense in them a desire for individual recognition.

It was during the Enlightenment era that the Romantic myth of the creative "genius" developed, associating creativity with high art, authorship, virtuosity, and the prodigy of the composer or writer, who possesses a talent that must be distinguished from the routine or ordinary and recognized as such by society at large. Prior to the Enlightenment, in line with today's understanding within ultra-Orthodox circles, creativity was considered divinely inspired, something humans could accomplish thanks to God. This then developed in the secular world into the notion of a special power among artists, who were often granted a mystical status. In the twentieth century, the myth of the genius creator gained purchase in the celebrity culture performed in mass media and consequently became globally influential. This account of creativity lies behind the creation of the copyright system and the notion of intellectual property that is now normalized and globalized. Creativity has been and often still is defined through the celebration of individuality thanks to a combined process of professionalization, institutionalization, and mediatization.

In music, this understanding of creativity particularly influences the cult of personality surrounding composers of art music and performers of popular music. Within the academic study of the topic, scholars in psychology and education have been at the forefront of research. Psychologists investigate how creativity and talent develop cognitively, while scholars in education explore how different pedagogical techniques can encourage and stimulate creativity. In anthropology and ethnomusicology, criticism of the hegemonic Western conception of creativity—as both a productive and a receptive process—stresses that creativity has a collective nature. These disciplines focus on non-Western cultures and explain the creative expressions of the "other" as a collective experience conceptualized as tradition. However, the work of sociologist Howard Becker in 1982 blurred the lines between Western and so-called non-Western (or "folkloric") creativity—between creativity as an individual process and creativity as a traditional, collective experience. By interpreting Western artwork as emerging not only through individual creation but also through the interaction of artists, collaborators, and audiences, Becker decentered individuality in the Western discourse on creativity and introduced the idea of the collective process.[5]

Working with a private performer such as Toby as well as her clients and fellows, I realized how they all embrace the idea of creativity as a collective process publicized among women and girls only. They portray the hidden nature of this process as an important part of their Orthodox womanhood, allowing them to create new sounds, arrangements, and ideas for music and performance that follow the norms of *tsnius.* For some, these private performances are emancipatory, developed as new techniques to negotiate their desire for individual recognition while maintaining strict religious norms. These women and their spaces of performance encourage us to rethink creativity as a gendered collective process that absorbs the individual. They underline how creativity and, more broadly, the arts, even when they are marketable, can be tools both for connection with the community and for individual satisfaction. Female-only creative spaces within conservative religion are often perceived as oppressive, and much research at the intersection of creativity, gender, and religiosity depicts female agency and liberation to be the result of public performances.[6] But the existence of an informal *frum* female market of entertainment and artistic productions suggests that creativity can be cultivated and is shaped by religious norms; the combined expressions of womanhood and religiosity through the arts offer an implicit critique of the Western secular feminist perspective that assesses agency according to public representation. An individual/communal, modern/traditional, Western/non-Western, secular/religious, public/private schism dominates both the ultra-Orthodox and the liberal secular canons. Within the ultra-Orthodox canon, creativity is envisioned as communal, traditional, private, and potentially non-Western. Within liberal secular discourse, the culture of individualism and exposure is the quintessential model through which to conceptualize creativity.[7] Yet through collective creativity, ultra-Orthodox Jewish women who perform in private places instigate change on the individual level by deciding who they are, how they will express themselves, and what they consider the spectrum of possible practices for ultra-Orthodox women and girls living in twenty-first-century North American society.

Motivated by the valorization of an education that brings *parnasse*, women and girls have created this new musical market while thinking about their collectiveness or their sisterhood, and how it is connected to Orthodoxy and religiosity. In doing so, they maintain the traditional structure of Orthodoxy by prioritizing service and collective creativity, but they also present new avenues for maintaining sisterhood, making *parnasse*, and gaining economic agency and publicity. On the other hand, because they are creating an informal market circulating across borders that allows them to gain economic agency, they also show the potentiality of the free market in the arts for female and conservative groups, and the importance of considering the individual within the collective.

Contrary to previous scholars who see ultra-Orthodox performance as a social, educational, religious process and as a communal raison d'être that excludes art for its own sake,[8] I argue that the latter's creative process—and any creative process for that matter, whether in religious or secular spaces—results from a combination of meanings where creativity in the arts is maintained by broader economic, social, and cultural mechanisms for their own sake. The women performers considered in this chapter justify their exploration of the arts and its publicity essentially as having social and economic rationales. Yet, Toby's interview offers an example of how this informal music market has also emerged as a celebrated and therefore empowering part of ultra-Orthodoxy, underlining how "gender-restricted markets" can be liberating when they foster a multifaceted approach toward creativity.

This chapter examines five feminine performance scenes—proceeding from the most traditional to the most avant-garde—that highlight the aesthetic transformation of the *frum* female art worlds impacted by the digital, revealing multiple forms of collective creativity. In this ethnography of the private performer, we discover how she develops a complex apparatus to make her arts advertised, appreciated, and marketable while respecting a strict interpretation of *tsnius* and *kol isha*. The five scenes of performance explored here illustrate the various shapes the informal *frum* female market takes and the ways in which it reinvigorates ultra-Orthodoxy. In their secluded spaces, these women find creative responses to their aspirations for visibility, novelty, and change, broadly reflecting how they are impacted by the ultra-Orthodox and broader society's economic, social, and digital environments.

The School Performance

One evening in January 2019, a few weeks after Hanukkah, my former piano students performed on stage for an annual school play. Their mother, Rivka, invited me to the occasion. Ever since we had met in 2016, Rivka had spoken about this play, which occurs every three years: "The girls perform every year during the holidays or at the end of the year.

THE PRIVATE PERFORMER | 63

There is often a singing, acting, and dance part with an exhibition of their paintings. But the one happening every three years during Hanukkah is very special. It is the professional one." The play is a private event for women and girls from the community. While more conservative girls' schools, such as in Satmar, define private events as restricted to students and teachers, excluding family members (mothers, aunts, or grandmothers) from the audience, Rivka's school hosts private events by limiting the sale of tickets to female members of the community. Inviting someone from outside, like me, is not a simple task; it requires strong ties and trust because privacy is essential to the event's sustainability. With permission, I was able to attend not only the play but also rehearsals. The director of the school also introduced me to the play's producers, songwriter, choreographer, sound engineers (women with home recording studios), and the woman I call "the archivist" because she collects and preserves video and audio recordings of women-only performances across communities. She is known as the "technology lady."

During that performance, I witnessed a creative universe that aesthetically echoed my own high school experiences with acting and dancing, but with distinctive norms regarding the celebration and advocacy of feminine creativity. This private feminine universe undergoes constant renewal at the hands of the women and girls in charge of the performance, often former students themselves, who borrow, adapt, and transform performative elements they discover in other creative spaces within and outside the community. These women and I discussed for hours the process involved in the making of the school play I attended on that day. Malky, a Montreal woman who contributes regularly to school performances, wanted to make sure that I understood the distinctive nature of creativity in her community:

> When people say that we are not creative, and can't be artistic, or that we do not have a sense of aesthetics, this is false. We do not learn as you do in the school of arts, we do not show it in public, and people do not know about it, but we do not want anyone to know. We have our own spaces where we experiment. Maybe these spaces are limited because the play is happening every three years, but it is because we do not have enough time to do everything, and it is a huge production that is costly. We are busy women!

Around 6:30 p.m. on the day of the play, Rivka and I arrived at a secular francophone high school where they were holding the performance. We were greeted by staff who guided us toward the performance hall. At the entrance, students from the Hasidic girls' school collected our tickets and gave us the booklet of אני חומה (*Ani Homa*, the title of the play, meaning "I am a barricade" and implying "I am fortified") with a one-sentence Yiddish description below the title translated as "a musical drama for *mesirut nefesh* [self-sacrifice] and strength." The booklet was written mostly in Yiddish, except for some advertisements in English and French depending on the business (French was used by francophone Jewish business owners). It provided the names of all participants, including the main organizers and producers, here labeled as "leaders," who received an honorarium for their work. These "leaders" coordinated the acting, music, technical support, props, and costumes. The booklet listed the names of performers according to their positions (choir, dance, song), with some in bold to highlight their special roles. Following this list were almost a dozen letters of appreciation celebrating the girls' talent and praising the quality of their performance. These letters acknowledged every single participant equally; no distinction was made between leading and secondary roles. The lyrics of five songs came next, without the names of lyricists or composers, as if they were traditional songs. The booklet also included messages from parents and families from abroad who paid fees to celebrate the girls' talent, show their pride, and financially support the production. Some businesses also paid a fee and were rewarded with an advertisement sized in proportion to their contribution.

The lights dimmed; the show began. Following the common themes of musicals produced in ultra-Orthodox schools, the script tackles the struggles of Jewish families to keep their faith in ancient Greece, stressing that Jews fought against the *yetzer hara* (bad inclination) that encouraged them to abandon their commitment to Judaism. The girls onstage are dressed with colorful and elegant clothing, makeup, and jewelry. While the play repeats the typical story of the challenges Jews encountered to follow the *derekh* (path), challenges common to *Yiddishkeit* throughout history, its novelty and the participants' creativity lay in its costumes, choreography, musical arrangement, and production. The script, written in English by a woman from New York and translated into Yiddish by the play's "leaders," was the starting point for the creative process of all the women involved in the play's production.

The first facet of the play that caught my eye was the costumes. Unlike boys' schools, which do not have the problem of casting opposite-gender characters because the plays have no female characters at all, girls' schools cast their own students in male roles. Since girls are not allowed to wear pants according to the *tsnius* norms followed in many ultra-Orthodox schools, the costume designers and directors for this production worked together to develop the performance of masculinity: they used makeup and body language, and they created clothing that would allow the audience to distinguish genders despite the all-girl cast. Jewish male characters had *peyos*, hats, facial hair drawn with cosmetics, and a distinctive bulky skirt. The costume team designed and tailored dresses and accessories to near-professional theater standards, and parents and girls participated in the process.

After the costumes, my attention turned to the choreography and stage occupation. While I knew there was a tradition of girls' performances at schools, camps, and seminaries, I did not expect such strong abilities from the young choreographers. The dark and graceful dances by small groups included modern jazz dance movements. Moving from circle to line, line to circle, and diagonally, the girls were doing *chassé*, *passé*, *plié*, *étiré*, *glissade*—graceful movements with their arms and heads, with a semblance of arabesque and attitude. As I discovered after the performance, the choreographers were influenced by professional dancers in Rachel's Place, the internationally recognized Broadway-style musical series produced for and by Orthodox women in New York, as well as their experiences at summer camps. Some of the girls had attended Orthodox girls' camps specializing in the performing arts, while others had taken lessons with professional dancers privately or at dance schools for Orthodox women. However, such lessons (which take place in more liberal ultra-Orthodox communities) would be controversial, and girls would not publicly acknowledge taking them. The play's sophisticated dances were accompanied by an instrumental playback downloaded from YouTube, while the collective simple dances used hits prerecorded in the home recording studio of Myriam, a woman from the community.

Regarding the vocal aesthetic, the absence of projection in their technique drew my attention. Contrary to Hasidic male singing, the girls did not project their voices and essentially mobilized chest voices. However, the final sound on stage appeared strong, boisterous, and resounding when the girls sang collectively, but also because all the solos were prerecorded or amplified with the microphones. The concept of *tsnius* expressing itself in terms of the performing girls' bodies, and thus implicitly their voices, had clearly come to affect the vocal aesthetics of these young girls. Nevertheless, with a studio where the voice can be transformed, adjusted, and amplified, another sound can be produced without transforming the performance of the self, anchored in *tsnius*, on stage.

Music and singing, which include melodies and harmonies, appear to have been the least creative elements of the performance, as they were not original compositions. However, here, musical creativity derived from the selection of melodies, their production in the studio, and the composition of new lyrics. The girls' individual talent displayed through the solo was recognized and acknowledged, but to prevent vanity, the community celebrated it as a collective trait. The recorded and live sections combined solos and duets with improvisations done within the choir performances that serves as the play's centerpiece. The choir represented cohesiveness, collective strength, and belonging, Rivka explained: "The most important thing we can give them is to be proud of who they are and where they are coming from. They create ties, from what I have seen. We cannot only have all these strong and powerful kids shining, but there should also be social power and the choir allows it. In small groups, we are giving them the chance to use their specific talents, but the most important is the social bonds."[9]

The choir is the embodiment of sisterhood, a sentiment that lies at the heart of the performances for girls developed by Sarah Schenirer, the founder of Orthodox Jewish schools for girls, discussed earlier. This is also the traditional space where girls can produce a powerful sound without learning how to project their voices. Beyond the social impact of community singing, community choirs are empirically connected to health and well-being because personal reward intersects with community feeling.[10] This connection to health and well-being that music allows has impacted the development of private education in the arts within ultra-Orthodox feminine circles, as we will see.

Throughout the two-and-a-half hours of performance, no special acknowledgment singled out soloists or other individual contributions; instead, the girls were celebrated as a group. Although some had solo parts, and therefore the chance to shine independently for a few seconds or more, their individual performances always blended into a collective one. Even the ownership of the lyrics, script, and music was conceived of as collective. The school plays are the foundation of the ways that creativity is traditionally received, experienced, embodied, and transmitted in feminine ultra-Orthodox circles. Because the performance occurs in an educational setting, the plays act as a central tool reinforcing the sense of feminine Orthodox cohesiveness while recognizing individual talent.

The Band

Married women are known for having fewer opportunities to perform than girls because of the centrality of the educational setting for performances. Moreover, the social roles of mothers and wives are traditionally perceived as contradicting with the figure of the performer visible and audible on stage.[11] Nevertheless, married ultra-Orthodox women do have opportunities beyond school and summer camp. For example, *tsedakah* (fundraising) events are occasions where women often sing, backed by recordings or alongside live female instrumentalists. From 2010 to 2020, the acclaimed Rachel's Place Productions organized performances by and for ultra-Orthodox women, headed by Miriam Handler, known as an expert in translating Broadway performances for ultra-Orthodox female contexts.[12] Because these performances were filmed and distributed by a major industry label and widely available on DVD and, since the pandemic, in streaming format, the female performers were often *baalei tshuva* or recognized as coming from more "modern" or "liberal" ultra-Orthodox families. Women from more conservative circles were rare. As Rivka noted, "The *frum* lady usually does not perform. She does not have the time for it, she is busy taking care of her home, her kids, or working, and

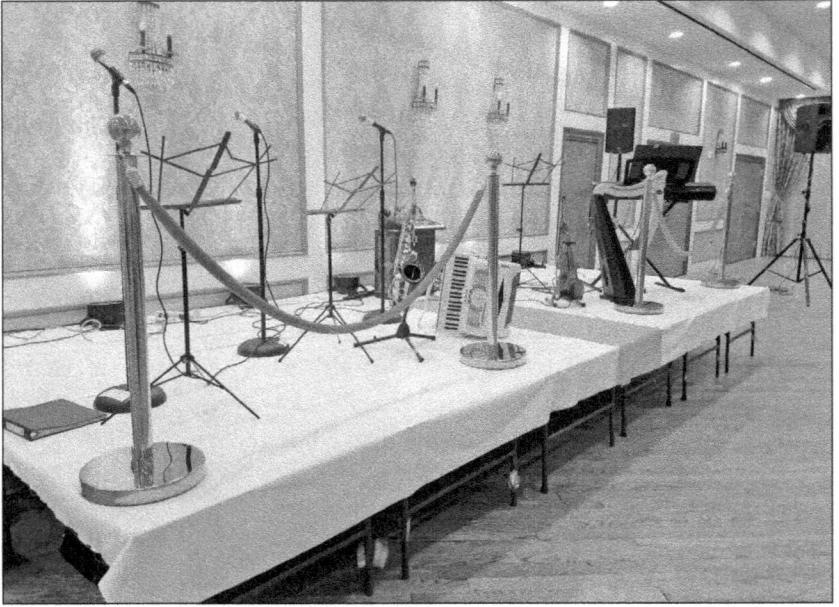

Figure 3.1: Photo of Toby's band before a concert (credit Toby).

the arts for women had not been traditionally seen as a possibility for *parnasse.*" Others mentioned that many view performing as an inappropriate practice for women as it conflicts with *tsnius*, which explains why most Hasidic women do not participate in the performing arts. Nevertheless, I had heard from a friend about Toby's band, referenced in the introduction to this chapter. When I met Toby, I discovered a new reality, contradicting what I had heard until then. Though this reality is admittedly a marginal one, it underlines the cultural, social, and economic changes occurring in the arts in ultra-Orthodox female circles.

Toby's band is well known in KJ. In the last decade, they have performed for many new mothers from across North America while they stayed at Aishes Chayil, KJ's postnatal care hotel resort. Their performances are part of a program to entertain these women during their stay in exchange for a small fee. The band does not have an official name, but it is often labeled "the Monroe group" (after the town of Monroe, which lies next to KJ) or "the instrument group." The lack of an official name was intentional, designed to limit the group's exposure. Toby wanted to protect band members from potential voices of opposition: "Without a name, we stay informal, and we do not officially exist. If someone does not like our idea, he does not have our name to write *pashkevil* against us [a broadside or poster often posted with rabbinic endorsement on a public wall located in an ultra-Orthodox community]."

The band usually plays traditional songs in Yiddish and Loshn Koydesh (as noted earlier, a mix of Hebrew and Aramaic, essentially consisting of religious texts and prayers), which are already familiar to the audience, and creates its own arrangements with original instrumental solos using the saxophone, harp, or violin. The group includes three singers (Toby, Ruchy, and Gelly), a guitarist (Leah), and a keyboard player (Devoiry or Yocheved); Toby also plays multiple instruments, in addition to preparing the program, selecting the songs, and writing the scores. Some of the band members know how to read sheet music and play accordingly, but most learned to play by ear.

While Toby has developed a creative environment where she serves as the leader and central creator, the performance represents a communal project that does not defy the norms of *tsnius* according to her community and can therefore be consumed. When creating a new song, the musicians normally get together to try out arrangements, harmonies, and solos. The singers work together to refine their voices; the keyboard player improvises and selects the effects, and the guitarist plays various chords to find the appropriate rhythm to reinforce the harmony. If the vocals are too much in unison, Toby encourages harmony to produce a choir-like effect. Since the band has different keyboard players and singers, the performance varies according to their own ability to improvise or take creative risks. As Toby put it, "Some ladies are more independent than others, more experienced and talented than others, with various creative ideas. But we work as a team. Others have creative potentials, but they are not used to developing it, so I am pushing them to develop it. Many are just following my guidelines and instructions. At the keyboard, for instance, I have someone who is playing basic chords, while another can improvise and bring novelty each time. But you can't really tell on stage because we always present our performance as a collective effort."[13]

Although everyone contributes individually, the cohesiveness of the group is essential, and the success of this communal effort has led them to expand their audience beyond the Aishes Chayil hotel. While they never record their performances (they are marketing themselves as a unique live music band), their audience has increased due to word of mouth. As the Monroe band became popular, they were invited to perform at various other private events and summer camps, becoming an important symbol for many other communities—the band represents the feminine expression of creativity and talent for married women while staying in accordance with *tsnius* and avoiding exposure to the outside world. In Toby's ten years of experience, she has only once encountered any backlash: the band was invited to perform its usual program for the opening of a new *mikveh* (ritual bath), and one woman in the audience asked for the performance to stop, feeling it was inappropriate to listen to women singing and playing instruments. The organizer of the event who hired the band called a local rabbi for advice on handling the situation. The rabbi then authorized the resumption of the performance without singing.

In conservative circles, performances by and for women encounter subjective reactions influenced by religious authority, which is a structure that every member of the community—including women—contributes to maintaining, reinforcing, or altering, depending on their views of tradition and novelty. Despite the one brief episode of pushback that came from another woman, Toby uses music performance as a tool to subtly disseminate new ideas and possibilities without destabilizing tradition. She emerges with the group on stage, reminding her female audience of the social and cultural role played by music—to reinforce community and to foster new ideas about women and the arts. And since they receive a fee in exchange for their performance, the band also participates in the increasingly profitable market of female entertainment. This entertainment scene is still small, but is gaining visibility with increased advertisements in many women's magazines published in hard copy and online, showing the arts as an avenue for some women to build a business and make *parnasse*. The potential of this entertainment scene derives from its educational role outside the formal school system because most ultra-Orthodox women in the arts make their living essentially as private educators.

Private Programs

As private lessons in the performing arts have multiplied in the last twenty years, some women have created private studios in which to teach singing, music, and dance, institutionalizing the teaching of the arts in the community. These programs initially catered only to girls, but married women have now become regular participants. Freida, a Hasidic dancer and painter from Brooklyn, invited me to participate in her dance class in the basement of a Williamsburg building. Our lesson was for local mothers, almost entirely from Hasidic backgrounds, and was part of a program for low-income mothers to engage in leisure activities free of charge thanks to public funding and health insurance supporting mental and physical health; the program is run by a local organization that supports childcare for young children. On the morning of my class, about twenty-five women were present, from young mothers in their twenties to more mature women in their fifties. The students represented various skill levels and physiques, wearing skirts, long-sleeved shirts, running shoes, and hair coverings ranging from *shpitzel* (headgear with multiple layers including net, turban, and scarf) to short *sheytl* (wig).[14] Before class began, I asked some of them why they chose to participate. They said they attended just for fun and to stay in shape. Freida did not inform the sponsoring organization of the specific content she would teach during her classes. The organization had hired her three years earlier to offer workout classes, and she took the opportunity to expose women to choreography and dance. Nobody ever asked her about her training, nor the style and technique she uses.

Freida is known as a talented dancer, but her journey with dance has been quite different from that of many ultra-Orthodox women. She attended classes outside her community, where she learned to dance using a creative practice centered on one's individual ability to reproduce a dance genre and adapt it into one's own style. Freida grew up in what she called a "typical" Hasidic family in New York and attended a Hasidic Yiddish-language school. Due to her interactions with the liberal arts world, she might be considered a nonconformist, or even living a double life without life-changing doubt, to use the terms coined by anthropologist Ayala Fader in her work on ultra-Orthodox Jewish doubters and secret lives. Freida first learned to dance at school, with a Sephardic *baal tshuva* professional dancer, and then by taking dance classes in various studios in New York, ending up with a degree in dance from a major performing arts academy. She does not advertise her professional training. Unlike arts schools in the liberal secular world—where an instructor's training is knowledge essential to clientele who want to know the traditions, styles, and genres they will be learning—arts programs in most ultra-Orthodox circles do not discuss training. This is partly due to the taboos surrounding interactions with the outside world, but it might also reflect the way creativity is thought to emerge from within the community as a collective good, for which it is not relevant to trace the origin.

Freida wanted to expose women to sensuality through dance by integrating new movements into her lessons. To do so, she slightly adapted the movements and presented them as personal techniques to improve physical health and well-being. The workout was structured around different styles inspired by modern jazz, Zumba, and mambo. At one point, Freida folded her torso forward at the hips and lifted her leg up high. "This experience is perfect to stretch your legs and gain the flexibility to move your entire body," she said. Toward the end of our class, the focus shifted to the upper body. She stuck out her chest and undulated it from front to back and left to right, explaining that rolling the thoracic cavity alleviates stress by liberating the tensions in these parts of the body. The ultra-Orthodox dancer is not supposed to move her hips, to undulate her upper body, or lift her legs up high, as it would not be *tsnius*. However, none of the women in the class contradicted Freida or expressed discomfort, having accustomed themselves to the choreography and accepted it as a method of relieving stress. Evoking health benefits has allowed Freida to bring new movements to the class without disturbing her students' sense of propriety. For Freida, these classes are not about challenging *tsnius*. On the contrary, she feels that learning about their bodies will give these women the necessary tools to embrace and understand *tsnius* better. She hopes that the increased popularity of these classes will eventually provide them with more knowledge about their bodies, which will help them not only as wives and mothers but also in gaining agency.

Contrary to what Freida learned throughout her professional training, her class is not about dance, sensuality, and expression. Through the medium of dance, she found a creative way to introduce new movements and bodily expression to these women, encouraging them to adapt the movements in such a way as to make them their own. The class contributes to their physical, mental, and even spiritual well-being, as Freida stated. In the class, she discussed the connection between self-care and spirituality, and its correlation with agency: "If you take care of yourself, of your body and your mind, you will be a better woman, mother, wife, and you will be able to serve Hashem." While discussing her creative strategies to make this community dance class a space where women can cultivate their creativity and personal well-being, Freida explained the following: "When I teach movements they are not used to, or that could lead them to think it is immodest, I emphasize the benefits for their physical and mental health. If at first, they are uncomfortable or surprised by these new moves, I always remind them about the role of these movements for their body, their life as a mother and wife, and implicitly their *Yiddishkeit*."[15]

Here Freida highlights the creative process by which artists adapt individualized knowledge to fit collective norms. This discourse that connects creativity, well-being, and health with religiosity resonates with the psychotherapeutic revolution that influenced American religions, particularly evangelical Christianity in the 1980s and 1990s, and ultra-Orthodoxy in the early twenty-first century. As Ayala Fader has pointed out, psychological knowledge has been combined with Jewish ethical writing to legitimize therapy and integrate into Jewish faith popular psychology and its emphasis on self-esteem and growth, with Rabbi Abraham Joshua Twersky, trained as both a rabbi and a psychiatrist, as the key architect of this enterprise.[16] In this context, some ultra-Orthodox women invested in the arts have embraced research in psychology focusing on the positive role of creativity for health and well-being in order to legitimize and normalize their practice. Women like Freida assert that their private practices serve the well-being of a new generation of women and girls and thus, implicitly, the future of *Yiddishkeit*. More specifically, the topic of fitness and dance as an agent of self-improvement, health, and well-being across many age groups in society has been documented in various fields.[17] For instance, neuroscientists and psychologists have stated that beyond improvements in physical fitness and cognitive abilities, the positive effects of dance include a strengthening of group coherence, an increased willingness to help others, and an improvement in successful rehabilitation as well as accident prevention.[18] Beyond academic research demonstrating the positive effect of dance on health and well-being, popular knowledge also embraces this idea in our society, including that of ultra-Orthodox spaces where yoga, dance, and other forms of exercise are becoming increasingly popular among women, revealing the impact of this global culture of body and well-being on religious communities.[19] While the growing popularity of these classes has been analyzed as a global phenomenon, anthropologist Julie Archambault-Soleil reminds us to complicate our understanding of these global trends by focusing on their specific manifestation in local contexts.[20] While the emergence of private programs in entertainment and the arts among ultra-Orthodox women echoes this global trend, it also reflects how creativity in this context—understood locally as a collective practice—is moving toward an individualized expression of health and well-being connected with religiosity and spirituality.

These private programs were created by women who generally had only participated in school and summer camp productions or *tsedakah* events, all of them searching for professional and economic opportunities outside the formal school system. All the studios I visited were in a basement, garage, or room in a home, where lessons were offered to women regardless of age, marital status, or the philosophy of their community regarding the interpretation of Jewish text, also known as the *hashkafa*.[21] The idea of cultivating talent outside the confines of formal schooling is a new phenomenon in ultra-Orthodox Jewish feminine life. While it does grant flexibility to women with creative ambitions since they can operate outside the control of religious authority, these women constantly endure pressure to avoid interpreting *tsnius* and *kol isha* in the "wrong way," which would harm their businesses and reputations. The line between the opportunity to innovate and the possibility of disturbing the established religious order is extremely thin, and to prevent any backlash, many women decide to participate in artistic endeavors under the radar of religious authority.

As an example of the possible controversy, rabbis recently came out against a music studio established by a Hasidic woman from Williamsburg, Esti.[22] In the early 2020s, Esti opened a music studio offering instrument classes and musical gatherings, also known as *kumzits*, for women and girls only, in a closed space. Around the time of Hanukkah, in December 2021, a well-known *dayyan* (person knowledgeable about Talmudic law, or a Jewish judge) and a rabbi, both from Satmar, published a long text drawing on sources from older rabbis claiming that women gathering to sing together should not be allowed, as this practice has never been done in the past. They also stated that women should not look for new sources of entertainment and should be satisfied with their domestic duties in the comfort of their homes. Following the circulation of the text, Esti canceled the Hanukkah *kumzits* event, hoping the tension would blow over after a few weeks, and did not announce any closure of her business, hoping that this incident would not force her to lose her clientele.

Rabbinical authorities—who always oversee programs at formal girls' schools—do not supervise these private programs and private performances, nor do many women consult them or ask for approval, fearful of an order to cease their activities or shutter their businesses, as happened with Esti. These women, in fact, also invoke *tsnius* to justify such reservedness—specifically, the obligation to maintain privacy. As many told me, this is a "do not ask, do not tell situation." One dance teacher explained, "I am an adult and I do not need someone to tell me what I have to do. I know the *halakha* [Jewish law]; I can decide for myself regarding my own choice, and I know I am doing the right thing. Everything has to do with my relationship with God, and no one else. I am my own rabbi! I do not need recognition from a rabbi. If one day I need a rabbi to give me a *hekhsher* [approval],[23] I will find the proper rabbi."

By affirming that she can find an appropriate masculine voice of authority to legitimate her practice, and that she is doing the right thing, the dance teacher reminds us that Orthodoxy is a constant negotiation between collective norms and individual needs that could potentially reshape these norms. Moreover, by justifying her choice with the claim that she has the support of God, she reiterates that religion is an immaterial belief manifested in multiple material forms, whether sounds, objects, bodies, or senses.

Despite the recent backlash experienced in Williamsburg by Esti, these programs generally prove to be successful, given the number of studios emerging across communities. This success certainly stems from the alignment of the tradition of collective creative performance with the cultivation of individual talent in private lessons and the growing need for women's and girls' entertainment even though some extreme rabbis are in opposition. The normalization of the culture of self-care, in which the arts, food, and sports become central to physical and mental well-being, as well as public funding for these private programs to support self-care for low-income families and people with developmental disabilities, has been a major factor in this growth. Lastly, the fact that religious authorities are rarely consulted by the women I have encountered may also be a cause. The discourse on self-care at the intersection of the arts prevents most of the tensions and controversy. According to Sarah, a New Yorker who offers music lessons, during her childhood in the 1990s, only families able to pay and willing to learn from non-Orthodox Jews or *baalei tshuva* artists, in very private and almost secretive settings, could sign up for these classes. In Sarah's conservative community, *baalei tshuva* were not acceptable teachers as they came from outside the community, bringing with them forbidden ideas. Most of the girls taking music lessons at this time often struggled to fit in with their peers. Today, all kinds of girls from various ultra-Orthodox backgrounds join these programs, led by women born and raised in the same community. New developments include performing arts studios and advertisements for them in local and international Jewish magazines catering to Hasidic Yiddish communities. Zalman, a Hasidic singer from Brooklyn who occupies a position of leadership in his community, reflected,

> Even though some rabbis are voicing their opposition to this practice as it brings new ideas, they won't be able to stop this growth. It is already very popular; they can do nothing about it. The most extreme rabbi might continue to voice their discontent; they will say how everything new is *assur* [forbidden], but they use this narrative only to serve what they want. It might be harder for women living in these more conservative communities; but they will advertise their businesses orally by the word of mouth instead of doing internal advertisement. Some of them, if discovered, might struggle for their kids if they go to these schools, but now with the growth of diversity within the *frum* world, they still can have their kids in other Haredi schools. And at the end of the day, if the business was already very successful, it means there is a demand and a need,

so extreme rabbis won't have that much weight. You see, only two rabbis were writing this statement against Esti; it is not unanimous.[24]

Many factors lie behind this shift, the first of which is the growth of the middle class and the development of what Haim Zicherman and Lee Cahaner label "modern ultra-Orthodoxy."[25] While the education system for Orthodox girls in North America has concentrated on isolating children from secular North American culture and media, the Orthodox world filled that vacuum with kosher news and entertainment principally controlled by men. Magazines, comics, audio recordings, and even films flourished, all with kosher content validated by renowned rabbis, but this media only featured male characters.[26] This led to an increased need for kosher content and entertainment aimed specifically at women and girls. The rise of private lessons in the performing arts to stimulate and nourish talent and creativity represents part of this broader phenomenon.

A second factor behind the emergence of these lessons is the digital revolution, including the consumption of the Internet. While the Internet and other new technologies have been described as *yeytzer hora* (inclination to do evil), ultra-Orthodox religious leaders could not avoid this revolution—for professional and pragmatic reasons. They have shaped it according to their norms, and developed filters for computers and cell phones to limit the Internet content that can be consumed. By defining their Internet use as professional, many women use it to learn about music and many other art techniques while staying in the comfort of their homes and making *parnasse* to maintain their family. They then offer programs based on this knowledge to women and girls in the broader ultra-Orthodox community.

Third, the positive discourse in the secular education system surrounding the benefits of creativity and extracurricular activities for child development has begun to influence the ultra-Orthodox educational system. While ultra-Orthodox schools have their own curricula, many girls' schools adopt aspects of secular teaching, consulting regularly with education specialists to adjust their programs. In schools offering extracurricular activities in the performing arts, girls are allowed and even encouraged to cultivate their skills beyond the classroom. As many interlocutors told me, both women and men, their communities value creativity adapted to *tsnius* more highly than they did a decade ago. This is even the case for *shiddukhim* (matchmaking). A "good girl" is no longer defined by her ability to fit in but also by being talented and beautiful.[27]

Fourth, this new discourse on creativity relates to the value of the arts for mental health and psychology, and more broadly the adoption of psychological frameworks in ultra-Orthodoxy. Research on creativity and well-being (understood as a combination of physical and mental health) largely occurs in the field of psychology, and ultra-Orthodoxy has incorporated a large body of knowledge from American popular psychology.[28] In this context, educators have used the arts as a teaching tool for neurodiverse children as well as those struggling with mental and physical disabilities. Social organizations finance these programs in the arts, and some women-owned studios now participate in these social programs, such as that supported by New York State's Office for People with Developmental Disabilities (OPWDD). One advertisement in Kiryas Joel's *Balebusta* magazine, for example, promotes a woman's extracurricular classes for children and notes the acceptance of OPWDD, a process adopted by many small businesses.

One of the pioneers of these creative private enterprises is Malky Giniger.[29] An educator, performer, singer, and composer originally from Flatbush, she belongs to a Modzitz Hasidic family (Modzitz is known as one of the most musical Hasidic dynasties). Trained by various professional musicians from both within and outside her community, Giniger started the program Voices of Youth in 1992, offering piano and voice lessons. In 2003, she rebranded the studio as the Ratzon Program,[30] expanding its reach by establishing franchises across North America and Israel. Giniger hires various instructors, often her former students, and offers lessons in music (voice, piano, guitar, violin), drama, art, crafts, dance, and sewing. In her most recent advertisement, Giniger brands herself as a singer, actor, and songwriter who turned "girls who could not sing, dance, act or perform into concert soloists and polished actors." In her advertisement, Giniger explores the language of the arts for their own sake.

Today such schools owned by women from various *hashkafa* flourish across the globe without necessarily having requested rabbinical endorsement, as the statement by the two Williamsburg rabbis referred to earlier reveals. Many of these women are self-trained (often with the help of online videos), some others took private in-person or online lessons with professionals, and very few have degrees in the arts. While Malky Giniger and other women belonging to more liberal communities that encourage success and professionalism advertise their programs online, women in conservative circles announce their programs via word of mouth and in local magazines through group lessons, emphasizing fun and community rather than professionalization or the fostering of individual talent.

The women running these programs are negotiating constantly between their ambition to celebrate talent and the need to maintain their students' humility. As Toby—the founder of the band discussed earlier, who also offers music lessons in her own studio—put it, "It became extremely easy for kids to perform on stage, and it could possibly inculcate a sense of pride and lack of humility. We do not want this. We are trying our best to teach children music without compromising humility." To align their project with both the traditional concept of collective creativity and their desire for novelty, they designate the private lesson as the place for the cultivation of individual talent with the goal of improving well-being.[31]

In her studio, Toby offers individual lessons for keyboard and violin, emphasizing creativity as a method of improving self-esteem. She shapes her teaching to individual needs, but, as noted, when her students play for the public, they do so as part of collective performances. Creativity results from an individual investment but manifests collectively. Even if Toby does not deal with the restrictions of *kol isha*, as she is not teaching voice but instruments, she nevertheless illustrates how feminine creativity takes the form of communal performance. Performances before an audience constitute an important part of girls' school curricula, but after the age of twelve, in most conservative Hasidic circles (such as Satmar schools) girls stop acting, singing, or dancing in front of anyone from outside the school, including parents. In this context, the "private" space is reduced to classmates and educators (though some Hasidic schools have recently decided to relax this norm). With performances organized in a private hall, Toby expands the circumscription of the private space established by religious authority in the school, providing additional venues for her students to express themselves creatively while still presenting such events as restricted to limited audiences. She believes in the power of creativity and music to improve personal well-being, and that because only those with common values will participate, her project will not be challenged or disrupted. Regarding the issue of privacy and publicity in relation to the arts, she notes that she operates in a kind of gray area for which tradition has few answers:

> This is not a *halakhic* question, but this is about the *tsnius* norms within our community regarding singing or playing instruments for women and girls. There are a lot of gray zones in what I do as it is not part of our tradition. Because it has not been done before and there is no *halakhic* issue, people are not sure about it. Bringing a new concept into the tradition is always challenging and you never know how it will be received. But I still do it according to the collective norms, and I make sure to not disturb anything. I concentrate on educational, social, and emotional support with the arts. I do not advertise for women's entertainment in local magazines like the woman in Williamsburg did with her *kumzits* Tuesday evening.

Toby did not know what to expect as an educator participating in the informal entertainment market. She realized the demand but was uncertain of how others might receive her program. While some of her clients at first had doubts about instrument lessons, they signed up in large numbers, and her clientele has grown immensely in the last ten years. More recently, instead of performing with her band at Aishes Chayil, Toby has invited her most talented students to play violin for the audience there. To help them prepare, she created a phone line where the students can listen to the songs and practice individually at home or together in a group.[32] Today, teaching musical instruments is Toby's full-time job, and it brings *parnasse* to her family. But she does not view her musical activity only as a business; she also sees it as a gift from God that allows her to serve her community. When asked about the success of her business, Toby evokes the social role of music and the current need for opportunities to cultivate the talent of women and girls—not necessarily in the form of performances, but as an outlet allowing them to express their feelings.

From the perspective of humanistic and positive psychology, stimulating creativity serves as a pathway to well-being and self-actualization.[33] Toby and her fellow music teachers embrace this approach to justify their projects. While the concept of the "mad genius" assumes a connection between creativity and mental illness, the literature also suggests that creativity might serve as a possible protection against such illness, mitigating psychological abnormalities and even channeling them into optimal functioning.[34] Toby and others adopt these arguments from popular psychology; they serve not only the woman or girl who just needs a creative outlet but also the one suffering from mental illness or disability. Such ideas have spread to other art forms, too, such as dance. Dance has always been significant in the lives of women and girls in ultra-Orthodoxy, but the global emphasis on well-being, the body, and creativity has recently resulted in the popularization of programs in dance, exercise, and even yoga.[35] While such women-led programs increasingly find coverage in community journals and magazines, these articles often underline the potential threat to conservative members of the community. The article in *Balebusta* about Toby's private musical program ended with an opinion disclaimer and a note of caution. As translated from Yiddish by Malky Goldman, the disclaimer stated, "We do not take a position on the content of this article. Everyone should ask for the opinion of their rabbi about playing or studying music." This comment—written in a very small font and seemingly insignificant—serves to protect the editorial board from any conservative backlash and is a telling reminder of such programs' precarious position in the community, especially in places such as Kiryas Joel. On the one hand, these articles continue to celebrate women and their contributions to these artistic fields, but on the other hand, there remains potential resistance to the cultivation of creativity with regard to changing practices of *kol isha* and *tsnius*. Somewhat ironically, these private programs and studios allow the individual cultivation of creativity thanks to their representation of it as a collective practice. This new scene in performing arts education impacts not only the ways women and girls learn and teach the arts but also the spaces and formats in which they perform and consume them, spaces that are reinvigorated and strengthened by the digital.

The Home Studio

A few months after the school performance I attended in Montreal, I met Chaya, one of the play's directors. Chaya regularly directs productions at schools and summer camps and she knows a great deal about the arts scene in her community. In our conversation, we discussed the transformation of the art scene in the previous decade—specifically, the growing number of home studios owned by women. All the schools and camps that Chaya has worked with organize recording sessions at these studios to create the playback for their performances. It became a custom, she told me, and it allows girls to have a "more professional" sound, resulting in "better performances" on stage when they must also act and dance. These women-owned studios mean that they no longer need to use studios owned by men and consequently struggle with the issue of *kol isha*. Very few women in Chaya's community are experienced instrumentalists, and most of those who are play only a handful of acoustic instruments, such as guitar or piano, which makes it difficult to produce music independently with an arrangement that includes many instruments. In the home recording studio, instruments and music theory knowledge are unnecessary because one can create instrumental playback with a computer. For women who do not play instruments, the studio has generated new ways to produce music outside the educational performance scene. Chaya told me, for example, how common it is for girls to book a session to record a new composition in the studio, then offer the final product, with a "professional arrangement including an orchestra in the background of the singing," as a gift to others. It has become very popular for girls to send these songs to friends and family for *simkhas* (family celebrations). The female home studio changes the relationship women and girls have with music. It provides a safe space for them to celebrate, record, and then disseminate their creative products. According to Chaya and others, the studio has also become an economic necessity in the community, and its use by schools and summer camps encourages women and girls to build home studios as a method of making *parnasse*.

The home studio cultivates economic, cultural, and social agency among women and girls. While songwriters, choreographers, play producers, and educators have used private studios to make *parnasse* and participate in the informal entertainment market for quite some time, the woman-owned home studio is a new and unique tool that has expanded the raison d'être of this informal market. It allows women to commodify their creativity while remaining outside the conventional entertainment industry and moving beyond the tradition of live educational performances. Computer-generated instrumental playback expands their opportunities by reducing the need to find female musicians or collaborate with men.

The studio owner both competes and collaborates with women and girls invested in schools and private arts programs, challenging their monopoly over creative production while also providing sound for their performances. It is tempting to interpret the phenomenon of the home studio as a discursive project challenging religious authority since it came about largely as a result of the Internet, which ultra-Orthodox religious authorities generally disapprove of (especially its use by women), as will be explained in detail later. However, it also represents the normalization of women's use of the Internet for professional purposes and for *parnasse*.[36] While very few women I met expressed a feeling of pride that they were able to build a home studio *without* the Internet at home—by downloading and sending files from other places—many explained that they were more efficient with the Internet, even though they had to use a filter limiting access to only professional resources. Others simply ignored such restrictions, asserting that they were perfectly capable of overseeing their own Internet practices and that they did not need anyone telling them what to do. Among the women criticizing religious authorities for their control over Internet access, most of them are supported by their husbands, sometimes even influenced by them. However, some women act almost secretly, knowing their husbands would disapprove of their use of the Internet without filters, using the gender-segregated dimension of the *frum* female art worlds as an argument to prevent their husbands from accessing their creative spaces.

The digital turn arose from the development and use of digital technologies in science and the humanities. It created controversy in many religious circles (including ultra-Orthodox circles, where it led to a "crisis of religious authority") and led to the emergence of the female home studio and the creative shift it enabled. This turn and its impact on the music industry are generally presented in one of two ways.[37] More specifically, the passage from the first to the second digital turn[38]—which included increased consumption of the Internet on any interface and with several methods of interaction (voice, social media, chat, etc.) around the globe—drastically changed the music industry, the system of copyright, and the consumption of music. Some scholars view this second digital turn as dangerous, as it increased rates of hacking, illegal reproduction, and appropriation of sounds and images, and diluted intellectual property and copyright laws.[39] Others expound on its potential for increasing access to groups outside the industry.[40] In discussions about the latter perspective, scholars have particularly neglected the potential of this technological revolution to dismantle the gender, racial, ethnic, and social inequalities that structure the industry.[41] Indeed, it allowed for the participation—at a very low cost—of individuals typically excluded from the industry, notably women. The voices of those who previously gave only live performances could now be recorded and disseminated beyond the physical performance space, constructing a sense of belonging without physical proximity or physical contact.[42]

This revolution ultimately did not deconstruct the hierarchies of the industry. Yet, it is important to recognize that it allowed minorities and marginalized groups to use low-cost materials to create their own content and disseminate it via informal networks rather than mainstream media. It contributed to the miniaturization and wider distribution of recording, editing, mixing, and producing equipment (laptops, digital recorders, etc.) among both musicians and filmmakers.[43] It also enabled individuals and communities, in the comfort of their homes, to create low-budget music, as well as video productions, exploring social and other issues ignored by the mainstream music and film industries. The second digital turn resulted in independent music and films that circulated through alternative networks, offering new financial and artistic possibilities.

Benefiting from the increased access of the second digital turn, in the mid-2010s, a critical mass of ultra-Orthodox women began investing in home studios. At first, acquiring the technical knowledge needed for music production required contact with individuals outside the community, including Jewish and non-Jewish men.[44] Combined with the ability to self-train by observing others in the studio, watching YouTube videos, and attending online or in-person classes, women's ability to manage the home studio without interaction with men meant that they could create their own market, defined by their own interpretation of the norms of *tsnius* and *kol isha*. With a computer, editing software, a few microphones, a pop filter, a digital audio workstation, studio monitors, some cables, and an Internet connection, women can record and adjust out-of-tune voices and download MIDI-based soundtracks from websites to mix with recorded voices.[45] While popular media in North America has portrayed ultra-Orthodox women as technologically illiterate, there has emerged a coterie of ultra-Orthodox women producers who are technologically savvy and who even engage in translocal collaborations. The most basic element of their production is the instrumental background track: a combination of percussion and a variety of instrumental playbacks produced electronically, often based on a downloaded MIDI file, to which is added the recorded voice (sometimes modified with effects such as reverb, backup vocals, distortions, or choir). Furthermore, in addition to acting as a space for production, the home studio is also a space for socialization. They meet, discuss, sing, play, listen to music, debate, and exchange in a secure, soundproof space where they cannot be overheard or disturbed by outsiders, particularly men.

Women's home studios vary according to the goals and professional expertise of their owners. Girls typically start with a small studio in their bedroom, as it requires very little investment and allows them to make money fairly quickly. After marriage, some of these young women professionalize and dedicate a specific room in their home to recording. A few women even invest in a semiprofessional studio, with different rooms for musicians and singers to record simultaneously, as well as a separate space for production equipment. Very few, however, build professional studios that would produce results equivalent to those within the established music industry.[46] Moreover, there are not many women investing in audiovisual production, which often requires a full team for each step of the production process. Those who do, as we will see, must often engage with the broader film industry to make their production profitable. All of them learn the technique of music and film production by taking in-person or online classes, with a mix of amateurs and professionals, often Orthodox men working in the music or film industry—but increasingly with Orthodox women now that they have gained knowledge in the domain.

Through the digitization of sound, music recorded by women and girls spreads across borders via email, WhatsApp message, unlisted YouTube video, and even via phone lines they can call to listen to recordings. Studio owners have developed these methods of informal mediation without rejecting collaborations with industry professionals, from whom they often buy sound resources such as MIDI audio files for their playbacks on websites without crediting them. The studio owner is a point of reference for women and girls who wish to materialize their creativity in recordings, and the studio converts collective creativity into a market product available via informal networks.

While the studio owner mediates the distribution of music, the agents of distribution are individuals who receive the digital files, either for their own leisure or to create businesses. In Montreal, I used the services of one agent of distribution named Chevi, the "technology lady" known to all the women and girls I met locally. I did not have the chance to meet her in person, but we interacted over the phone several times as she helped me access the audiovisual archives of a Hasidic school. Chevi provides the service of converting CDs or DVDs into digital files. She collects audio and video recordings of performances produced in schools and summer camps across the globe, as well as other kosher content that women and girls bring to her. She rents out tablets and MP3 players filled with kosher entertainment to the local *frum* communities.

This digital distribution has also led to the construction of a common heritage shared transnationally. The dissemination and adaptation of Benny Friedman's 2019 song "Charasho" by Hasidic girls and women has been a particularly telling example. A few months after the release of the hit song (composed by Yitzy Waldner with lyrics by Aliza Spiro), the principal of a Hasidic girls' high school in Borough Park took the melody and recorded it with her own lyrics. The new song narrated her struggles with her school's closure while explaining the need to be resilient and accept the situation as God's will. Sung by girls from the same school, the song was recorded, arranged, and mixed in a studio in Borough Park. The refrain addresses the main themes of the song:

> Yes, I can accept this plan.
> I accept, I accept it's how Hashem wanted it to be.
> And I trust that it must be designed with love for me.

Yes, it's hard, and it hurts. It's so tough, but so am I.
I say yes to Hashem's plans. I won't ask why.

Titled "I Accept," the song circulated via email, WhatsApp, and some girls' Hasidic school performances. It rapidly became a hit among women and girls in schools, summer camps, and dance and gym classes across North America, and even the UK and Israel, yet remained unknown to the male community. In January 2020, Elisha, a woman in her seventies from Borough Park, was inspired to write a Yiddish version of the song. She kept the message of resilience and acceptance, replacing the word "accept" with "understand" to relate the song to a traumatic event in her family. The idea of understanding adversity was then extended to the pandemic, which broke out a few weeks later. The song, entitled "Ich farshtei" (I understand), was recorded in another woman's studio in Borough Park and distributed not only via email to schools but also over a phone line for women established by Elisha. The MP3 files of "I Accept" and "Ich farshtei" circulated without the names of either the singer or the lyricist, and only with the name of the home studio owner, listed alongside her email and phone number.

Ultra-Orthodox women and girls have thus found a way to mobilize technology for the purposes of creating and communicating across borders, participating in the digital revolution while embracing *kol isha* and *tsnius*. According to Chaya, it is the restrictions of *kol isha* and *tsnius* that keep the most talented girls "down to earth." The home studio is a great example of how ultra-Orthodoxy adapts to the technological digital revolution to serve the community, and how women can use the tools provided by this revolution to acquire artistic and economic agency, and to a certain extent independence. The second digital turn has transformed the production and consumption of music in the ultra-Orthodox female world; to the live performances whose raison d'être was religious and educational it has added a digital market where music beyond its traditional raison d'être can exist.

The participation of women in alternative networks of production and distribution has contributed to the general conception that women do not participate in the music industry. However, they continue to exist alongside and even borrow from this industry. In fact, some studio owners have even decided to produce music *for* the industry. As with music in informal economies across the globe,[47] the informal ultra-Orthodox women's music market illustrates how women have constructed a niche that is neither within nor set against the music industry dominated by males, but rather influenced and reshaped by it.

The Writers' Room

The practice of not publicizing the names of composers, lyricists, or scriptwriters underlines a distinctive understanding of the Western concepts of ownership and copyright.[48] Notions such as "author" or "work" are inoperative in many creative and performance contexts where borrowing has always constituted important elements of creativity.[49] The notion that copyright requires the production of a "new" work must be handled carefully, as the concept of novelty is subjective and contextual. As many authors point out, "Artists' appropriation of other artists' works is an integral and longstanding part of creative production."[50] In ultra-Orthodox circles, women have developed a distinctive model of ownership that embraces this process of borrowing. In the creative spaces presented in this chapter, women and girls understand creativity as a collective process in which all participants become creative subjects. Each female composer or writer is paid according to her contribution, but she does not own it. After she delivers it to her client—be it a young girl, a married woman, a school, a summer camp, or some other organization—her work belongs to the community and is performed and disseminated as such. The origin of the work rarely matters so long as it is labeled "Jewish and kosher."

When authorship is remembered, it is usually granted to the lyricist, who is often presented as the composer of the song—though "composer" here is not understood as the person who writes the melodies or arrangements. Instead, what women have described to me as being the "good" and "talented" female composer is the one who can write lyrics and find the "right" melody to resonate with the message of the words. I thus use the term "songwriter" to denote the lyricist. Songwriters compose on demand, for women and girls and even for men, requesting a fee that varies according to the task. The one who selects the melody is also not necessarily the one writing the lyrics, and each step requires a separate fee. Some women do this work to make an extra income on the side. For others it represents their main source of revenue. In the case of plays, scriptwriters are paid for writing an original script, but the use of a previously performed play is often offered free of charge. Very few women, however, compose original melodies; the custom is to select a well-known male Jewish hit or a melody from non-Jewish sources, not reveal the origin, disregard the composer, and write new lyrics. Female creators often use the filter of the male industry to ensure that the melody they select has already been validated as "Jewish and kosher." These melodies are imitated, reproduced, or appropriated, adapted to new lyrics, and integrated into a new work, constituting the first steps of creativity.

Clients typically request songs of these women for a *simkha* such as an engagement, wedding, bat mitsva, or graduation. Their lyrics often evoke God's presence or the power and beauty of *Yiddishkeit*. Once the female creator makes *parnasse* producing her work, she is rarely recognized and does not take part in a system of copyright. The creative value of the work lies in the novelty of the lyrics, and so these women do not appear to prioritize the preservation of the creative past. This collective principle governing the ownership of music (or, more broadly, performances of any kind) prevails in certain male contexts as well, but it is strongest in conservative female circles since their music market is informal and separate from the mainstream industry.

This attitude toward ownership can be explained by three factors: oral tradition, *tsnius*, and the absence of copyright. First and foremost, music in Orthodox circles is essentially the domain of an oral tradition. Here, orality means that individuals learn music aurally via live performances or recordings; music is not materialized, preserved, or transmitted in writing. Female composers, musicians, lyricists, and singers memorize and disseminate their compositions through live performances and audio recordings on MP3 players, CDs, or cassettes. None of them work with sheet music, and musical literacy is a rare trait among both female singers and female instrumentalists. Songs are not transcribed nor available in scores or recordings found in the broader industry.[51] Such a tradition resembles what ethnomusicologist Anne Dhu McLucas identifies as the backbone of much of America's musical heritage, in the repertoire of tunes and in the melodic and harmonic content, all of which descend from a sort of oral and unwritten tradition.[52]

Second, the norms of *tsnius* dictate either authorial anonymity or the disclosure of initials only, because ownership and intellectual property exhibit individual creativity. According to these codes, the aim of creative work is not to encourage personal growth but to enrich the community. Thus, it should not be presented as an individual process or individual success. Women and girls should not seek fame; crediting them by name as individual creators might lead to narcissism. In this context, modesty takes the form of a rejection of individual attention. However, this does not mean that they are not recognized and publicized as individual creators. On the contrary, publicity is crucial to their economic success; it is merely that publicity does not become individual glorification. These women act behind the scenes, and in so doing gain appreciation, as well as economic and social power, in their circles. The strict norms of *tsnius* lead to a displacement of authorship from individual to collective.

Lastly, this informal market functions without an official copyright system; instead, creators do not own their work but rather profit only upon the initial delivery of their services. The model of copyright and authorship that persists internationally today was a Western invention of the nineteenth century—developing from the earlier notion of literary copyright—that made a fundamental distinction between the author, the work, and the work's intellectual property rights.[53] In the ultra-Orthodox context, as I have explained, ownership of creative products is essentially collective, and artistic works become detached from their initial creators. However, as such traditions are subsumed into the international music industry, they enter a now-globalized system of copyright and intellectual property. The Orthodox male pop star, for example, emerged when male artists creating kosher music formally entered the music industry. But for women, the norms of *tsnius* and *kol isha* prevented this entry, so their creations circulate in informal networks where copyright and intellectual property do not exist. The production and consumption of this informal market thus has a very different logic from that governing the music industry. It reveals a connection among music, performance, and people that departs significantly from the concepts of individual creation and individual ownership.[54] As the legal expert in copyright Margaret Chon has stated, "The scholarly critiques of the romantic author focus on current copyright law's excessive reliance on possessive individualism, claiming that this overreliance then influences copyright doctrine to ignore or devalue collaborative and collective forms of authorship."[55]

In the last decade, the democratization of ultra-Orthodox female music effected by home studios has transformed the process by which women and girls create their art, and this—informed by and overlapping with notions of belonging—has in turn impacted the traditional concept of collective ownership.[56] In June 2019, before traveling to summer camps in the Catskill mountains, Chaya, one of the directors of the Montreal Hasidic school play I had attended that January, was looking for a new song for the summer play she was producing. A friend in New York recommended a song she had heard in a Hasidic school play in Monsey. Chaya contacted the school to obtain the recording. Following the established norm in ultra-Orthodox female circles, they sent her the material by email without mentioning the composer's name. Because Chaya needed an instrumental playback, she asked a few girls from New York to record the song prior to their arrival at one of the camps she would visit. Chaya retained the melody but changed the lyrics to address the topic of *shabbes* and rendered them in Yiddish instead of the original's English. Since the studios where the girls usually record were all booked, they decided to work with another woman whom they did not know. In her studio, the girls began to sing, yet after a few seconds, the woman studio owner identified the melody as a composition of one of her clients. She then stopped the recording session, refusing to record the song without authorization from the original composer. According to Chaya, this was a very unusual practice, but it is apparently becoming increasingly common to request permissions. After Chaya explained that it was to be used in a summer camp performance, the composer granted the request in exchange for eighty dollars.

Like the composer in this example, some female creators increasingly insist on individual ownership of their work and control over how it is used. Influenced by the kosher music market and in particular the disparity between their income and that of male creators, some women defend the notion of intellectual property as one of their rights. The growing demand for female entertainment engenders rivalry, and a competitive environment rewards those who guard their creative work more fiercely. While they do not earn a lot of money by claiming such ownership, that claim nevertheless indicates a desire to control their work and its dissemination. As sociologist David Arditi has noted, despite the fact that most composers do not earn much money through copyright, they continue fiercely defending it.[57]

Women shared with me many stories of this shift in attitude concerning authorship transcending the borders of their community. A lyricist altered a client's agreement regarding the right to reproduce a song without her consent; a filmmaker contacted women involved in the unauthorized circulation of her films in another country; other women debated how they might transform notions of intellectual property as the demand for kosher entertainment for females grows. In short, there is little doubt that the informal market has been influenced by the broader entertainment industry's commodification of music and film. Collective ownership still dominates—female studio owners continue to download and record different lyrics over new, male-composed hit songs—but the materialization of songs in the studio leads female composers, songwriters, and studio owners to search for ways to expand their businesses, brand their names, and control the reproduction of their oeuvre. In other words, the digital turn gave rise to the individualization of performances and the notion of authorship. Girls entering the studio want to leave with "their" version; composers and lyricists write into sale agreements new clauses protecting their work, and female studio owners apply digital signatures to the files of their completed songs.

Furthermore, with the birth of the home studio, the market no longer centers only on social service and education but also on individuals' aesthetic and creative needs. My ethnography has thus revealed seemingly opposite trends in current understandings of creativity within the feminine entertainment market. Importantly, it has also revealed that these trends are not antithetical. With the help of the studio owner, individual creativity emerges from and enhances the collective creativity that prevails in schools, summer camps, and private programs. Rather than consider the collective and individual conceptions of musical creativity (and by extension, musical intellectual property) as in tension with one another, as ethnomusicologists Mats Johansson and Ola Berge did in the context of Norwegian folk music,[58] here the two systems coexist, responding to distinctive attitudes toward *tsnius* and *kol isha*.

Subversive Creativities, Sisterhood, and Publicity

My ethnography with private performers illuminates the creative process in conservative circles and the way women understand novelty without destabilizing tradition. I was able to identify three meanings of "creativity":[59] first, it refers to an ability to forge new ideas, materials, or performances through a variety of religious norms and practices; second, it describes a collective experience through which the individual can gain publicity if the creative product is framed as serving the collective; third, it is an umbrella term for performance and the arts.

In creating an informal entertainment market for women and girls only, the private performer expands the potential for creativity in earning *parnasse* and acquiring publicity thanks to technology. Two economic regimes emerge from this creative process: one promotes collective ownership, with the individual participating only as a member of the group, such as educators in schools, camps, and private programs, as well as the musical band described above; the other upholds intellectual property, authorship, and individual recognition, as we have seen with the home studio owner, the writer, and the composer.

Ultra-Orthodox women's efforts to expand creativity and develop an informal musical market resonate with the second economic regime, echoing the homogenizing and normative influence of globalization toward the intellectual property agenda pushed by the World Trade Organization.[60] However, ultra-Orthodox women have shaped the local manifestations of these trends to make them acceptable within the ultra-Orthodox world while also seeking publicity. They remain outside the industry; they are publicized because they serve the well-being of girls and women; they keep their production at the informal level, and they combine the two systems of authorship to satisfy the most conservative voices. This integration of Western intellectual property law works against individuals who wish to retain the traditional system of collective ownership. It creates a competitive market in which women and girls must select one regime or negotiate with both to strengthen sentiments of sisterhood within, and by means of, this informal music market.

The conceptualization and expansion of ultra-Orthodox female creativity—all of which takes place in private spaces—reveal how the digital and technology redesign traditional paradigms of publicity within Orthodoxy. Even in the most conservative circles, there are possibilities for women's publicity and the opportunity to become a knowledgeable figure in the arts, while maintaining strict religious norms. The interplay between tradition and modernity, in particular its effects on women's music practices, resembles what ethnomusicologist Anne Rasmussen found in the sonic environment of Indonesian Islam.[61] She argues that musically active women are more traditional than modern, and that modern constructions of Islam—particularly those fueled by a reformist impulse—actually damage traditional ways. Tradition is not a limitation but an opportunity for Indonesian women. Similarly, tradition in the ultra-Orthodox context explored in this chapter, for the private performer, does not limit women invested in the arts, but rather shapes the ways they incorporate technology and the digital into their practices, not as a tool for reform but as an opportunity to work within tradition while expanding notions of creativity and individual development. Viewing the private creative spaces of ultra-Orthodox women and girls through a Western liberal feminist lens, where agency is attainable only with public performances accessible to all, would obscure rather than illuminate these developments.

From the school performance to the writers' room, the creative process of these women is guided by a rigorous understanding of *tsnius* and a tradition of communal music making, embedded in the mixed processes of descent, dissent, and affinity, to echo the ethnomusicologist Kay Kauffman Shelemay's tripartite analysis of musical communities.[62] The private performer traditionally creates artistic spaces for girls and women who share common descent as Hasidic or Litvish, in private schools and summer camps. She pursues this process by performing with the musical band, recording in the home studio, and composing in the writers' room. With the emergence of the digital, the private performer was also able to integrate authorship and copyright, to create new opportunities for girls and women to explore the arts with private programs, a process of dissenting from what originally existed. Lastly, the private performer also collaborates with other performers across borders for her recordings and compositions, and to advertise her private programs and music bands, but she does it on the basis of artistic and personal affinity.

THE PRIVATE PERFORMER | 95

Instead of interpreting *tsnius* and *kol isha* in their circles as restrictive, the private performer considers them to be normative tools in her training, creative process, and mechanism for publicity.[63] Women's publicity and creativity are thereby decoupled from public and individual performances subject to the liberal gaze. By viewing publicity as necessary for economic success within an exclusively female arts sphere, the private performer does not create a counterpublic that contradicts and challenges the Orthodox public media. Her desire for promotion and longing for becoming a renowned figure in the very private domain of the *frum* female art worlds are not meant to create an alternative public to her exclusion from the Orthodox public space and media. Rather than influencing the ultra-Orthodox public space, she instead pursues strategies to exist parallel to these public spaces that are accessible to both genders, and to publicize her business in the ultra-Orthodox feminine network. The private performer uses technology to do so—through the dissemination of interviews and advertisements in the media and the creation of booklets of productions happening in schools or for *tsedakah* events, as well as the cooperation of technology ladies and home studio owners in making connections through word of mouth. By doing so, she transforms this private space into an informal market, known to a female audience that consumes it. The *frum* female private performer challenges understandings of private and public spaces in anthropology, which attaches visibility to political life and invisibility to domestic life, as well as the feminist theorists who envisage women's eagerness for exposure and publicity as counterpublic.[64] In the context of religious studies, she complicates the binary that we usually embrace between the feminine private and invisible space and the masculine visible and public space, forcing us to think beyond the binary. She is also demonstrating a fine distinction by which one can gain publicity by making oneself visible without disclosing one's face or name, making the private space a space where publicity is possible while the invisibility of its raison d'être is maintained.

Creative production by these women has not one raison d'être but many. Some women, such as Freida or Toby, subscribe to the idea of art for its aesthetic value, an outlook sustained by a discourse focusing on its social, educational, and economic role. Many women and girls rely heavily on this discourse, since creativity for its own sake conflicts with the language of *kol isha* and *tsnius*. Furthermore, the democratization of music production and distribution introduces us to women who want more than to insert their individual creativity into the collective. For some, the notion of authorship in this informal market did not satisfy their desire for recognition of their talent and right to retain their intellectual property, and they decided to surpass the informal market and participate in the kosher entertainment industry. These women label their niche within the industry "for women and girls only" or *"kol isha"* to proclaim their Orthodox Jewishness, as we will see in the next chapter.

Because creativity is traditionally experienced as collective, it reinforces both sisterhood among women and girls and ties to Orthodoxy. As we saw, Sarah Schenirer, as a visionary and leader for females' empowerment through education, has demonstrated this for girls at schools and summer camps,[65] but the digital revolution expanded the range of these effects beyond the local. Women and girls now exchange a corpus of their studio-produced songs through email, phone calls, WhatsApp, and YouTube, as well as physical forms that are collected, carried, and distributed by women as they travel within, between, and across communities. The process of music production by and for women engenders a sense of pride within them that is shared across these communities.

The private performer no longer works solely at the local level to create new hits for annual performances at schools or summer camps. She engages a repertoire of songs produced by women or men, MIDI files, scripts, and arrangements circulating across borders. As Toby explained in the *Balebusta* article, she takes pride in seeing women and girls connect with each other through music, a creative exchange that extends across many boundaries. She reaffirmed this in a private conversation with me, asserting that music played a key role in building community beyond just Kiryas Joel. Through a shared definition of *tsnius* and *kol isha* and the music-making and distribution processes that derive from them, the women and girls depicted in this chapter join a collaborative community of like-minded individuals in KJ, Montreal, Williamsburg, Borough Park, and other places. The digital, embraced and adapted by ultra-Orthodox Jewish women, accelerated their awareness of belonging to a transnational community, one that transcends affiliations to specific Hasidic branches, Litvish local communities, or general localities, but still affirms their shared identity of being descended from Eastern European Orthodox Jewry. This process of expanding sisterhood beyond religious affiliation has been reproduced by *frum* female creators searching for fame. But these women profess and perform a different expression of *tsnius*, and therefore take a very different path, aspiring to celebrity through established industry routes.

4

The Celebrity

Making the Kol Isha *Industry, Conceiving a Modest Public*

> I am not a singer because I want to be a celebrity. I think
> about it as a mission. Because girls need to be inspired, and
> to have healthy role models to preserve their integrity as
> Jewish girls.
> —Bracha Jaffe, November 2020

The cover of the January 13, 2021, issue of *Ami Living*, a weekly magazine for ultra-Orthodox women, reads, "A Studio Grows in Brooklyn: Rochel Leah Reifer Creates Music and Helps Others Create Their Own." The story within positions Reifer, a Hasidic woman from Borough Park who built a home recording studio in her basement, as a success story, part of the growing phenomenon of ultra-Orthodox women becoming entrepreneurs and professionals in the domain of the arts, entertainment, and technology. Respecting the norms of the ultra-Orthodox press, *Ami Living* did not show Reifer's face in its pages but did publish her full name (an approach contrary to that followed by the magazine *Balebusta*, as we saw earlier). The story presents her creativity, curiosity, and musical talent as vehicles for serving and supporting others in the community. Reifer started out as an autodidact, reproducing the songs of others, and later received music lessons for a short time with the support of her parents. The story depicts this training as a major factor in the launch of her music career, carefully underscoring that she has had religious support from Rebbetzin Goldberger, who is the principal of Bnos Zion of Bobov (a private Hasidic school for girls) and the daughter of the Bobover *rebbe*.

To counterbalance Reifer's professional accomplishments, the article's author, Musia Kaplan, suggests toward the end of the piece that Reifer's domestic role remains a "top priority":

Aside from her musical career, Rochel Leah is a busy wife and mother of four. Like most working moms, she sees each day as a balancing act. "Chinuch" [Jewish education] is a full-time job . . . Her family is her first priority. She insists on being there to welcome the kids when they get home from school and makes sure to prepare supper before her husband's arrival. A few years ago, she decided to get rid of her smartphone so she could have peace of mind outside the studio . . . Her dedication to music will never override her devotion to her family. Thankfully, the two usually don't conflict. Rochel Leah's family loves and supports the music studio that is growing in Brooklyn. And the melodies that pour forth bring joy and inspiration to all.[1]

Although the publication acknowledges Reifer's fame and therefore promotes the success of women in the arts, the publication also reminds readers that the main duty of an Orthodox woman is to be a mother and a wife, with a focus on home and family.

Reifer is one of many *frum* female artists and celebrities whom I have encountered participating in the emerging formal market of performances for and by women. Unlike the informal music market that exists in private spaces, discussed in the previous chapter, this new, formal market is part of the kosher music and film industry. It involves professional recording studios, producers, digital stores, managers, booking agents, and record labels, as well as women and girls labeling themselves *frum* female artists. These women offer live and online performances as well as films and other musical content. Their products are available in stores on CDs, DVDs, and USB drives as well as online on downloading files, and streaming and video sharing platforms, all distributed by the same mainstream corporations that handle music and films produced by Orthodox men.

The women and girls who are creating this new industry of unique visual and sound aesthetics are following the path of Orthodox Jewish male singers and actors who have defined the kosher entertainment industry thus far. Yet while male celebrities have already reshaped ultra-Orthodoxy to conform to North American consumer culture, *frum* female artists introduce a new element: they are adapting the industry to the norms of *tsnius* and *kol isha* by finding new strategies to create a modest public space with the digital and technology. In doing so, they translate celebrity culture into Orthodoxy, reminding us of the economic and social capital women have with which to reshape Orthodox womanhood in a manner aligned with American capitalism, modernization, and popular feminine culture.[2] This development resonates with the more democratic concept of the celebrity brought on by the digital revolution.[3] This new feminine industry, which I label the *"kol isha* industry," can either threaten or buttress traditional ways of life, but *frum* female artists themselves advocate for a new role model that recognizes the arts and creativity as tools that need to be promoted, utilized for their own gain, and nourished. Nevertheless, the debate resides in the ways this use, promotion, and nourishment are done; this varies from one artist to another, as we will see below. While some perceive the role of the female artist—signifying fame, vanity, and self-promotion—as individualistic and antagonistic to *tsnius* values, others believe it to be a noble profession, focused on service to women and girls in the community, that does not conflict with a woman's primary duty to care for her family.

Comparable to what scholars have observed regarding male Orthodox cantors,[4] *frum* female artists make the choice to stay within the prescribed mold of their community while experimenting with the development of a modest public scene on social media. Contrary to men, who were and are able to experiment with their artistic development on the mainstream secular artistic scene with mixed-gender audiences while staying connected to their community through their performances at the synagogue and thereby developing a double career, women are limited by the norms of *tsnius*. These norms prevent them from performing in front of mixed-gender audiences if they want to pursue their careers within Orthodoxy, a space where they have their audience and can become famous. In opposition to male singers and artists, if they crossed the line of the secular venue, they would be totally excluded from their Orthodox audience.

In order to be recognized as a kosher entertainment product—CD, DVD, or YouTube video—featuring ultra-Orthodox female artists, the product must be labeled "for women and girls only" or, when the production involves singing, *"kol isha,"* warning Orthodox male audiences that the content is forbidden to them. The women themselves must negotiate with other rules of *tsnius* that forbid images of their faces and bodies from being displayed on their products and their distributors' websites.[5] Nevertheless, any web search for these *frum* celebrities using their names will almost always surface photos published by themselves on social media platforms, as well as in online advertisements. The space in which they perform and publicize their work is neither private, because their music and films are available online or recorded, nor fully public, as they deliberately exclude male audiences and sometimes have private social media accounts. I identify the artistic space of the *kol isha* industry as a modest public space, distinct from the Orthodox public space, as they do not wish to replace or oppose the public kosher industry dominated by males. Their aim is to complement the work of men in the industry. These female artists seek professional recognition to transform the educational and social role of the arts in ultra-Orthodox Jewish society into an economic one. Among the *frum* female artists that I have met, some have thousands of followers on their Instagram profile, hundreds of thousands of views on their YouTube music videos, are known across borders, receive publicity from both Orthodox and secular public media, and are able to charge decent honorariums for their artistic services. They push for normalizing women's copyright and fame, and promoting the arts for social change and for their own sake. These women are perceived as celebrities by many of the women and girls I have met, taught, and collaborated with. A clear desire for artistic publicity, combined with distinctive labeling as *frum* artists, highlights a broader shift in the professional positions available to women and girls, revealing structural changes in the ways religious groups are able to shape private and public spaces in the digital era.

"*Frum* female celebrity" might seem like an oxymoron—and the most conservative circles still forbid such lifestyles to their members—but these women's productions have become increasingly popular within ultra-Orthodoxy. As English academic and scholar in film studies Richard Dyer has taught us,[6] celebrity culture is bound up with the conditions of global capitalism in which the stars are examples of the way people live their relation to production in capitalist society. The birth of the *frum* female celebrity is a great example through which to understand how ultra-Orthodox women as performers and spectators have transformed their relationship with cultural production, and how conflicts within Orthodoxy surrounding gender, individualism, and community can be mediated. But since the triumph of the individual contravenes *tsnius*, many women in the arts initially resisted this model. Nevertheless, the celebrity culture model today prevails among a group of *frum* women I have encountered in person and online, mainly located in the United States, who mobilize it to further their artistic careers. They use social media to create and amplify their fandom, sharing both professional and personal stories to forge an emotional bond with their fans. The twenty-first-century pop star model on social media transforms the figure of the celebrity from powerful and famous to intimate and familiar.[7]

This chapter brings us to the rise of what I have designated the "*kol isha* industry" and the birth of the *frum* female celebrity. Almost all of the women discussed in this chapter are supported by their husbands and their families to engage in such novel adventures. None of them are single, all have between two and seven children, and all started essentially according to the norms in the community, performing for charity almost for free and educating for schools and summer camps, ultimately developing a business for their *parnasse* as artists. These women desired professional opportunities in the arts but also wished to maintain *tsnius* and *kol isha* while becoming recognized and known as artists and professionals. To this end, they incorporated, adapted, and indigenized celebrity culture and stardom to Orthodoxy.[8] Celebrity is produced by the interaction among media, star power, and public opinion.[9] These women have drawn on their experiences in education and the performing arts to become professionals in the arts, embracing and valorizing traditional positions while remodeling them as tools for self-empowerment and economic agency. The *frum* female celebrity acts upon the society in which she exists, simultaneously defying certain norms, reinforcing others, and blurring the divide between masculine and feminine practices in contemporary ultra-Orthodox communities by creating a modest public art space. The arts thus serve as a tool to reinforce religiosity and community, but also to disclose the negotiations made by women to shape celebrity according to their primary role as mothers, a position granting them financial capital and autonomy.

A formal market of recorded and live performances now exists alongside the informal one maintained by the more conservative women discussed earlier; it is an integral part of the kosher music and film industry, available in Jewish shops across the globe as well as online. What were once hobbies for these women became careers, setting the stage for new models of womanhood that transcend the normative role of the working woman, a role that constrains them to renown that is gained not by revealing their faces and voices in entertainment media but only by serving their communities as *rebbetzins* (rabbis' wives), educators, therapists, social workers, mothers, and wives.

Women, Celebrity Culture, and the Kosher Entertainment Industry

The *kol isha* industry emerges from and complements both the formal kosher entertainment industry dominated by men and the informal market made by women. Women in this industry work with a variety of other industry professionals, such as songwriters, audiovisual engineers, and booking agents, as well as record labels, performing rights organizations, and retail and digital stores. Through a process of professionalization, individualization, and commodification, *frum* female artists turn live, unmarketable performances into a new economy. This new industry reinforces gender segregation in that the broader entertainment opportunities it provides exist in an environment restricted to women and girls. Yet, the availability of female-made products in online and brick-and-mortar stores also involves a degree of self-promotion and public self-display that conflicts with traditional models of modesty.

These artists also challenge norms regarding access to secular popular culture, opening the door to sounds, images, and ideas that spread rapidly through different social media platforms over which religious authorities have little control. The *kol isha* industry is part of the digital economy and follows the broader social and cultural logic of Orthodoxy, which it reifies, reproduces, and transforms all at once. In this context, digital technology takes on a dialectic role: it reifies Orthodoxy transnationally while also reinventing the ultra-Orthodox female aesthetic as a commodity.

The shift to the digital in music production not only impacted concerts at schools and summer camps, as we saw earlier, but also contributed to the monetization of women's performances through commercial recordings, musicals on DVD, music videos, and cinema. Before the digital turn, it was almost exclusively *baalei tshuva* women who recorded and distributed albums as professionals in the arts. Trained at secular professional musical schools, they moved from secular stages to Orthodox ones, bringing their knowledge and experience to ultra-Orthodox circles. These women include Ruthi Navon Zmora, an Israeli singer who performed on Broadway and recorded her first album in 1988; Julia Blum, who recorded in 1990; and Kineret Sarah Cohen in 1998. The first generation of women born in ultra-Orthodox circles to enter the music industry were Rochel Miller, a Yeshivish woman who grew up in the Bronx; Malky Giniger, a Litvish woman from Brooklyn who attended Bais Yaakov; and Chanale Fellig-Harrell, a Lubavitcher woman from Florida who now lives in Israel. This generation of female singers was a small group collaborating out of necessity with mostly male producers and sound engineers. In the 1990s, women such as Giniger and Fellig-Harrell had difficulty marketing their music to Orthodox circles. Now, they work as professional composers and singers with their own home recording studios, while their albums appear widely in stores and online as well as in the press, responding to the needs of a consumerist ultra-Orthodox middle class.[10]

In addition to recording albums, this first generation often performed live for female audiences at charity events and recorded musicals that they sometimes sold on DVD. The concept of the *frum* female musical as a marketable product emerged under these conditions, as some realized that screening DVDs of previous performances was cheaper than hiring artists to perform live again. During this development, some artists saw an economic opportunity and began to film their musicals in real settings—as they do in cinema—instead of on a stage.

Because screenings of women's live performances had become acceptable practice in certain circles, these new films sparked little controversy. They exposed women and girls to a new form of entertainment. While more "adventurous" women decided to access the formal market—working with distributors and creating labels for their DVDS that marked them as "for women only"—others kept their productions in the informal market.

With the emergence of portable video equipment in the 1980s and the democratization of digital filmmaking in the first decade of the twenty-first century,[11] independent production companies proliferated, allowing smaller communities to access film-production technologies to tell their stories and explore issues important to them.[12] These companies offered affordable services due to the miniaturization of production technologies and the low cost of materials, which led to the development of community cinema that included films made by ultra-Orthodox women. While few of these *frum* female filmmakers had professional training, they often worked closely with these companies during the production and postproduction stages. The first generation of filmmakers thus learned mostly through experience rather than formal instruction, but the growing popularity of these films is leading to professionalization and further careers for women in a niche cinema space.

The emergence of the *kol isha* industry has brought to light several ambiguities and transformations within Orthodoxy. First, even though access to the Internet is limited to business use, such access opens the door to non-kosher knowledge and cultural content. As we saw earlier, creativity traditionally arises from a collective process, which is different from the understanding of creativity in Western artistic scenes centered on the individual. However, by integrating models of celebrity culture,[13] *frum* female artists offer other ways to be creative. Second, until the early twenty-first century, women's and girls' voices were not commonly recorded for commercial purposes, to prevent men from accessing them. Finally, rabbinic authority in ultra-Orthodox circles traditionally prohibits the consumption of film, television, and other video-recorded content. Because the *kol isha* industry resulted from a paradox between the proscriptions of religious authority and the practices of individuals, its success encourages us to think about the changes to authority in religious settings brought about by the digital.

These female celebrities are swiftly becoming role models within the realms of music production, performance, and women's cinema. I use the term "celebrity" to refer to individuals in regional and specialized markets with thousands of devoted followers on social media, online, and at live events. Celebrities and stars are firmly constructed through "local politics and ideologies, film industries, linguistic contexts; they are signs of local cultural codes, gestures, languages, attitudes, and ideas."[14] In other words, followings limited to ultra-Orthodox circles (rather than a broader demographic) do not preclude celebrity; rather, local and specific publics are an integral part of celebrity. Although these religious female celebrities' influence remains fragmented and limited, it is nonetheless essential to consider it as a text that reflects the conditions of the society from which it emerges.[15] Committed to strong gender segregation, these celebrities carve out places for themselves from the hardwood of complementarianism while molding the culture of celebrity to female Orthodoxy.

The path to celebrity typically emerges from activity within a single artistic role—singer, studio owner, filmmaker—but these categories are not siloed off from one another. Women such as Devorah Schwartz, Bracha Jaffe, Chayala Neuhaus, and Malky Weingarten, whom we will meet in this chapter, have achieved fame thanks to their personalities, original productions, and ties with professionals in the music and film industry as well as institutions in their Orthodox communities, social media, and cultivation of audiences and fandoms. These four women epitomize the *frum* female artist and celebrity within the *kol isha* industry and introduce us to new ways of interpreting visibility and private and public spaces with the digital.

The Modest Public Space

In 2020, when the COVID-19 pandemic began, *frum* female singers increased their online presence, offering livestream concerts, posting daily on Instagram, and releasing a large number of music videos. That summer, the ultra-Orthodox organization Bonei Olam, which assists couples struggling with infertility, produced its first music video for women and girls. *Frum* female singers Bracha Jaffe and Devorah Schwartz were selected and performed "Vzakeini" (a religious word appearing in some Jewish prayers, meaning "you should grant us merit"). Jaffe and Schwartz posted the YouTube link on their respective Instagram accounts, where they each had thousands of followers. Jaffe initially had a private account when I started my ethnography and Schwartz a public one. Throughout the years, Jaffe went back and forth between public and private, and at the end of 2022, her account was public. Within a few months, the video, labeled "for women and girls only" on YouTube, had reached more than three hundred thousand views, becoming the most popular YouTube video by a *frum* female singer at the time. The song also moved to the top of Schwartz's popular songs list on Spotify. In the video, both singers perform in elegant and modest black dresses covering their collarbones and elbows, with pearls accenting their ensembles, and two long, stylish *sheytl*. At the start of the video, both artists enter a professional recording studio decorated with candles. Bracha Jaffe starts to play on a grand piano while Devorah Schwartz begins to sing. In some parts of the music video, they walk through a forest with children while the lyrics address the theme of motherhood. Closing their eyes and raising their hands when saying the word *"vzakeini,"* the artists perform, grounded in their interiority, as powerful, modest, and elegant, embracing a musical professionalism palpable in their vocal technique and performance.

This music video, financed by an ultra-Orthodox organization, appears to normalize the performances of *frum* female artists online, but it actually resulted from controversy. Bonei Olam's "Vzakeini" reveals how famous female singers have pushed Orthodoxy to authorize unconventional or subversive practices. Rather than ostracizing performers using social media to promote their work, the organization saw an economic potential with these productions. The video also exemplifies the creation of a modest public space where *frum* female celebrities advertise their productions to a broader audience for their *parnasse*. Contrary to the private performer, who follows strict norms of *tsnius* by not revealing her name or her face, the *frum* female celebrity attracts individualized attention in an unprecedented manner.

Bonei Olam originally commissioned the song "Vzakeini" from composers Baruch Levine and Miriam Israeli in January 2020 for the organization's annual fundraising campaign. Its release came in the form of a music video featuring Levine and fellow Orthodox star Benny Friedman alongside the New York Boys Choir and Shir V'shevach Boys Choir.[16] The fundraising campaign was presented as a global women's movement, the "Vzakeini Movement," encouraging women from around the world to donate one dollar a week to support a childless couple in need of in vitro fertilization (IVF). As maternity and family are central to ultra-Orthodox women's lives, infertility treatment is highly encouraged and supported. Because of strict gender segregation in the community, ultra-Orthodox organizations organize exclusive events and, more recently, global campaigns targeting women, in which they deliver messages often celebrating motherhood, *tsnius*, *chinuch* (Jewish education), women's empowerment, and unity. The goal of the Vzakeini Movement was to reach eighteen thousand women—a number reflecting both the mystical meaning of the *chai* (חי), which is eighteen according to the numerological system of *gematria*, and the cost of IVF treatment (eighteen thousand dollars)—and harness the power of their prayer when lighting their *shabbes* candles on Friday nights.[17]

Since the campaign was targeted at women, the well-known Hasidic songwriter Miriam Israeli wrote lyrics about women's faith and the lighting of candles for *shabbes*, as well as the hope of women wanting to become mothers, who ask in prayer to be "granted merit" (*vzakeini*). But when the music video was released, it showcased male singers Benny Friedman and Baruch Levine as the stars of the campaign. The organization received tremendous backlash on social media from *frum* female advocates for the publication of women's faces and voices. These women were outraged by the release of a song addressing women's issues without any visual or auditory representation of women themselves. Bonei Olam had taken a conservative approach to *tsnius* and *kol isha*—with a particular aversion to the broadcasting of women's voices—no doubt because the organization serves various *hashkafot*, including the most conservative. The song's writer, Miriam Israeli, also embraces this approach, as her response on YouTube in April 2020 made clear: "In response to those who protest the absence of women in the video: Allow me to speak on behalf of tens of thousands of Jewish women who choose to influence family, society and history with wisdom, diplomacy, and discretion. We don't desire or need public exposure, and we view modesty as a privilege, not a burden. This is our choice. Please respect it."

Nevertheless, despite Bonei Olam's conservative stance on modesty, the organization responded to these demands with action, though admittedly without making a public statement. First, they asked Devorah Schwartz to write a version of the song inspired by the circumstances of the COVID-19 pandemic, so as not to eclipse the original, but this version was never recorded. Then, seeing an opportunity in the many new online events for Orthodox women and girls during the pandemic, the organization arranged a livestream concert with Schwartz and Jaffe performing a new version of the song. Both singers promote (though more by their actions than by their discourse) an interpretation of *tsnius* and *kol isha* that places the responsibility for men to avoid accessing female faces and voices onto men's shoulders. Instead of holding the concert as an exclusive Bonei Olam event, the organization arranged it through the Ohel Sarala initiative, a section of Bonei Olam created in 2017 to support childless couples. The Orthodox Jewish press advertised the concert both in print and online with two different posters: one with the singers' faces, and the other without.[18] The former was a response to the criticism that women could already use such images for their own publicity and on their social media accounts, while the latter served to satisfy the organization's more conservative clientele.[19]

The livestream attracted thousands of viewers across the globe, and its success no doubt encouraged Bonei Olam to later produce a music video for the song starring the two singers. However, the organization never published or promoted this video on its social media accounts, likely for fear of conservative backlash. Only Jaffe's and Schwartz's social media accounts have advertised the video—which is labeled "Bonei Olam Vzakeini—For Women and Girls Only"—allowing the organization to remain mostly invisible.

While Bonei Olam itself does not support the visibility of women in music videos or the celebration of their fame, it needed *frum* female singers to maintain the legitimacy of its campaign as a global women's movement. As it turned out, the decision to invite two of the most celebrated and respected professional female singers of the ultra-Orthodox music scene—Jaffe and Schwartz are often considered *frum* versions of the classic North American pop star—was not exactly hazardous to the organization's cause. The group capitalized on these women's fame to reach thousands of supporters without alienating its more conservative audience. Before these events, Bonei Olam most likely failed to realize that their social media campaign's target audience included a female contingent vocally critical of women's invisibility in ultra-Orthodox media. Most women with conservative views on this matter, here represented by Miriam Israeli, consume less social media content than this activist crowd, so a fundraising campaign on social media should ideally be marketed more toward the latter group. Whether the organization erred in its marketing of the campaign or in not realizing the power of *frum* female celebrities and activists, one thing is clear: female celebrities are currently shaping the way celebrity culture impacts ultra-Orthodox society, beyond the male gaze as well as the traditional figure of the famous *rebbetzin* and woman educator.

The recent popularity of *frum* female singers has allowed some of them to independently produce highly successful live concerts, attracting the attention of organizations, such as Bonei Olam, in search of marketing opportunities. In the same way that celebrities sell products and commodities,[20] *frum* female singers sell the organizations that sponsor them. Although earlier *frum* female singers such as Malky Giniger, Rochel Miller, and Kineret Sarah Cohen had also performed for such organizations and indeed pioneered the *kol isha* industry, they could only develop a fan base locally or through international tours when they participated in these *tsedakah* events, since they had no mediatic presence they could control. With the development of social media, Schwartz, Jaffe, and their peers attract fans from far beyond the circles of these organizations, integrating into Orthodoxy the model of the digital celebrity who is using social media to create a direct and intimate relationship with her fandom. Because they always follow the norms of *tsnius* by advertising their shows as "for women and girls only" and performing with hair coverings and modest clothing, and because they wield massive influence through the global fan base they have built online, they compel Orthodox organizations such as Bonei Olam, who want to benefit from their global reach and recognition, to reposition themselves in the domain of women's entertainment.

Social organizations are now increasingly capitalizing on this trend, producing high-quality music videos with professional *frum* female singers for their fundraising campaigns and thereby implicitly acknowledging and institutionalizing the figure of the *frum* female pop star perceived as a celebrity by the women of the community. One video that epitomizes this development features Bracha Jaffe singing the original composition "Stronger All as One" for the Food Fuels Refuos campaign of Chesed 24/7, an organization that provides services to the sick, elderly, developmentally disabled, and others facing similar challenges. It begins with a short prelude that introduces a sick woman searching for food in her home. Then Jaffe, singing in English treated with vocoder technology over a pop electronic track, appears on screen wearing a black skirt, black and white top, black leather jacket, and white boots. With pink lipstick and her long *sheytl*, she sits at a computer in an office, using the Internet to search for the Chesed 24/7 website. After making an online donation to the organization, she closes her computer, leaves her office, and drives her car to a hospital, pulling a trailer with "Chesed 24/7" plastered on it. Once there, she delivers food to patients out of the trailer with the help of other women, all of whom are dressed modestly. Throughout the video, Jaffe exemplifies the modest, fashionable, and independent modern ultra-Orthodox woman. But in addition to transmitting new norms regarding *kol isha* and *tsnius*, the video also demonstrates the professionalization of such music productions by *frum* women; the dancing of Jaffe with other women and girls is choreographed by professional dancer Rhonda Malkin (who has also worked with Devorah Schwartz), and the song itself is produced and arranged by classically trained Israeli pianist and composer Shai Bachar. Both Chesed 24/7 and Jaffe released the video on their YouTube channels.

The pioneers who have produced such music videos include the *frum* female singers Shaindel Antelis, Nechama Cohen, and Franciska Kosman. But they released their videos between 2011 and 2014 as part of an underground scene in which they were building a community without the support of Orthodox organizations. Nevertheless, since late 2010, these artists too have professionalized themselves, incorporating celebrity culture into Orthodoxy by mobilizing and embracing mediatic and professional tools, as well as digital marketing strategies. Appearing on social media such as YouTube, dressed according to the norms of *tsnius* and claiming the creation of a space "for women and girls only," the *frum* female singer and other artists using these online platforms are creating a modest public space.

The Singers

Among *frum* female performers, Devorah Schwartz has one of the largest social media presences and online fan bases, no doubt due to an artistic persona that combines her many talents—not only singing but also dancing and acting. Growing up in a very musical and artistic Hasidic family in Flatbush, Brooklyn, in the 1980s, Schwartz began learning dance and gymnastics at the age of five in private schools established by *baalei tshuva* women who were professionally trained outside the community. As a teenager, she worked for three years as a dance choreographer, counselor, and performer at Orthodox summer camps, where she met Malky Giniger, who would later offer her the position of dance director at Ratzon, the arts school she founded for women and girls in Flatbush. After she married, Schwartz became increasingly attracted to a career in performance that includes singing and dance. She began professional voice training in 2013, taking lessons with Juilliard alum Steven Schnurman. The choice of a male instructor might be considered controversial due to *kol isha*, but for Schwartz and her supportive husband, the professional context mitigated such concern. In 2016, she not only rebranded herself as a singer and performer but also founded her own Sunday arts school, Devorah's School of Arts (DSA), offering classes in dance, voice, and drama.

As part of her rebranding as a singer, Schwartz joined multiple mediatic platforms where she advertised her products and services. In 2016, she created accounts on Facebook and Instagram, and the latter has become her preferred platform. Instagram, where she labels herself a "Singer, Musical Artist, and Voice Teacher" with *"KOL ISHA"* at the center of her profile (@devorahschwartzofficial), allows her to develop a community of fans by regularly sharing visual and audio content related to her voice training, performances, and collaborations. Browsing Schwartz's Instagram page, one discovers her eclectic use of various musical aesthetics, including covers of English-language pop songs (by Barbra Streisand, Celine Dion, Josh Groban, and Whitney Houston, as well as songs from Disney films), modern Hebrew hits (by Simcha Leiner, Shmuel Iungar, Yoni Z, Berri Weber, Avraham Fried and Ari Hill, and Benny Friedman), and traditional Jewish songs in Hebrew and Yiddish. Her videos and photos capture moments in various settings across North America, the Caribbean, and Israel: recording studios, theaters, concert halls, cruises, hotels, private homes, outdoor venues, schools, summer camps, and community centers. Moreover, she also posts music videos in which she performs alongside Dobby Baum, Nechama Cohen, Chanale Fellig-Harrel Franciska, Bracha Jaffe, Dalia Oziel, Eli Ryp, and many other artists, helping to build a collaborative online community of *frum* female singers.

In addition to this aggressive social media rebranding of herself as a singer, Schwartz released an original album—recorded at Chayala Neuhaus's studio—in April 2019 under the Orthodox Jewish record label Aderet. Advertised in all popular Orthodox Jewish newspapers, it was available in Jewish stores across North America, Europe, and Israel, as well as online for downloading and streaming. After its release, Schwartz self-financed the production of music videos for its songs. For both the album and these music videos, she invested in a professional team of technicians, composers, and artistic directors, wanting to demonstrate that *frum* female artists could produce high-quality music products.

Schwartz's decision to make her music videos public on YouTube (though explicitly labeled "for women and girls") proved pivotal. She knew that doing so would not meet with unanimous approval, but she had the sanction of some religious leaders, giving her confidence that such entertainment practices would eventually become normalized even in the most conservative circles. Moreover, the decision came as a response to the circulation of a private video without her consent:

> I wanted to become a singer. I made a private promotional video that I sent to camps, to friends, and relatives. The video traveled all over the world without my consent. This viral video put me on the map unintentionally. Then I thought, if people are going to share my video without my permission, I am going to deliver what I want to the public. When you perform, everybody has a phone or a camera and can post it easily. I'd rather control my image and my message. If I provide images and videos, people won't feel the need to upload videos of me performing. For the ones saying that I am making men sin, this is their problem, not mine. All my videos and channels are "for women and girls" or "*kol isha*." This is not my responsibility at this point. (personal interview, December 2020)

Schwartz's opinions on public music videos are shared by other *frum* female singers, including Nechama Cohen and Franciska—two pioneers in the production of publicly accessible music videos[21]—as well as Chaya Kogan, Shaindy Plotzker, and Chanale Fellig-Harrel all of whom post online content. By putting "*kol isha*" or "for women and girls only" in the titles of these videos, or even just in the video description (as is the case with some video produced by Franciska and Esther Freeman), these singers advocate for an understanding of *kol isha* that makes the consumer, rather than the creator, responsible for engagement with the content. They aspire to offer what they call a "professional artistic experience" with sounds and images, analogous to what male singers have offered since the creation of YouTube, and to participate in the industry within the constraints of their female-only audience. Following the model of the twenty-first-century pop star, Schwartz promotes herself and her products online without an intermediary. She is in direct contact with her fan base and controls her own image. In 2021, her Instagram account grew to over twenty thousand followers, making her one of the most prominent *frum* female performers and singers.

Live performance constitutes another aspect of Schwartz's music career, and she is regularly invited to perform at summer camps, schools, and private events for charity (*tsedakah*).[22] For these performances, she adapts to the aesthetic and religious expectations of her clients when deciding the style of her wig, makeup, and sometimes even clothing. In the last two years, she has developed new strategies to maintain her own artistic vision without the interference of any sponsoring institutions, performing in self-produced concerts and online events offered directly to her fans. Her "Chanukah Spectacular" of December 2020, coproduced by composer Mirel Bennett, was one such online event. Schwartz and Mirel collaborated with a team of professionals, including choreographer Rhonda Malkin, dancers from the New York dance company the Rockettes, inspirational speaker and master of ceremonies Yaffa Palti, and a professional production company for the recording, editing, and mastering of the concert footage. They advertised the show a few weeks in advance in Jewish magazines and on social media, where it was shared by many *frum* female singers and influencers. Thousands of people from Mexico, Canada, the United States, the UK, France, Australia, and Israel attended the online concert, which is now available for purchase on DVD. While this was not the first independently organized concert to feature ultra-Orthodox professional singers and dancers, it was the first to receive extensive coverage on social media and in the ultra-Orthodox Jewish press.[23]

Schwartz is part of a new generation of professionally trained ultra-Orthodox singers and musicians who use digital media to achieve greater fame. She integrates celebrity culture into Orthodoxy through the incorporation of its forms, processes of production and publicity, and consumption patterns. Unlike the first generation of *frum* female singers, who remained largely invisible to the press while being known and recognized as important figures in the arts, these singers use common pop star strategies to grow their followings, yet they also remind

Figure 4.1: Devorah Schwartz with the dancers at the Chanukah
Spectacular, December 2020 (credit Sarah Mugrabi; special thanks
to Devorah Schwartz for the photos).

Figure 4.2: Poster of the Chanukah Spectacular, December
2020 (credit New Marketing Creative in Lakewood, New
Jersey; special thanks to Devorah Schwartz for the photos).

their audiences that they are not simply performers, as their voices are vehicles of God's presence.

Although Schwartz's, Jaffe's, and others' particular model of celebrity embraces *tsnius*, they are aware of the limits of tolerance or acceptance in conservative communities. Nevertheless, many of them have expressed the belief that God granted them their talent, and so they must use it to transmit his message. They have therefore sought out a professional education in the arts,[24] and their professionalization has been furthered by many artistic and entrepreneurial strategies. The *frum* female singer has become a highly visible and audible figure of the *kol isha* industry, with a growing fan base that makes her appealing to many organizations for marketing purposes, even if such organizations do not necessarily support this modernization, digitalization, and publicization.

The Studio Owner

At the height of the COVID-19 pandemic in January 2021, on the Instagram page of the renowned C-note Studios—a music studio in Lakewood, New Jersey—a simple but dramatic promotional video was posted. A single tree silhouetted against a faint mountainscape and reflected in a pool in the foreground announced the release of the single "Ein Od Milvado" (There Is No Other). Two names float across the top of the graphic—those of Devorah Schwartz and Chayala Neuhaus— even though in the accompanying music video the two women appear only after four minutes have elapsed. One of them is filmed only from behind, her face never visible.[25]

Neuhaus, the owner of the C-note Studios, is a singer and songwriter herself. The single advertised in the image is a contrafactum, a song in which new lyrics have been substituted for the old without substantial changes to the music. The original song was a hit composed by the Israeli Orthodox male singer Mordechai Shapiro. The new lyrics, written by Neuhaus and sung by Devorah Schwartz, address the feeling of insecurity many people experienced due to the pandemic. The music video, which was viewed more than thirty thousand times in five months, tells a story centered on the secular print media during the pandemic; in between the lyrics that pop up across the screen, imagery reveals various headlines and recreations of COVID-19 newspaper stories before

Figure 4.3 and 4.4: Devorah Schwartz, *Pessakh* concert in Israel, 2022, for the organization Daily Giving (credit Chaim Tuito; special thanks to Devorah Schwartz for the photos).

shifting to photos of landscapes, ending with the destruction of these journalistic articles as they transform into texts of the psalms. By the end of the clip, Schwartz is presented, appearing singing with headphones on in the recording studio, then the C-note Studios logo appears, followed by photos of the studio space and the song and production credits. The music video concludes with a short advertisement for C-note Studios in which Neuhaus is heard describing her facility and marketing her new offering of online training in the art of recording and sound engineering. After almost four minutes of video, Neuhaus's face remains unshown. Devorah Schwartz, on the other hand, expanded her visibility for a few months after the release by providing a video dance tutorial dedicated to this specific contrafactum.[26]

This music lyric video comes at the apex of Neuhaus's success in the industry. She has translated the culture of celebrity to the *kol isha* industry by holding tight to ultra-Orthodox norms such as concealing—to a point—women's faces and singing voices while ignoring others, for example, by branding her full name and being on social media to expand her business. The first generation of women studio owners learned music production through online classes with experts outside of their religious circles and as autodidacts experimenting with the technology themselves.[27] But Neuhaus and women like her are changing the role of women in the field of music production. In her career thus far, Neuhaus has moved from private to public, from amateur to professional, from unmarketable to marketable, and from the arts for entertainment to the arts for her own sake and for *parnasse*.

Neuhaus holds a reputation as a famous studio owner and songwriter not only in the *kol isha* industry but also in the kosher music industry more broadly. She initially became known in the industry by producing albums for boys, representing one among a network of professional female studio owners—to which Rochel Leah, mentioned in the introduction to this chapter, also belongs—who have distinguished themselves by breaking into the male music market through behind-the-scenes productions. Because of her reputation as an upholder of conservative norms, she has found success in both conservative and modern ultra-Orthodox circles. Like most *frum* female artists, Neuhaus explains her talent as a part of her family heritage and a gift from God. She started her musical journey at a very young age and was always supported by her parents, who encouraged her to pursue a professional music education focused on classical music. She took private piano lessons for years with various teachers, both Jewish and non-Jewish but all classically trained at professional schools of music. Through this training, she was introduced to diverse genres, including classical, jazz, and pop. She debuted in the field of composition at the age of eleven, using her tape recorder to memorize lyrics and the melodies created on a keyboard. As those in her circles began to recognize her skill as a composer, she started writing songs for performances in schools and summer camps. In her teens, she broadened her clientele, composing on demand for newly engaged girls (*kallot*) and other events for a small fee. As she explained, "It was my hobby, my passion, and I could make a little bit of cash with it, but I never thought about it as a career. At that time, nobody thought about music and composition for women as a profession, as a serious career in the industry."[28]

Neuhaus is one of the female studio owners discussed earlier who have transformed the informal market of women's performances by investing in portable materials to create and record music. Around 2006, she was teaching English and history at school, giving private music lessons at home, and composing on the side when she decided to quit her day job to focus on her music career. She set up a semiprofessional home studio, and music production became her main source of income. At first, Neuhaus only worked on the private and informal music productions of girls, providing compositions and instrumental playbacks, as well as training for women and girls who wanted to build their own home studios. But this did not satisfy her, and she sought to participate in the larger, male-dominated music industry, which had only a few women composers working behind the scenes.

In 2015, Neuhaus acquired the necessary tools to produce her first professional album, *Miracles*, as a composer and studio owner. When I interviewed her in March 2021, she said her goal was to "share her music with the world," but due to her strict observance of *kol isha* and *tsnius*, she needed a male voice to interpret her songs. Therefore, she used that of Dovid Pearlman, a young boy from the famous Miami Boys Choir. After this album was available for purchase in stores and was a great success, her clientele grew significantly, and she needed a larger space for recording. In 2017, she built a professional studio and hired professional technicians (both women and men) for mixing and mastering. C-note Studios—as she named her venture—specialized in composition, and Neuhaus opened an Instagram account to increase the studio's exposure.

In 2018, Neuhaus recorded her second album, *Miracles II*, this time in collaboration with Doni Gross, a well-known producer, composer, and arranger of music by male Orthodox singers. They recruited Yehuda Kirschner, another boy in his teens, to provide vocals. While album covers for music by male artists usually feature a photo of the artist himself, Neuhaus's first two albums did not follow this model, instead using that established for female artists, whose faces do not appear on album covers. Thus, no human appears on the cover of either album, though Neuhaus's name appears in a larger font than the singers' names. However, an important shift occurred between the two releases related to how the albums are credited. For *Miracles* (2015), the album follows the usual conventions for music collaborations between men and women, meaning that only the initial of her first name appears alongside her family name (C. Neuhaus) and that the album is registered on streaming platforms under the name of the singer, Dovid Pearlman. For *Miracles II* (2018), however, the album cover displays Neuhaus's full name, her studio's name appears in a larger font than that used for other credits, and streaming platforms credit not the singer but her (again using her full name) as the primary artist. The record label Aderet, located in Brooklyn and specializing in Jewish music, produced and marketed both albums.[29]

While neither album featured Chayala Neuhaus's voice, they established her brand in the general kosher music market, positioning her as a producer and composer serving emerging boy stars. With *Miracles II* she accomplished a major shift and centered C-note Studios as the hub of her music work, making known to all (including men) her artistic contribution to the Jewish music scene and, more specifically, studio recording and production.

In 2018, as professional women singers gained greater popularity and acceptance, Neuhaus contributed to the debut album of Devorah Schwartz, who was at the time a new singer and dancer in female Orthodox circles. This was her first collaboration with a *frum* female singer, and she not only recorded and produced the album but also composed half of the songs, including the hit "Chana's Song," which reached

Figure 4.5: The cover of Devorah Schwartz's album *I Believe in Me*, 2019 (credit Yocheved Herzog; special thanks to Devorah Schwartz for the photos).

thousands of views on YouTube. She has continued to collaborate with Schwartz on a regular basis. Although both artists have distinct ways of establishing their brands in the *kol isha* industry, their artistic collaboration is mutually beneficial. Using the face and voice of a female celebrity allows Neuhaus to expand her clientele and promote her work as a composer and producer to the growing *kol isha* industry, while Schwartz benefits from the expertise of a woman composer and producer whom she trusts to develop her artistic persona. Throughout the years, Neuhaus collaborated with another famous *frum* female singer, Bracha Jaffe, composing the song "This One." The song was released as a music video, filmed as a high-quality production in Israel and Macedonia with Shai

Bachar, Jaffe's producer.[30] Their collaboration expanded to a live concert in November 2022 benefiting the organization Ezer Mizion. For the occasion, Bracha Jaffe was the main host and Neuhaus was presented as a guest star, alongside a renowned *rebbetzin*, a master of ceremonies, a dance performance group, a child soloist, a teen sensation, and an all-women band.[31]

In 2021, Neuhaus composed and wrote "A Yid," a song that echoes the struggles encountered during the pandemic (lost lives, sickness, closing of schools), for Hasidic male pop star Benny Friedman. Doni Gross produced and arranged the song, which was released as a single on social media in February 2021. The music video opens with the credits, first listing Neuhaus, whose name also appears on the promotional poster for the single. The song was available on YouTube, Vimeo, and Instagram, and on streaming platforms under the name of Benny Friedman, but with a promotional poster that highlights Neuhaus as the composer. Friedman and Neuhaus also promoted the release on their respective Instagram accounts, tagging each other on the posts. On YouTube, the music video reached almost 140,000 views within a month, more than any of Neuhaus's previous videos had received in such a short time.

On April 30, 2021, during the Jewish holiday of Lag Baomer, a deadly crowd crush occurred when pilgrims—mostly ultra-Orthodox Jews—to the tomb of Rabbi Shimon Yochai in Meron, Israel, fell on a slick passageway floor while exiting the tomb. Forty-five men and boys lost their lives and around 150 others sustained injuries, making it the deadliest civil disaster in the history of the state of Israel. This tragic event affected ultra-Orthodox communities around the globe, especially since many of the victims came from abroad. A few weeks after the event, groups started singing and recording Neuhaus's song "A Yid" in various schools, *yeshivot*, and seminaries, and it became an emblem of perseverance in the face of tragic events. Its lyrics, originally conceived as responding to the pandemic, resonated strongly with these affected communities, who sang it at their annual performances and recorded their own covers. Versions in English and Yiddish were recorded in Montreal, New York City, London, and Jerusalem, including two music videos made by women artists—one by Dobby Baum and her sister Frimi (May 2021), and another by Devorah Schwartz with her student Esther Sara Zuskind (June 2021).[32]

In the fall of 2022, Neuhaus entered a new stage of her career, emerging as a *frum* female celebrity alongside other *frum* female celebrity singers to organize a major live concert advertised and promoted on social media by other *frum* female singers, never with her face or voice exhibited. Neuhaus organized a major concert for women and girls only, Miracles Live, a title echoing her album's name. The concert was benefiting the organization Bridges, dedicated to facilitating temporary host homes for children whose families are going through a crisis. She performed and sang her own compositions alongside other female guests such as Mindy Blatt and the all-woman band *melodica*. The concert was held at the Ritz Theatre Edison in New Jersey, with transportation available by bus from Borough Park, Lakewood, and Monsey; the venue was a packed room with girls and women dancing, singing along, and bouncing with joy and passion.[33]

The promotion of Neuhaus's name alongside those of emerging stars and acclaimed celebrities such as Devorah Schwartz and Benny Friedman has allowed her to emerge as a celebrity herself, the famous composer and producer who acts behind the scenes and works with the most talented singers. Unlike most female songwriters, who are only celebrated privately for their work—such as Miriam Israeli, who for a long time used only an initial for her first name in her branding—Neuhaus appears prominently not only on the covers of these music products but also through media coverage in newspapers and on social media. While she wanted to embrace this fame to advance professionally, artistically, and financially, she kept her face and voice hidden from the limelight, exemplifying the uniqueness of the modest public scene.

> I did not need to share my face with the world to build my brand. In a way, there was less pressure than today. It is hard work to keep up the profile, to build it, to be the face, to smile, to perform all the time. I did not have this pressure when I started. It did not exist. Only very few female performers existed, Malky Giniger, Kinireth, Rochel Miller, but they did one or two shows in a year, that was all. It did not exist. When social media arrived and some Orthodox women started to use it for their business, I had to reinvent myself. I am not a singer, and my bread and butter come from writing, composing, and producing. I had a brand before,

but it was not largely distributed. Producing and distributing my album brought me a much bigger clientele. (personal interview, April 2021)

Neuhaus is creating a new model for women's fame in the *kol isha* industry, gaining recognition as a female producer and composer for singers of both genders. In this model, women do not remain invisible in the creative process but rather sit at its core, even if their faces and voices go unseen and unheard. As a figure of authority in music production and songwriting for both genders in an industry where women were almost nonexistent until recently, Neuhaus elevates women's music to the same level as men's, underscoring the professionalization of women in the arts.

The figure of the professional female studio owner, exemplified here by Chayala Neuhaus, embodies the artistic entrepreneurship that underlies both the *kol isha* industry and the general kosher music market. Alongside the *frum* female singer, the studio owner—who is not only a technician, as in the case of the educator, but also a songwriter and producer—has become a key proponent of the quasi-normalization of the *kol isha* industry.

The Filmmaker

In November 2020, I was in Borough Park, Brooklyn, on the set of *Hush Hush*, assisting the production team, which was an all-woman crew. Malky Weingarten—a filmmaker and actress well-known in Orthodox female circles—wrote, directed, and produced the film, in which she was also acting. She hired her friend Chaya Sarah to manage the production and postproduction process. Chaya Sarah is a Hasidic woman and self-taught filmmaker, producer, and songwriter. In fact, the cast and crew are self-trained except for lead actress Mimi Friedman, who has a degree in filmmaking, and Weingarten herself, who attended the New York Film Academy and the School of Visual Arts in New York. The all-woman crew is a first for Weingarten, as she usually works with professional production companies comprised mostly of men. That day, we were shooting at her home, debating the central message of the film, which addresses the taboos and stigma associated with mental illness in the context of *shiddukhim* (matchmaking). The camera operator expressed her strong skepticism about the scene and more broadly about the script, opining that the women were misguided to think that open discussion of mental health is truly possible in the community, but Weingarten asserted that candid discussion would diminish the associated stigma. The film's dialogue in some places clearly condemns the way the community deals with mental health issues. Evidently, Weingarten wanted to address such issues head on and encourage people to seek help.

Film serves as an appropriate medium for testing *frum* taboos. Since its origins in the early twentieth century, cinema has been considered quintessentially modern by the ultra-Orthodox community for its representation of Western culture, importation of foreign values to Orthodoxy, and cultivation of celebrities.[34] For some ultra-Orthodox individuals, DVDs of films and musicals transgress religious norms regarding the representation of female faces and bodies. Despite prohibitions against it, the feminine film industry has become an established genre within ultra-Orthodox cinema, a global (though contested) product that celebrates the creativity of ultra-Orthodox women, with its directors often granted the status of auteurs. DVD covers for these films almost always display only the name of the filmmaker; no actors or other individuals are billed (see figures 4.6 and 4.7). The rise of this market is related to the digital turn that democratized film production, allowing marginal communities to create and sell their own content. Rabbinical disregard, which could be interpreted as approval, might be explained by the economic opportunities of these productions, their development within the community (rather than by the mainstream film industry), and, most importantly, the increased need for female entertainment.

In the middle of the shoot back in Borough Park, Weingarten received a text from popular YouTube celebrity Peter Santenello, who was creating a series on Hasidic Judaism in New York. He needed the face and voice of a Hasidic woman who would agree to be interviewed for a video in this series. He received Weingarten's contact information from Shloime Zionce, a Hasidic YouTuber who writes for an important Orthodox Jewish magazine. She hesitated to accept his invitation, concerned about "being instrumentalized by secular media to serve the discourse that portrayed Hasidim as oppressive toward women."[35] Yet the recent increase in these "negative portrayals" also encouraged her to

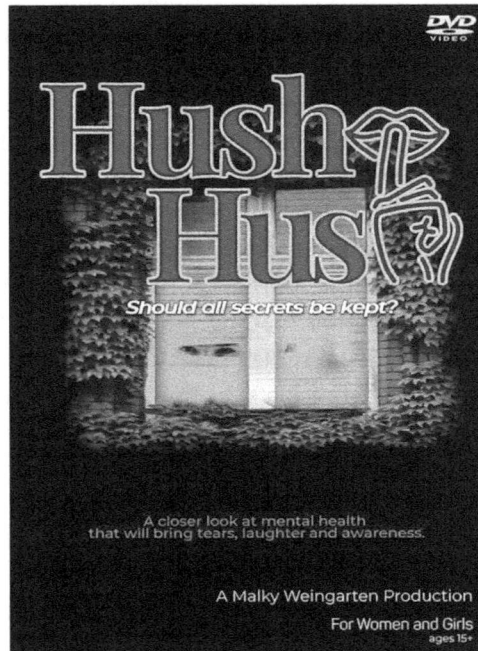

Figure 4.6 and 4.7: DVD cover of *Mali* and *Hush Hush*, films by Malky Weingarten (credit Malky Weingarten).

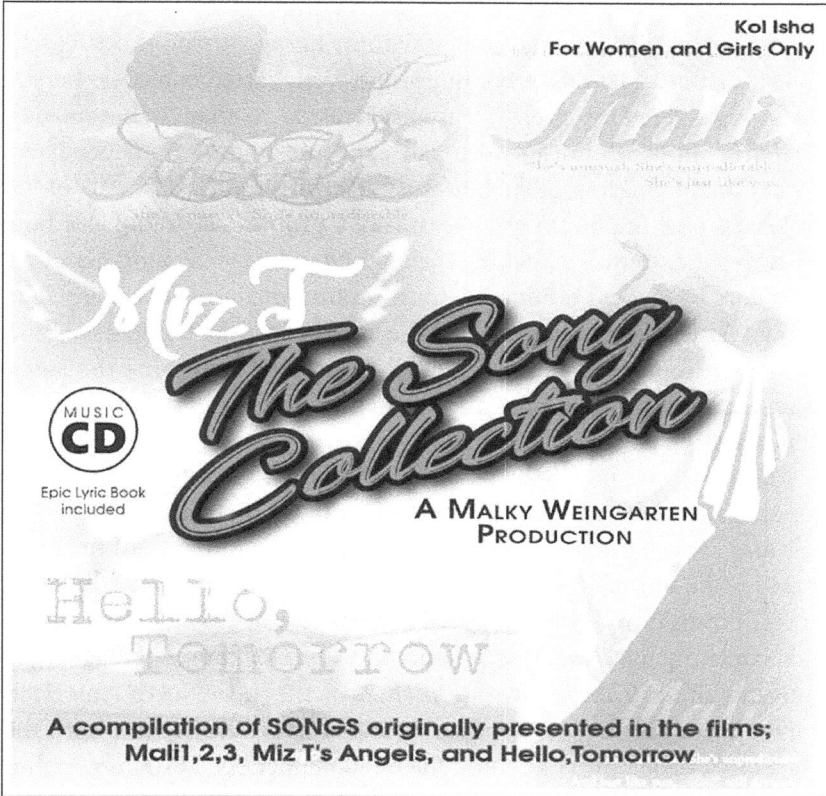

Figure 4.8: Album cover of the songs produced for Malky Weingarten's films (credit Malky Weingarten).

take part and to convey a "more positive" narrative to secular audiences. Despite her hesitation, she felt honored by this public recognition of her role both within and outside her community. On my departure, she informed me that she had accepted the invitation. The video was released on YouTube in mid-December 2020, and in less than five months, it had received more than 780,000 views, making it one of the most-viewed videos on Santenello's channel.[36]

Weingarten can take such risks as a filmmaker and public spokesperson certainly because of her position as a celebrity. With a solid community of fans and a marked ease interacting with people from different backgrounds, she is one of the rare *frum* female artists to engage publicly with secular audiences and individuals. Having gone from private local performances to transnational stardom, known throughout North America and to a lesser degree in Europe, Weingarten considers herself (and is considered by others) an atypical Hasidic woman. In her movies, she defies her community's norms by exposing stigmas on neurodiversity and mental illness.[37] She famously treasures the Hasidic way of life while also pushing boundaries within it, a prominent example of how this new generation is remaking the *kol isha* industry. Among her other endeavors to discuss taboos and push boundaries, in November 2022 Malky Weingarten was featured by the famous Hasidic homemaker and creative entrepreneur Raizy Fried, who has over forty-nine thousand followers on her Instagram platform, in a video in which she discussed preparing teenage girls for puberty.[38]

Weingarten is among the first women to turn the arts into a professional career, creating *frum* female cinema to entertain women and girls and convey moral messages. She entered the industry in the mid-aughts while in her early thirties, after more than a decade performing for her community as a comedian and dancer at private local events and producing live events for schools and summer camps. She emerged alongside other *frum* female filmmakers as this new North American market grew, echoing earlier developments in Israel that saw both the first *frum* female filmmakers and the establishment of a program in film production for ultra-Orthodox women at the Ma'aleh School of Film and Television.[39] *Frum* female cinema serves as a useful tool for conveying moral messages, entertaining women and girls while reinforcing *Emuna* (faith),[40] and supporting women in the arts financially. As this industry took shape, Weingarten saw an opportunity to further her career by providing not just service to her community—in the form of her live performances—but also products for consumption (her films) that could reach a broader, transnational audience.

Although she would eventually branch much further out, Weingarten initially followed the path taken by other *frum* female filmmakers with backgrounds in education and the performing arts. She began by filming her live performances and selling them on DVD, then considered filming on location instead of on stage, which led to her first movie, *Passing Inspection*, in 2009. Weingarten cowrote and codirected this film with her sister, Toby Tessler, and hired a professional crew for production and postproduction. While working on this film, she also wrote the script for her first independent movie, *Mali*, about a neuro-diverse girl. The script was based significantly on Weingarten's own life with her son, who had been diagnosed with Asperger's syndrome and who struggled for acceptance in society and his community. The film, made in 2013 and released on DVD in 2015, achieved tremendous success within the community. Weingarten subsequently adapted the concept for a series of the same name following the girl as she transitions from girlhood to motherhood.

The funding and promotion of these films for such a niche market requires community support and personal investment. Like others engaged in community film production, Weingarten prioritizes keeping film budgets low since they are community funded.[41] Working in the independent film industry, she avoids government guidelines and restrictions but needs family, friends, and the broader community to help sustain her productions. She expertly navigates the various taboos associated with both *frum* female cinema generally and the sensitive issues she addresses, finding appropriate partners that allow her to minimize affronts to the community, such as organizations that work with disability, autism, and mental health. The logos and promotional videos of these organizations appear in her films, lending them legitimacy. For example, Project Menucha, which supports children with disabilities, sponsored her first three films, while *Hush Hush* ends with a promotional video for an association that aids Jewish women with mental illness.[42]

Typically, the best exposure for filmmakers such as Weingarten comes from the annual *Khol Hamoed* screenings, which occur over the week leading up to Jewish holidays, during the intermediate days of Passover and Sukkot. These emerged first in the 1990s with screenings of live performances on VHS, then in the following decade shifted to Israeli and US *frum* female cinema. Weingarten works with a distributor connected to local Orthodox agents who organize the events, renting spaces for several nights and charging a fee for admittance. These screenings, which almost always reach full capacity, have essentially become a tradition in ultra-Orthodox female circles, and they provide filmmakers with the largest portion of their income as well as the opportunity to disseminate their films transnationally.

On October 16, 2019, I attended one such screening in Borough Park for the movie *Hello, Tomorrow*. The film's coordinated launch took place in major cities across North America and Europe, with ultra-Orthodox communities in the United States, Canada, England, and Belgium gathering for four nights in a row for the event, which sometimes even began in the afternoon. Upon arriving, I found an audience of hundreds of women and girls enthusiastically applauding Weingarten as she took the microphone to introduce the film. According to many of her fans, her popularity stems from her willingness to engage with difficult topics and the simple and direct way she communicates her films' messages.[43] She acts in her own films and includes a personal message in which she explains each one's raison d'être. Unlike other *frum* female filmmakers, she builds à more personal relationship with the women and girls who watch her films; at screenings she is unable to attend in person, she produces a tailored video message that runs before the film, also mentioning the legal and *halakhic* implications of film copyright. Weingarten is a strong advocate of intellectual and artistic property within the community, familiarizing younger generations with the concepts of authorship and creative rights for artists. For her, there is no contradiction between religious commitment, a profit motive, and the celebration of individual creativity.

Before the screening of *Hello, Tomorrow*, Weingarten introduced its topic—the Holocaust—and explained how *Emuna* helped survivors endure such tragic events. The film takes place in the past, but she extends her discussion of *Emuna* to the present, reminding her audience about the power of having God in their lives when confronting difficulties. At the end of the screening, a very elegant woman with a short wig approached Weingarten to congratulate her and express how pleased she was with the filmmaker's endeavors, on account of the great need for kosher entertainment for women and girls. A few months earlier, this same woman had invited Weingarten to the office of her school and explained that according to the standards of her community, the girls she advised cannot participate directly in these productions. However, those same girls were present that night at the screening. Some no doubt simply enjoyed the film while understanding that they, as ultra-Orthodox girls, are expected to do no more than watch, but others may dream of

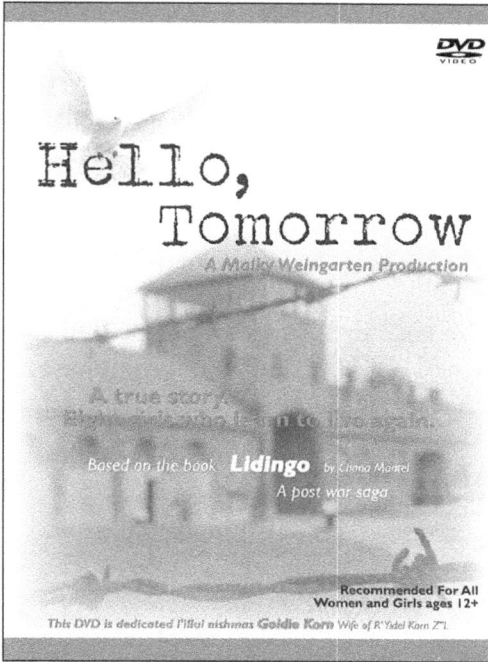

Figure 4.9: Cover of the film *Hello, Tomorrow* (credit Malky Weingarten).

taking part in the industry. Weingarten paves the way for the latter to be accepted and even celebrated by the others.

A film sometimes has two or three screenings before its DVD release. Some filmmakers, such as the famous Israeli Dina Perlstein, do not release their movies for sale after the screening period, for economic reasons or *tsnius* concerns. Weingarten's films typically appear on DVD a year and a half after their first screenings. During the pandemic, Weingarten premiered her movie *Hush Hush* online via a streaming platform since a great majority of her fandom now followed her on social media and online. She went on to launch her movie online in 2022 as the cost-benefit ratio of premiering online was more advantageous, even if she lost part of her more conservative audience that does not have Internet connection at home. Because her films have a strong musical component, she also releases their soundtracks, recorded in Rochel Leah's studio. Nigun Music, an important distributor of Jewish creative media, handles distribution for all her products. The DVDs are available online and at shops specializing in music and films, as well as at Jewish supermarkets across North America and Europe, demonstrating her work's transnational appeal and popularity.

Local, national, and international Orthodox newspapers advertise Weingarten's film screenings and DVD releases, while women and girls from places such as Montreal and New York mention her as an example of success. She also has a daily presence on social media and appears in secular media such as BRIC TV, a nonprofit community TV channel and digital network that in 2018 aired a piece on her by documentary filmmaker Rebecca Israel titled "Malky Makes Movies." In 2020, the documentary was nominated for a New York Emmy in the category Religion, Program Feature/Segment.[44]

Weingarten uses social media to reinforce the relationship she has fostered at screenings and on her DVDs between filmmaker and audience. She is one of the rare Hasidic filmmakers with an online presence, with more than ten thousand followers on her public Instagram account and thousands of views on YouTube. Her posts often document appearances at events such as community gatherings that promote her films. One such event took place on March 19, 2019, in a supermarket in Lakewood, where Raizy Fried organized an exclusive event to promote Malky's movie *Mali*. As seen in the reel of photos and videos from the event on Weingarten's Instagram, the venue was absolutely packed with women and girls of all ages excitedly asking her questions and sharing their praise for the film.

Malky Weingarten occupies a distinct position within the *kol isha* industry as a woman who has brought celebrity culture to ultra-Orthodox female cinema. She has found success by cultivating her persona and brand, engaging with an interested public, and shrewdly utilizing the media.[45] With her eccentric personality and fashionable way of being *frum*, novel films addressing difficult topics and implicitly critiquing her community, and social media presence, Weingarten exemplifies what the political scientist Rachel E. Stern has defined as the indigenization of celebrity culture in Orthodoxy. She is not the only famous *frum* filmmaker, but she is the only one addressing taboo subjects in her oeuvre

Figure 4.10: Malky Weingarten on March 10, 2019, in Lakewood supermarket, Instagram account, March 10, 2019 (credit Malky Weingarten).

and reaching out online (even outside the community) as an influencer. In contrast to Neuhaus, who adapts celebrity culture to Orthodoxy while concealing her image because of *tsnius*, Weingarten transforms this culture into an indigenous Orthodox experience where the exposure of her face and voice beyond her community is accepted. Engaged with secular audiences while respecting ultra-Orthodox norms by limiting access to her films and other content, she effects an Orthodoxification of celebrity culture, allowing her to advocate for the transformation of those norms and of internal and external perceptions of Orthodoxy. Within the community, her films demonstrate that women can succeed as artists and engage with secular audiences. Outside the community, her transnational celebrity status challenges the image of the deprived, secluded, and unhappy Hasidic woman often presented in mainstream secular media.[46] As a famous woman with a strong public commitment to her faith, community, and Hasidic way of life, she broadcasts a progressive image of ultra-Orthodoxy detached from the religious establishment.

Cinema is no longer a new medium for ultra-Orthodox women. With several filmmakers now in competition, audiences expect an increasing degree of professionalism on screen. Women are transitioning from hobbyists to professionals in the cinematic arts. Mimi Friedman, for example, who started her career as a teenage actor in the *kol isha* industry, wants to help transform *frum* female cinema into a "professional stage" where new careers can emerge.[47] While many women in the original generation of *frum* female filmmakers gained experience by observing professional teams, collaborating with *baalei tshuva* women from the mainstream film industry, or taking sporadic lessons, the next generation seeks a "professional industry" where both the narrative and the aesthetic of the movie represent the *frum* female world with all of its intricacies.

Tsnius, the Global Market, and the Orthodoxification of Celebrity Culture

Artistic performances by ultra-Orthodox women are usually characterized as private, live, collective, unrecorded, unmarketable, and outside the conventional entertainment industry. *Tsnius* and *kol isha* tell women to produce content collectively for only female audiences, while the global culture of celebrity prompts them to be visible to the most people possible, to be elegant, and to be glamorous, with a high value placed on physical appearance.[48] Ultra-Orthodox institutions remind women of their primary role as spiritual wives and mothers, connected to *Hashem* (God). Still, celebrity culture encourages professional careers, marketable productions, individual accomplishment, and liberal and secular values. The journeys of Devorah Schwartz, Bracha Jaffe, Chayala Neuhaus, Malky Weingarten, and other *frum* female celebrities in the arts establish a new reality: the integration of women's music, film, and creativity into the kosher entertainment industry, where fame and professionalism—previously associated only with male performers and considered detrimental to *tsnius*—now constitute important elements of productions for and by women that encourage us to reconsider the nature of religious publicity and publicity itself.

For the thousands of women and girls worldwide consuming these artists' products, they are celebrities, influencing ideas about body image, career aspirations, motherhood, and even politics among ultra-Orthodox women.[49] The term "celebrity" accurately characterizes the new economic, social, and cultural potential that fame brings to these artists who advertise religion in a modest public space. Although *rebbetzins* have been and still are celebrated in the ultra-Orthodox sphere, the *kol isha* industry has produced a version of female celebrity that transcends the figure of the mother, wife, or spiritual leader, as well as the format in which she can exist—with her voice, name, and face on display in a modest fashion. The *frum* female celebrity is reinventing ultra-Orthodox women's roles by integrating the principles and conventions of religious communities with capitalist logics.[50] This process echoes what scholars have observed globally with other religious groups, most notably conservative Christians.[51]

The arts produced by *frum* female celebrities, which many see as unconventional and subversive, circulate around the globe through both online and traditional media. As a result, the informal market that is the traditional format of the *frum* female art world, as we saw earlier, has been transformed—from emphasis on the collective to recognition of individual artists, from private performance to public YouTube videos and streaming. Thus, a section of ultra-Orthodox women's artistic space has been revamped into a global commodified industry. Ultra-Orthodox women and girls worldwide consume *kol isha* media by attending *Khol Hamoed* screenings, watching live performances at *tsedakah* events or summer camps, ordering CDs and digital music files online, or even just surfing the web. This feminine artistic space has a presence on YouTube, Instagram, and even TikTok, as well as in local and international Jewish magazines, where stars, films, performances, and educational programs are advertised. This new industry does not contradict its origins in the education system and the traditional collective space of women's performance. Rather, it transforms these institutions, translating external values and processes into an ultra-Orthodox context.[52]

The famous women presented in this chapter are—for the most part—middle-class wives and mothers whose families support their professionalization, mirroring the strategies used by pop stars. On the other hand, as Jewish press coverage indicates, the community accepts, consumes, and even celebrates *frum* female artists because they conform to the traditional Orthodox image of women, committed to serving the community and God with their music. While the performances by *frum* female artists on stage, screen, and the Internet do, in some ways, contradict the ultra-Orthodox norms of *tsnius* and *kol isha*, both women artists and religious authorities acknowledge the growing need for professional training and production in the arts (including technical aspects like sound engineering, mixing, and studio production), allowing artists to flourish within the boundaries of "the system."

Translating celebrity culture into ultra-Orthodoxy highlights two elements of modern society molded into ultra-Orthodox circles: the celebration of the individual and the growth of the ultra-Orthodox middle class.[53] Echoing Nomi Stolzenberg and David Myers in their analysis of Kiryas Joel as a North American phenomenon, I argue that the *kol isha* industry confirms that ultra-Orthodoxy in North America is a product of its society, and I would add, of global capitalist society, as demonstrated by the translocal network of followers and artists located across the globe and participating in this new economy. This translation of culture occurs within the constraints of ultra-Orthodoxy embraced by the artists, demonstrating what I call an Orthodoxification of celebrity culture: a dynamic process of adaptation, indigenization, and integration.[54] Here, I borrow the terminology of Rachel E. Stern, who sees the translation of human rights within the female inheritance movement in Hong Kong on a continuum ranging from adaptation to adoption.[55] Adaptation means the most minimal borrowing; adoption is full reproduction, and indigenization is a process in between. Contrary to Stern, in the ultra-Orthodox context, I argue that there is not a total adoption; instead, I designate the process closest to adoption as integration. These artists maintain their status as *frum* female artists because they push the boundaries of the system, but they never surpass those boundaries, as would be the case in adoption. For instance, without strict restrictions concerning their audience when it comes to performance, they would not be part of the *kol isha* industry (which is exclusively for women). The careers of the women described in this chapter fall into various places along this continuum, illustrating the many facets of this Orthodoxification. Devorah Schwartz and Bracha Jaffe represent integration, endorsing the mechanisms of celebrity culture (without fully adopting it) by performing publicly online and reaching a transnational audience,[56] while still respecting the norms of *kol isha* regarding the warnings about the online performance, and by also deciding who is permitted to see and hear their live performances. Adaptation finds its avatar in Chayala Neuhaus, who aggressively promotes her brand without exposing her face and by using men's voices. Finally, Malky Weingarten, who represents innovation at the margins of Orthodoxy, embodies the indigenization of celebrity culture, introducing new practices such as exploring sensitive topics and promoting herself outside Orthodox circles.

The success of women in this industry still depends on the encouragement, acceptance, and even active participation of their husbands and families. The industry itself remains dominated by patriarchy and unequal remuneration, echoing the gender pay gap that persists throughout North American society and beyond. Despite complementarian claims of the equal spiritual worth of men's and women's artistic activities, this supposed equality does not manifest financially. Some argue that this is the case because these women do not perform for men and thus have a smaller audience, but others refute this point on the basis of equal pay for equal work. None of these *frum* female artists earn as much as their male counterparts, and many actively seek to redress this inequity.

Unity, Common Affinity, and Authority

The *kol isha* industry has engendered new processes of community building among women and girls. Inspired by Kay Kaufman Shelemay's tripartite framework on building community based on processes of descent, dissent, and affinity, I suggest that the increased role of technology in the ultra-Orthodox musical scene has given rise to a community based on common (economic and technical) necessity and affinity. In summer camps and schools, women and girls mobilize music to reinforce sisterhood based on common affiliation, logics of geographical space, and local community belonging—a process of descent and dissent.[57] *Frum* female artists form a community based on a shared artistic professionalism and will to transform conservative norms of *tsnius* and *kol isha*. The community built by the collective artistic experience hinges not on belonging to a specific community within Orthodoxy but on a common desire to succeed in the arts and to serve as new role models for girls and women as artists. Contrary to experiences in schools or summer camps, alliances among *frum* female artists form due to professional expertise and the common necessity to connect with artists with whom they have affinity. Their performances are no longer localized to a community based on common descent; rather, artistic communities are today shaped by professional, economic, and creative interests that transcend ethnic and geographical boundaries. The arts—once a purely collective experience anchored in religiosity, education, and entertainment—now provide *parnasse,* career opportunities, and for some, fame. The *kol isha* industry fosters a new model of womanhood and girlhood in which *tsnius* and fame coexist. Through this industry, women and girls redefine ultra-Orthodoxy so as to embrace their new practices and countenance their new communities, remodeling what is usually described as religious authority. Their negotiations of modesty and fame lead to new forms of agency and positions of authority in the arts. Many ultra-Orthodox organizations partner with them on social media to engage a broader swath of potential supporters—specifically, middle-class women.

The artists owe much of their success to their respect for local cultural codes. They can translate celebrity culture into Orthodoxy because they hold tight to certain ultra-Orthodox norms (even while challenging or ignoring others). They all are dressed modestly, covering their hair according to the norms of their community; they are almost all married with kids in religious schools; and they all disseminate messages to reinforce the cohesiveness of being women and *frum.* Neuhaus kept her face and voice out of the picture; Weingarten limited her audience to women and does not stream her movies on YouTube, and Schwartz promoted religious organizations while employing a *kol isha* label. While they use different strategies, reflecting their singular ways of performing womanhood, these artists all carefully balance the sacred and the taboo in their work, challenging their relationship with what they view as a conservative interpretation of *tsnius* and *kol isha,* simultaneously acknowledging under a different model its importance publicly with the label "for women and girls only."

Media entrepreneurs want celebrities involved with their projects because their involvement will help attract audiences.[58] While historically the celebrity's public profile was controlled by a third party such as a public relations firm, the emergence of social media has drastically transformed this dynamic, allowing *frum* female artists to shape their own public image according to their individualized expressions of *tsnius*. This involves acknowledging the commodified status of the *frum* female artist as well as the potential personal costs of fame. Moreover, as celebrity-commodities, these artists aspire to benefit the entire community, as demonstrated by Devorah Schwartz and Bracha Jaffe. This process requires meticulous care in choosing forms of Orthodoxification of celebrity culture that increase the value of the commodity within the industry without sacrificing those aspects of celebrity.

The future of the *frum* female celebrity is difficult to predict as she emerges from a flux of public expectations, media representations, and self-fashioning. That unpredictability makes celebrity culture a suspenseful, interactive, and serial drama.[59] One thing, however, is certain. The *frum* female celebrity now coexists and engages in constant dialogue with the collective, private artistic space. Even though the private performer may contest the raison d'être of the modest public with new advertisement strategies, she still consumes its content. The idea of art for its own sake, or for the artist's glory, has found a place in new cultural norms alongside more traditional ones. With their fame and social media presence (where no religious leaders censor their words and actions), *frum* female artists now transcend their artistic role, becoming subversive actors advocating for women's empowerment and for changes within Orthodoxy.

5

The Influencer

Advocating for Changes, Forging the Cyberfrumenist Counterpublic

> What kind of message are we sending our daughters and sons when they look through a magazine and there are no female faces to be seen? We all know that a picture says a 1,000 words. Just the name of a woman is not enough.
> —Adina Miles-Sash, #flatbushgirl, Instagram post, May 2017

On February 9, 2021, Dalia Oziel, a *frum* female singer with over fifty thousand followers on Instagram,[1] posted a video exposing the story of Chava—a "chained wife," known as an *aguna*, who has been waiting ten years for a divorce. According to Jewish law, only men can grant a divorce. Thus, marriage is not dissolved until a bill of divorce, a *get*, is granted from the husband to his wife. When the husband does not want to grant a divorce, or cannot because, for example, he disappeared during a war, the wife becomes *aguna*. Pressure from religious authority or from powerful individuals who have the potential to socially marginalize the man who does not want to give the *get* has traditionally proven to be a significant strategy. In June 2018, Chava had created an Instagram page to bring attention to her plight—using the handle @free_chava—but it only ever acquired a few followers. In 2021, she got the idea of reaching out to Dalia, who is well respected in Orthodox women's circles and has a high number of followers on social media, to raise awareness of her case. Since ultra-Orthodox Jews, and more specifically women,[2] had increased their presence on social media since the pandemic began in 2020, she hoped that an online campaign would have a significant impact.

Dalia began by posting virtual flyers with information about Chava's husband, Naftali Eyal Sharabani, allowing her followers to contact him in different ways to pressure him to give the *get*. By sharing his contact information and whereabouts, she was also putting pressure on other members of his community to encourage him to cooperate with Chava. Finally, she organized a fundraiser through the global collaborative platform raising funds for all Orthodox Jewish–related causes, the Chesed Fund—"*chesed*" referring to the idea of benevolence, compassion, and love between people and toward God. Dalia raised more than $87,623 for Chava,[3] and assembled a team of women advisers to assist her in the process of attempting to obtain a *get*.

As the movement grew, Dalia escalated her social media activism against Naftali. On February 25, she organized a campaign called "Pink Out Thursday" with the hashtag #freechava. She posted ten photos concerning Chava's story and the issue of *get* refusal, which she framed as abuse. Dozens of ultra-Orthodox female artists and professionals in various domains, who have social media presences (including Hasidim and Litvish) across North America, Israel, and the UK, then posted and reposted the content using the hashtag. The page @free_chava grew to over a thousand followers, many of whom participated in the "pink out" by posting photos of themselves wearing pink. Dalia had thus succeeded on two fronts. She had mobilized people to support Chava's cause across borders, and had motivated other ultra-Orthodox artists, who are usually very quiet about such political and controversial issues, to take part in a campaign exposing matters of women's abuse.

In the following days, Naftali seemed cooperative and entered discussions about giving a *get*, but he soon abandoned these efforts and went into hiding. This prompted the movement to shift to a broader scale, exposing more supporters of women obtaining a *get* in the Orthodox community. Dalia's followers used social media to pressure these men by commenting on their posts and speaking out against them. At the same time, for International Women's Day on March 8, 2021, male Orthodox influencers such as Mendy Pellin and Berel Solomon began using their social media platforms to engage more men in the conversation about *agunot* and *get* refusal. Mendy Pellin initiated a campaign called #blueoutmonday, in which several men recorded themselves saying the words, "Dude, let her go, free Chava." While some *frum* women frame their support for this campaign as feminist, Dalia Oziel rejects the term "feminism" while remaining in conversation with feminist action. She emphasizes "girl power" and "unity," reminding her followers that "we

Figure 5.1: Poster used for the social media campaign #freechava.

won't stop," "we won't be silenced," and "we are stronger together." On International Women's Day, Dalia posted a video thanking men for their support and clarifying to her audience that this was not a women's issue but an issue that concerned every Jew, one for the entirety of *Klal Yisrael* (the Jewish people).

The movement sparked by Dalia's actions on social media shifted into real-world activism when crowds began to gather outside the homes of *get* refusers across the United States. Multiple *agunot* were freed after their ex-husbands yielded to pressure from social media, protesters, and rabbis during this social media campaign. Although Chava had not yet received a *get* as of the end of 2022, the movement gained momentum and encouraged members of the Jewish community to take action against *get* refusers. Dalia is still raising awareness and sharing hashtags. Women who are active on social media—as well as men who present themselves as women's cause advocates—continue to join the movement. On Monday, March 16, 2021, the famous Hasidic comedian

Leah Forster, who was alienated from Orthodoxy and has almost eighty thousand followers on Instagram, posted a cover of the song "Rehab" by Amy Winehouse. However, she inserted lyrics that evoked Chava's story and those of other *agunot*, changing the refrain and exaggerating the English accent of her Hasidic character Tichel Tuesday by transforming "husband" into "m'usband": "She's trying to get a *get* from M'usband, but he says no, no, no." The song reached forty thousand views within two days.[4] Adina Miles-Sash, a well-known social media activist and writer with over sixty thousand followers on Instagram, took the cause seriously and participated in in-person activism. In the fall of 2022, she even appeared in the second series of the Netflix TV reality show *My Unorthodox Life*, alongside two other women activists, Amber Adler and Hadassah, to discuss the issue of *agunot*.

Ultra-Orthodox women artists such as Dalia Oziel represent an emerging online community of *frum* female artists and celebrities who mobilize social media to advocate for women's empowerment and structural changes within Orthodoxy. Through this process, they create a counterpublic space to the public ultra-Orthodox media—a space where they are not overseen by religious authority. As we saw earlier, *frum* female celebrities use social media to promote their work; in this chapter, we will see how they also use it to promote cultural, social, and political ideas that contradict ultra-Orthodox norms concerning *tsnius, kol isha*, and women's roles. By maintaining a consistent online presence through regularly engaging in contentious subjects, *frum* female artists and celebrities normalize social media use within certain ultra-Orthodox circles while simultaneously rebelling against traditional practices, influencing their audiences on these issues. Their online performances address various subjects (e.g., feminism, racism, beauty, Orthodoxy) in an attempt to entertain, educate, influence, and debate with their followers and the emerging community of *frum* female artists. They also portray a common cultural heritage, represent new and diverse modes of professional development—both online and offline—and promote products and services of other businesses. In other words, they are becoming influencers, are defining and presenting themselves as such. Their audience goes beyond their local ultra-Orthodox community, as they also attract the attention of non-Orthodox and even non-Jewish audiences. However, by discussing controversial topics on social media, often navigating between public and private accounts, these women routinely disobey religious leadership, contradicting norms established by the Jewish ultra-Orthodox press vis-à-vis exhibiting women's faces and voices, as well as discussing controversial topics.[5] While some religious leaders accept the use of technology and the Internet for work and economic purposes, as we have seen with the celebrity, the majority have declared it a clear danger and developed various strategies to block access to certain websites, applications, and contents. These leaders argue that the Internet is especially dangerous for women, and they constantly warn younger generations of its perils.[6]

When religious leaders engage in a war to control their communities' access to the Internet, they are experiencing a crisis of religious authority, as anthropologist Ayala Fader has outlined. Reflecting this crisis of authority, Instagram, which started to become especially popular in 2013 (and exponentially so since 2016), has developed into a hub where *frum* female artists and celebrities engage in subversive discourse while promoting their artistic endeavors in writing, music, dance, and film. Instagram now serves as a prominent, albeit sometimes secretive, forum for women to observe *frum* female artists and celebrities without having to expose their names and faces in their profiles. In a sense, it is a social media platform perfectly tailored to their privacy needs. The secret consumption of Instagram, and of social media more broadly, reveals certain paradoxes embedded in religious practices. In this context, social media use in the most conservative circles is something that women tend to know about but do not discuss. The *frum* artists, on the other hand, use social media openly. Because they present themselves as professional, their social media presence has become normalized, as is the case for other *frum* female business owners. These women constitute a digital community engaging in personal and collective transformations online, with a strong desire to have an impact beyond the digital space, as exemplified by Dalia Oziel's digital activism. With their thousands of followers, they use media platforms to do more than promote their own work, seeking also to influence their audience to engage in behavior and media consumption oriented toward what they often present as women's empowerment deriving from complementarianism, family life, and religious leadership in society. The women described in this chapter relate to the Haredi feminist movement in Israel, described by gender studies scholar Tanya Zion-Waldoks, which endorses the rei-magination of individual lives and communal structures. They under-stand their personal lives as political; they form a collective criticism of their communities that is directed toward radical change.[7] Some of them oppose liberal feminism, criticizing its tendencies to universal-ize women's experience, echoing the feminist discourse of decentering the "West" that is defended by postcolonial and decolonial feminist scholars.[8]

The account of Dalia Oziel's activity on social media presented above helps to shed light on the peculiar phenomenon of ultra-Orthodox women mobilizing social media, specifically Instagram, as a tool for empowerment and social change. It is useful to examine this phenom-enon by looking at two central issues: the performance of *tsnius* through images and voices online, and the function of social media as a trans-formative space where women create new discourses and practices about agency within Orthodoxy. Social media act as a counterpublic transformative space for *frum* female artists and influencers,[9] one in which they challenge religious norms while reinforcing Orthodoxy as a practice that should transcend the norms established by some religious authority. The term "counterpublic" refers to a group's attempt to cre-ate a discursive and subversive arena as an alternative to the dominant public sphere, which in this case is embodied by ultra-Orthodox public media and press, as well as the discourse of religious authority and lead-ership on the use of social media and the Internet. This concurrent act of challenging and reinforcing Orthodoxy online involves new expres-sions and understandings of Orthodox women's empowerment that is in dialogue with cyberfeminism. This movement advocates for women to appropriate and take control of Internet technologies to empower themselves in their respective societies.[10] Because their cyberfeminist practices are defined by a claim to transform Orthodoxy and the *frum-keit*, I have adopted the term "cyber*frum*enist" to characterize it. The online performances of these artists travel across borders, strengthening and accelerating the sense of belonging to a global Orthodox commu-nity defined in terms of sisterhood, while mediatizing and fashionizing new standards of beauty, femininity, and religiosity. Whether these stan-dards have common expressions or are as diverse as the Internet itself depends on how these women negotiate their roles as creative artists and entrepreneurs, as well as their relationship with religious authorities: rabbis, school directors, and directors of seminaries, as well as anyone who might complain or report to religious authorities their supposedly deviant actions in order to stigmatize them.

An Internet of Paradoxes

As we have seen, although ultra-Orthodox Jewish leaders broadly denounce and forbid access to the Internet—which they consider to be a *yeytser hora* (evil inclination)—and more specifically social media, they have also come to realize its economic potential and its necessity for business.[11] Like other conservative religious groups,[12] ultra-Orthodox Jewish leadership—except Lubavitch, which has embraced the Internet in accordance with its mission of outreach toward secular Jews—has a contradictory relationship with the Internet. Social media blur the lines between representation, participation, and reception of information and knowledge beyond borders. It allows religious groups to constantly redefine themselves and build decentralized communities around the world.[13] While such technology can serve as a new platform for proselytizing, it can also function as a pathway for supposedly problematic moral or secular content to invade the home.

The tensions resulting from the possibilities and dangers of the Internet have led to a field of paradoxes between public norms and practice. To counter these paradoxes, religious leaders have made a strong distinction between the Internet, its content, and its materialization (the electronic devices through which one accesses it) and have implemented new strategies to control it. Among material technologies, for example, the smartphone, in particular, became a dangerous object—typically considered *assur* (forbidden)—because it could easily connect one to the Internet while resting in a pocket, invisible to others. Computers and tablets, on the other hand, are not as portable or discreet and are therefore safer objects. Thus, while the Internet is now an integral part of the professional lives of most ultra-Orthodox Jews, material access to it remains extremely regulated.

Content must be filtered and koshered to prevent the consumption of material deemed *assur*, such as that relating to sexuality, drugs, violence, chatting, dating, and so forth. To that end, software emerged in the first decade of the twenty-first century aimed at blocking websites, applications, and emails that pertained to or addressed *assur* topics. Several anti-Internet organizations appeared among ultra-Orthodox communities across the globe. In North America, their activities reached an apex in 2012 with a large, male-only anti-Internet *asifa* (rally) at New York's Citi Field, where thousands of male religious leaders and followers gathered in the stadium to discuss the danger of non-kosher online content. The event, somewhat ironically, was broadcast live on the Internet to communities across the globe (and therefore was viewable by all genders).

The first Citi Field rally did not result in universal compliance among Hasidic men concerning Internet restrictions or online behavior, but it did lead to the development of new strategies to regulate the Internet and the access it provides to the wider, non-kosher world. Emerging from the rally, leaders focused on the education of future generations, especially women, who began participating in rallies where they were taught about their moral responsibility to protect their homes and children. In May 2018, I was present when the *rebbe* and the *rebbetzin* of Hasidic Belz visited the ultra-Orthodox community in Montreal during Lag Baomer, discussing—among other things—special programming for women in the evenings, including a gathering to address the topics of the Internet, social media, and smartphones. Several women expressed their satisfaction with the discussion, as it comforted them in their choice to escape smartphones and social media, or even merely access the Internet while at home. During my various discussions with members of the community, social media networks—notably Facebook—were presented to me as "heretic spaces," where one might encounter uncontrollable waves of secular ideas, words, sounds, and images. A particular concern was the potential for online interactions that might lead someone to become a doubter or even an OTD ("off the *derekh*," one who has left the community).

Some ultra-Orthodox women, however, are conflicted about Internet use. Many of them working in the film and music industries need to access the Internet: to send emails and video or audio files, to download files, and to collaborate with other artists and industry professionals. Their unease can be palpable, as it was with Yitty, a woman who was hesitant to disclose her Internet usage to me. Although she has a computer at home, Yitty consistently told me that she did not have access to the Internet. One day I asked her how she was able to download music files for the film she was shooting.

> YITTY: I connect my computer to the Internet via a cable.
> RODA: Oh, great, but from which modem?
> YITTY: From the building.
> RODA: Okay, but where exactly?
> YITTY: I have it in a specific room, just dedicated to it! So, this is not in the home.[14]

Only after my third attempt did she respond to my question. We both smiled, but Yitty was embarrassed, blushing furiously as she confessed to the room with Internet access; she felt it necessary to reiterate—and establish absolutely—that her home was Internet free. I told her that I appreciated her struggle: on the one hand, she needed to access the Internet from home to facilitate her business, while on the other hand, she wanted to adhere to the guidelines of her Hasidic community. When she began making movies, she initially only had access to the office of a family friend. She refused to buy a smartphone but needed a stable Internet connection at home, having recently opened a social media account under her company's name. The business's hours of operation were very limited, and it was difficult for her to manage her schedule. It became much more convenient to set up access at home, something she and her husband decided to keep hidden from their younger children.

Certain ultra-Orthodox religious leaders target women by citing the need to combat the threat of the outside world to protect their homes and to prevent their children from accessing the dangerous Internet, especially from using social media for personal purposes. But like Yitty, some women need to bypass these norms, and they have developed two main strategies to do so. They either avoid discussing the issue altogether and simply use the tactic, as Yitty did, of ignoring the restrictions while disengaging from discussions about this paradox, or they justify their use by evoking professional and economic reasons. This is the case for dozens of artists who use Instagram, ignoring the debate among religious authorities, as well as for the thousands of ultra-Orthodox women and girls who follow them—an audience that grew significantly after the start of the pandemic in 2020. In June 2022, years after the Citi Field rally, a similar gathering was organized by religious authorities. This time, the targets were women, revealing that the political actions implemented in the previous ten years by religious authorities had been unsuccessful. Although many conservative women do not consume social media, the authorities could not prevent increased participation in social media by some of these women. None of the women discussed in this chapter deleted their account; in fact, one of them even made explicit criticisms about the gathering, and most of them increased their online presence and follower count following the months of the rally.

Frum female artists connect through social media on a regular basis. Since registering children for school requires that parents disclose what access they have to the Internet from home or via smartphone, they often buy a second phone that they keep hidden from the school's authority, or they simply justify their social media use by declaring it necessary to their careers. Women endorse new types of professional attitudes and discourses. They promote careers in the arts and nontraditional concepts of beauty, with unusual colors, accessories, and modern design, as well as progressive views on marital relationships, with husbands in charge of domestic duties. They also act as influencers, promoting businesses that serve their women's communities. By doing so, they reinvent the practices of Orthodoxy, gender, and capitalism, contributing to the broader phenomenon that Kira Ganga Kieffer identifies as a new form of capitalism that is gendered feminine.[15] Thus, while the majority of religious authorities clearly and staunchly oppose the use of social media apart from professional purposes, the emergence of digitally active ultra-Orthodox women artists and influencers—most notably on Instagram—complicates the field of paradoxes arising from the discourse surrounding these technologies and the realities of their use.

Ultimately, these artists have established a mostly women-only online space, even when they have a public account, as they rarely engage with men. They usually disregard men's participation in case of a comment, reinforcing the idea of an exclusive feminine space. Even if they do not all use explicitly adversarial rhetoric, such as criticizing religious authority and norms to claim that their use of social media offers an alternative to the discourse produced by religious authorities, their online activities and appearances—in sound, text, and image—are fundamentally subversive. As anthropologist Ayala Fader has documented, some ultra-Orthodox Jews who harbor doubts about the religious system and authorities created a counterpublic by making blogs where they anonymously published their criticisms. She labeled this counterpublic a "heretical counterpublic space" because of the reception of these bloggers by religious authority. Similar to the way the "heretical counterpublic space" reproduces the exclusion of women from the ultra-Orthodox public sphere,[16] *frum* female influencers and their followers mobilize Instagram and other social media in a way that mirrors the gender segregation established in ultra-Orthodox communities. Nevertheless, unlike in the heretical space of the blogosphere, the exclusion of men from the social media of ultra-Orthodox female artists and influencers creates a transformative space for women in which they—even as they are sometimes viewed as heretics—aim to reinforce Orthodoxy, transforming it from within by creating a new market associated with women entrepreneurship in nontraditional spaces of the arts through their actions online. By connecting to the Internet at home through their computers, sometimes posting photos or videos with their children (though rarely with their husbands) and discussing subjects beyond those related to their professional duties, women resist religious leadership that has tasked them with preventing their children from accessing the Internet and using social media for personal reasons. Their resistance to religious authority, although not voiced in any explicit way, manifests in their online action.

These artists and influencers are not merely challenging religious norms but also, somewhat paradoxically, reinforcing religious observance by presenting themselves as performing for women and girls only, respecting and valorizing the "benefit" of *tsnius* and *kol isha*. They appear with hair covering, skirts or dresses covering their knees, and blouses up to the elbows and collarbone; advertise their profile and performance as "*kol isha*, for women and girls only," and sometimes have a private profile where they can control their followers. They are inventing a new Orthodox feminine. It may be for this reason that religious authorities have not inveighed heavily against these women, their followers, and their market. While defying conservative religious authorities about their views on *tsnius*, domestic life, and the publication of women's faces and voices, *frum* female artists online strengthen Orthodoxy by offering new opportunities for feminine religious expression, belonging, and marketing. The number of online events for Orthodox women and girls has increased since the late 2010s, growing exponentially in the early months of the coronavirus pandemic, when live performances as well as film screenings were canceled across the globe. According to the social media users I interviewed, there are diverse explanations for why this trend goes largely unopposed. Some assume religious authorities broadly felt that they had won the battle against the Internet by convincing younger generations not to use smartphones or social media. Because Chabad-Lubavitch accepts and embraces the Internet for the purposes of outreach, many ultra-Orthodox Jews feel that they are justified in using it for other reasons. Finally, certain women explained that Instagram and Twitter have essentially been considered marketing tools—a use that rabbis and *rebbes* have deemed acceptable.

Although many groups and individuals consider Instagram a publicizing tool, it was initially designed to create a more connected world through photography and to improve the "mediocre" quality of photos taken with mobile phones by popularizing filters.[17] By making visible and audible their faces, voices, and religiosity on Instagram, ultra-Orthodox Jewish women create a subversive online space where they can challenge religious norms and reinvent the concept of *tsnius*. Moreover, these women—who belong to the Hasidic communities of Bobov, Satmar, and Belz, or from conservative Litvish backgrounds opposed to the use of social media—increasingly join the Lubavitch women's force, who are active and present on social media and exist in their own press and modest public space. By doing so, they are creating a global and pluralist Orthodox community. In this way, *frum* female influencers act as transformative agents of ultra-Orthodoxy, navigating beyond the norms dictated by their own religious circles regarding the consumption and production of social media.

In the context of what many ultra-Orthodox Jews, and particularly Hasidim, label a crisis of leadership, social media allows individuals to become alternative voices of authority, creating innovative ways to engage in a participatory society. With the disappearance of the generation of *rebbes* who survived World War II and rebuilt the Hasidic world in North America, many conflicts erupted concerning the transfer of power and religious authority, resulting in the multiplication of Hasidic branches or an absence of centralized leadership, as is the case for example with Chabad-Lubavitch and Breslev.[18] Internet use is now prevalent even outside Lubavitch circles, so much so that one might consider it an integral part of ultra-Orthodox life despite admonitions against it. Instagram, in particular, has become an extension of the private ultra-Orthodox female artistic space. Here and elsewhere across social media, *tsnius* is fashioned, performed, empowered, standardized, and marketed for the consumption of other women and girls. Because rabbis must approve printed and digital content published in ultra-Orthodox circles and thus *frum* female artists cannot depict women's faces or bodies in the public Orthodox media, the visual expression of *tsnius* online became a central tool for *frum* female artists to promote their work.

Performing and Standardizing a New *Tsnius* Online

As we have seen, many *frum* female artists and entrepreneurs have received training in their respective fields from outside their communities. Their mentors are often strangers to the ultra-Orthodox world, and sometimes even to the Jewish world, and, unaware of the controversy around doing so, expose them to social media to promote their art to the growing online community of Orthodox women and girls. Instagram became the platform par excellence for these women because it allows them to highlight their creations' audio and visual dimensions. This social media advertising exposes the faces and voices of unique and fashionable Orthodox, Hasidic, or religious women—advocating new forms of *tsniusness* that embrace entrepreneurship, public exposure, and individual creativity.

Out of approximately thirty *frum* female professional artists and influencers I have identified as the most popular on Instagram,[19] a majority opened their accounts around 2016—a period when the platform rebranded itself,[20] created the Instagram story,[21] and increased its popularity—and justify their online presence as necessary for their careers. They are from Litvish and Hasidic backgrounds, navigating between public and private online forums while showcasing diverse performative expressions of *tsnius* involving dress, body language, and expression (makeup, hair covering, movements) and singing about topics normally considered forbidden.

There is a perceptible pattern to their initial appearances online. At first, they generally publish photographs of the products associated with or created by their art, such as instruments, cameras, food, DVDs, CDs, and published writings. After a few weeks or sometimes months, they post photographs of their faces or full-body portraits, progressively adding messages to their followers in the accompanying text or videos posted separately. Once reaching a certain number of followers, they often begin using the platform to advertise other *frum* female artists as well as Orthodox Jewish businesses that target female audiences, such as *sheytl* salons, fashion designers, makeup shops, restaurants, spiritual coaches, wellness centers for women, or grocers. The decision to make their profile public or private often depends on numerous factors, including their interpretation of *tsnius* and *kol isha*, the nature of their target audience, the advice they receive from both female and male religious authorities, and the potential impact on their families. Moreover, they sometimes switch their account settings from private to public, or they might post some photos and videos publicly but secure other content with a password or as unlisted videos on YouTube.[22] For instance, some women started with a public Instagram account but set it to private after receiving flirtatious messages from male followers. As one dancer told me, allowing only women and girls to follow her gives her more liberty to perform online. Others who began with a private account opened it to everyone once their followers grew to over five thousand.

As professionals, *frum* female artists are highly respected within their ultra-Orthodox communities, often serving as teachers of their respective specialties. On the other hand, their celebrity status makes them outliers. They occupy a peculiar position within their respective communities; their online activities contravene established norms set by the religious authority of rabbis and *rebbes*, and yet they are still celebrated, admired, and invited to participate in collective religious life by performing for their community. After all, they acknowledge, respect, and embrace Jewish Orthodoxy, and more specifically their own Litvish/Yeshivish or Hasidic traditions.

The online performance of *tsnius* unifies these artists of various religious affiliations, but I wondered whether these affiliations manifested in disparate ways or had common expressions. More stringent prescripts might be expected regarding the dress code for the Hasidic

Yiddish-speaking world—such as the Satmar, Bobov, Gur, Belz, and Skver. I anticipated a formal, more conservative, "old-world aesthetic," including dark fabrics and robust prints, very light makeup, tops covering the elbows and the collarbones, skirts or dresses three to four inches below the kneecaps, and short wigs with hats or *tikhels*.[23] Hasidic clothing practices involve a complex set of negotiations in which the interpretation of Jewish modesty produces an attractive and fashionable yet distinctive female Hasidic aesthetic.[24] While Hasidic women are in general extremely invested in the preservation of this refined elegance—typically referred to as the European style—the appearance of some of them on Instagram in longer wigs (without a hat), colorful and stylish clothing, and pinkish or reddish makeup significantly departed from these standards. Such an expression of *tsnius* might represent a threat to their communities because it calls attention to the female body in a way that is at odds with Hasidic observance; indeed, it is often viewed as symbolizing the sin and indecency of American secular culture.[25]

Dobby Baum is a London-born singer and composer who has lived in Borough Park in Brooklyn since marrying a Gur Hasid in 2016. With over ten thousand followers, Dobby has an active social media presence, notably on Instagram. She initially had two separate accounts on the platform—one personal, where she posted almost every day and which was private and restricted to women and girls only before it became public, and the other, which has been public since the beginning, devoted to the Brooklyn Girls' Choir, which she founded in 2017. Dobby posted for the first time on September 16, 2016, on her private account, sharing a poster of her August concert at the Palgai talent camp for girls, which took place just a few months after her move to Borough Park. Already known in London for her work in music and performing arts while still a teenager, she—as a young artist in her twenties—needed to make a name for herself in New York and more broadly in North America. Thanks to her older siblings in the music industry, notably her brother, the music producer Gershy Schwarcz (Edgware Studios), Dobby was familiar with technology. At first, she posted *affiches* for her concerts and videos of her private vocal training, studio recording sessions, and piano instrumentals. In May 2017, she posted a photo and video of herself in which she appears with a *sheytl* reaching to the shoulders while demonstrating vocal types. In June she

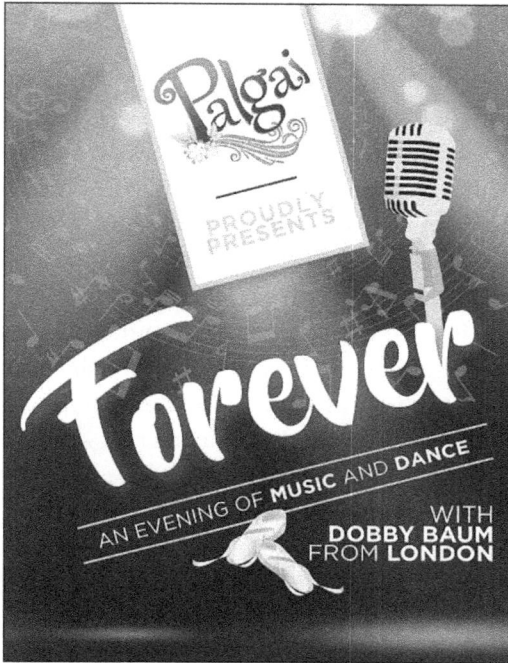

Figure 5.2: Dobby Baum's first posts on Instagram
(credit Dobby Baum).

introduced her followers to her voice with a rendition of "How Far I'll
Go," a song written by Lin-Manuel Miranda for Disney's 2016 animated
feature film *Moana*, tagging the video as "one of her favorite songs" and
playing an accompaniment on the piano. In 2019, and even more so in
2020 during the pandemic, Dobby drastically increased her online presence and transformed her appearance, wearing bright pink or red lipstick, shiny or colorful dresses, and longer *sheytl*.

The changes in Dobby's performance of *tsnius* corresponded to her
burgeoning career, branding, and growing popularity. It was in the fall of
2019 that Dobby released her first album, *Rejuvenate*, and a few months
into the lockdown due to COVID-19, she created *The Dobby Show*, where
she invited Orthodox female artists from around the world to discuss their
art and to sing. The show greatly increased her popularity within ultra-
Orthodox circles, even in the most stringently conservative communities.
As her followers grew, Dobby began communicating with them regularly

and advertising cosmetic brands and *sheytl* stores as well as other artists. On March 26, 2020, she released her first music video, "It Is Meant to Be," a composition responding to the COVID-19 crisis, produced as a family collaboration with her brother (Gershy Schwarcz a well-known producer and music studio owner in the Orthodox Jewish music industry), her sister-in-law, her husband, and a niece from the UK. Dobby made the video available on both of her Instagram accounts, where it was posted with the caption *"Kol Isha."* Not long after its release, she posted the video on YouTube, setting it as unlisted, allowing only people with the link to access it and making the video untraceable through keyword searches. Through this process, only individuals she personally transmits the link to have access to the music video. As it was her first music video, Dobby was unsure how to disseminate her artistic musical work while respecting the norms of *kol isha.* By making the video unlisted, she prevented disapproval for exposing her voice to the public.[26]

While the global pandemic generally devastated arts scenes and ended live performances, Dobby, as well as many other *frum* female artists, was able to reinvent herself and create an online community. She was a pioneer in the making of this community. She got an agent, toured the West Coast during the summer of 2020 and the South in the summer of 2021, acted in a film aimed at ultra-Orthodox women, produced other music videos that are now available to anyone, with the label "for women and girls only," and collaborated with other well-known Orthodox female artists to produce more online content.

One example of such collaboration is Dobby's frequent communication with the filmmaker and dancer Malky Weingarten (@Malky_Media), discussed earlier. Like Dobby, Malky had opened an Instagram account to expand her audience, an action she took in September 2017, three years after the release of her first movie, *Mali.* She had heard about the potential of social media to reach new fans and to connect her with her nonreligious friends in the film industry. When I met Malky, she was in her forties. She had not grown up with technology, as Dobby had. For the first year of her online activity, she published only simple posts or short excerpts of various media relating to her work. These included excerpts from her films, behind-the-scenes photos, calls for auditions, screenshots of emails from fans, and videos of her dancing while cooking and of dancing classes for girls set to Israeli music.

In January 2018, she made an important shift in her online engagement. She not only posted content about her work addressing important social issues (specifically, aging and disability) but also started a dialogue with her followers. The discussion that followed touched on a broad range of topics. It included her experience writing scripts, the growth of female Orthodox music and film, her children (including the struggles of her autistic son and her daughter's wedding during the COVID-19 pandemic), her travels to Hasidic summer camps, her travels abroad while shooting a friend's film, her visit to Georgetown University upon my invitation in February 2020, and the impact of the pandemic on her work. Beyond documenting her personal journey, Malky also uses Instagram to debate various contentious issues such as leaving the community; women's agency, roles, and rights; mental health; poverty; depression; the representation of Hasidic women in the media; and *tsnius*, contrasting her expression of modesty with that of the conservative Hasidic community to which she belongs. For example, on January 9, 2018, she published a photograph of herself with a very short *sheytl* and dark hat, very light makeup, small earrings, and the following caption: "Sometimes when I do gigs in Hasidic schools/camps they request I dress accordingly!! I love nothing more than feeling what it is like to be different than what I am! Also . . . I'm an actress, remember? I love to dress up!!!"

By likening her ensemble to a costume, Malky here stresses the performative nature of *tsnius*. In July 2019, she returned to the subject, posting a live video (available in her Instagram stories) about her experience entertaining girls at Hasidic summer camps, in which she included two photos of herself wearing a short *sheytl* and another of her in a *shpitzel*. She also invited her followers to weigh in on the matter: "Sometimes the camps need me to adhere to a dress code. This is the getup I was given for my first camp. What do you say?" This sparked a conversation in which she engaged directly with fans about the different dress codes within Orthodoxy. Summer camp organizers often ask her to perform in more modest clothing and with her hair fully covered, and her video on Instagram broached that issue as a topic of debate with her followers.

A few months before this episode, she had posted a photo with a sticker on her lips that read, "Who says I want to fit in?" The following comment accompanied this:

I decided that the ability to "fit in" comes along with a certain type of personality. Some find it harder, and some have no issues. Being put in a box works for some people. It feels freeing for them. All their choices are made—it eliminates a lot of heartache and makes their life simpler. Lucky them. And then there are the personalities that to them a box feels like a prison. They don't function well. It's like their wings were cruelly cut off. And that's why thankfully, our creator, who created all those personality types, loves us all equally, and loves to watch us find ourselves. In the box. Or outside it. You have his permission to "fit in" or "fit out."[27]

Appearing in a long, flamboyant chestnut *sheytl*, orange lipstick, eyeliner, and discreet, elegantly applied eyeshadow, Malky is telling her audience that she does not fit in with the Hasidic circles she encountered while posting in January 2018 and July 2019. However, since this fashion style is embraced by other ultra-Orthodox female artists on Instagram, she is one of many such artists contributing to the normalization of a new model of *tsnius*, a model anchored in the image of the stylish Orthodox woman with a long, fancy wig, colorful makeup, and varied clothing designs—all of which differs greatly from the image of the traditional Hasidic woman. Whether merely walking, biking (something that Hasidic women, even if they do it, often do not admit to), or preparing for a live performance or dance class, Malky consistently promotes this more fashionable *tsnius* appearance on social media. Of course, this performance takes place on the streets of Borough Park, but by disseminating it online, Malky reaches a broader audience far beyond her own neighborhood, an audience eager for this new model of *tsniusness*. Respecting the general codes of *tsnius*, such as keeping the hems of skirts and dresses below the knee, she allows herself some flexibility regarding rules about leggings or tights (which is prescribed dress in most ultra-Orthodox circles except Lubavitch), sweaters covering the elbow, unconventional accessories such as sunglasses, sport watches, and caps, and colorful clothing including greens, oranges, blues, and pinks.

The Instagram journeys of Malky and Dobby parallel those of other ultra-Orthodox female artists. Their online performances evolve toward a fashionable and consumable expression of *tsnius* while also respecting—when necessary—various ultra-Orthodox interpretations of modesty. When @Malky_Media teaches or performs at Hasidic camps, she follows their rules, wearing a *shpitzel* or a short *sheytl*, speaking mostly in Yiddish, and keeping her bright lipstick in her pocket. Meanwhile, when she posts on Instagram for her followers, she performs *tsnius* in bright colors and long *sheytl*, with leggings sometimes replacing her tights. The result is a style of modesty that she defines as her own. When Malky writes that she does not fit in, she refers to the Hasidic community she has been affiliated with since childhood and through marriage. Her expressions of *tsnius* set her at odds with this group's cultural norms. In so doing, Malky participates alongside Dobby and other professional artists in the standardization, through social media, of a new performance of *tsnius*, embraced by women coming from various Orthodox communities.

While one might think to observe in all this the creation of a pluralist, transformative space allowing for many voices and unique expressions of *tsnius* and *kol isha*, with a distinction between Litvish, Lubavitch, and other Hasidic worlds, there is in fact another kind of homogenization occurring. And the resulting form of *tsnius* resembles the fashionable and consumable version of Orthodoxy present in some Lubavitch and Litvish circles, where styles of *tsnius* are characterized by flexibility and modernity. Indeed, even while rabbis from more conservative circles reiterate and reinforce restrictions regarding the size of *sheytl*, colorful or fashionable clothing, and makeup, stores and cosmetic businesses in ultra-Orthodox neighborhoods increasingly advertise modern fashion trends and display female models with long, natural hair. These trends in ultra-Orthodox modest clothing parallel those in secular fashion magazines such as *Vogue, Fashion, Cosmopolitan*, and *Elle*. While Malky and Dobby represent two different generations, they engage in similar behavior on Instagram, acting as influencers and participating in this new, nonnormative standardization of *tsnius* as part of a network of artists and their followers—all of them Orthodox Jewish women—who defy the rules established in their Hasidic conservative communities.

These women's transformation of *tsnius* is in line with the theory of the gendered self as a performance that is interactional and influenced by audience.[28] *Frum* female artists on social media adapt and transform themselves according to the response of their online community. Moreover, the performer, too, is a spectator of the self, altering her performance according to her own perceptions of it. The social codes of these artists' wider ultra-Orthodox communities remain embedded in their performance of *tsnius*, but their participation in the online community alters this self-expression. As new media experts have stated, social media gradually and slightly change our behavior and perception, as the content we consume influences how we present ourselves. Social media expand religious practices and communities beyond traditional social interactions in schools and/or religious spaces.[29] The forms of *tsnius* performed online have thus taken shape in this nexus of self-perception, online consumption, and interactivity between ultra-Orthodox female artists and their followers.

Throughout this process, a constant need for individual expression emerges that includes a desire to not fit in or to expand the frame of "fitting in"—to express and suggest, through word, image, and sound, a different way of being ultra-Orthodox. This desire challenges the institutions from which it originates, yet still produces a narrative that echoes a collective experience of Jewish ultra-Orthodoxy. Many Hasidic and Litvish female artists began their online activity by challenging the codes of modesty of their own communities, but as they progressively embraced a modern, fashionable Orthodox image—a figure presented as not fitting in with Hasidic circles, one who is preoccupied with fashion, individuality, and self-promotion—they nevertheless produced another in-group, a new community to fit into, in the counterpublic space of their online interaction.

Counterpublics

In addition to standardizing new *tsnius* norms, *frum* female artists use online networks to defy and criticize their religious communities' expectations of their social roles as women, artists, and, in some cases, activists. While, as we have seen earlier in the book, these communities do offer platforms for women to be creative and opportunities to become professional artists and celebrities, the kosher mainstream creative industries do not incorporate social media, and so these women perform in a counterpublic space that they have constructed in opposition to the mainstream representation of women in the Orthodox Jewish press and Orthodox popular culture, where we never see their faces and rarely hear their voices. Within these counterpublics, they maintain their Orthodoxy but express criticism in the hopes of engendering broad changes in women's public representation and social position.

In 2017, Adina Miles-Sash, known as @FlatbushGirl on social media, launched a bold online campaign with the hashtag #FrumWomenHave-Faces. Adina defines herself as a Litvish girl from Flatbush with a Hasidic influence, as her mother grew up in Borough Park with a Satmar father. She launched the hashtag campaign with a statement about the absence of women in the Orthodox Jewish press alongside a photograph of herself with two elderly women: Esther Lenchevsky, her husband's maternal grandmother, and Lea Adler, her own maternal grandmother, both teachers in the ultra-Orthodox system since the 1970s. Adina viewed Esther and Lea as mentors who passed on sacred information about Jewish femininity to subsequent generations.

The hashtag #FrumWomenHaveFaces went viral, responding to what Adina describes as the erasure of women from Orthodox Jewish media.

Figure 5.3: Adina Miles-Sash (known as FlatbushGirl) launching the social media campaign #FrumWomenHaveFaces (credit Flatbushmedia).

This initiative stands in opposition to the norms of her upbringing established by both male and female ultra-Orthodox leadership. Adina mobilized social media against this interpretation, suggesting that it is a male's responsibility to distance himself from such content if he feels uncomfortable looking at a woman. In her arguments, she resorted to religious rhetoric, referencing Jewish texts and ideas such as the notion that to be Jewish—and more specifically, to be a Jewish woman—is to bear the responsibility to "repair the world" (*tikkun olam*) for subsequent generations.[30] Her campaign led to many debates within Orthodoxy regarding the difference between public and private spaces in the context of *tsnius*, with some individuals reaffirming the stricter rules of ultra-Orthodoxy and others, such as women who created a website entitled "Keep Women in the Picture," combating this interpretation.[31]

As a storyteller and public advocate for women's rights and changes within ultra-Orthodoxy, Adina has received much support but also criticism by others.[32] She openly challenges religious authority on her public Instagram and YouTube accounts, criticizing ultra-Orthodox Judaism and more specifically women's roles and stringent codes of *tsnius*. On Instagram, she addresses taboo subjects such as *shiddukhim* (arranged marriage), birth control, *taharat hamishpachah* ("family purity" laws), domestic violence, sexual education, attitudes toward the LGBTQ community, individuals who have left the Orthodox community, and, more recently, the issue of *get* refusal.

Adina first appeared on YouTube on December 25, 2015, and on Instagram six months later, on June 6, 2016. Her accounts on both platforms are public, and she eventually began posting comedic videos about women in Orthodoxy, often with a satirical, ditzy, or slightly sardonic tone. In one of her first satirical videos (posted January 18, 2017), she highlights the judgment of authorities about various forms of modesty within the Hasidic Yiddish world, acting in a skit alongside Riki Rose, a Satmar singer and actress who dissociated herself from the ultra-Orthodox community and performs Yiddish theater with other former community members.[33] Her first appearance on Instagram was a video identifying her as a mother, wife, daughter, and entrepreneur, accompanied by text asking, "Which roles do you identify with the most?" In 2018, when she started her bid for district leader in the 45th New York State Assembly District, she progressively took a more activist tone. Her posts began to state more explicitly her criticisms and her desire to challenge religious authority. In a video produced by NowThis News and posted to her Instagram account on November 19, 2018, she specified, "There is no board of rabbis who need to approve a post before it goes up. This space of social media is really leading to an explosion of females taking back their voices."

In May 2018, Adina was interviewed on BRIC TV, a Brooklyn-based nonprofit community TV channel and digital network,[34] to talk about her journey from getting a master's in literature to the creation of her social media company, Flatbushmedia, and her persona as a female Orthodox social media influencer. She created this persona to attract more clients for her company but received much criticism, primarily from *frum* women who viewed her social media activity as a threat to their "lifestyle." Her response to such criticism took a conciliatory tone but strongly reaffirmed her position: "My goal is not to shatter the system, I think there is a very important role in tradition in the family unit, in the culture, in our tribe, I think those things are beautiful. It is just where it limits girls reaching their potential and understanding their power as female rather than their weaknesses as female."[35]

Adina would go on to reveal that her mission embraces more than just cisgender, heterosexual women. A few weeks after her TV interview, she posted with transgender OTD activist Abby Stein and challenged followers, "Ask yourselves, what is so scary about having open dialogue with the LGBTQ and OTD communities?"

But there is a cost to these social media challenges to ultra-Orthodox norms and their arbiters, especially if one wants to run for public office in the very community one criticizes—a cost that led Adina to seek out a community of like-minded individuals online:

> I was willing to take the first wave of backlash from the male elected officials from within the Orthodox community, so that the path can be more easily walked upon by the next girl. I lost clients, I lost friends, I lost family; it is my duty for the girls who come after me to recognize that change is painful. And, like, I just, I am looking for those girls to take the torch from me and keep going and inspire the next generation of girls to do the same thing. (NowThis News, posted on November 19, 2018, on FlatbushGirl Instagram)

Figure 5.4: Adina Miles-Sash with transgender activist and former Hasidic community member Abby Stein, May 25, 2018 (credit Flatbushmedia).

Beyond her social media activism, Adina materializes her dedication to creating change through "real life" activism. For instance, in December 2019, she planned a participation in a comedy show for New Year's Eve, with Leah Forster, one of the most famous *frum* female stand-up comedians who has been marginalized since the exposure of her attraction to women, and Riki Rose. Participating in the activist-oriented comedy show came at the cost of increased marginalization from Orthodox organizations. However, it also afforded her and the other two women much media coverage. The event was to be hosted by Garden of Eat-in, a kosher diner in Flatbush. Still, the venue had to cancel due to a rabbi's threat to revoke its kosher certification because Forster is openly lesbian. Adina Miles-Sash played a major role in the public discussion around the event's cancellation. She stood by Forster and posted a video on December 10, 2019, announcing the relocation of the event to a bigger venue in the center of Brooklyn. This video received almost forty thousand views, and the mainstream media eagerly picked up the story. Four days later, Adina posted a statement by the Vaad Hakashrus of Flatbush (a council of rabbis in charge of *kashrut*)—the same organization that had initially prevented the restaurant from hosting the event—stipulating that discrimination according to sexual orientation should not happen. As Adina mentioned, the reversal of the situation is undoubtedly a result of the restaurant owners' apprehension regarding the legal consequences that their business would face due to their involvement in such discriminatory practices.

Adina regularly participates in in-person activism, using social media to raise awareness and create a community of support. For instance, in 2020, she joined the forces of Ezra Nashim to raise money for this organization, became an EMT, and volunteered for the organization. Ezra Nashim is an all-female Orthodox Jewish volunteer ambulance service established with the aim of offering urgent care services to women by women. This initiative became controversial after the project was launched in 2012. In 2021, the call from Dalia Oziel about *agunot* brought Adina to social media activism and to participation in demonstrations in front of the homes of *get* refusers. Even though her in-person activism became a part of her practice, the attention she receives has mostly been thanks to her social media activism, and has mostly come after her online activism.

Adina Miles-Sash is one of the rare ultra-Orthodox women who describe themselves as a feminist, espousing a feminism that is distinct from the Jewish liberal one and the modern Orthodox one. Although the Orthodox feminist movement in North America is often characterized as primarily made up of modern Orthodox women, Adina and other Hasidic and Litvish women represent an ultra-Orthodox feminist challenge to their communities' restrictions of female status and female agency. Orthodox Jewish feminists advocate for a more egalitarian approach to Jewish practice within the bounds of *halakha*, campaigning strongly for a greater leadership position for women in the synagogue. Meanwhile, Adina and her counterparts—who are often reluctant to use the term "feminist" as they seek not only equality but also gender complementarity—embrace issues such as women's rights to higher education, to drive, to use birth control without approval by religious authority, to divorce, and to enact alternative expressions of *tsnius* that include growing their hair and covering their head with a long *sheytl*. Indeed, many Orthodox feminists have already acquired these forms of autonomy, while ultra-Orthodox communities continue to stress conformity to established norms. Although Adina situates her action as a transformation of ultra-Orthodoxy from within, she has drastically departed from ultra-Orthodox public discourse about women's role, public position, and representation, while never criticizing the heart of Jewish law. In conversations with women in positions of leadership in the educational system for various ultra-Orthodox high schools and seminaries in New York and Montreal, they evoked Adina as someone who challenges their own authority as well as the position and images of Orthodox women: "We are transmitting values and ideas to our girls, but someone like Adina Miles-Sash, via the social media, can just emerge and suggest an alternative to our voices, not only by doing things but by disseminating ideas online. Trying to prevent girls from accessing social media is not enough anymore. We need to address the issues presented by persons such as Adina Miles-Sash, and to reflect on new ways for consolidating our authoritative voice."[36]

With more than sixty thousand followers on Instagram, Adina is known as a celebrity inside and outside ultra-Orthodox circles, having been featured in the *New York Daily News*, the *Jewish Chronicle*, *The Forward*, the *Jewish Week*, the *Times of Israel*, the *New York Post*, *Sputnik News*, the *Daily Mail*, NowThisNews, and Netflix. She is a controversial figure who pushes the boundaries of tradition by using social media to expose the lives of ultra-Orthodox women and girls. These acts of exhibition are acts of disobedience that challenge established religious authority, but questions remain about the impact of this social media campaign on the religious system itself. Some women or girls think that Adina Miles-Sash's social media advocacy encourages other women to engage with and reflect on topics such as women's education and leadership roles. Though educators in schools and seminaries condemn Adina Miles-Sash's statements and attitudes—explaining to their students that she does not respect their "standard of modesty"—they now have no choice but to address the issues broached by her in the counterpublic space that is social media.

Adina Miles-Sash is perceived as a controversial figure but takes a conciliatory approach. Making an important distinction, she criticizes not tradition itself but the social roles that have been established based on tradition. She uses the language of inclusion, representation, and freedom borrowed from the discourse of liberal universal feminism, while at the same time distancing herself from that ideology by emphasizing the "beauty" and importance of tradition. Adina Miles-Sash represents a challenge to feminists such as the philosopher Serene Khader, who advocate for decolonizing universal feminism. She is one of those "other" women coming from a non-liberal and potentially non-Western environment (in the sense of not embracing the Enlightenment), living in North America within a globally connected world, and having developed a reflexive relationship with her community, due as much to the development of online publics as to liberal feminism. On the one hand, Adina Miles-Sash advocates for a nonideal universalism, as she promotes a feminism within Orthodoxy that respects *halakha*; but on the other hand, she adopts a missionary feminist approach by casting her activism as the dismantling of women's oppression derived from patriarchal tradition. It may be that Adina Miles-Sash carefully negotiates these feminist currents to save face in the community to gain legitimacy.

Frum female influencers and creators like Adina Miles-Sash bypass their communities' restrictions in their ability to promote their work and disseminate ideas that criticize socioreligious norms within Orthodoxy. Social media allow them to avoid the surveillance and interference encountered in public spaces, and to develop transnational online networks to discuss women's issues and promote new discourses and practices. Adina Miles-Sash may be one of the few using the term "feminism" on their Instagram accounts, but the majority of ultra-Orthodox women within this counterpublic advocate for "female power," a feminist expression in all but name that echoes the strategies implemented by women who are spiritual entrepreneurs and coaches.[37] While often used to defy religious authority, the counterpublic space can also reinforce a religiosity in which these women become alternative figures of female authority and examples of femininity.

Cyber*frum*inism(s)?

Engaging with *frum* female artists and influencers online, ultra-Orthodox women produce knowledge and discourses on topics such as women and creativity, the economy, relationships, marriage, motherhood, and femininity—on all of which they act as their own authority in their domain of expertise. In these spaces, they are mobilizing the rhetoric of women's rights and empowerment, creating a conversation with feminist discourses online even while not engaging with the literature. Drawing on the work of sociologist Jessie Daniels and communication studies scholar Radhika Gajjala, I refer to their practices as cyberfeminism(s) to underline the variability in the relationships between gender and digital culture, and characterize them as viewing cybertechnologies as a tool women should appropriate in an attempt to empower themselves.[38] This cyberspace allows them to reveal ultra-Orthodox female faces, bodies, and voices, and more specifically their private social, cultural, and artistic lives, which have been stereotyped by the public secular media and made invisible by the public ultra-Orthodox media.

Chany Rosengarten, who has more than ten thousand followers on her public Instagram account, is a writer and life coach advertising "New Perspectives on Female Power." She grew up in the Hasidic community of Skver (officially, the village of New Square) in Upstate New York. Many know her as a poet in both Yiddish and English and as a writer for the Orthodox press on subjects such as Hasidic upbringing, marriage, relationships, cultural differences between Israeli and North American Jewries, and the defense of her childhood village against detractors. After spending a few years in Israel, where she took professional courses in writing with the Orthodox Jewish writer Sarah Shapiro, she relocated to a more diverse and "modern" ultra-Orthodox community in Monsey (in Rockland County, New York) and established herself as a professional *frum* female writer and life coach offering courses on self-confidence, self-love, sexuality, relationships, money, and business. She took marketing and business classes, and her teacher recommended that she open social media accounts on Facebook and Instagram to engage a broader audience and prospective clientele in preparation for launching her first novel, *Promise Me Jerusalem*.[39] In October 2015, Chany opened her

Instagram account, first posting photos of landscapes, food, and flowers. It was not until January 2016 that she finally provided a photo of herself. She then began to increasingly post photos of her face and body, appearing with various hair coverings (such as a *sheytl* and a hat, a *shpitzel*, or a longer *sheytl* descending past the shoulders). Chany initially shaped her online persona around the concept of individual choice,[40] with quite strong religious or spiritual connotations, evoking the female's position at home as one of empowerment. As she progressively stepped away from this religious persona, her discourse on female power became broader and more inclusive through the absence of religious references, certainly to attract followers beyond ultra-Orthodox Jewish circles.

In the summer of 2017, she joined FlatbushGirl's social media campaign #FrumWomenHaveFaces and asked her followers for their thoughts on the publishing of women's faces in the Jewish press. For Chany, the decision to publish her photo and appear publicly on Instagram was an informed individual choice entangled with the requirements of her profession. As she mentioned during a private conversation, she considers social media a marketing tool. Still, she acknowledges that most women in her community do not want their faces published in magazines or online. Drawing on the past to explain that Hasidic practices and traditions change, she encourages her female followers to reflect on this issue:

I want to thank @flatbushgirl for the courage it takes to ask questions. Because questions are part of our tradition. And while questions without clear answers are scary, it is important to raise them when we see them. Ask, dear women. Because not only do #frumwomenhavefaces

Frum women also have questions. And answers.

And wisdom.

And shared experience that we receive from one another when we dare to discuss what matters to us.[41]

In the fall of 2017, Chany further pushed the idea of individual choice, adding the phrase "freedom to choose" and tagging Adina

Figure 5.5: Chany Instagram photo used for her post on July 10, 2017 (credit Chany Rosengarten).

Miles-Sash (@flatbushgirl). In contrast to earlier posts in which she merely questioned her followers about their understanding of women's abilities, she became increasingly specific about her own conception of them. She encourages women to live beyond the judgment of others, to feel free to act as they want, and to be the person they aspire to be, all the while interrogating the internal tension between the desire or freedom to choose for ourselves and the consequences of these choices: "We choose our experiences. We choose how we show up in this world, and which restrictions will define us. What is it that you would be and do if nothing stood in your way?"[42] In an Instagram TV video posted on January 2020 that she dedicates to "the Experience of Freedom," she uses the *parasha* (weekly reading of a portion of the Torah) for the week to make her argument.[43] In other words, she inscribes the concept of individual choice or freedom into her version of Orthodox Judaism. However, in another video that she published several months later titled "How to Have Boundaries with a Society That Judges You,"[44] she does not employ any religious or spiritual references, suggesting that her followers limit how much ultra-Orthodox norms can impact their lives if their individual choice is not respected.

A few weeks later, Chany posted about women's privilege to be at home and bake challah, defining this action as empowering women. While she reinforces gender roles with this post—using the expression "we know our place, we accept our essence"—she embraces a role for women that stresses their influence, power, and complementarity to men. Chany envisages women's agency in terms of autonomy within the framework of tradition—that is, something that women can have when they are empowered economically and emotionally. Following what postcolonial feminist scholars such as Saba Mahmood (2005) have stated, Chany's adherence to the patriarchal norms of ultra-Orthodoxy parochializes the key assumption of feminist universalist theorists about freedom, agency, and autonomy.

On May 24, 2018, Chany posted a photo of an article published by *Lohud*, a local secular newspaper serving the New York counties of Westchester, Rockland, and Putnam, where she is presented as "Author, Hasid, Feminist."[45] The article was published in the printed newspaper and online, accompanied by a short video containing one of the few references to "feminism" that appears on her social media accounts. While hundreds of women liked and commented positively on her Instagram posts, often thanking her for acknowledging "the beauty of the community," one follower questioned her supposed alignment with feminism:

Lol, when I saw the word Feminist, I [was] like really? No, especially when writing about an amazing Orthodox Jewish Young Woman, Wife, and Mom that seriously takes what Hashem has commanded us to do Seriously. You take Seriously Chany, doing Mitzvahs every day. From small to major. The same with Tikkun Olam. Those who have actually taken the time to read your work, your amazing book know this to be B'H [Barukh Hashem, meaning thank God] absolutely True. A better title would be "True Woman of Valor"! Every day you live the prayers & blessings written on the Ketuba, and in the Woman of Valor Prayer. Thanks for always sharing & being Chany!!!

Chany's ideas about freedom of choice within a religious framework empowering women progressively evolved toward a concept of female power liberated from religious reference and authority. She presented agency as internal, discreet, introspective, and processual: "Myth: strong women are vocal, high-profile and born knowing what they want and how to get it. Truth: strong women have the courage to get to know themselves. They have the courage to expect more. They have the courage to be who they are."[46]

Chany also engages with taboo subjects such as sexuality and marriage, becoming an authoritative voice on such matters through her work as a coach and motivational speaker. In May and June 2020, she posted photos of herself with captions acknowledging the heavy burdens that come from having a spouse who "has [an] addiction," "has an affair," "is on the autistic spectrum," one "whose rage is disturbing" or "whose attention is fragmented," encouraging women to take time to care for themselves and offering herself as a support for them in this process. Her advice for those in intractable marriages is firm: "The 'healthy' thing for women in very difficult marriages is to leave."

Chany's path from religiously inflected freedom of choice to broader understanding of the concept has potentially been part of a business decision, allowing her to market herself to those outside the Orthodox (or even broader Jewish) community. Still, since a majority of her followers are Orthodox women, they are the primary recipients of her message. And this message—her conception of choice and freedom—is now aligned with a notion of empowerment in which individuals establish boundaries to protect themselves from the consequences of their choices. In 2020, Chany published her second book, *The Boundary Is You: A Guide to Creating Boundaries by Loving Yourself More*, and posted a screenshot of Amazon.com presenting it as a "New Release in Feminist Studies."

As part of this more inclusive approach, Chany contributed to an edited volume alongside eleven other women from various backgrounds discussing their personal battles with self-identity, discrimination, financial disparity, divorce, and sexual trauma. The book, *Saving Lives While Fighting for Mine: Stories to Empower Women to Win*,[47] was edited and published by the African American evangelist and author Ayanna Mills Gallow in October 2020. In it, Chany is presented as "a wife, mother of

four young children, #1 Amazon bestselling author and powerful motivational speaker," with no reference to her Orthodox Jewish religious
background.

Chany does not intend her project to criticize the position or role
of women within Orthodox Judaism, or more specifically within
ultra-Orthodox Judaism, but to start a public conversation about
"women's right" to make their own choices. She encourages them to
choose whether to have their face published in magazines or online,
to choose the kind of relationship they want, the number of children
they want, and when to have them, to think about their professional
development—in short, she asks them to take back the authority to
make important decisions in their lives beyond the norms of their environment. Aligned with feminist autonomy theorists,[48] Chany Rosengarten wants women to develop their ability to reflect on and evaluate
their relationship to traditions, and to think about the multiple choices
they have as women even in the ultra-Orthodox world. She has been
presented to me as an example of female empowerment using social
media to accomplish her goal and a source of inspiration for other
ultra-Orthodox women seeking economic, social, cultural, or intellectual growth. Yet by focusing on the potential of women to earn money,
regain authority, and liberate themselves from abusive relationships
without evoking the inequalities that often structure these oppres-
sions, she is also neglecting the less educated and prosperous women
who are unable to move away from these relationships, often women
who are also unable to use her private service. As a coach and inspirational speaker, Chany may not be extending her message beyond these
more privileged women. As an influencer who created a counterpublic platform, she reaches beyond her selective clientele, who ironically
allow her to maintain her position as a global ultra-Orthodox female
influencer thanks to their participation in her business.

Chany abandoned her active presence on Instagram in October 2021
and redirected her followers to her mailing list if they wanted to follow
her. She attributed her decision to algorithms of social media platforms
that are now controlling our behaviors. While Instagram was initially
an authentic way for her to communicate new ideas about female empowerment and autonomy, and to create an online community, she felt
she was not authentic anymore in her actions, envisaging the platform

as a business one. She did not erase her social media presence, as she keeps her YouTube channel. She sends a weekly newsletter, and her Instagram account is still active, with sporadic posts. As a woman who started using social media because of her criticism of religious norms and society, she exited social media as a global citizen critical of our liberal society and an exemplar of our use of the digital. Without denying the potential of social media, she acknowledged the need to challenge it and to reinvent herself as aligned to this new world she now belongs to. The potentiality and impact of her voice as an influencer may take new forms that are still difficult to envisage.

Chany is one of the rare ultra-Orthodox female artists I discovered on Instagram to exit social media during the pandemic. For many of them, the pandemic became instead a springboard upon which to increase their online presence and audience. When the COVID-19 pandemic hit North America in 2020, many *frum* female artists were preparing concerts, inspirational talks, performances, and other types of events for *Khol Hamoed Pessakh* (referring to the intermediate days between the beginning and the end of Pessakh, also known as Passover). While some of these women were already using Instagram to market themselves, COVID-19 drastically increased the use of the Internet in ultra-Orthodox circles. As children were out of school and had very few places to be entertained, *frum* female artists began offering online entertainment. This represented a tectonic shift in the way *frum* women engaged with their audience. They gave informal online performances and collaborative online concerts, produced and posted more music videos than ever, and organized online talent shows. Dobby Baum was a central figure in all this, as discussed earlier. She encouraged women and girls around the globe to take part in online activities and advocated for a global community of *frum* female artists unrestricted by denominational or geographical borders. On March 9, Dobby promoted a *Khol Hamoed Pessakh* event and added a video story on the Brooklyn girls' choir page tagging her personal account: "Yesterday it was International Women's Day, and that means celebrating women, changing history. And we are actually changing history by making the very first *Khol Hamoed Pessakh* concert. *Frum* female singers all together, five singers, the Brooklyn girls' choir, which has never existed before. It has never existed before—a choir for *frum* girls here in America performing live.

We are celebrating it on International Women's Day. If you live abroad and you won't be able to attend the concert, just a little something to make our concert happen, thank you so much."[49]

On March 17, she announced the rescheduling of the concert to *Khol Hamoed Sukkot* (around September–October), almost certain that the large gathering would then be possible. Ultimately, the concert became an online performance, scheduled for October 6, 2020.

At the outset of the pandemic, Dobby had to reinvent herself and her work practices. Even though Internet and social media access at home is controversial in ultra-Orthodox circles, the consumption of online kosher entertainment at home increased drastically during the first few weeks of lockdown, and Dobby capitalized on it, providing free kosher entertainment for women and girls. In April 2020, she started weekly online performances and other activities, using Zoom and InstaLive to launch online concerts and *The Dobby Show*, which featured the collaborative performances of *frum* female artists—professional and nonprofessional, women and girls—from the UK, Israel, and the United States. They exchanged stories of their artistic and personal journeys and discussed topics such as *kol isha* and the professionalization of *frum* female performers, as well as women's economic inequalities in the kosher art industry. This online presence drastically increased the number of her followers, from approximately four thousand in March to almost eight thousand in October. In her discussions with other female artists, she constantly stresses the need to promote, encourage, and recognize female talent in the community. The online concert was produced in the Brooklyn video studio Flowmotion TV,[50] and concertgoers gained digital access upon registering for tickets on the InPlayer platform. A professional advertisement was released on October 1, 2020, on YouTube, Instagram, and Facebook and circulated through WhatsApp groups and individual social media accounts. The announcement framed the concert as the "most exciting event in the history of Jewish music."[51] On October 9, Dobby posted a video of the concert rehearsal (now with almost twenty-five hundred views) with the following caption echoing the initial announcement of March 8: "'We're MAKING history, women and girls full of glory, until we meet once more, let our voices SOAR!!' You can still buy your tickets if you haven't yet watched this momentous change in *frum* female History!!!!"[52]

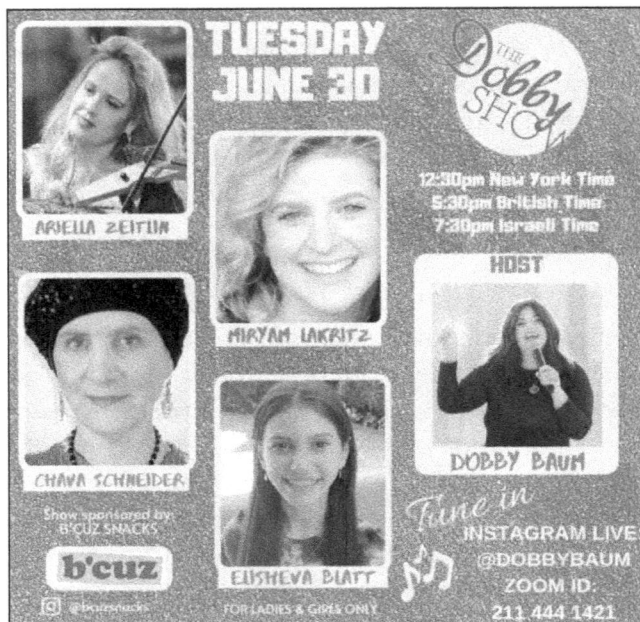

Figure 5.6: Poster made by Dobby Baum for her *Dobby Show* (credit Dobby Baum).

Framing support for *frum* female artists as a response or contribution to International Women's Day and to Jewish history transmits a feminist message. Dobby even privately defined herself as a Jewish feminist woman. Moreover, with her online advocacy and popularity, she challenges perceptions of cyberspace's utility. This is not merely a space where one can deviate from Orthodoxy—as the religious leadership in many Hasidic and Litvish circles continues to claim—but a space where women and girls can reinforce their religious commitment while finding ways to criticize, condemn, defy, and transform gender norms and practices. Dobby's followers regularly ask her how she navigates her work-life balance, and she often responds that her husband is a strong collaborator in her artistic development. He also takes care of her children while she is teaching, performing, and studying. Her conversations with other artists address women's equality in the music business, and she advocates for equal remuneration even if they perform for women only.

Since Dobby navigates technologies within her prescribed role as a *frum* woman and entrepreneur needing to reach the broadest female audience possible, she embraces power that is exercised through women's fulfillment of prescribed gender roles while extending and transforming the normative role of women artists.[53] As Khader stated, "Western feminists often assume that feminized power is an inferior form of power and that investment in it signals a failure to desire the forms of power that would end women's domination."[54] Postcolonial feminists, instead of dismissing less obvious forms of agency, recognize that women do not have to participate in male power structures to be liberated. While Dobby mobilized a liberal universal feminist framework by associating her action with International Women's Day and advocating for equal remuneration and equal access to high-quality productions, she also breaks away from that discourse to carve out her own place within ultra-Orthodoxy, addressing a women-only audience and differentiating herself as a "Jewish feminist." She by no means rejects the restrictions of *tsnius* that result in unequal access to performance opportunities, but rather uses the rhetoric of *tsnius* to maintain her religiosity while gaining agency—an example of feminized power. In line with this feminized power, Dobby also joined Dalia Oziel's campaign against *get* refusal.

Dobby and other *frum* female artists borrow from cyberfeminist discourses to advocate for female empowerment within ultra-Orthodoxy through social media. Their criticism of the community in the counterpublic space tackles various issues, from gender inequality in the entertainment industry and the press to birth control, divorce, and social pressure to conform, or takes the form of revealing what women do and think about. Contrary to Euro-American cyberfeminism,[55] this counterpublic cyber*frum*enist space does not focus on technology's role in creating gender hierarchies, nor does it encourage women to engage with new media technologies to dismantle gender inequalities. For example, none of these artists seek to perform in front of mixed audiences or to dismantle the Jewish law that requires men to give the *get* or women to cover their hair. Rather, this is a space in which women's personal experiences can be narrated, in which female power and agency can be observed in the decision to have a public or private account, and in which feminist consciousness can be fostered through the promotion of female autonomy in the context of gendered complementary practices and roles.

Decentering Religious Authority, Normalizing Online Activity, and Women's Solidarity

The figures of Dobby Baum, Adina Miles-Sash, Chany Rosengarten, and Malky Weingarten discussed in this chapter illuminate the marginal but growing phenomenon of *frum* women using social media to transform ultra-Orthodoxy from within. Even though they target a female-only audience, as mothers and wives, they also impact the world of men who see them acting on these platforms, creating social media content, and disseminating new ideas about women's positionality within ultra-Orthodoxy. Ultra-Orthodox Jewish women use Instagram and other platforms for professional, educational, spiritual, and social reasons, thereby defying their communities' norms, which forbid both the use of the Internet for nonbusiness purposes and the presence of women in media. At a broader level, these tensions reveal new approaches toward authority and autonomy in our everyday digital lives.

These ultra-Orthodox artists, singers, and influencers court controversy by displaying their uncovered faces and unmuting their voices on social media. Even if they normalize their public online presence by justifying it as related to their businesses, they engage with subjects that transcend these businesses, producing alternative standards of *tsnius* and *kol isha*, and thus paving the way toward distinctive understandings of Orthodoxy and religious authority in the digital era. They are able to do so thanks to the particularity of their tool. As media scholars Oren Golan and Michele Martini demonstrated, a visual social media platform such as Instagram has the ability to shorten and transform the social distance between the media producers and their followers. This new relationship can lead followers to engage with or commit to a specific visual practice.[56]

The variety of ways in which these women express subversive ideas about the public dissemination of female faces or voices highlights the many choices involved in being a *frum* woman seeking greater agency. There are profound differences in the activist vocabularies they employ, the topics they discuss, and the stances they take. For example, even the labels they use to describe themselves vary; they may define themselves as feminists, women offering new perspectives on female empowerment, activists, or inspirational voices. Interpreting these women's actions through the lenses of various feminist tropes—including religious feminism, feminist autonomy,[57] universal liberal feminism, and postcolonial feminism—I aspire to complicate our understanding of North American Jewry and the intersections of feminism and religiosity within it. Postcolonial feminists argue that women living in non-Western countries are not represented by mainstream feminism, which universalizes a Western experience—imagining women's agency solely in terms of being publicly visible—without taking into account other forms of feminism. Media studies scholar Radhika Gajjala has noted that cyberfeminism and, more broadly, online content by women are not the products of the subaltern but of the privileged, of those who can speak and write and acquire the technological literacy and resources required. However, this privileged group exposes the silenced, the unsaid, and the cannot-be-said to disrupt hegemony and authority.

Some ultra-Orthodox women may lament being misrepresented on mainstream mediatic Orthodox platforms, but they do not use the counterpublic space of Instagram to directly challenge these representations. To do so would be to pursue the dismantling of gender roles in Orthodoxy, a goal of many OTD artists. However, they do indirectly challenge these public representations. Chany, Malky, Adina, and Dobby might certainly be considered among the privileged minority that is aware of the consequences of marginality within certain ultra-Orthodox communities, yet they have created a space that disturbs the traditional discourse of religious authority concerning social media and women's images or voices. As social media influencers, they are all well-known beyond their online community, invited to promote products and services of businesses and corporations, but also to present their artwork for talks, concerts, screenings, or workshops for women's and girls' events in ultra-Orthodox circles in North America and beyond. This counterpublic is an alternative to the dominant public discourse within ultra-Orthodox Jewry, where there is a "war" against the Internet and social media as well as strong opposition to the publication of women's faces and voices out of respect for the rules of *tsnius* and *kol isha*.

These women are altering hegemonic narratives about the invisibility of ultra-Orthodox Jewish women, proposing new role models, and embracing the digital turn. For them, Instagram is not only distinct from male religious authorities—like all other ultra-Orthodox private female spaces—but also a space where they act as voices of authority, reconstructing the female Orthodox community and negotiating its cultural and social boundaries.[58] This counterpublic space acts as an agent for reframing women's practices within ultra-Orthodoxy, changing the shape of the public space that previously excluded them from representation and, at a broader level, altering the vision and public image of ultra-Orthodoxy itself. Since 2012, the religious leadership has tried hard to limit the use of the Internet and implement stricter rules for accessing it, but it has not been able to anticipate or control the surge of online counterpublic spaces that challenge its authority. Unlike the Jewish blogosphere described by anthropologist Ayala Fader that is considered a heretic space, the *frum* female counterpublic is a transformative space that is suitable *within* the religious system due to the business needs of *frum* artists. Even if the most conservative groups will present this counterpublic space as unorthodox and try to shut it down, as the anti-Internet rally of June 2022 targeting women demonstrated, it is generally assumed that it is not a heretical space because its raison d'être is essentially to maintain Orthodoxy. Indeed, far from being heretics, *frum* female artists and influencers disseminate avowedly Orthodox words, images, and ideas. They desire to transform ultra-Orthodoxy rather than cast it off, and they use social media to express this desire and to model it through their own personal transformations.

Like the formerly ultra-Orthodox artists we will meet in the following chapter, *frum* female artists and influencers distinguish themselves by creating a unique persona while consolidating themselves as a group through a shared vision of online self-empowerment. Social media allows for the mobilization of this simultaneous (even paradoxical) reinforcement of individuality and the collective because its users can maintain some privacy for their "public" personas through the use of private accounts. By circulating fashionable *frum* women and a discourse on feminized power within *frumkeit*, Instagram both normalized *frum* females as unique individual leaders in their respective fields and fostered a virtual imagined community with common concerns, experiences, and beliefs—similar to what Gajjala observed among diasporic postcolo-nial groups.[59] This virtual community, consisting of female artists from around the world, reinforces global belonging to Orthodoxy through a new model of *tsnius* in which women are in control of their images and voices, deciding when, where, how, why, and with whom they want to share them. In their own words, these artists and influencers often char-acterize the resulting solidarity as a sisterhood of women bound together by common experiences and concerns for the future as they use social media to challenge authority.

These women are engaged in what feminist scholars have described as the reshaping of religious hierarchies and traditional authority,[60] al-lowing the emergence of female voices of leadership that do not require the endorsement of male rabbinical authority. Indeed, such positions of leadership instead depend on mutual recognition and self-produced media. On the other hand, the broader acceptance of these women's ac-tivity and the absence of any backlash against them is explained by the fact that they remain within spheres that ultra-Orthodoxy perceives as "feminine" and address a female-only audience. Exploring the visible and audible performance of the *frum* female influencer who generates follower affinity on Instagram invites us to decenter the way we ap-proach religious authority. Scholars working on religious authority have discussed the role of charisma in religious leaders in overcoming the limitations of legal and traditional leadership. *Frum* female influencers are not legal or traditional religious leaders, but they act as charismatic leaders in the domain of Orthodox arts and activism, incorporating tra-ditional Judaism and religious references into their self-performance. As religious studies scholar Paul Gifford would put it, they are delivering a religious experience that ultimately constitutes a form of authority that influences its followers.[61]

As this audience grows, and with it, a variety of new artistic opportu-nities and collaborations, Instagram and other social media normalize the visible and audible publicity of *frum* women beyond their religious circles. The *frum* female influencer is a result of the crisis of authority that anthropologist Ayala Fader tackled in her work with ultra-Orthodox Jews who have religious doubts and created a counterpublic heretical space. The *frum* female influencer also represents a new phase in the crisis of authority brought about by digital technologies in traditional religious environments, characterized by the new ways conservative religious women create and legitimize new forms of charismatic feminine leaders that may impact the religious system beyond the counterpublic.

Malky, Dobby, Adina, Chany, and others are transforming the ultra-Orthodox Jewish landscape in ways that prompt religious leadership to reposition itself and reformulate its discourse on the use of technology, the Internet, and social media among women and girls. But even though these artists and influencers defy religious norms, they do not destabilize gender hierarchies in religious spaces, which would transcend the boundaries of the acceptable. Moreover, their impact has spread beyond the realm of social media; in the last few years, the nonprofit organization Penimi, which works with schools, educators, and individuals to "develop non-judgmental curricula for practical support to navigate technology and contemporary culture while remaining steadfast to religious values" (www.penimi.org) has drastically increased its programs and offerings.

Scholars of digital religion have argued for more comprehensive analyses incorporating both online and offline religious contexts.[62] Heidi Campbell, for example, defines digital religion as the technological and cultural space that blends or integrates online and offline religious domains,[63] stressing that online properties affect offline praxis, but not in a universal form. Oren Golan and Eldar Fehl, for another example, have focused on the use of social media to change religious communities.[64] On the other hand, Stewart Hoover and Nabil Echchaibi, have suggested viewing online religious expressions as "third spaces," implementing various types of "in-between-ness."[65] This "in-between-ness" exists between public and private, authority and autonomy, individual and community, and it is becoming the source of identities, ideas, claims, and solidarities that have the potential to affect the offline world. This chapter has suggested the potential impact of this "in-between-ness" on the offline world, as well as the use of social media by *frum* female influencers to transform their community, but it has also highlighted the creation of a distinctive counterpublic space that maintains its independence from the offline Orthodox world. Its protagonists have consolidated an online community that does not require offline interaction and does not necessarily want to affect the offline world. Therefore, we must consider the unique circumstances of these communities and their online practices, particularly since the pandemic has dramatically increased online activity and encouraged new forms of digital life. Online and offline spaces should also be considered as separate, each with its own raison d'être. Online practices might interact with and nourish offline experience, but it is also essential to recognize their autonomy.

The *frum* female influencers may transcend religious norms on Instagram, but in the offline world the challenges are greater, and the stakes are higher. Chany did not return to New Square after living in Israel; she now lives in Monsey, where her children attend an ultra-Orthodox school for those whose parents from Satmar, New Square, or other more conservative religious systems no longer fit into their communities. Dobby recently moved to Monsey, something she had thought about for years, searching for a more "diverse and inclusive" Orthodox neighborhood outside of Brooklyn. The Hasidic girls' camp in the Catskills where she had performed for years has canceled the event following her high presence on social media during the pandemic. While the camp's reasons for doing so have not yet been explained, Dobby assumes that her activity on Instagram and YouTube, as well as the recordings she has released on music streaming platforms, certainly had an influence.

Nevertheless, it remains to ask just how much these *frum* female influencers and artists impact their broader Orthodox communities, and to do that we must look at their interactions in offline religious environments. Instagram may normalize and transform their personal lives, choices, and self-perceptions, but can we envision a form of legitimation that would be transformative not only in the counterpublic space of the Internet but also in women's public offline spaces? Legitimation must transcend social media, entering the private spaces where artists can move beyond sisterhood and be acknowledged by mainstream religious authorities. For some *frum* female artists and influencers whom I encountered throughout several years of research, success—which they define in economic, social, and cultural terms—continues to derive essentially from their online lives. Their work and ideas infiltrate real-world spaces indirectly and informally, but they are too modern to be invited to certain official performances at camps and schools. *Frum* female artists are not yet changing the system, but they are important agents in the diversification of the ultra-Orthodox Jewish landscape, creating communities for like-minded women in both the digital and the physical worlds. Among the *frum* female artists and influencers for which the counterpublic was not sufficient to their artistic and personal development, some decided to break away from ultra-Orthodoxy. The ones who did break away often aspire to be recognized as public artists who transcend the social norms of their religious worlds. The expectations of a *frum* life as women and artists were impossible to maintain. Yet through this process, they have ironically ended up reapproaching religious and secular liberal worlds.

6

The Public Artist

Legitimizing Hasidicness, Diversifying Jewishness

I am still Hasidic, and I will always be. This is not only who I
am, but it is in me.
—Malky Goldman, July 2020

In New Yiddish Rep's staging of the play *Got Fun Nekome* (*God of Vengeance*), Malky Goldman's role was a far cry from her Hasidic upbringing
in Mea Shearim, Jerusalem. As Raizl, a Jewish prostitute, Malky traded
her everyday clothes for a hot pink romper with a black corset. Her
décolleté, red skirt with black flowers, black tights, and high-heeled
boots were extensions of the character. Her body language followed
suit as she flirted with clients by playing with her legs to offer a better view of her flesh. On March 22, 2017, at the Theatre at St. Clement's
in Manhattan, I saw Malky act in front of an audience eager to see the
modern version of a controversial play written by Sholem Asch in the
early twentieth century.[1] Exploring Orthodox Judaism, prostitution, and
same-sex love, the scandalous play is set in a brothel owned by Yankl, an
Orthodox Jew who is trying to marry off his daughter to a yeshiva student while she falls in love with one of the brothel's prostitutes. While in
many ways foreign to Malky's former life in Jerusalem, the play overlaps
with that experience in two key respects: its use of the Yiddish language
and its exploration of Jewish Orthodoxy.

 Got Fun Nekome received extensive media coverage for featuring
native Yiddish speakers in a play about Orthodoxy itself; the *New
York Times*, for example, declared it "An Incisive Play about Hasidism, with Actors Who Lived It."[2] Like Malky herself, many of her
castmates also grew up in ultra-Orthodox families, primarily Hasidic
ones. They, too, belonged to a community of ultra-Orthodox Jews who
broke away from their religious path and were subsequently labeled

Figure 6.1: *God of Vengeance*, New Yiddish Rep, March 2016. *Left to right*: Malky Goldman, Mira Kessler, Melissa Weisz (photo and credit: Ronald L. Glassman).

"off the *derekh*" (OTD). Unlike the *frum* women artists presented in the previous chapters, who express themselves in private, semiprivate, and counterpublic spaces, Malky and her peers performed for a general audience. Because their work is public-facing, I categorize them as "Hasidic public artists." The actors in *Got Fun Nekome*—Shmully Blesofsky, Lili Rosen (credited as Eli Rosen), Luzer Twersky, and Melissa Weisz—had all married in their communities, divorced, abandoned a lifestyle they could no longer pursue, and begun careers in the performing arts, capitalizing on their fluency in Yiddish and their life within the Hasidic world.

Beyond participating in this theater scene that legitimizes Yiddish as a living language, Malky and her peers also act on screen, producing Hasidic characters in mainstream film and television for public audience. In many of these public representations, Hasidic women have been portrayed as backward, oppressed, and uncreative. Writers and producers outside ultra-Orthodoxy often orientalize and sensationalize these religious women's narratives and reinforce Western feminist liberal tropes,[3] as they also do with Islamic women. As Mireille Rosilio reminded us, many in liberal circles have experienced the uncomfortable silence that occurs when they are confronted with people who expect them to agree with stereotypes about others who are presented as incomprehensible or deviant.[4] But what happens when one is no longer stereotyped or visibly Jewish—due to changes in one's appearance or presentation that permit a kind of passing in society—but one's peers continue to be?

In their work, many Hasidic performers must compromise on the representation of Orthodoxy and gender equity that they produce; they must resign themselves to "playing the industry game," whether as actresses, consultants, art directors, producers, or writers. By accepting these terms, Hasidic women public artists are mediators between two worlds, allowing them to reshape both Hasidic public culture and the representation of religious minorities on screen and stage. While in previous chapters we discovered how artistic productions are used to reinforce, defy, and transform Orthodoxy *from within*, in this chapter we see how artistic productions are mobilized not only to move away from Orthodoxy but to transform it *from outside*, albeit while inevitably feeding stereotypes on certain occasions.

Some ultra-Orthodox women exercise agency by breaking with religious authorities and finding a new authoritative force: the art industry. These public-facing performances exist alongside those limited to women community members, which we explored in previous chapters. The Hasidic women who do not follow Hasidic life anymore and participate in these public-facing performances do not (necessarily) cater to women and girls but move away from religious norms. In their everyday lives, their appearance and dress do not connote Hasidicness: they do not wear *sheytl*, *tikhel*, or skirts, nor do they shave their heads (a custom among many Hasidim). They are openly nonbelievers, casting off the markers of Jewishness in favor of the same clothing worn by North American secularists and liberals. Generally, however, as they may come back to their families and communities from time to time, they reembrace and embody Hasidicness out of respect, a process that keeps them allied with the community.

For her part, Malky remains a painter in her Hasidic community and has been teaching women and girls there for years. Several nights a week, she leaves her apartment in a black dress covering her elbows, knees, and collarbones, thick stockings, flat shoes, and a *tikhel* covering her hair. In these Hasidic clothes, she joins her students at her art garage in the back of her parents' home between Flatbush and Borough Park. There, she guides them in producing still-life, landscape, or portrait paintings using photos for reference, but she also encourages them toward less conventional abstract art. Some students—Jewish and non-Jewish, men and women—also learn art history, as Malky introduces them to the aesthetics and technique of various art schools. Malky knows that most students, even the most talented, will not become professional artists. But she is also conscious of the increasing number of artistic opportunities in their communities, the growing number of Instagram accounts used by female painters to promote their businesses, and the new art studio, Shtetl Gallery, opening in Williamsburg for Hasidic artists, including women.[5] Malky does not discuss her public life with her clients or her family. Some of her siblings are fans and follow her career in theater and cinema, but she carefully restricts with whom she discusses her outside life. She navigates carefully between these disparate social universes, following the norms and rules of each while within it, thereby performing two Malkys: one *frum*, the other secular.

The Hasidic public life is a space of tension. Part of this tension stems from recognizing aspects of Hasidic female cultural identity, such as shaving and covering the hair, restrictive clothing styles, lack of access to certain knowledge, or extreme gender segregation, as sources of external embarrassment once one exits the community. This embarrassment about a certain aspect of Hasidic life, echoing a form of archaism or ignorance in the collective memory of OTD individuals, often reinforces the stereotype of Hasidic identity. However, for former Hasidic artists, it is also a source of capital that is envisaged as common sociability among exiters sharing the same sentiment, a process that Michael Herzfield characterizes as cultural intimacy.[6] The Hasidic woman public artist acts as a "legitimate" figure for mass media and for Yiddish theater, putting on display a culture that is—for many—an object of mystery, fascination, and otherness. As North American cinema and theater increasingly require characters to be played by actors of corresponding racial, ethnic, gender, sexual, and religious identification,[7] Hasidic public artists find a niche in embodying Hasidicness for public audiences and need to conform to these new norms in the entertainment industry. They use acting and consulting to gain agency in re-creating themselves,[8] and the arts are a facilitator of their economic, social, and cultural transition.

The participation of Hasidic women artists in this emerging public culture has led them to investigate new creative means, expanding this culture by providing more realistic and plural depictions of Hasidicness to contest the oft-portrayed image of the invisible ultra-Orthodox woman as antifeminist, backward, and silent. In their work of creating this public culture, these women design and traverse a broad terrain of new relations, activities, and experiences that cannot be themselves public, yet comprise essential aspects of this public culture.[9] Drawing upon anthropologist Andrew Shryock's reflection on the intersection between cultural intimacy and mass mediation, this chapter presents the onstage and offstage lives of Malky Goldman and Melissa Weisz, two leading OTD women artists performing Hasidicness. Their journey is at the center of this chapter because I was able to participate in the making of their public cultural lives over several years. I joined them for online readings and theater rehearsals during the pandemic, festivals, and film shootings. I participated in several informal and formal gatherings in various settings (homes, restaurants, organizations, etc.), spending hours in conversation over the phone, on WhatsApp, and while staying at Malky's New York homes. Ethnography allows us to glimpse a broader reality through the prism of individual lives, and thus this ethnography centered on Malky and Melissa reflects what is happening in the lives of other women artists "trying to make it out there," some becoming public figures of pride for the OTD community and symbols of Hasidic feminine legitimacy in North American cinema and theater. The integration of OTD individuals into North American mainstream media—and more specifically, Yiddish cinema and theater—has created a new genre in public culture.

Hasidic Public Culture in North America

The OTD artists I have met left their communities for various reasons. Many of them were already artists within their communities, as was the case for Malky, and pursue performance careers that transcend their ultra-Orthodox identities. And yet, they seem preoccupied with what they perceived as and referred to as legitimate or authentic representations of their communities. Over the years, I discussed the idea of legitimate or authentic representation with Malky, Melissa, and many of their peers, including men, trying to understand what they implied by this very subjective concept. As former Hasidic Jews, they were able to translate the culture for a public audience, while Hasidim do not traditionally engage with secular media and cinema. And they knowingly acknowledged the responsibility that came with publicly performing Hasidicness. Authenticity correlates with the legitimization of the representation. In other words, an authentic representation is expressed by someone who has an experience from inside, who is coming from the community, or who has captured the experience from within to create the representation. In this debate about the representation of minority identities, scholars in performance studies, ethnomusicology, and film studies have argued for structural changes, visibility, and inclusion of performers from minority groups so that they are represented. In the early 2000s, critiques concerning the legitimate representation of Hasidic characters were connected to Jewishness; now, the focus falls instead on Hasidicness.[10] This shift drastically altered the meaning of legitimacy in this context, greatly affecting the representation not only of ultra-Orthodox Jews but of minorities in general in the mass media.

North American representation of Jewish culture has been largely homogenized, separated into a simplistic binary of Jewish and non-Jewish. As Nathan Abrams stated in his analysis of Jewish representation in film, cinema tended to define Jewishness in secular ethnic rather than religious terms.[11] Even though early cinematic representations of Jews were predicated on nineteenth-century racialized notions of Jewish identity,[12] they rapidly shifted to simply obscuring Jewishness altogether, with Jewish Americans becoming white, invisible, and assimilated to society.[13] Jews involved in cinema hid their ethnic and religious heritage to widen the appeal of their productions. As Abrams points out, we can count a few exceptions, with *The Chosen* (dir. Jeremy Kagan, 1981), *Yentl* (dir. Barbra Streisand, 1983), and *Driving Miss Daisy* (dir. Bruce Beresford, 1989), "but the general trend was to render Judaism invisible, or where represented, de-Semitised, de-contextualized, universalized, caricatured and only very occasionally realistic."[14] When Orthodoxy was represented, it was usually Hasidic and more broadly ultra-Orthodox, as Hasidism is the most obviously distinctive branch of Judaism. Prior to this moment, the performance of Hasidicness on stage and screen had represented an ostensibly visible and obvious religious minority. Occurring as a way to make visible religiosity that distinguished Jews from white Americans, this representation conflicted with the assimilated Jew passing as white.[15]

We can trace the multiple meanings of the imagery presented in screenings of Hasidicness—and more broadly, of Orthodoxy—as it changed through time. Since assimilated and invisible Jews or non-Jews often made these representations, they often combine rejection, nostalgia, and the romanticization of Hasidic culture, thereby orientalizing Hasidic life from yet another angle. For instance, in Yiddish theater written by secular and assimilated Jews, the figure of the Hasidic Jewish man often served to critique, mock, or romanticize religious culture and mysticism.[16] In the cinema of the 1970s, Jewishness qua Hasidicness highlighted ethnic revival and multiculturalism.[17] In the late 1990s and early 2000s, cinema presented the ultra-Orthodox Jewish man in a proliferating range of extreme guises: as a murderer, gangster, drug smuggler, rocker, intellectual, or clergy member.[18] All these representations were contextualized within the broader interest in ethnic and religious minority groups.[19] Still, these voices from within ultra-Orthodoxy were ignored, silent, or inaccessible, because insiders were unwilling to engage with secular society.

Throughout the development of this Hasidic imagery, male characters remained central, while women were often characterized as objects or as visible only through their connection to a religious man.[20] Cinema of the twentieth century rarely features Hasidic women characters in primary roles, since unlike Hasidic men's clothing (which visibly marked them as Hasidic), Hasidic women's clothing is more ambiguous and might be interpreted as simply culturally neutral modest attire.

Contrary to other racial, ethnic, gender, and sexual minorities searching for public recognition in North American cinema and mass media,[21] Hasidic and other ultra-Orthodox Jews did not engage with their depictions. When the movement emerged for better representation of minorities in casting and for awareness of cultural appropriation, it appears that Jewish identity was enough to grant legitimacy to the representations of Hasidicness. During the Broadway revival of *Fiddler on the Roof* in 2004, Alfred Molina, a non-Jewish actor, was chosen to play Tevye. The decision was heavily criticized. Yet these criticisms concerned his non-Jewishness, not his position as non-Orthodox, implicitly suggesting that a non-Orthodox Jew would have sufficed to play the role, when in fact the tension and misconceptions between Orthodox and non-Orthodox Jews can be extreme.[22] So can we assume that a liberal and secular American Jew would have the background and knowledge to understand and play the role of an ultra-Orthodox/Hasidic character, especially knowing of the tension between liberal and Orthodox Jewish communities in North America?

In the late 2000s, the performance of Hasidicness progressively shifted as OTD communities and institutions emerged. Several individuals published their stories during and after transitioning from Hasidic to secular culture, which brought greater visibility to these organizations searching for donors. Some even became bestselling authors.[23] Many were already performers in their communities and were searching for exposure in the broader, mainstream entertainment industry. These OTD narratives caught the attention of filmmakers and other industry professionals. Ultra-Orthodox Jews began to be hired as consultants or actors (though typically for secondary or minor roles), legitimating the depictions of Hasidicness made by outsiders. Today, for many in the film and theater industry, working with Jewish actors is not enough; performers of Hasidicness must have deep knowledge or personal connection with the Hasidic world to prevent the criticism of cultural appropriation. This shift has been a way to simultaneously recognize the struggles of Jews leaving ultra-Orthodoxy and open doors for them to the entertainment industry.

This new Hasidic public culture that former ultra-Orthodox Jews participated in took various forms: documentaries, films, television series, and even reality shows. Those financed by mainstream media or produced by outsiders often keep to a common narrative, focusing on religious women's trajectory through suffering and distress.[24] The productions that do not reiterate this hyperbolic portrayal are usually produced in Israel, certainly because of the closer reciprocity between religiosity and liberal ideas in society at large as well as the growing institutions serving Orthodox Jewish artists—as in the case of *Shtisel* (2021), for which the third season was produced and distributed by Netflix after the show's success in Israel for the first two seasons—or they are short films or smaller productions, but these are not as popular as the sensationalist depictions.

Visual media have never been as instrumental in our society as they are today, supplanting texts as the primary method of knowledge acquisition and taking the form of a global billion-dollar film industry.[25] Viewed in the comfort of our own homes through streaming platforms, visual media and streaming have become an incredibly influential tool in the making, reinforcing, or contesting of representations and narratives about identities.[26] As the leading platform, Netflix has succeeded in reaching a global audience, contributing significantly to viewers' knowledge and perceptions of many topics. With the growing mediatization of ultra-Orthodox Jewish life in North America on this platform, which is almost exclusively depicted through the experience of leaving the community, Netflix allows viewers to learn about the community through the gazes of those who have left it.

Within this new public culture, four North American productions have received special attention in their national context as well as internationally, all of them available on popular streaming platforms. Three were distributed by Netflix as "Netflix originals"—meaning that they are exclusive to its platform, and sometimes fully financed by the company—and the fourth is now available on Amazon Prime.

These four productions were acclaimed by critics, received international coverage, and disseminated a global image of Hasidicness tinted with realism and legitimacy on account of having OTD actors, consultants, and interviewees. The representation of Hasidicness on screen goes beyond these four productions, but these recent and globally distributed media loom large, and their focus on women's suffering hugely impacts the depictions of Hasidicness in the public space, disseminating a global representation centered on the religious women who need to be saved by secularism, liberalism, and a feminism that sees women's agency exclusively in terms of her public exposure.

			Major North American Productions Featuring Ex-Hasidic Women		
Release Year	Name	Distribution	Genre	Creation and Direction	Country
2014	*Félix et Meira*	FunFilm (available on Amazon Prime)	Fiction	Directed by Maxime Giroux; written by Maxime Giroux and Alexandre Laferrière	Canada
2017	*One of Us*	Netflix	Documentary	Directed and written by Heidi Ewing and Rachel Grady	USA
2020	*Unorthodox*	Netflix	Miniseries (inspired by Deborah Feldman's 2012 autobiography)	Directed by Maria Schrader; written by Anna Winger and Alexa Karolinski	Germany/ USA
2021	*My Unorthodox Life*	Netflix	TV Reality	Executive producers Jeff Jenkins, Ross Weintraub, Reinout Oerlemans, and Julia Haarts	USA

In this new Hasidic public media, the focus on women's suffering and liberation developed alongside the orientalist gaze after 9/11, when the figure of the oppressed Muslim woman became central to mainstream media.[27] Through the figure of the terrorist, Islam was presented as a threat to the nation and mediatized as an uncivilized culture in which violent male despots oppress subdued women.[28] Even though the representation of the Middle East has multiple dimensions, including an exoticism that renders the Islamic world as a place of Western desires, the image of the Muslim woman covering her hair with a *hijab* is often perceived and presented by certain liberal feminists as the collective emblem of backwardness, oppression, and abuse.[29] While some scholars argue that the ten-year period following 9/11 saw a tendency to reconstruct more convincing Muslim and Arab cinematic characters,[30] the narrative of the Muslim, and especially the Muslim woman, who needs to become assimilated (like other minorities in the United States) and be saved by the "West" is still preeminent.

Hasidic women are also figures of otherness in contemporary North American society, presented as controlled by men and hiding beneath modest clothing and hair coverings. Yet as opposed to the Muslim woman, who is often made to embody a subject foreign to the West, the figure of the Hasidic woman embodies a firmly North American (and growing) demographic. Ultra-Orthodox Jews may exemplify fundamentalism, but contrary to Islam, this fundamentalism can be more easily transformed to become liberal, secular, and white, as exemplified by secular and liberal Jews. Some minority groups toward whom American cinema has been prejudicial have received better representation through Americanization,[31] but ultra-Orthodox Jews still embody the mystery of the American other.

In these public media representations, women's narratives of suffering in religious communities and of the need to exit appear particularly central. Scripts nourishing liberal feminist views on women and religion while simultaneously taking a sensationalist tack by offering the "legitimate" and "authentic" voices of suffering women who needed to leave their community have successfully engaged a general audience. Using sensationalist means to attract the largest number of viewers/readers and to bring attention to a cause is nothing new, as stated by media scholar Mitchel Stephens and economist Alberto Gabriele.[32]

By exposing the suffering of women who left their Hasidic communities and by using the presence of Hasidic women actors who left these worlds, media producers amplify the voices of these individuals and their communities, while also imbuing their media products with a feeling of authenticity and legitimacy. Because ultra-Orthodox Jews do not engage with public mass media, those who leave the ultra-Orthodox world become legitimate voices on public screens and scenes. Even though they are not observant of Orthodox Judaism anymore, these individuals often defend their Hasidic/Orthodox culture and identity, firmly insisting on their ability to deliver a complex and unromanticized image of its reality. If in the past Jewish actors were able to portray Hasidic characters, the industry of film and theater does not seem satisfied anymore; the cultural reality of a Hasidic Jew is now acknowledged to be drastically different from that of a secular, liberal North American Jew. The recognition of internal diversity within these broad racial and ethnic categories has thus become central to the public representation of minorities.

The Actress-Consultant

In 2017, during my months of research and exploration of the Hasidic underground scene in New York, I met an OTD actress and consultant for cinema and theater: Melissa Weisz. She invited me to her Williamsburg apartment. We chatted for hours about her transition out of Orthodoxy and her experience as a lesbian, her loyalty to Hasidic Jews, her admiration of religious women, and the arduous, powerful, and liberating nature of the public art industry. Despite choosing to leave her religious life and community, Melissa has a good relationship with her family. She regularly attends *simkhas*, visits her parents and siblings for Jewish holidays and *shabbes*—during which she wears *tsnius* clothing—and even works on a podcast with her father. Having grown up in what she describes as an open-minded Satmar family in Borough Park, Melissa speaks of her childhood as joyful, vibrant, and animated, and describes her sisters as passionate women, full of opinion. As she mentioned, Melissa was considered to be an atypically curious Hasidic girl. She wanted to learn more about Jewish law and texts. She went to seminary in English where she studied before getting married, which is uncommon for a Satmar woman. When she returned from seminary, her parents made a *shiddukh* with a boy similar to her in this respect of not being "typical." She married at nineteen, fought to keep her hair rather than follow Hasidic culture and shave it, explored secular film and other media with her husband, and enrolled in Touro College, a private Jewish university with Orthodox leadership, to study psychology. Melissa and her husband agreed on not immediately having children; they were both looking for a different life, one outside the boundaries of stringent Hasidism, which would have expected them to get pregnant right after the marriage. After four years of marriage, her husband wanted to have a family and at that point, when she had begun to increasingly pursue activities outside the norms of Orthodox life, they were on different paths. They divorced. She described her marriage as loving and cooperative and speaks about her ex-husband as someone she cares for, who was devoted and supportive of all her choices.

Melissa's aspiration for a different path encouraged her to move away from her family and community circles, and then to search for an apartment on her own. She heard about Footsteps, an organization offering various services to people who have chosen to leave their ultra-Orthodox communities. The organization helped her to find an apartment and then assisted her throughout the transition to secular life. In 2010, Lazer Weiss, a former Hasidic Jew and her boyfriend at the time, was working on the Yiddish translation for the movie *Romeo and Juliet in Yiddish*, in which he also acted. He invited Melissa to audition for the role of Juliet. The film's director, Eve Anneberg, a secular Jewish writer, director, and producer, had been seeking a female Hasidic Yiddish speaker for the role. Anneberg had started the film project in 2006, after discovering the weekly gathering called "Thursday Night Chulent," founded by Isaac Schoenfeld in Brooklyn in the 1990s.[33] Thursday Night Chulent is an informal gathering where ultra-Orthodox Jews who feel that they do not fit in their communities meet and socialize with others like themselves as well as with non-Orthodox Jews and non-Jews curious to know more about Hasidic lifestyle. Inspired by this underground Hasidic scene, Anneberg wrote a script for a film in which she imagined Hasidim acting. While Melissa had planned on pursuing a career as a therapist for children with special needs, she was selected for the role, and this opened a new path.

Throughout the years, Melissa has often struggled with the decision of whether to accept or reject artistic projects. Working primarily with outsiders, she has been confronted by a new form of expression involving the exposure of women's bodies, the misrepresentation of Hasidicness, and the difficult rules of the industry. The dilemmas she has faced have required that she negotiate between multiple worlds while trying to be both critical of and faithful to her Hasidic "tribe" and not provoke her potential audience from within the community, including her own family.

Several members of the cast selected by Anneberg for *Romeo and Juliet in Yiddish* were Hasidic Jews, many of whom were transitioning toward leaving ultra-Orthodoxy or simply stood at its margins. For the shoot of the love scene, Anneberg engaged an Oscar-winning cinematographer and, thinking about how to capture Melissa's and Lazer's love affair, suggested a seminude scene to Melissa. While Anneberg had not initially thought about integrating a seminude scene, during the shooting she decided otherwise.[34] The director's and the cinematographer's desire to glimpse Hasidic intimacy, sexuality, and bodies—specifically, women's bodies—echoes the gaze that looks upon the nude female body, especially the "oriental" and "unknown" female body, as beautiful. The romantic scene and the partially exposed body of Melissa, a once-Hasidic woman sensualized on screen, transcend the codes of *tsnius*, and prevent an official Hasidic audience from engaging with the film, including Isaac Schoenfeld, who played a rabbi but accepted the role only on the condition that the film not contain nudity.

Through analysis of anthropological and literary texts, Meyda Yegenoglu demonstrates how the desire to penetrate the veiled surface of "otherness" is constitutive of hegemonic and colonial dynamics. In the context of the power dynamic between Hasidic and liberal Jews, even if Anneberg aspired to create dialogue between the two groups, her decision to unveil the Hasidic bodies while assuring some of the actors that she would not use nudity echoes this hegemonic dynamic. This power dynamic between the secular American Jewish filmmaker and the religious Hasidic Jewish actor exemplifies how our model for analyzing religious, ethnic, and racial identities should be complicated. The category "Jewish" is not sufficient to describe what is at stake regarding the power relations here. This example is particularly interesting in that it amplifies the need to use an intersectional analysis to map power relations and inequalities between the representation of minorities and the larger "unmarked" dominant culture on screen and on stage.[35]

It was during this period, when it came time to be credited in the film, that Melissa, whose given first name is Malky, became Melissa Weisz. She wanted to stay anonymous on paper, to have a less Hasidic name, and to feel "American." *Romeo and Juliet in Yiddish* premiered at the Lincoln Center in New York and won the Gerhardt Klein Audience Award at the Berlin Jewish Film Festival in 2011, a success that impacted Melissa's future, opening the doors to an emerging Hasidic actor–led cinema. Despite any misunderstandings on set about the seminude scene, in 2021 the film was named by Rotten Tomatoes one of the ten best-filmed adaptations of *Romeo and Juliet* of all time, and it prompted the Yiddish New Wave, which features Hasidic and formerly Hasidic actors.

Melissa's transition to the secular world was not easy. She had to navigate a world that she was unfamiliar with, learn new codes, develop new relationships, and then adapt to yet another system, that of the film industry, often characterized by the exploitation of women's bodies.[36] In

THE PUBLIC ARTIST | 199

2016, a few years after her transition from a Hasidic to a secular life, Melissa came out as a lesbian and recorded a video for *NBC News*.[37] As she describes her exit from the Hasidic community, it does not resonate with the scandalous stories of women victims and male abusers that are portrayed in mainstream media.[38] Her journey involved an amicable divorce (where love yet remained) and a family accepting of her coming out as a lesbian. She is now a public artist who works with the media, theater, and film industries while publicly criticizing structural gender inequalities and the lack of women's voices in both societies, the one she left and the one she chose. The success of *Romeo and Juliet in Yiddish*, one of the first productions to cast Hasidic Jews, opened the door to this emerging art scene, with new roles for Hasidic actors, such as Melissa's role as Ruth in *Félix and Meira*, the acclaimed Canadian film written and directed by the Quebecois filmmaker Maxime Giroux.

Maxime Giroux knew nothing about Hasidim but was curious about and charmed by their culture. He was inspired by living in the Montreal neighborhood of Mile End, where the largest Hasidic community in Canada resides alongside other Quebecers, whether francophone, anglophone, or allophone.[39] With screenwriter Alexandre Laferrière, Giroux imagined a love story between Félix (a Quebecois man) and Meira (a Hasidic woman). Meira joyfully discovers secular music and clothes and flirts with the secular and francophone Félix, an independent but lonely man. For Giroux, the film was a way to learn about Hasidic culture. First, he hired a woman who grew up in the Chabad-Lubavitch communities in Canada to serve as a consultant on the script's first draft. Later, great care was taken with casting, and he and his team hired and worked closely with Melissa and another Hasidic actor, Luzer Twersky. Despite his collaboration, stereotypes concerning Hasidic women's personalities and experiences were part of the script and even discernible on screen.[40] Melissa initially read the script for the lead role and auditioned a few weeks later. She remembered being enchanted by both the love story—a well-articulated narrative in which she recognized the Hasidic world—and the welcoming attitude of the production team:

> When I read it, I recognize[d] a form of authenticity, meaning that some part of the script I could relate to, and I understood the world they described. I believe[d] the world the characters I was reading about were

in—something that does not happen that often with a script written by outsiders. For instance, in the Hollywood movie *Disobedience*, directed by Sebastian Lelio with Rachel Weisz and Rachel McAdams as actresses, I could not recognize these people and their world. They were not Hasidic, I know, they were Litvish, but I also lived among this community in Manchester, and I could not recognize them.[41]

However, Melissa was somewhat dismayed to learn that they decided to give her a smaller supporting role in the film. Her personality did not fit with the role of Meira, they told her—she was too tall, too striking, too passionate, too sharp, and not Hasidic enough. They had certainly been extremely respectful of what she had to say about the script, but they also had a very clear idea about the type of Hasidic woman and actress they wanted for the main role. Influenced by stereotypes of religious women as invisible, backward, and oppressed, the producers imagined Meira as short, slightly curved, shy, disempowered, and lost—someone who would find agency and freedom through her relationship with Félix. The narrative of the invisible religious woman finding liberation thanks to the secular white man is part of many on-screen narratives, a trope this film could not escape despite the input of a Hasidic woman consultant. In terms of casting, Giroux was also concerned with finding actors who might raise the film's profile; he had heard about Israeli secular actress Hadas Yaron, who had just won the Volpi Cup for Best Actress at the Venice Film Festival as well as Best Actress at the Ophir Awards (often called the Israeli Oscars). She was eventually cast for the role.

Melissa's consulting work influenced several aspects of the film, including body language, dialogue, Yiddish, set design, and costume. Still, she was not able to alter their ideas about Hasidic women's personalities, specifically concerning those women who desired to leave the community. Indeed, due to her regular consulting work with filmmakers wanting to cast Hasidim in their projects, Melissa has observed several patterns regarding the way Hasidic Jews are perceived and portrayed:

People have weird ideas about how someone looks Hasidic, and even more one who wants to leave. They often told me that I do not look Hasidic, because I am too tall, too blond, and I have blue eyes. My story is not the one fitting the expectation. I know women suffering in the community, but I also know women suffering in the industry. Women who want to leave are often portrayed experiencing trauma, abuse, or depression; and simply reinforcing the stereotype about us OTD as well as the way the community sees us. But my story, and one of many others, is not about that. This idea of weakness is at the core of the narrative, and I still do not understand why it is so hard to go beyond such stereotypical portrayals to sell a story about Hasidic women. I remember even that for the shooting of *Romeo and Juliet*, Eve Anneberg makes me responsible for a mistake on purpose during the shooting of a scene. She told me that she wanted me to be weaker and confused as she imagined the role of Juliet speaking in Yiddish. Is it Juliet that has to be confused and weak; or is it Juliet, Hasidic, who has to be?

Felix and Meira premiered at the 2014 Toronto International Film Festival, where it was extremely well received, winning the Award for Best Canadian film as well as many other awards and nominations.[42] It was selected as the Canadian entry for the Best Foreign Language Film at the eighty-eighth Academy Awards. The film was acclaimed by a broad audience,[43] with critics pointing to the male protagonist's loneliness and presenting the narrative as about "two lost souls seeking love" or "two alienated characters."[44] Others interpreted the film as evidence that the Hasidic community does not permit women to feel alive,[45] while yet others believed it succumbed to the cliché of the secular man rescuing the oppressed religious woman who has a sense of obligation to her community.[46]

In the end, despite its aims, Giroux's film did not contribute to the visibility of Hasidic women. Regrettably, Giroux missed an opportunity to give voice to Hasidic women, who might have given more nuance to the depiction of these women's experiences. Giroux and his team fell into the same trap they imagined their character was caught in. While it is true that a film is a product often dictated by the law of the market, when art portrays identities, it also shapes collective memory and creates stereotypes that are not without consequences.

Melissa Weisz never expressed this thought; she always felt that the team was extremely respectful and receptive to her ideas. But our long conversation about gender roles and gender dynamics in the film industry brought me to this connection and revealed a certain paradox. Melissa was always aware that her position as actress-consultant would be part of the narrative that would facilitate the film's claim of legitimacy, and that her contribution might reinforce incorrect and harmful stereotypes about Hasidicness within the North American collective imagination. Nevertheless, she was also mindful of the fact that it would open doors, potentially leading to new professional and economic opportunities where her contributions might have a greater impact on the public narrative about Hasidic women. Indeed, following the film's success, Melissa was interviewed about her personal trajectory, which contrasts greatly with that of Meira.[47] She also imagined that the public would see the paradox of gender hegemony within the film industry, something that continues to push her to collaborate more with women and advocate for their visibility in film and theater.

After the success of *Felix and Meira*, Melissa took another step in claiming her identity: she came out as queer. Now an OTD public figure and a testament to the success of the organization Footsteps,[48] Melissa has focused on writing, producing, and acting for projects that offer empowerment and voices to Hasidic women in the arts. To counter the dramatized images of Hasidic women found in mainstream media, she joined forces with Malky Goldman to create a production company, Malky Squared Productions.

The Art Director-Actress

An artist recognized in both the religious and secular worlds, Malky Goldman occupies a distinctive position. Her constant movement between religious and secular artistic lives puts her constantly to the test. Even now, she has never been able to choose between them. Her journey from Mea Shearim painter to Toronto International Film Festival–attending Hasidic public artist underlines former Hasidic women's agency within the arts and aspiration to transform their artistic environments.

Born in the ultra-Orthodox Jerusalem neighborhood of Mea Shearim, Malky moved to Borough Park, New York, with her parents as a teenager. At the time, Malky was already an atypical girl for a dynastic rabbinical family. Well-behaved at school, she also loved painting and was charming yeshiva boys who came to her father's home for study. Her painting followed the norms of Haredi art: religious men, still-life objects, or geometrical forms. At twenty-two, she married a Hasidic boy from Williamsburg and shaved her hair, covering it with a *shpitzel*, as is the custom in her family. Malky had not wanted to marry this boy, but her parents, coming from a rabbinical dynasty, wanted the best for her and were certain it would be a good match. Malky divorced him a few weeks after the wedding and claimed her independence, demanding that she be able to rent her own apartment. Her parents, feeling guilty about the unsuccessful *shiddukh*, agreed to the arrangement and never again discussed her commitment to Hasidic life. She began searching for new ways to explore the world and the arts beyond the Hasidic model. She joined Footsteps and enrolled in Touro College to study fine arts, developing new friendships with women and men who had experienced similar clashes. At Footsteps, she met Melissa Weisz, who was starting her career as an actress, and with whom she established a cherished relationship that would lead to professional partnerships.

While doing so, Malky continued to teach fine arts within the Hasidic community, wearing her *shpitzel* and *frum* clothing. With her *frum* students, she discusses philosophy and themes such as freedom and choice, and she pushes many of them to innovate: to paint abstract art or women's faces (even if they must hide the painting in their bedroom), and to explore the "impossible." As a divorcee without children, Malky is not worried about her reputation. Her studio is private, and even though her fine arts classes are open to anyone in the community, she primarily works with clients who met her before her marriage, as well as with at-risk individuals or those having "special needs," as they are labeled in the community—those searching for experience outside the box.

Though all these changes were happening in her life, Malky never "came out" as OTD to her clients, nor to her family, always visiting them as her *tsnius* self. She often laughs about her "two parallel full lives," as she calls them. She does not hide her secular life; she is visible in films, at festivals, and in newspapers, but does not force the ones she loves to see her without a hair covering, in jeans and a short top, as she believes many of them would be extremely hurt. They also do not search out information about her other life; "don't ask, don't tell" is her mantra when she describes her relationship with her family and her clients. Some of

Figure 6.2: Malky in her Brooklyn studio, September 2020 (credit Yoseph Horowitz).

them know about her artistic life outside the community—they watch her performances and follow her on Instagram—but Malky is uncomfortable discussing it openly with them. Navigating both universes is not without its difficulties, but she wants to effect change in the community and believes in the potential transformations she can make from within her family and community.

Malky's first gig as an artist in the film industry came from her connection with the underground Hasidic scene in Brooklyn—specifically, Isaac Schoenfeld's Thursday Night Chulent, which had also inspired Eve Anneberg, as we saw earlier. She became a cultural and artistic advisor during the shooting for the film *Fading Gigolo*, written and directed by

John Turturro. Turturro needed someone to guide Vanessa Paradis in her performance of the Hasidic widow Avigail, but also to consult on costume and set design. Schoenfeld, who was already consulting on the film, immediately thought of Malky due to her position in and familiarity with both secular and Hasidic worlds. Malky spent hours reading the script with Paradis and consulting on other aspects of the film, even providing her own paintings to decorate Avigal's home. She was unfamiliar with the film industry but passionate about cinema. She imagined it as another professional path in addition to her work in fine arts. At the time, she had just transferred to Hunter College and had started to take acting classes there and at the Susan Batson Studio, opening the doors not only to the film industry but also to the Yiddish theater.

Yiddish theater has entered a new phase thanks to a community of native speakers who have advocated for the use of Hasidic Yiddish onstage—people like Malky. In the summer of 2016, Miléna Kartowski-Aïach, a French anthropologist and performer specializing in Yiddish theater searching to connect with native Yiddish speakers, sent out a call for OTD artists in New York to take part in an experimental theater uniting ultra-Orthodox and secular worlds.[49] The project, entitled Fray mit an Emes (Free with a Truth), was a collaboration among Footsteps, the New Yiddish Rep, and the Workmen's Circle in which actors would explore their journeys away from the Hasidic world,[50] reenacting their experiences and struggles in their mother tongue in Yinglish (mix of Yiddish and English primarily spoken by Hasidic women). The week-long experimental theater lab was concluded by a public work session at St. Mark's Theater. Almost all participants joined the New Yiddish Rep, and so the secular French scholar's project served as a bridge that allowed these Hasidic performers to develop partnerships in an entirely new cultural milieu—Yiddish theater—through which they could expand their opportunities and contribute to the diversification of the Yiddish language in public culture. A few months after Kartowski-Aïach's project (which extended into 2017), Malky and Melissa were recruited for God of Vengeance and various other plays and films, though they would continue to be challenged by gender inequality in the distribution of roles.

Theater was the start of Malky's journey into public performance, but her aspiration was to pursue a career in film. One film jump-started

Figure 6.3: Experimental theater, July 2016. *From left to right*: Melissa Weisz, Malky Goldman, Goldie Hoffman, Lili Rosen, Luzer Twersky (credit Ralph Gabriner).

Figure 6.4: Experimental theater, July 2016. *From left to right*: Malky Goldman, Luzer Twersky, Goldie Hoffman, Lili Rosen, Melissa Weisz (credit Ralph Gabriner).

her career, and I was lucky enough to witness her in it. On November 29, 2018, I arrived in Brighton Beach, Brooklyn, for the shooting of *The Vigil*, a Hasidic horror movie written and directed by Keith Thomas. One of the executive producers was Danny Finkelman, an Orthodox film director who in 2009 founded the production company Sparks Next, which specializes in Jewish Orthodox and Hasidic cultures. Malky had been working with Finkelman for several years as an art director, associate producer, and actress. As one of the executive producers of *The Vigil*, he introduced her to the production team as a potential set designer, Yiddish consultant, and actress. The director wanted to work with Hasidim but knew it would be difficult to do so with someone with no experience with the industry. Since three of the producers were modern Orthodox, they considered the perfect choice to be OTD actors who did not publicly criticize Orthodoxy or Hasidic culture. Malky was one of the rare artists navigating between both worlds—an OTD woman still working in and connected with the community—who met all these criteria.

Malky was thrilled by the project. Not only was she acting, but she was also credited as an associate producer. She described the script as brilliant, and there was little need to make the weighty decisions that ensured her community was portrayed with complexity. As she put it, "It is the first Hasidic horror movie. It is a new way to portray Hasidic culture, connected to the Holocaust, to mysticism, to the culture without sensationalism, without women in need of liberation, and with a group of people from different Jewish backgrounds on the production and acting crew." The story is about Yakov Ronen, a recent Hasidic departee, who serves as *shomer* for a night (watching over a deceased member of his former community) and is targeted by the *Mazzik*, an invisible demon from Jewish folklore. Malky plays Sarah, an OTD woman who flirts with Yakov as she helps him in his transition. It was her first role in a feature film—a Hollywood indie with a budget of approximately a million dollars—for which she was the second-billed woman actress.

The Vigil is full of suspense as well as references to Hasidic culture. It draws from a tradition of portraying Hasidim in unusual settings and using mystical references, and it benefits from hiring practices that privilege representation of the minority portrayed on screen. Writer-director Keith Thomas is a secular Jew, and he imagined the film with

Hasidic Jews speaking Yiddish to grant the film legitimacy.[51] Because the suffering of former Hasidic Jews and notably women is not part of the narrative, the script was perceived as "neutral" in its depiction of Hasidicness, at least by the cast, crew, and critics.

On that day in late November, Malky invited me to experience more closely the shooting of the film. When I arrived, she was preparing the *peyos* (sidelocks) of Dave Davis, who had the lead role of Yakov Ronen, and was verifying the details of the set, which was meant to be an old Hasidic home. I was told that the house where most of the shooting took place had been owned by a deceased *frum* couple. The production team decided to retain all the home's original objects and furniture to give a faithful representation of a home owned by Hasidic Holocaust survivors. Malky brought in her Hasidic paintings to decorate the walls. Because the leading actor was a nonnative Yiddish speaker, Malky sat for hours with him, reading the script and working on his Hasidic male Brooklyn accent. She also advised him on body language, Hasidic life, gender dynamics, and the experience of leaving the community. The goal was to allow Davis, a secular Jew, to incorporate and internalize a Hasidic habitus.

The entire team was extremely welcoming toward me. Producer Raphael Margules, who specialized in horror movies, guided me through the house. He explained how the film would refresh the image of Hasidim and was very proud to let me know that shooting only occurred from Sunday to Thursday, as they did not work on *shabbes*, something extremely rare in the mainstream film industry. When we went to dinner, he happily mentioned that all the meals were kosher. As a modern Orthodox Jew himself—marked as such by his black *kippa*—Margules needed to create a comfortable place for religious Jews. Malky was used to working in an Orthodox setting. Still, it was a new experience for her to be part of such a diverse team, uniting Hasidic, modern Orthodox, conservative, and secular Jews with OTD as well as non-Jews—women and men, all working in front of and behind the camera.

However, despite the presence of women in the cast and on the production team, the cast and the crew were essentially male. When Raphael Margules talked up the religious inclusivity on the set and the absence of sensationalism, he did not seem to be aware that the absence of women could be subject to public criticism. He also did not mention how the film might be perceived as reproducing gender inequality because women had only secondary roles. Of the twenty actors and extras, only four were women, and all had minor roles except for Lynn Cohen, who played the female lead. As an octogenarian, Cohen did not represent the same threat to Hasidic gender dynamics that a younger woman might. Having gone through menopause, she could not be *niddah* (a woman's status during menstruation or a woman who has menstruated and not yet completed the requirement of immersion in a ritual bath, the *mikveh*), and it is not even clear whether she represents a Hasidic woman in the film, as there are only close-up shots of her, and her hair covering (or any other markers of identity) cannot be discerned. The two other women in the main cast are Malky and Lea Kalich, both portraying OTD individuals and appearing for only a few minutes in the entire film. There was also one woman among the extras, Bluma Gross. Thus, the absence of any explicitly Hasidic woman on screen may be taken to replicate their invisibility in public culture.

Malky was therefore not faced with the dilemma of representing Hasidic women in a good light, as they were not depicted on screen. Instead, as a producer, she established the pronunciation of Yiddish, the set design, and the costumes according to Hasidic norms, while as a supporting actress (even though she appears only briefly), she gained some visibility within the industry. While in her previous project Malky often felt creatively constrained by the need to depict Hasidic women, in filming *The Vigil* she felt liberated, able to portray a female character more disconnected from Jewish and Hasidic life.

The dilemma Malky faced with *The Vigil* was not about the representation of Hasidic women but about the lack of women's representation more generally. Nevertheless, while she is vocal about gender inequality in the film industry and mindful of the gender imbalance in the project, she also recognizes the exposure she received from it. As someone still connected to the community through her artistic and teaching work (though no longer religious herself), Malky represented religiosity. She also brought a woman's face and voice to the otherwise masculine production team, a gender imbalance that was quite conspicuous at the film's premiere at the Toronto International Film Festival, where she was the only woman on the entire team to be present. The industry is such that, though they might disagree, performers must play by the rules of those who have the means and authority to make success happen, an act that—as we will now see—Malky and her professional partner, Melissa, embraced when they were contacted by the director of the acclaimed Netflix miniseries *Unorthodox*.

The Players

One of the most controversial projects in which Malky and Melissa played the roles of Hasidic women, and felt conflicted about doing so, was the German-American Netflix limited series *Unorthodox*, produced by German filmmaker Alexa Karolinski. The series aired in April 2020, just as the pandemic and the restrictions that resulted from it pushed everyone further into digital spaces. Thousands of people from all over the world watched the series, which narrates the painful departure of Esty from her Hasidic community, family, and husband in Williamsburg, and her subsequent journey to Berlin. During this unprecedented virtual global moment, the very culture of the women I work with and write about was distributed globally through this show. Writer-director Karolinski, inspired by the real-life story of Deborah Feldman, based the script on Feldman's memoir. But in order to grant the film even further legitimacy, Karolinski and her team also mobilized former ultra-Orthodox Jews to serve in secondary roles, as extras, and as consultants.

Although Deborah Feldman's memoir was a bestseller, it caused controversy among ultra-Orthodox exiters. Some envied the success of the book—one of the first autobiographies by an OTD woman—while others thought she only wrote what she needed to write to be successful, and yet others felt betrayed by her, describing her writing as voyeuristic and dishonest. When I began my research in 2015, I remember finding her book and Shulem Deen's successful memoir in many New York bookstores, where they were marketed as "must read" autobiographies. When I would bring up the books in conversations within OTD circles, some women personally recalled interactions with Feldman that took place during and after her transition from ultra-Orthodoxy, but did not recognize her journey as she portrayed it in the book,[52] especially her description of her husband and her entourage.

Malky and Melissa appear in the miniseries. Malky understood the positive force of the narrative but also had concerns. Hasidim in

Williamsburg would be depicted as uncreative, fundamentalist, and backward, secular Jews and non-Jews in Berlin as brilliant, cosmopolitan, progressive, and artistic. Malky was worried about her participation in such a project, especially since she would be credited as the primary consultant. At the time, she did not know it was a Netflix production, and she demanded a high consultancy rate to make sure that any internal struggles she might have would at least be remunerated. The team, however, decided to work with a man who had already been cast for the show as the rabbi. Nevertheless, when the team came to Brooklyn to shoot the Williamsburg scenes, Malky was brought on as a cultural advisor. Familiar with Hasidic shopping in Borough Park, she bought the male costumes and the necessary accessories for the scene of Pessakh (Passover). At the request of the production team, she also auditioned. They did not have a specific scene for her, but they wanted to offer her an appearance. Melissa was also cast and advised them on an informal basis for the *mikveh* scene.

During the shooting in Brooklyn, Melissa and Malky were the only two actresses from a Hasidic background. All the other female roles were given to secular Israeli Jews. When the miniseries came out, Melissa and Malky were tagged on social media and publicly thanked. But behind the scenes, the two were less enthusiastic. During our conversations at the *shabbes* table, over the phone, and on Zoom, they were very anxious about the show's impact on the perception of Hasidim. Despite the welcome reception it found on social media among many exiters, Melissa remained critical, voicing her lack of power in such circumstances. Malky was silent when the show came out. She did not advertise it or post anything on her social media account. And she would prefer to not engage in a public conversation about it. Throughout our exchange, she made it clear that she participated mostly for the credit on IMDb and so that she might add it to her biography. In other words, she did it for her career, and having only a small role, she could not have much influence on the final product. We had several conversations about specific scenes. Even though her own wedding night was something she would rather forget, Malky complained that the sex scene between Esty and Yakov reproduced another negative cliché: "Now it was not anymore having sex through a sheet that people will remember about Hasidic people, but having sex without pleasure, without respect for women's bodies, and with family pressure." These sensationalistic depictions concern Malky—she agrees that they can generate conversation, but she also reflects on the harm these exacerbated representations, which do not leave space for other types of images, could do to her own family and community.

For her part, Melissa was invited twice to discuss the miniseries at public events. While acknowledging the beauty of the show's aesthetic, the talent of the actors, and the realistic details in the marriage scene, the costumes, and the mise-en-scène, she also criticized the elements that misrepresented the experience of Hasidic women. In an article by Catherine Genest in *Elle Quebec*, Melissa explained that she has a very good relationship with her parents, and while she is very critical of the Satmar environment in which she was raised, she also wanted people to learn about other aspects of the community.[53] When Lani Santo, the chief executive of Footsteps, asked her to comment on the untold story of the show, Melissa took the opportunity to provide a little more nuance to understandings of Hasidic life:

> It is [a] one-person story. And I think that when people do not know many people of that community, they don't get a sense, they see that story as the way all Hasidic are. The thing I want to talk to is that there was a lot of pain and joy for me. Growing up in a large family, there is so much noise and life; it is not just the serious things you see. People who live in New York often think of Hasidic women as meek, and I think there is so much passion that we do not get to see as much. There is a noise, joy, love, fighting, music, songs, dance; there is life, and that is the part that exists in the community. [In the series] Williamsburg was portrayed [as] bleak, while Berlin was beautiful. I think there is a lot of nuances in Hasidic communities, in any communities, in the humanity, and this is what I would say.

From the first day we met, Malky and Melissa criticized the mediatization of Hasidicness by outsiders who are not familiar with the Hasidic world. *Unorthodox*, even though they participated in it, was the icing on the cake. In this German-American drama, a Hasidic neighborhood in New York—a neighborhood founded by Holocaust survivors—was depicted as obscure and backwards, while Berlin, whose twentieth-century

Figure 6.5: Malky and Melissa in the short film *Tzadeikis,* written and directed by Emily Cheeger, which was shot in 2018 and premiered at the Toronto Jewish Film Festival in 2020 (credit Emily Cheeger).

history is difficult to ignore for many, was portrayed as bright, with no reference to historical German xenophobia or antisemitism. Granddaughters of Holocaust survivors, Melissa and Malky were uncomfortable with the images projected in *Unorthodox.* Ultimately, they both acknowledge that it is a constant dilemma to participate in the entertainment industry, a system that is difficult to access and to change, and that they must at times simply play the game.

For these two women, it is not only a question of outsider versus insider but of understanding nuance and producing accurate artistic representation instead of sensationalistic cinema. And some projects on which they have worked have indeed accomplished this, such as Swedish filmmaker Emily Cheeger's short film *Tzadeikis,* in which both women acted. Growing up in a secular Jewish environment, Cheeger had always been interested in the Hasidic world. As a film student at NYU, she wanted to capture this world on screen. She immersed herself in the Hasidic world of Borough Park, living in the neighborhood and developing many friendships with people in the community, and it shows in her original script for *Tzadeikis.* It allowed her to depict the intricacies of Hasidicness while at the same time offering an artistic version of it, something Malky and Melissa wish to see more of. Nevertheless,

Cheeger's project is an outlier among the many scripts for which Malky and Melissa have been consultants, cultural advisors, and actresses.

In a phone conversation in January 2022, Melissa reminded me why the representation of Hasidic Jews in these media matters, and why they continue to participate in the hopes of effecting change: "When we will gain exponential visibility and power, and when we will have Jewish Hollywood actors from the Hasidic culture, the narrative might change. For now, we do what we can, and we also believe in all our past and current project[s] with the indie movie and community cinema. People think that Jews are all the same, but they are not; and it is important to recognize this diversity, the same as you have in any other community and society."

The Creators

Through their exploration of the industry, Malky and Melissa realized that they could use their Yiddish expertise and Hasidic feminine life knowledge to transform women's representations. They established their own production company, Malky Squared Productions, so the projects they worked on might be free from Hasidic narratives produced by outsiders, engaging implicitly with the broader debates about cultural appropriation in the arts. The company's goal was to support and create projects that give voice to women and better address their stories on stage and on screen, contributing to the diversification of North American representations of Hasidicness.[54] They branded themselves as feminist creators and imagined producing and writing as ways to avoid the frustrations of working with outsiders and provide more accurate representations of women, and especially women in religious minorities. As creators, they eschewed stereotypical representations that reinforce gender clichés, but they must also compromise with actors and others behind the scenes. Their work—motivated by a desire to see Hasidicness represented in public culture—brought them back into the community in surprising ways, as we will see.

The two women began by collaborating with Pearl Gluck, a pioneer in making independent films on Hasidic culture for a general audience. As a filmmaker and professor of film studies at Penn State University, Gluck is a leading figure in Hasidic cinematography. She grew up in a mixed Hasidic family in Williamsburg and Borough Park, and her filmmaking journey began with a collection of stories connected to her roots. Her first production was the documentary film *Divan* (2004), which followed her expedition from Brooklyn to Hungary in search of a couch that had been in her family for years. In this and other projects, both documentary and fiction, Gluck used her experiences and the stories of other former Hasidim to depict Hasidicness with nuance and complexity.

While reconnecting with her roots in the early 2000s, Gluck met other OTD individuals, including some who were creators like her. Back in the 1980s, when she had decided to take a different *derekh* from the one outlined by her Hasidic parents, no supportive groups or institutions existed. Her journey was an individual one, and it was only almost two decades later that she encountered an OTD community. Wanting to depict realistic Hasidic life on screen, she insisted on casting former Hasidic Jews. In 2012, she produced the short film *Where Is Joel Baum* (2012), which features Luzer Twersky, who introduced her to other artists in Footsteps, including Malky and Melissa.

Gluck describes herself as an activist working through the arts to counter the negative portrayal of Hasidic women in media. She uses film to disrupt, ask questions, and tell stories. When she met Malky and Melissa, the three women instantly hit it off, sharing similar opinions and goals. Collaboration among the three artists and their two productions companies (Gluck is the founder of Palinka Pictures) resulted in two short films written by Gluck: *Summer* (2018), which Malky and Melissa coproduced, and *Castle in the Sky* (2022), for which they consulted on the script. Both films address women's lives and agency, the first through narratives of teenage girls exploring their sexuality, and the second through the story of adult women doubting their religious life and exploring the secular art scene. These three women, then, having left their communities, now seek to produce a public culture for Hasidic women, representing their intricate human adventures, their doubts about religion, their choices, their sexual and romantic lives, and their diverse interior beings. They are reshaping Hasidic public culture from within and giving it a feminine dimension.

After the success of *Summer*, which was acclaimed and rewarded at various festivals, Malky and Melissa embarked on another creative venture: the writing of a women-only play for the New Yiddish Rep. This New York theater company had hired them for *God of Vengeance*. The project resulted from a tumultuous exchange between Melissa and David Mandelbaum, the theater's artistic director, about the lack of women's roles and representation in Yiddish theater. Responding to Melissa's feminist critique, Mandelbaum asked her to read *Women's Minyan*, a script by the American-Israeli playwright Naomi Ragen. He proposed that she and Malky translate the play into Yiddish and produce it for the New Yiddish Rep. Both women were extremely moved by the writing, but they adapted it into Yinglish rather than translate it into Yiddish, drawing on experiences they had witnessed among their peers in Brooklyn. Mandelbaum was thrilled by the integration of Hasidic Yiddish in his theater and encouraged the two protagonists in the creative process. Based on the true story of an ultra-Orthodox woman in Israel who fled from her adulterous and abusive husband and was deprived by rabbinical courts of her right to see or speak to her twelve children, *Women's Minyan* resonated with Malky and Melissa. The play became an opportunity to represent the personalities of women whom they themselves knew—and lived with, loved, criticized, or despised—in a public performance. Nevertheless, they kept the custody battle at the core of the narrative. Malky and Melissa embraced this chance to write something about the people still living the life that they had left but still respected and felt affection for.

They began writing the play in late 2017 and named it *Di Froyen* (The Women). It is the first Yiddish play written in Yinglish for a general audience by and about women from the Hasidic world, tackling issues of abuse, agency, and modernity in contemporary North American Hasidic society. It is also a catalyst for the transformation occurring in the public culture of Hasidicness and represents the potential of the arts to create dialogue, even if it involves conflict, among individuals from within the community, those who left, and outsiders. Resulting from artistic, economic, and political debates and choices, *Di Froyen* also reminds us that the arts have raisons d'être that go beyond aesthetics; artworks are the products of markets, and artists must participate in these markets to make their art.

The writing and production of the play involved many debates, disagreements, and compromises about the images and messages Malky and Melissa wanted to include. They both agreed to be careful about the way in which abuse, which is a taboo issue in the community, should be tackled. They did not want the play to contribute to an anti-Hasidic sentiment. This dilemma led them to focus on representing complex and unique personalities for their characters. For these characters, they imagined women they knew in real life and imagined how they would react to the situations depicted in the play. Although the play openly criticizes rabbinical authority, as the abuser comes from an elite rabbinical family, it also emphasizes the ways women contribute to and are complicit in the system, while still being potential agents of change. Thus, while the play depicts abuse, the resistance to acknowledgment of women's suffering, and the weight of men's influence in this culture, it also stresses sisterhood and the desire to create change. Inspired by *Women's Minyan*, *Di Froyen* casts men as invisible, present only through women's conversations about them.

To describe abuse by mirroring the way it is addressed in Hasidic circles, Malky and Melissa created the character of the social worker, Victoria, who would be responsible for verbalizing and elucidating the taboo. As a liberal Jewish woman, this character embodies the dispute between secular and Orthodox Jews and exposes one of the most contentious topics in ultra-Orthodoxy: the clash between Jewish and secular courts. In the play, a Hasidic woman named Pessah Leah comes to visit her children after two years of being banned from visitations by the Jewish court (Beth Din). She is accompanied by the social worker Victoria, who acts as a mediator and translator of the secular court's final decision regarding her visitation rights. The women of Pessah Leah's family welcome her when she arrives, but they deny her rights to visit and express doubt in different ways about her story of abuse. Only one woman, her sister-in-law Hindie, holds back. Perceived as Pessah Leah's ally, Hindie confesses to also having been a victim of her brother. Her revelation marks a turning point in the play and a shift in attitude among the five women, who begin defending Pessah Leah. Pessah Leah leaves the house after her mother-in-law calls Rabbi Aaron, who is presented as the leader and decision maker of the community, to let him know that the lies are over: "Aaron. No. No we didn't send her away. Just the opposite, we know everything! And now we are taking her to see her children. Don't threaten me, Aaron. Don't you fear God? You don't scare me, Aaron. I'm only afraid of one thing: God in heaven, *Hakudesh Burech Hu* [God be blessed]" (English translation by Malky and Melissa).

The play premiered as part of the Yiddish Book Center's Decade of Discovery: Women in Yiddish initiative, at the end of January 2022. It was promoted online and on social media with an image that portrayed Hasidic women as underwater and in darkness, perhaps perpetuating the idea of their inherently oppressed status. David Mandelbaum was involved in designing the promotional poster, but by summarizing the play as one that "lifts the veil on the plight of women in an abusive relationship within the Chasidic community," he neglected the women's agency discernible in the play and erased feminist messages. The advertisement is broadly indicative of how, although Mandelbaum had created this artistic opportunity for Malky and Melissa, there were constant political, economic, and artistic negotiations between them.

While Mandelbaum certainly considered how such language might attract a secular audience, he did not know that the ultra-Orthodox community had been discussing similar issues to those raised in the play: abuse at the hands of religious leaders. In November 2021, sexual abuse allegations publicly emerged against the famous rabbi and author of children's literature Chaim Walder. Walder had been a revered personality, and his case shook the ultra-Orthodox world. It was not the first time that abuse within the Haredi world was publicly exposed; it was, however, the first time such allegations were leveled against someone who embodied elite Haredi society. Called by the Jewish court of Safed in Israel to present himself to face these accusations, Walder refused and took his own life on December 27, 2021. Following his death, tensions were high between religious leaders who claimed that *lashon hara* (disparaging speech) had killed him and others who supported the victims and condemned the religious leaders' response as disgraceful. A further shock came when one of Walder's victims took her own life a few days after his suicide. Some were silenced, and others tried to cover up the scandal, but the mediatization of the tragedy led to fierce debate within *frum* families and communities in the United States, Canada, Europe, Israel, and beyond. *Frum* women spoke out about the need to change attitudes toward abuse, abusers, and their victims. Many artists discussed the ban of Chaim Walder's book, threw out the copies that

Figure 6.6: Poster of *Di Froyen* (credit Vitaly Umansky).

they had in their homes, and debated the broader issue of the artistic product's entanglement with the personality of the artist.[55]

While Malky and Melissa argued for months about the ending of the play, whether it should have an idealistic or a contentious conclusion, this schism ultimately changed each woman's perspectives. Melissa envisioned the end as an apotheosis in which all the women stood in support of Pessah Leah in a sort of reproduction of Hasidic sisterhood as a feminist statement, whereas Malky imagined disagreement among them to give the finale a more realistic tone. Ultimately, Malky agreed to the happier, harmonious ending. Neither of them imagined that their play would put them on the front lines of a very public debate. The discussion in ultra-Orthodox circles following these events caused Malky and Melissa to see their play as something more than fantasy; conversations like the one they depicted on stage could happen—indeed, *were* happening—within the community. Surprised by the changes they saw and by the responses of women to the cascade of events, they began holding a Q&A session after each showing of *Di Froyen*. In these sessions, Malky and Melissa spoke about the correlation between the play and reality, bringing together novices and experts of the Haredi world.

Toward the end of the play's run, a survivor of Chaim Walder wrote a letter to Rabbi Ron Yitzchok Eisenman, rabbi of Congregation Ahavas Israel of Passaic.[56] The letter was published a day after the play's final performance, in the online ultra-Orthodox magazine *Voz Is Neias* (What's New).[57] It contained a criticism of ultra-Orthodox education, specifically of the idea that rabbis are beyond reproach, an idea the letter writer had been taught in school. The letter goes on to advocate for changes in the way rabbis and, more broadly, religious institutions are perceived and presented, changes that Malky and Melissa's play also addressed. The play became relevant not only to Hasidic public culture but to Hasidic communities themselves, where debates now occurred about the future of Chaim Walder's book, the issue of sexual abuse, and the need to let victims speak out.

These events forced Malky and Melissa to think about new opportunities for the future of the play and for their reciprocity with the community. They have considered staging a performance in Brooklyn, in Borough Park, for Hasidic women, and even using ultra-Orthodox actresses—something that is now very possible, as we have seen. *Di*

Froyen may have been written as an idealized depiction of the potential for change within the community, but contemporary events transformed Malky and Melissa's imagined scenario into a sort of realism. The future will tell us whether they achieve their wish of Hasidic women performing the play, but the conversation has already begun, with desire expressed on both sides. As Malky told me after the publication of the victim's letter discussed above, "We wrote *Di Froyen* thinking about the art imitating life; we now hope that the life will imitate our art."

The Public Culture Dilemma

Malky's and Melissa's journeys from Hasidic marriages to North American public stages and screens epitomize the conflicted decisions made by other former ultra-Orthodox women whom I have met to enhance their careers as public artists. They took roles and participated in projects written by outsiders to gain visibility, even though these projects reinforced the very stereotypes that they were fighting against. As actresses, consultants, and art directors, they found themselves locked into images that orientalized and invisibilized the Hasidic women to whom they wanted to give voice. Some of their attempts to combat stereotypes in the industry wound up contributing to them. The paradoxical outcome of all this is what I call "the public culture dilemma."[58] This is the same predicament faced by many other minorities underrepresented in mainstream media. They aspire to better and more diverse representations within the mainstream entertainment industry.

Writing and producing for independent cinema and theater, these creators contribute to our understanding of pluralism within minority groups, challenging the homogenization of such minorities that often occurs in the industry. They embrace Jewishness as a plural category encompassing ethnic, racial, linguistic, economic, and social differences, defending Hasidicness as a separate category that is itself diverse. In this definition of Hasidicness, the observance of *halakha*, Jewish law, is not part of these women's self-identity, as I would say is the case for many of these former Hasidic actors, including men. Hasidism is presented and defined as a singular cultural expression within Judaism disconnected from *Emuna*, belief, and faith. These representations of Hasidicness are not created by liberal Jews who live alongside Hasidim in Brooklyn but remain ignorant of and judgmental toward their way of life. Instead, a more pluralistic representation arises from working with actors and consultants who come from these Orthodox communities, challenging assumptions about Jewishness among the North American public. In 2005, Henry Bial spoke about a double coding that isolates Jewish and non-Jewish audiences but does not recognize and legitimate various Jewish subcategories such as Hasidic, Sephardic, Orthodox, and Jews of color, revealing how the single label "Jewish" does not suffice. To borrow Bial's idea of coding according to the audience, there are multiple codings, which expand the Jewish/non-Jewish binary, and the performance of Hasidicness adds a level of complexity to the concept of double coding. Being Jewish does not have the same impact as being ultra-Orthodox or Hasidic—or even, more specifically, as being an ultra-Orthodox woman.

Hasidic public culture made by outsiders goes beyond the simple action of reinforcing stereotypes. The engagement of outsiders with Hasidic culture can be framed as a means to reshape North American cinema to include more religious, ethnic, and racial diversity. Here I am inspired by the work of anthropologist Erica Lehrer, who analyzed the Polish Gentile engagement with Poland's Jewish heritage not as a superficial fad (as some imagined) but as an opportunity to reimagine the country in pluralist terms. Malky's and Melissa's participation in *Romeo and Juliet*, *Felix and Meira*, *The Vigil*, and *Unorthodox* constituted a step toward writing and producing themselves, where they imagined their contribution to Hasidic public culture in pluralist terms, aiming to diversify and complicate representations of Hasidicness and religiosity on North American stages and screens.

As we saw in previous chapters, women artists who remain inside and serve ultra-Orthodox communities ignore or negotiate with religious authorities to gain agency within the ultra-Orthodox system. This chapter has described negotiations with leaders in the neoliberal arts and entertainment industry, and artists who gained agency by breaking their ties with religious authorities. Artists must always participate in the politics of the industry, and women have a distinctive position in this game because those in charge remain primarily men. They therefore need to capitalize on their gender difference and singularity, adjusting to the norms of their respective systems. From their exit from ultra-Orthodoxy to their entry into the secular art world, Malky and Melissa used the arts as a tool to gain agency in their process of becoming new selves and to facilitate their economic, social, and cultural transition.

Melissa and Malky maintain their attachment to Hasidic culture despite not being visibly marked as Hasidic, and they believe that to understand and accurately portray a culture, one needs an insider's sensibility and knowledge. However, they also acknowledge that changing the industry from within requires them to compromise. Ultimately, the public culture dilemma of underrepresented minorities increases minority presence in industry leadership, even though these representations are sensationalistic. Nevertheless, with ultra-Orthodox Jews, as well with as other self-secluding minority groups such as Mormons or Amish, one may argue that the public culture dilemma is unsolvable because those within such groups refuse to engage with this public culture. The example of Melissa and Malky complicates this argument, as does the recent social-media campaign #myorthodoxlife, created by *frum* women to counter the "negative" portrayal of Orthodoxy on the reality television show *My Life as Unorthodox*.[59]

At first, I imagined the private and public ultra-Orthodox performers as operating in different, perhaps even opposite, manners, but I observed many similarities in the ways they navigate and use their role as women creators in their respective societies. Both use creativity to reshape women's professional and economic opportunities in subtle ways and face the dilemma of their new positionality. The private performer negotiates with religious authorities and disguises the arts as a tool for education, while the public artist negotiates with the entertainment industry and brings realism to religious women characters. Private performers such as Toby and Chaya, discussed earlier, subscribe to the idea of art for its beauty and pleasure, while focusing on the social, educational, and economic role of their creations. Meanwhile, the public performer similarly subscribes to the (impossible) idea of art for its own sake, yet must also respond to the social, economic, and cultural reality of the moment. Malky and Melissa encourage a rethinking of public culture as a means to create new bridges between Orthodoxy and liberal society, catalyzing intricate experiences that might impact social realities from both inside and outside Orthodoxy.

Malky and Melissa are artists who left the Hasidic community, who left their lives as Hasidic wives and potential mothers accountable for the future of *Yiddishkeit*. But when one considers their constant engagement and reciprocity with the Hasidic world, what exactly did they leave behind? They left their marriages, their former partners, their *frum* clothing, and their *sheytl* and *shpitzel*, the last of which they sometimes take back up when they return to visit their family, but they are still connected to the *frumkeit* in various ways. They left their belief in religious authority, their commitment to Jewish laws, religious organizations, schools, and the social and economic services structuring the communities they grew up with. However, they did not leave the part of themselves that matured as a child, as a teenager, and as a young adult, enjoying painting lessons (whether as a teacher or a student), food, Yiddish songs, dances, the sound of children playing, and many other aspects of the ultra-Orthodox world today that allowed them to rise in Yiddish theater and the North American entertainment industry.

Postlude

Arrival: Women Remaking Orthodoxy in the Digital Age

From the stage of a live comedy club to her online performances on Instagram and TikTok, the acclaimed *frum* female sketch comedian Leah Forster, who came out as a queer lesbian living outside Orthodoxy, provokes her audience with humor and satire about the intricacies of Orthodox life. With a variety of references to Hasidic and Orthodox culture—and often performing in distinctively Jewish-accented English—she offers a sharp and provocative social analysis of religious life that is consumed by a variety of Jewish and non-Jewish audiences, including the Haymish Hasidic community. Forster adopts the roles of various ideal-type female characters and engages with diverse subjects and taboos such as *shiddukhim*, work-life balance, coupledom, divorce, modesty, mental health, and motherhood. Her main character, Tichel Tuesday, an old-fashioned *balebusta* Hasidic woman from Williamsburg, has regular epiphanies about creating various businesses in her basement. With this character, Forster parodies the monetization of many activities present in Hasidic circles. Other personas include Shira Dvora, the single, "open-minded Litvish girl" from Lakewood, who is desperate to find a husband and struggles to balance being hip with respecting tradition, and Pessy, the fashionable Hasidic woman who moved from a conservative to a more liberal Orthodox neighborhood and is now divorced, and who misleads her family about her dedication to Jewish law and to modesty.

With humor and wit, Forster exposes the multiple faces of and paradoxes within Orthodoxies while advocating for the acceptance of OTD and queer identities within religious spaces. By performing as these characters, Forster—who left Orthodoxy because she felt restricted in her sexual and artistic life—traces the permeability of the artistic spaces depicted in the previous chapters. Her comedy and trajectory within and outside of Orthodoxy exemplify the network of exchange and contact among the many women I have met and discussed in this book. Her career brilliantly encapsulates how the many *frum* female artistic spaces analyzed in this book distinctly intersect with one another while maintaining their own function and logic.

I met Leah Forster in May 2019 at a café in Flatbush, Brooklyn. Well known as a *frum* female comedian whose stand-up routines incorporate music and song, she had on that day just come from an interview with a documentary film producer. The latter was interested in showcasing her journey from *frum* artistic venues to secular entertainment media. A few days before this encounter, Leah had been recruited for a private event by a *frum* woman from Borough Park, the neighborhood where she had spent her childhood. During our conversation, Leah discussed how she maintained many of her relationships with other *frum* female artists, even though she has been marginalized since the public exposure of her sexuality as a lesbian. Among her over seventy thousand Instagram followers are all the *frum* women invested in the arts discussed in this book. Like her, they post regularly on that social media platform. For many of them, the line between the way they can perform in private and the way they can perform in public spaces is clear. It is a matter of audience. One either limits one's performances to Orthodox circles or seeks out venues where those outside the community might discover one. With this ostensibly sharp division in mind, Leah is one of the artists who blur the line between these different spaces, revealing how the private, modest public, counterpublic, and public art spaces overlap and imbricate even though they exist as separate and distinct spheres.

Leah Forster inhabits a space both within and outside Orthodoxy. She began her career as a *frum* private entertainer and celebrity, and she now performs at comedy clubs for mixed-gender audiences. I first heard about her from some of my Hasidic women friends in Montreal, many of whom believed her to be a great example of women's creativity, originality, and success. After all, Leah became one of the most famous entertainers in the *frum* female world. She was a key figure in the growth of the entertainment scene for and by ultra-Orthodox women in North America, and she has traveled across the globe to perform at packed theaters. She has acted in famous women-only professional productions, sung alongside well-known *frum* female singers, made thousands of girls and women laugh at summer camps, and produced dozens of exclusive musical comedy shows.

Leah's fame spread beyond the ultra-Orthodox community in 2018, when she fell under scrutiny by the secular media, including *CBS New York*, the *New York Daily News*, *The Forward*, and *The Advocate* as rabbis forced two kosher restaurants in Brooklyn to cancel her show because of her sexuality. While Leah was indeed in a relationship with a woman, she had never revealed this information to her fans. At this time, some media outlets presented her as a Jewish Orthodox lesbian comedian, a label she never publicly claimed. Within Orthodox circles, someone had already exposed her private life by posting on social media a photo of her hanging out at a lesbian bar in Manhattan. In 2016, the post went viral within her community and resulted in her resignation from a teaching job at a Hasidic girls' high school and her rejection by some members of her family. At the time of the exposure of her private life without her consent, only her closest friends and collaborators in the *frum* female art worlds knew her sexual orientation. For years, she had two lives; one building a reputation as a high school teacher and comedian in the community, performing around the world; and another spending time with secular friends, pursuing education outside the community, and exploring her sexuality. When Leah was outed in 2018, she had already announced her "retirement" from women-only entertainment. She was transitioning to a life outside the norms of ultra-Orthodoxy: pulling her daughter out of Orthodox school, covering her hair with a hat instead of a wig, and wearing pants and tank tops on certain occasions. As long as her two worlds did not collide, she was perfectly fine, she said. Nevertheless, after a few years of navigating both worlds, her double life became increasingly burdensome. She decided to retire from her career in the *frum* female public space rather than come out publicly about her rejection of the lifestyle required by ultra-Orthodoxy.

After the 2018 scandal, Leah progressively built another career among mixed audiences far from the radars of ultra-Orthodox institutions. Today, ultra-Orthodox religious authorities have prohibited their members from following Leah Forster's comedy, watching her DVDs, or listening to her musical comedy albums, all of which became taboo. However, many Orthodox Jewish stores I visited still carried her work in various formats, on both their physical and their online selling platforms, and I met some ultra-Orthodox Jews who both attended her shows in Manhattan and invited her to perform at private (and unpublicized) events. Women with smartphones or access to social media also mentioned the popularity of Leah's new online comedic persona, "Tichel Tuesday" (*tikhel* being a reference to the headscarf worn by Orthodox women), satirizing Hasidic women in their everyday personal and professional lives, notably their struggles as mothers and wives. Today, Leah Forster uses her notoriety as a stand-up comedian to act as an influencer transforming Orthodoxy and public perceptions of it. With over a hundred thousand followers on Instagram, and over thirteen thousand followers and 130,000 likes on TikTok in June 2023, Leah has fans among a diverse Jewish audience and some non-Jews as well. Through all of this, she has often aligned herself with a certain type of Jewishness connected to Orthodoxy—based not on religious practice or observance of Jewish laws but on cultural identity and affinity.

An Ecology of Orthodoxies

Leah Forster's story—that of a dissident artist achieving fame in multiple *frum* female art spaces—complicates ultra-Orthodox categories of belonging. Her case also reminds us of the consequences and limits of exposing subversive practices in these contexts. Throughout this book, we have discovered how the private performer, the celebrity, and the influencer defy social norms through the arts to offer new ways of Orthodox womanhood. They are all aware of the limits dictated by their Orthodox communities and work within these limits to engage their creativity without being excluded. Leah Forster, too, followed this process, but revealing her subversive sexuality crossed those limits and led to her exclusion. On the other hand, we have learned how the experience of exclusion can be instrumentalized and politicized outside Orthodoxy to consolidate secular and liberal norms and discourse. The publicizing of Leah's subversive sexual practices resulted in professional and economic opportunities, allowing her to expand her audience to include men as well as women, both Jews and non-Jews. In their rhetoric, both Orthodox and secular spheres reinforced the boundaries of belonging to their systems, but individuals' lived experiences highlight the nuanced paradoxes of these spheres and the spaces between them existing within and outside Orthodoxy.

The strategies women use to gain visibility in the arts, earn *parnasse*, and transform Orthodoxy from within and without depend on the particular Orthodox space in which they operate. Even though many women were able to navigate from one space to another—as private performers, celebrities, influencers, or public artists—they performed differently in these spaces. The performance, voicing, and visibility of female Orthodoxy is thus contingent on not only individuality but also, most importantly, the collective expectations of the immediate audience. Forster changed strategies as she passed through different boundaries of belonging—first, within Orthodoxy, as a stand-up comedian for women only; then, outside Orthodoxy, for a mixed-gender audience. Initially considered a *frum* female celebrity, she retained some Orthodox fans when she began her career outside the community, encouraging her to maintain bridges between these multiple worlds. Because she transitioned from being an internal to an external celebrity, Forster does not belong to a specific chapter in this book, but rather represents movement between the worlds the chapters explore. While each chapter focused on the strategies women developed in specific environments—the private, the modest *tsnius* public, the counterpublic, and the public—these categories are not siloed, and some women, like Forster, transcend them.

I have written this postlude as a story of arrival that mirrors the prelude, an arrival led by the ethnography: the rethinking of Orthodoxy through women. While the book has underlined how ultra-Orthodox and former ultra-Orthodox women invest in specific artistic spaces to reshape Orthodoxy, this postlude concludes with a discussion of the broader implications of these women's artistic investments for the future of Orthodoxy and of the interactional dimension of these spaces—something hinted at throughout the book. The *frum* female art worlds reveal the multiple shapes of Orthodoxy and the interconnection and interdependence among them and with society at large. With their translocal dimension, *frum* female art worlds reveal how the ethnographic study of groups within conservative religious communities can help us understand how modernity reshapes religion, and vice versa.

As we have seen, the private performer consumes art from the modest public and the counterpublic spaces, often looking to the public space to understand how she is represented. Such was the strategy of some of the women performing in a band or owning a dance studio. The *frum* female celebrity, meanwhile, feeds the private performer with her productions, often participating in the counterpublic when there is a social media campaign—she likes, reposts, or tags the campaign, and connects with the public artist by watching her perform or hiring her for other productions. Our examples here are various online postings normalizing women's participation in arts businesses, as well as the social media campaign to force husbands to give Jewish divorces to their wives (#freechava), criticism of public representation of Orthodoxy (#myorthodoxlife), or advocacy for the publication of women's faces (#frumwomenhavefaces). While the public artist can perform in the modest public space, she is also inspired by the private performer to translate Orthodox female life to a public audience outside of Orthodoxy, sometimes cooperating with the influencer to transform Orthodoxy from within, as Malky Goldman, Melissa Weisz, or Riki Rose did.

I thus see the four artistic spaces presented in this book as part of an ecology, as described by the anthropologist Gregory Bateson.[1] As the schema in figure P.1 describes, there is both connection and division within each space. I envisage each space as related but having a distinct purpose and mechanism. By using the term "ecology," I draw on the theoretical work of social scientists, who borrowed the word from biologists to describe how social structures of certain environments interact with each other.[2] In line with this thinking, this ecology of Orthodoxies is connected to the broader social ecology of North America and the world. The four spaces (private, modest public, counterpublic, and public) are like heterogeneous elements; each space is necessary to produce equilibrium in redefining publicness and privacy according to and beyond the dictates of religious authorities. With these dynamics of change occurring in each space, the art worlds and conservative religious worlds coexist despite their divergence. This interconnected model of Jewish Orthodoxies can be useful for understanding other religious groups who define themselves as creators of alternative modernities.

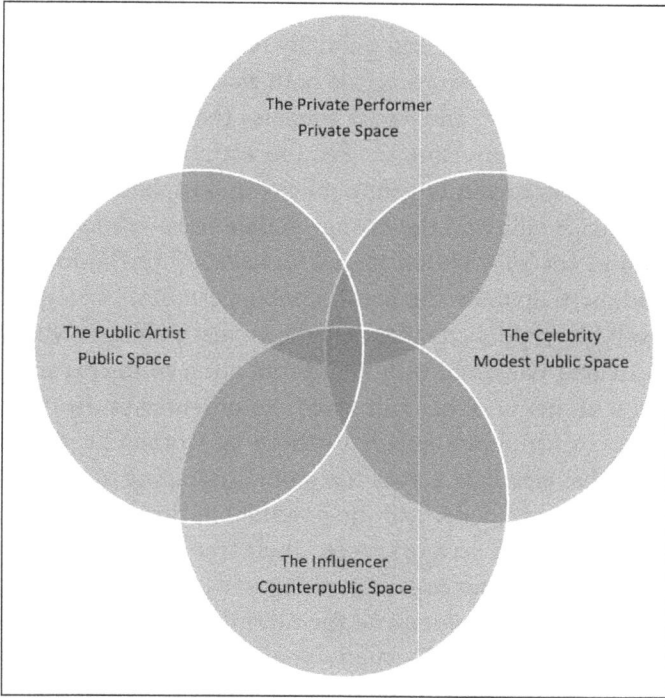

Figure P.1: Diagram illustrating the zones of contact and separation between the four artistic spaces discussed in the book.

Art Worlds, Religious Worlds, and the Digital

Art worlds and religious worlds in conservative circles might appear to be incompatible.[3] Art worlds serve as places to transcend norms. In some cases, the arts have occasioned a break with, transformation of, or reimagination of religiosity.[4] For instance, within Jewish Orthodoxy, singers sometimes seek out venues where they are not supposed to appear.[5] The dialogue between art and religiosity may challenge many Jewish male artists (especially singers) regarding the meaning of their performances. Nevertheless, their identities as performers have never been controversial, unlike those of women artists, whose raison d'être is to resist the norms of *tsnius*.[6] Conservative religious worlds compel invisibility, women's concealed names, faces, and voices, while art worlds require exposure, visibility, and publicity for art and artist. Despite this tension, *frum* female artists reconcile both worlds by mobilizing the digital, claiming economic and social agencies that allow them to inhabit Orthodoxy as they envision it. Female artists within Orthodoxies develop diverse strategies to gain publicity and expand their businesses through social media and the kosher female press while acknowledging *tsnius* and *kol isha*. The women who have left Orthodoxies, on the other hand, participate in the secular public, establishing legitimacy to create new types of publicity that defy the secular public, as Malky Goldman and Melissa Weisz did with their production company, and as Pearl Gluck did with many of her films and documentaries. In the cases of performances within and outside Orthodoxy, women produce sounds and images that circulate across the globe, reshaping what constitutes Orthodoxy. Their stories reveal the potential of the arts and the digital to redefine public and private spaces. Their transformations come with promises of financial success, provoking wider—and unpredictable—structural changes for women and their families.

My research suggests the many ways in which women embody ultra-Orthodoxy and reveals the diversity of perspectives they hold on agency and autonomy, as illustrated by their negotiation and creation of the norms dictated by their artistic spaces. In so doing, the research highlights the usefulness of translocal ethnographies in capturing the multilayered social realities within groups that are generating parallel modernities.[7] My approach contributes to the growing literature on how the digital is transforming public, private, and counterpublic spaces for women and religious groups. This literature often pits publicity against privacy and invisibility, positioning private space as the domain of the unknown or the hidden and the counterpublic as a space existing in resistance or opposition to the public. The experiences of the women in this book provide alternative narratives, showcasing the opportunities that the arts and the digital offer to reinvent publicness, even in spaces defined by restrictiveness.

This book has explored how women who grew up within ultra-Orthodoxy have become private performers, celebrities, influencers, and public artists. While the arts have always had a celebrated place within women's and girls' circles due to the religious and cultural functions that they serve, they have now become an informal market and an industry, contributing to women's economic agency. As part of this process, women have reshaped Orthodoxies by taking part in globalizing processes, the opportunities supplied by the digital revolution, and broader economic shifts. Ultimately, they have aimed to create alternative careers, sources of income, and new social positions for themselves.

The specificities of the *frum* female art worlds have broader anthropological implications regarding gender, religion, and the digital. These ultra-Orthodox women work to decenter the power men have within conservative religion by developing their own businesses—independent from religious authority and the secular entertainment industry. Although most of the women who stay within Orthodoxy receive support from their husbands to pursue a career in the arts, the resulting alternative economy remains their creation. Women who have left Orthodoxies, meanwhile, must by necessity work in an industry dominated by men, but have played an indispensable role in altering public perceptions of Orthodoxy by influencing depictions of Orthodox life and religion in entertainment media. Depictions of religiosity require the voices of religious women. Thus, religiosity has become a tool that women use to gain visibility, audibility, and agency.

The Post-Pandemic Public Life of Research in Anthropology

This book—and my research in general—navigates a particularly troublesome ethical quandary pertaining to research on conservative religious communities. Anthropological research ethics encompasses various questions related to how we select research topics, carry out fieldwork, analyze what we observe, disseminate our findings, and conduct any work with secluded communities who are themselves struggling with the balance of public and private in their lives.[8] As I wrote for publication and presented my research at academic conferences, in public lectures, and in the classroom, I had to think critically about the manner of my presentation. By writing and talking about the *frum* female art worlds, I expose to a secular public audience the hidden spaces, realities, and strategies of exclusively female artistic worlds. I write about women who will likely read what I write about them (and some already have) or hear of my work through op-eds, podcasts, or online conferences during the book's promotion. They will no doubt have strong opinions about it. The paradox is clear: even though their world remains secluded and the secular media does not advertise their artistic work, they all can have access to secular knowledge and many whom I have worked with do access it.[9] Hence, like the women described in this book, I have had to reconcile two worlds: the academic world that requires the publication and diffusion of research and the *frum* female art worlds that demand discretion, even though some women are particularly eager to gain publicity beyond Orthodox circles.

I understood—and it is important to mention—that the women who collaborated with me were willing to have a place in my book, which would help them gain the exposure and recognition they desired to influence perceptions of them among the secular public. Many of them have sought this kind of exposure elsewhere—for example, through the social media campaign using the hashtag #myorthodoxlife, which emerged after the release of the Netflix reality show *My Unorthodox Life*. This campaign provided an opportunity for *frum* women across the globe to share glimpses of their lives in the world rather than cloistered away, proclaiming that one can be both Orthodox and unoppressed. This was one of the few moments when Orthodox and ultra-Orthodox women spoke directly and publicly "to the world" (that is, the non-Orthodox world).[10] On the other hand, many of the *frum* female celebrities and influencers whom I write about understand that their precarious position might depend on the reactions of religious authorities, as their audience and clientele exist within Orthodoxy. Some were beyond caring what these authorities might think, but others were less certain, as they continued to collaborate with many organizations and institutions within the community. With a simple threat from important rabbis, they could lose clients. I needed to anticipate this and convince them that the collaborative aspect of my research meant that we could find a compromise between public exposure and the need for privacy.

Regarding the public life of the book, I decided to adapt the same strategies used by these women in their efforts at self-promotion, allowing myself some liberty to expand their visibility, but always in line with our agreement and my feminist approach. I wanted to respect their own processes of diffusion and dissemination of their artwork. For instance,

I do not expose the private performer's videos when presenting my research. Instead of hiding their names behind first and last initials, I use only their first name. When using quotations and visuals, I only present the advertisements in kosher women's magazines. For the *frum* female celebrity and the influencer, I use the music videos and audio they provide on social media and streaming platforms. I announce to my audience that they are "for women and girls only," thereby shifting the responsibility to men, who can choose whether it is appropriate to view or listen to the content.

I made these decisions based on collaborative research where, among other things, I shared my writing, copresented in the classroom or for public talks, and participated in the making of a community.[11] Ethnomusicologists and anthropologists of the arts are often confronted with such ethical questions about the diffusion of the material they have access to and use in their research. Sometimes scholars reveal this material to secular audiences with little reflection on how they do so. It is conventional to promote and educate others about the music and performances at the heart of our fieldwork. In the case of rituals and music that cannot be recorded in their original context, written descriptions typically suffice. In the context of material restricted to a particular community—or to a certain subsection of the community, as is the case with ultra-Orthodox women—these restrictions should be interpreted as meaningful for the community and those outside the community, such as academic audiences.

But unlike many of these scholars, whose subjects generally never see the resulting research due to language barriers or other access issues, I work and collaborate with women and members of their communities who do have such access. Moreover, the COVID-19 pandemic engendered changes in the way research is disseminated. Many previously in-person conferences and lectures have migrated online, where anyone can view them. Organizers broadcast these events on YouTube or Facebook, opening academia to a broader audience across the globe, and thus to the very communities and individuals that we study. The digital world, which facilitated both the emergence of *frum* female artists and my access to them, now grants them access to my analysis of their lives. In other words, if before the (scholarly) gaze went only in one direction with religious communities, now both sides observe each other, creating an interesting path for research—and especially anthropological research—in the twenty-first century. We must recognize and adapt to these changes in the dissemination of research. Our collaborators now have access to not only books and articles but various online versions of our research. The digital has drastically transformed the diffusion of scholarly work beyond academia, and as a result, our ethics cannot be dictated only by respect and trust; we must pursue collaboration and partnership.

The Future of the *Frum* Female Art Worlds

On June 21 and 22, 2022, a large *asifa* (rally or gathering) for *frum* women, organized by ultra-Orthodox religious authorities, occurred at the Prudential Center in Newark, New Jersey. The first night's events were conducted in Yiddish (for Hasidic members of the audience), and the second night's in English (for Litvish members). The event, entitled "Live Higher" (biblical Hebrew נְקַדֵּשׁ, *nekadesh*: sanctified), was an "Assembly of Emissaries for Women of the Jewish People" (with "Jewish people" understood to mean Orthodox Jews),[12] dedicated to the dangers of the Internet and social media. Rabbis organized this *asifa* to discourage women from accessing and using social media—specifically, Instagram. One of the largest and most powerful ultra-Orthodox companies involved in the "battle of the *nisayon*" (trial or test of technology) is TAG; they sponsored, advertised, and promoted the event. The company specializes in "cutting-edge technology to help filter companies come out with the best filters."[13] Their professed goal is to create filters for digital devices to block or allow content in line with the "Yiddishe values" described on the company's website. During the two days of *asifa*, dozens of rabbis attempted to convince women to avoid social media. As usual, their arguments involved *tsnius*, women's responsibility for the future of *Klal Yisrael*, and women's role as mothers and wives. Women received special instructions regarding the promotion and recording of the event. They were prohibited from photographing the event and from publicizing it on social media.

The effects of this event reverberated through ultra-Orthodox communities across the globe. Ultra-Orthodox and former ultra-Orthodox women reacted in a variety of ways, mobilizing narratives on feminism, women's empowerment, and oppression. Some of them—often those with physical, brick-and-mortar locations—decided to leave Instagram, letting their followers know that the *asifa* had influenced their decision. Many *frum* female celebrities, on the other hand, ignored the event, and influencers expressed their alienation from religious authorities, pointing out the hypocrisy that ultra-Orthodox men organized and advertised the event on their smartphones and computers.

The *asifa* was organized in an unprecedented moment, amid women's social and economic ascension due to the Internet, social media, and related technology. Ultra-Orthodox women justified their arts industry and its use of the Internet on economic grounds—it allowed them to build a profitable career—but their economic success and independence began to threaten religious authority. Most importantly, they represent a different role model for women that some religious leaders see as a menace to the system because it does not echo traditional expectations. While there are religious arguments for the stance promoted by the *asifa*, it must also be stressed that religious authorities maintain their position of power thanks to an economy they control. Indeed, if women are economically independent and able to disseminate a new, appealing image of *frum* women without the need for religious-authority support, the authority is thus losing power. The *asifa* is motivated by not only religiosity but also the economic power, autonomy, and agency women gain through the Internet, which religious authorities find threatening. The event illustrates the crisis of authority facing conservative religious groups. Many women I have met lack confidence in the religious authorities because they restrict economic and professional opportunities, wishing women to remain merely consumers (and not producers or creators) in an economic system they control.

Accounting for ultra-Orthodox women's lives requires moving beyond a notion of religious authority limited to religious practices, texts, and beliefs. The anthropology of religion should resituate the centrality of the economy as a parameter of analysis, as it is in the nexus of religion and the economy that alternative modernities arise. The Internet and social media have allowed new businesses and ways of generating income to proliferate across the globe, including for conservative religious groups, particularly women. In an era when access to the Internet and its link to surveillance and social control are at the center of fierce debates, ultra-Orthodox women and men find freedom and liberation thanks to the Internet. Even though they are aware of the surveillance and control that companies may have, their everyday life is dictated by the surveillance and control of religious authority anyway, a fact that makes the issue of surveillance on the Internet almost irrelevant or secondary.

The women described in this book exist on the fringes of the normative ultra-Orthodox world. Still, their work has increasingly reached more people within their communities—even among the most conservative circles. By suggesting that these women are reshaping Orthodoxy, I envision the *frum* female art worlds—marginalized though they are—as affecting many people beyond their own gender group, both within and outside Orthodoxy. Those who work in the arts professionally are often perceived as the exception in society, but artists and artwork significantly reflect and inflect social change, which is the case for the *frum* female art worlds. The future will show whether the emergence of this world results in broader social change or simply new ways to support the existing system, but the recent controversy around the use of social media by these women demonstrates that they are at least seen as attempting to effect social change.

There is little doubt that patriarchal and conservative forces that wish to control women and girls, censoring their bodies and their voices, will continue to exert pressure within ultra-Orthodoxy and elsewhere in the world, and that these forces will continue to claim and mobilize religious texts, laws, and ideas to justify such attitudes. However, I would view it as likely that due to economic pressure and alternative modernities, women will continue to use digital technologies to channel self-expression, economic agency, and autonomy.

Does this book capture a moment in the history of North American ultra-Orthodoxy that is only temporary, or will these truly structural changes have a long-term impact? It is hard to predict, but one thing is certain. These women will continue to circumvent norms and laws as they fight for the right to determine who and what they want to be, and the digital will remain one of their tools. Not only are these women reshaping Orthodoxy from within and from without, but they are encouraging us to rethink Orthodoxy with the digital and beyond the male paradigm. In other words, they are remaking Orthodoxy. This book tells a story about the strategies ultra-Orthodox and former ultra-Orthodox women use to redefine themselves as autonomous, creative, and empowered through the arts and digital technologies. Some of them may do it to simply find new ways to support the system; others, to criticize, challenge, or translate it. The future of *frum* female art worlds is in the hands of the women who shape them, their followers, and consumers. Leah Forster's drastic change from a *frum* female celebrity to a public artist still admired by some within the community serves as a great example of the surprises these women artists might offer.

As for a feminist anthropologist like myself who seeks to observe and capture the contrasting narratives emerging from these art words, the surprises reside in the ways these women have complicated my understanding of religious and secular womanhood in twenty-first-century North America, by revisiting the norms and exposing the margins of ultra-Orthodox life.

APPENDIX I

Rachel's Place Analysis

Year	Name of Rachel's Place Production	Name of the Original production	Original run date	Original run location (excluding tryout runs)	Original composer	Original lyricist	Original screenwriter
2011	Barons & Bankers	The Rothschilds	1970	Broadway	Jerry Bock	Sheldon Harnick	Sherman Yellen
2012	The Songs of the Hills	The Sound of Music	1959	Broadway	Richard Rodgers	Oscar Hammerstein II	Howard Lindsay Russel Crouse
2013	English To a "T"	My Fair Lady	1956	Broadway	Frederick Loewe	Alan Jay Lerner	Alan Jay Lerner
2014	That's My Nanny!	Mary Poppins	2004	West End	Richard M. Sherman Robert F. Sherman George Stiles	Richard M. Sherman Robert F. Sherman Anthony Drewe	Julian Fellowes
2015	The Kingdom of Aldecot	Cinderella	1957	Film	Richard Rodgers	Oscar Hammerstein II	Oscar Hammerstein II
			2013	Broadway	Richard Rodgers	Oscar Hammerstein II	Oscar Hammerstein II Douglas Carter Beane
2016	Shtetl	Fiddler on the Roof	1964	Broadway	Jerry Bock	Sheldon Harnick	Joseph Stein
2017	Jinji	Annie	1977	Broadway	Charles Strouse	Martin Charnin	Thomas Meehan
2018	The Bandman	The Music Man	1957	Broadway	Meredith Wilson	Meredith Wilson	Meredith Wilson Franklin Lacey
2019	Katalina	Anastasia	2017	Broadway	Stephen Flaherty	Lynn Ahrens	Terrence McNally
2020	Ragamuffin	Oliver!	1962	West End	Lionel Bart	Lionel Bart	Lionel Bart
		Les Miserables	1980	Palais des Sports	Claude-Michel Schönberg	Alain Boublil Jean-Marc Natel	Alain Boublil Claude-Michel Schönberg

APPENDIX II

Selected List of Women Invested in the Arts

Last Name	First Name	Categories of arts	Background	Private	Modest Public	Counter-public	Public	Chapter quoted
Anneberg	Eve	Film and Writing	Secular Jewish				X	The Public Artist
Antelis	Shaindel	Music	Litvish	X	X	X		The Ethnographer; The Celebrity
Baum	Dobby	Music	Hasidic	X	X	X		The Ethnographer; The *Frum* Female Artist; The Celebrity; The Influencer
Bennett	Mirel	Music	NI		X			The Celebrity
Blatt	Mindy	Music	NI		X	X		The Celebrity
Blum	Julia	Music	NI	X				The Celebrity
Cheeger	Emily	Film	Jewish				X	The Public Artist
Cohen	Kineret Sarah	Music	Litvish	X				The Celebrity
Cohen	Nechama	Music	Litvish		X	X		The Ethnographer; The Celebrity
Davis	Maayan	Dance	Litvish		X	X		The Ethnographer
Feldman	Deborah	Writing	Hasidic, now secular				X	The Public Artist
Fellig-Harrell	Chanale	Music	Chabad	X	X			The Celebrity
Forster	Leah	Music and Comedy	Hasidic	X	X	X	X	The Influencer; Postlude
Freeman	Esther	Music	Chabad	X	X	X		The Celebrity
Fried	Raizy	Entertainment	Hasidic		X	X		The Celebrity
Friedman	Mimi	Film	Litvish	X	X	X		The Celebrity

Last Name	First Name	Categories of arts	Background	Private	Modest Public	Counter-public	Public	Chapter quoted
Garbose	Robin	Film	Chabad	X	X			The Celebrity
Giniger	Malky	Music and Dance	Litvish	X				The Private Performer; The Celebrity
Gluck	Pearl	Film	Hasidic, now secular				X	The Public Artist; Postlude
Goldman	Malky	Film, Theater, and Visual Art	Hasidic. now secular		X		X	The Public Artist; Postlude
Handler	Miriam	Film	Litvish	X	X			The *Frum* Female Artist; The Private Performer
Hartman	Michal	Film	Litvish		X	X		The Ethnographer
Israeli	Miriam	Music	Hasidic	X	X			The Celebrity
Jaffe	Bracha	Music	Litvish	X	X	X		The Ethnographer; The Celebrity; The Influencer
Kay	Tzivia	Music	Orthodox	X	X			Acknowledgments
Kogan	Chaya	Music	Chabad	X	X	X		The Celebrity
Kosman	Franciska	Music and Entertainment	Litvish		X	X		The Ethnographer; The *Frum* Female Artist; The Celebrity
Miles-Sash	Adina	Social Media, Writing	Hasidic and Litvish		X	X	X	The Influencer
Miller	Rochel	Music	Litvish	X				The Celebrity
Navon Zmora	Ruthi	Music	Orthodox	X				The Celebrity
Neuhaus	Chayala	Music	Hasidic	X	X			The Ethnographer; The Celebrity
Not advertised	Chaya	Music and Dance	Hasidic	X				The Private Performer
Not advertised	Chaya Sarah	Music and Film	Hasidic		X			The Celebrity
Not advertised	Chevi	Music	Hasidic	X				The Private Performer
Not advertised	Devoiry	Music	Hasidic	X				The Private Performer

Last Name	First Name	Categories of arts	Background	Private	Modest Public	Counter-public	Public	Chapter quoted
Not advertised	Elisha	Music	Hasidic	X				The Private Performer
Not advertised	Esti	Music	Hasidic	X				The Private Performer
Not advertised	Freida	Music and Dance	Hasidic	X				The Private Performer
Not advertised	Frimi	Music	Hasidic	X	X	X		The Celebrity
Not advertised	Gelly	Music	Hasidic	X				The Private Performer
Not advertised	Goldie	Music	Hasidic	X				The Ethnographer; The *Frum* Female Artist
Not advertised	Leah	Music	Hasidic	X	X			The Private Performer
Not advertised	Malky	Music	Hasidic	X				The Private Performer
Not advertised	Myriam	Music	Hasidic	X				The Private Performer
Not advertised	Rivka	Music	Hasidic	X				The Ethnographer; The Private Performer
Not advertised	Rochel	Music	Hasidic	X				The Ethnographer
Not advertised	Ruchy	Music	Hasidic	X				The Private Performer
Not advertised	Sarah	Music	Hasidic	X				The Private Performer
Not advertised	Toby	Music	Hasidic	X				The Private Performer; The Public Artist
Not advertised	Yitty	Music	Hasidic	X				The Influencer
Not advertised	Yocheved	Music	Hasidic	X				The Ethnographer; The Private Performer
Oziel	Dalia	Music	Litvish	X	X	X		The Celebrity; The Influencer
Palti	Yaffa	Entertainment	Litvish	X	X	X		The Celebrity
Perlstein	Dina	Film	Hasidic	X	X			The Celebrity
Plotzker	Shaindy	Music	Litvish	X	X	X		The Ethnographer

Last Name	First Name	Categories of arts	Background	Private	Modest Public	Counter-public	Public	Chapter quoted
Ragen	Naomi	Writing and Theater	Modern-Orthodox				X	The Public Artist
Reifer	Rochel Leah	Music	Hasidic	X	X			The Celebrity
Rose	Riki	Music and Film	Hasidic, now Secular			X	X	The Influencer; Postlude
Rosen	Lili	Theater	Hasidic, now secular				X	The Public Artist
Rosen-garten	Chany	Writing	Hasidic	X	X	X		The *Frum* Female Artist; The Influencer
Ryp	Eli	Music	NI		X	X		The Celebrity
Schwartz	Devorah	Music and Dance	Hasidic and Litvish	X	X	X		The Celebrity; The Influencer
Shapiro	Sarah	Writing	NI		X	X		The Influencer
Shuster-man	Dalia	Music	Chabad	X	X			Acknowledgments
Tessler	Toby	Film	Hasidic		X	X		The Celebrity
Wein Harris	Rifka	Writing and Music	Hasidic and Litvish	X	X	X		The *Frum* Female Artist
Weingar-ten	Malky	Film	Hasidic		X	X	X	The Celebrity; The Influencer
Weisz	Melissa	Film and Theater	Hasidic, now secular				X	The Public Artist; The Postlude
Zuskind	Esther Sara	Music	NI	X	X	X		The Celebrity

Note: This list of the women invested in the arts mentioned in the book is in alphabetical order by last name. "Background" refers to the religious environment in which the artists grew up or how they self-identify today; these are not hermetic categories. The term does not refer to Jewish ethnic roots (e.g., Sephardi, Mizrahi, or Yemini) because ultra-Orthodox and Orthodox Judaism is a product of the Eastern European Jewish experience that only in the second half of the twentieth century became familiar to other Jewish ethnic groups. "NI" means "not identified."

APPENDIX III

Selected List of Music Videos with Frum *Female Singer*

Frum Female Singer	Name of Song	Date of Release	YouTube Channel	Number of Views (as of June 2023)	Language
Franciska https://www .youtube.com /@FranciskaMusic https://www. youtube.com/ @FranciskaMusic	Kol Haolam	June 27, 2017	Franciska	13,336	Hebrew
	Shiru L'Hashem	November 7, 2017	Franciska	22,788	Hebrew
	Misheberach	May 7, 2019	Franciska	453	Hebrew
	Vezakeni Legadel	December 21, 2019	Franciska	2,259	Hebrew
	Hamakom, with Esther Press and Ariella Zeitlin	April 12, 2020	Franciska	1,414	Hebrew
	Modim, with Devorah Schwartz	May 12, 2020	Franciska	1,750	Hebrew
	Keish Echad	August 27, 2020	Franciska	734	English and Hebrew
	Tov Lehodot, with Maayan Davis	December 10, 2020	Franciska	6,082	Hebrew
	If You Wanna Be, with Rahcel Sam	February 20, 2021	Franciska	3,661	English and Hebrew
	Vikar, with Maayan Davis Choreography	March 26, 2022	Franciska	4,839	Hebrew
	Elokai Neshama	December 20, 2022	Franciska	1,924	Hebrew

Frum Female Singer	Name of Song	Date of Release	YouTube Channel	Number of Views (as of June 2023)	Language
Devorah Schwartz https://www.youtube.com/@devorah-schwartzoffi-cial2546	Chana's Song	January 1, 2019	Devorah Schwartz OFFICIAL	109,388	English and Hebrew
	I Believe in Me	April 6, 2019	Devorah Schwartz OFFICIAL	262,124	English
	Riboin, with Esty Morelle (cover)	November 20, 2019	Devorah Schwartz OFFICIAL	65,490	Hebrew
	Rise Up, with Esty Morelle (cover)	November 4, 2020	Devorah Schwartz OFFICIAL	54,238	English
	Blessings (cover)	November 4, 2020	Devorah Schwartz OFFICIAL	31,989	English
	Tell Your Heart to Beat Again	November 18, 2020	Devorah Schwartz OFFICIAL	82,493	English
	Ein Od Milvado	January 17, 2021	Devorah Schwartz OFFICIAL	41,509	English and Hebrew
	Ein Od Mil-vado, Dance Tutorial	March 13, 2021	Devorah Schwartz OFFICIAL	65,358	English and Hebrew
	Pieces	December 11, 2022	Devorah Schwartz OFFICIAL	12,197	English
	Hold On Tight	February 26, 2023	Devorah Schwartz OFFICIAL	72, 597	English and Hebrew
	Just Want	June 29, 2023	TYH Nation, Thank You Hashem	8,718	English and Hebrew

Frum Female Singer	Name of Song	Date of Release	YouTube Channel	Number of Views (as of June 2023)	Language
Bracha Jaffe https://www.youtube.com/@brachajaffe5767	Psiotay, with Chaya Kogan (cover)	January 8, 2020	Chaya Kogan	312,112	Hebrew (English subtitles)
	Speechless (cover)	March 11, 2020	Yaeli Vogel	224,433	English
	Halev Sheli, with Devorah Schwartz (cover)	May 12, 2020	Bracha Jaffe, Devorah Schwartz OFFICIAL	19,074	Hebrew
	Ribo Medley, with Belev Echad	July 31, 2020	Bracha Jaffe	291,351	English and Hebrew
	Bonei Olam Vzakeini, with Devorah Schwartz	August 6, 2020	Bracha Jaffe	584,655	English and Hebrew
	Never Alone, with Shaindy Plotzker	June 6, 2021	TYH Nation, Thank You Hashem	744,493	English and Hebrew
	Shemesh, with Yaffush (cover)	February 20, 2022	Bracha Jaffe	50,024	Hebrew
	YID	April 12, 2022	TYH Nation, Thank You Hashem	357,402	English, Hebrew, and Yiddish
	YID, Dance Tutorial	June 11, 2022	TYH Nation, Thank You Hashem	35,469	English, Hebrew, and Yiddish
	Erev Shel Yom Bahir (cover)	February 4, 2023	Bracha Jaffe	14,777	Hebrew

Frum Female Singer	Name of Song	Date of Release	YouTube Channel	Number of Views (as of June 2023)	Language
Dobby Baum https://www.youtube.com/@dobbybaum	When I Look at You, with Bari Mitzmann (cover)	November 2, 2020	Barianna	50,232	English
	Rejuvenate, with the Brooklyn Girls Choir	August 4, 2021	Dobby Baum	9,597	English
	We Are the Power, with Aliza Loeb	August 4, 2021	Dobby Baum	21,973	English and Hebrew
	It Is Meant to Be	August 4, 2021	Dobby Baum	6,340	English
	Give Us Strength, in collaboration with Chazkeinu	November 22, 2022	Dobby Baum	5,116	English
	Ana Hashem (cover with Chana Ruchy)	December 18, 2022	Dobby Baum	7,801	Hebrew
	Shema (cover)	May 21, 2023	Dobby Baum	2,936	English and Hebrew
	Beautiful	June 25, 2023	Dobby Baum	12, 279	English
Nechama Cohen https://www.youtube.com/@nechamamusic	Heartbeat	July 21, 2013	Nechama Cohen	120, 806	English
	Inside Out	October 22, 2014	Nechama Cohen	173,611	English
	Fight Song (cover)	June 18, 2015	Nechama Cohen	19,242	English
	I Still Have You	December 12, 2018	Nechama Cohen	137,312	English
	Full Color, with Shaindel Antelis	August 9, 2020	Nechama Cohen	111,155	English
	Fighting for Me (cover)	December 31, 2020	Nechama Cohen	15,504	English
	When I Look At You (cover)	August 13, 2022	Nechama Cohen	12,570	English

Frum Female Singer	Name of Song	Date of Release	YouTube Channel	Number of Views (as of June 2023)	Language
Shaindel Antelis https://www.youtube.com/@shaindelantelis	All around the World	September 6, 2019	Shaindel Antelis	9,065	English and Hebrew
	Invisible	October 12, 2020	Shaindel Antelis	34,490	English
	The Sun Is Rising	October 12, 2020	Shaindel Antelis	665	English
	By Your Side	November 3, 2021	Shaindel Antelis	12,491	English
	Live Today	March 9, 2022	Shaindel Antelis	501	English
	Light Up the World	March 9, 2022	Shaindel Antelis	4,231	English
	Jump, with Maayan Davis (cover)	March 26, 2022	Shaindel Antelis	35,098	English
Shaindy Plotzker https://www.youtube.com/@ShaindyPlotzker	Ah-Yay, with Bracha Jaffe (cover)	May 17, 2020	Shaindy Plotzker	382,731	English
	Zachreinu	September 16, 2020	Shaindy Plotzker	268,645	English and Hebrew
	Burning Bright, with Bracha Jaffe	December 12, 2020	Shaindy Plotzker	115,498	English
	Holding On	March 9, 2022	TYH Nation, Thank You Hashem	222,080	English and Hebrew
	Fire	March 4, 2023	Shaindy Plotzker	29,926	English
Judith Gerzi https://www.youtube.com/@JudithGerzi	New Day	December 14, 2020	Judith Gerzi Music	9,134	English
	Burn Bright	November 30, 2021	Judith Gerzi Music	5,796	English
	Back to You	September 22, 2022	Judith Gerzi Music	2,214	English

Frum Female Singer	Name of Song	Date of Release	YouTube Channel	Number of Views (as of June 2023)	Language
Chaya Kogan https://www.youtube.com/@chayakogan8310	Hakol Mimcha	January 28, 2019	Chaya Kogan	401,921	Hebrew
	Your time (cover)	May 5, 2019	Chaya Kogan	300,514	English
	The Power Is You	July 4, 2020	Chaya Kogan	281.857	English
	Ani Ma'amina	June 18, 2022	Chaya Kogan	135,429	English and Hebrew
	Ani Ma'amina, Dance Tutorial	June 25, 2022	Chaya Kogan	14,914	English and Hebrew
	Battle Cry	December 12, 2022	Chaya Kogan	58,509	English
	One Nation	June 12, 2023	Chaya Kogan	2,210	English

GLOSSARY

Aguna (plural *agunot*): anchored or chained. The term is used to refer to a woman whose husband refuses, or is unable, to grant her a divorce (which requires a document known as a "*get*," according to Jewish law).

Assur: forbidden.

Baal tshuva (plural *baalei tshuva*): those who return or repent; refers to people who did not grow up keeping Jewish law, *halakha*, but are now doing so in compliance with the *halakhic* standards of the community they want to belong to. People who identify as *baal tshuva* often belong to Chabad-Lubavitch Hasidism and, to a lesser extent, to Breslev Hasidism.

Belz: Hasidic community found in the town of Belz in Western Ukraine.

Chabad-Lubavitch: one of the world's largest Hasidic communities, known for its outreach activities toward secular Jews.

Emuna: faith, belief, or trust in God.

Frum: Yiddish term meaning "religious" or "pious," used to describe Orthodox Jews.

Frumkeit: the world of religious or pious Jews, in Yiddish.

Gematria: the practice of assigning a numerical value to a name. The letters of the Hebrew alphabet involved have standard numerical values.

Get: a document presented by a husband to his wife in Jewish religious law that effectuates a divorce between a Jewish couple.

Halakha (adjective *halakhic*): Jewish law.

Haredi/Ultra-Orthodox Jews: branches within Orthodox Judaism that encompass Hasidic and Litvish/Yeshivish Jews, who have in common their strict adherence to Jewish law and traditions. They define themselves by their limited contact with the outside secular world.

Hashem: one of the terms used to talk about God.

Hashkafa (plural *hashkafot*, adjective *hashkafic*): refers to the philosophy or ideology that Orthodox Jews adopt to interpret Jewish texts. It plays a crucial role in the way they interact with the world and guides practical decisions such as at which school to register children, which synagogue to attend, and what community to live in.

Hasidic Judaism: a branch of Orthodox Judaism that originated in eighteenth-century Eastern Europe and spread rapidly, emphasizing mystical teachings, music, dance, and connection with God. After being widely persecuted in the Holocaust, Hasidic Jews have rebuilt their communities worldwide, with the largest communities being in Israel and North America. Each Hasidic community has a court (*hoyf*) that is usually named after its Eastern European country or town of origin and is led by a *rebbe* chosen through male lines of descent.

HAYMISH: "homey" in Yiddish; in some contexts, refers to Hasidim or Litvish/Yeshivish who do not associate with a particular Hasidic court or follow a particular *rebbe*, nor a particular rabbi.

HEKHSHER: certification; refers to the confirmation that a product has been certified kosher by a particular rabbi or group of rabbis. The term is often used in reference to food, but it also refers to literature and entertainment.

KASHRUT: Jewish regulations that prohibit the eating of certain foods and require that other foods be prepared in a specified manner (based on Jewish law).

KETUBA: marriage contract.

KHOL HAMOED: the intermediate days between the beginning and the end of Passover and Sukkot.

KIPPA: yarmulke, a brimless cap, traditionally worn by Orthodox Jewish males to fulfill the customary requirement that the head be covered.

KIRUV: act of bringing secular Jews to a more observant state.

KLAL YISRAEL: the nation of Israel in a spiritual sense in rabbinic Hebrew. Refers to Jews as a nation and is used to express Jewish solidarity in Orthodox circles.

KOL ISHA: "woman's voice" in Hebrew; refers to a man hearing the singing of a woman to whom he is not permitted to listen. The prohibition of *kol isha* arises from the fear that the sensuality of a woman's voice arouses men.

KOSHER: term used in Orthodox circles to describe food or any product (including music, films, arts) that has been approved by religious authority as respecting Jewish law.

KUMZITS: compound word in Yiddish meaning "come sit," referring to community sing-alongs in Ashkenazi Orthodox Jewish communities, often at a summer camp or getaway.

LAG BAOMER: Jewish holiday institutionalized by the rabbis, usually observed in May. The holiday is associated with the anniversary of the death of Rabbi Shimon bar Yochai and the celebration of the Zohar, which is the foundational work in the literature of Jewish mystical thought. It celebrates a break in the Omer (the countdown from the second night of Passover to the Jewish holiday of Shavuot, also known as Pentecost) and includes the holding of weddings, lighting of bonfires, and cutting of hair.

LOSHN KOYDESH: the language of holiness, referring to the ancient Hebrew used in the Torah, which is distinct from modern Hebrew.

NIGGUN (PLURAL NIGGUNIM): melody; refers to a religious musical prayer, or improvisation, with repetitive sounds such as "lai-lai-lai" or "yai-yai-yai" instead of formal lyrics. *Niggunim* are central to the worship of Hasidic Jews.

ORTHODOX: a collective term for religious Jews who are members of traditional branches of modern-day Judaism who are observing Jewish law (*halakha*).

OTD: off the *derekh* (meaning "path" in Hebrew); those who leave their Orthodox Jewish communities.

PARNASSE: an income or livelihood.

PASHKEVIL: an anonymous publication meant to incite, either as a poster hung discreetly or as flyers distributed secretly; can be intended either as gossip meant to hurt people or to enforce religious norms.

PEYOS: visible side curls worn by Hasidic males starting when they are three years old (all Orthodox men have *peyos*, but their visibility varies according to the group).

RABBI: a Jewish scholar and teacher.

REBBE: a male leader of a Hasidic sect.

SATMAR: Hasidic community originally from Romania (Satu Mare) known for its extreme conservatism, rejection of modern culture, and anti-Zionism.

SHABBES: a day of rest, prayer, and reflection that commemorates the seventh day of creation. It is observed every week, from Friday evening to Saturday evening.

SHEYTEL: Yiddish for "wig." Worn by married ultra-Orthodox women, for whom exposing their hair is forbidden except to their husbands.

SHIDDUKH (PLURAL *SHIDDUKHIM*): a system of matchmaking in which Orthodox Jewish singles are introduced to each other. The introductions change according to the customs of the community, the family, and, potentially, the individual. In Hasidic circles, the singles usually meet once or twice before being engaged, while in Litvish circles, they meet several times and even date.

SHPITZEL: type of multilayered head covering worn by Jewish women that consists of a partial wig and a headscarf; most common in conservative communities.

SHTETL (PLURAL *SHTETLAKH*): Yiddish for a small Jewish town.

SHUL: a synagogue.

SIMKHA: "joy"; used in Orthodox circles to refer to a life-cycle celebration (marriage, bris, bar/bat mitsva).

SUKKOT: Jewish holiday occurring between September and October celebrating the comfort of a shelter provided by God for the journey through the desert, the shelter being represented by the *sukkah*. The *sukkah* is a temporary hut built on an open porch or balcony where activities such as eating, studying, or even sleeping take place.

TALMUD: the central text of Rabbinic Judaism, which gives guidance on Jewish religious law and theology. Composed of both the Mishnah (oral traditions) and the Gemara (commentary on the Mishnah, the Hebrew Bible, and other writings).

TIKHEL: Yiddish for "headscarf." Typically worn by married Orthodox women to adhere to the codes of modesty.

TIKKUN OLAM: Jewish concept referring to various forms of an action intended to repair and improve the world.

TSEDAKAH: the moral obligation to do charity or the act of charity itself.

TSNIUS: modesty in dress and conduct.

YESHIVA (PLURAL *YESHIVOT*)/*KOLLEL*: Orthodox Jewish institutions of higher learning for men. In the ultra-Orthodox environment, *yeshivot* are the equivalents of middle and high schools, or seminaries attended by males before marriage, while *kollels* are seminaries frequented after marriage.

YESHIVISH OR LITVISH: ultra-Orthodox Jewish communities that trace their lineage to the *misnagdim*, led by the Gaon of Vilna and his students, who opposed the Hasidic movement when it emerged in the late eighteenth and early nineteenth centuries. Today, Hasidic and Yeshivish/Litvish Jews work together, share communal institutions, and often collaborate on issues of mutual concern.

YEYTSER HORA: the innate inclination to do evil.

YIDDISHKEIT: of Jewish culture or essence; the quality of Jewishness.

ZMIRES: medieval lyrics that are often sung during *shabbes* meals.

NOTES

CHAPTER 1. THE TRANSLOCAL ETHNOGRAPHER

1 There is a spectrum of practices regarding the publicization of females' images in the ultra-Orthodox press. The most conservative press does not publish any female faces, while others, such as the popular magazine *Mishpahah*, will publish the images of girls who are under twelve years old (age of bat mitsva, considered the age of maturity).

2 "*Frum*" is a Yiddish term meaning "observant" or "pious." It refers to the devotion of Orthodox Jews toward the Jewish law (*halakha*) and is used in ultra-Orthodox circles to refer to both Hasidic and Litvish/Yeshivish communities and individuals.

3 The term "*frum* female artist" has been mobilized by ultra-Orthodox women artists to define themselves and their community.

4 Religious authorities have different attitudes toward and interpretations of the prohibition of *kol isha* for boys. The restrictive age ranges from nine years old—the beginning of puberty—to thirteen years old, the age of religious maturity (bar mitsva).

5 Shaindy Plotzker reached out to her rabbi to make sure that it would be fine for her to advertise and publicize her musical work on social media under the label "for women and girls only."

6 See "Our Team" on the website of the company Vision & Hart: www.visionandhart .com.

7 Music video of the song "AH-YAY," by Shaindy Plotzker and Bracha Jaffe, 2020: https: //www.youtube.com/watch?v=B7TIWISAcBw.

8 Music video of the song "YID," by Bracha Jaffe, 2022: https://www.youtube.com/watch ?v=nxQQUNmIvsk.

9 Here, I echo sociologist Howard Becker, who developed the concept of art worlds to examine secular and liberal art as a collective action. Ultra-Orthodox women exist within what I call the "*frum* female art worlds"—the art worlds that differ from others because of their female and Orthodox dimensions, which have substantially impacted their origins and development. See Becker, *Art Worlds*.

10 Fader, *Hidden Heretics*, 1–27.

11 For more information on the establishment of ultra-Orthodox Jewish communities in North America after the Holocaust, see Deutsch and Casper, *A Fortress in Brooklyn*; Fader, *Mitzvah Girls*; Heilman, *Sliding to the Right*; Stolzenberg and Myers, *American Shtetl*.

12 Fader, *Hidden Heretics*, 1–27.

13 The Orthodox public media is the content available across communities evaluated by religious authority to make it kosher and is regulated by strict rules about the publicity of women's faces, names, and images. The non-Orthodox public media is television, streaming platforms, and the mainstream secular press.

14 My reflections on the impact of technology and social media on the redefinition of the private, public, and counterpublic spaces in religious communities were based on the work of the various media scholars, anthropologists, philosophers, and sociologists

who wrote extensively about the subject. Consult the bibliography under the heading "Public, Private, and the Counterpublic" to learn more.

15 Consult the bibliography under the heading "Women and Religion" to learn more about the works that have influenced me on the subject.

16 Bilge, "Beyond Subordination vs. Resistance."

17 About the criticism of liberal universal feminism consult Khader, *Decolonizing Universalism*.

18 The concept of *counterpublic* has been developed by philosophers such as Oskar Negt, Alexander Kluge, Peter Labanyi, and Nancy Fraser, and then mobilized by anthropologists such as Michael Warner, Francis Cody, Charles Hirschkind, and Ayala Fader to characterize individual and collective responses to exclusions from dominant publics. The term has been particularly central to the feminist critique of mainstream public sphere theory, to characterize women's response to exclusions by dominant publics with the goal of transforming them. For more information, see: Negt, Kluge, and Labanyi, "'The Public Sphere and Experience'"; Fraser, "Rethinking the Public Sphere"; Warner, "Publics and Counterpublics"; Cody, "Publics and Politics"; Hirschkind, *The Ethical Soundscape*; Fader, *Hidden Heretics*.

19 Ellen Koskoff was one of the pioneers to write about Hasidic women and music. See: Koskoff, *Music in Lubavitcher Life*.

20 Consult the works by Birgit Meyer and Annelies Moors, Ayala Fader, Matthew Engelke, and Charles Hirschkind in the "Public, Private, and the Counterpublic" section of the bibliography.

21 About kinship beyond blood see: Leite, *Unorthodox Kin*; Todne, Malik, and Wellman, eds., *New Directions in Spiritual Kinship*; Weston, *Families We Choose*.

22 For more information see: Batnitzky, *How Judaism Became a Religion*; Daniel Boyarin, *Judaism*; Jonathan Boyarin, *Yeshiva Days*; Stadler, *Yeshiva Fundamentalism*.

23 For more information see: Winston, *Unchosen*; Davidman, *Becoming Un-Orthodox*; Skinazi, *Women of Valor*; Fader, "Ultra-Orthodox Jewish Interiority, the Internet, and the Crisis of Faith"; Fader, *Hidden Heretics*; Cappell and Lang, eds., *Off the Derech*; Newfield, *Degrees of Separation*.

24 For more information see: Batnitzky, *How Judaism Became a Religion*; Boyarin, *Judaism*; Asad, *Formations of the Secular*; Nongbri, *Before Religion*.

25 Asad, *Genealogies of Religion*, 200–238.

26 Blutinger, "So-Called Orthodoxy."

27 Consult the bibliography under the heading "Ultra-Orthodoxy in North America" to learn more about the communities in North America from a historical, sociological, and anthropological perspective.

28 This crisis of authority is not the first one, as many others have occurred since the birth of Hasidism and the Yeshivish community (also known as Misnagedim at its birth), see: Fader, *Hidden Heretics*, 1–27.

29 In the last two decades, ethnographers have largely discussed and invested in multi-sited ethnography, studying transnational or translocal activities on site and online. Consult the bibliography under the heading "Transnational and Translocal Ethnography" to learn more.

30 Vaisman, "'She Who Seeks Shall Find'"; Taragin-Zeller and Kasstan, "'I Didn't Know How to Be with My Husband'"; Shuman, "Cutting Out the Middleman."

31 About online ethnography of religious groups see: Fader, *Hidden Heretics*; Kieffer, "Manifesting Millions"; Baumel-Schwartz, "*Frum* Surfing"; Boellstorff, *Coming of Age in Second Life*.

32 Stolzenberg and Myers, in their book about the history of the village of Kiryas Joel, are implicitly reinforcing the concept of the enclave by using the title *American Shteitl.*
33 Marcus, "Ethnography in/of the World System." About the spatial turn, see: Appadurai, ed., *The Social Life of Things*; Hannerz, *Transnational Connections.*
34 Hannerz, "'Transnational Research'"; Falzon, *Cosmopolitan Connections*, 16.
35 Smith, "Translocality"; Greiner and Sakdapolrak, "Translocality."
36 Oakes and Schein, eds., *Translocal China.*
37 Greiner and Sakdapolrak, "Translocality."
38 Deutsch and Casper, *A Fortress in Brooklyn.*
39 About friendship and fieldwork see: Taylor, "The Intimate Insider"; Tillmann-Healy, "Friendship as Method"; Van der Geest, "Friendship and Fieldwork."
40 I use the concept of an "underground" to characterize out-of-the-ordinary gatherings of ultra-Orthodox Jews that occur on the margins of established socioreligious codes and do not conform with religious leaders' expectations of social spaces. Such an underground is populated mainly by former ultra-Orthodox individuals, those who are transitioning, those who are marginalized, and others who lead double lives, meaning that they are secretly navigating between religious and nonreligious spaces. Several scholars have described and analyzed the process of leaving and living a double life: Winston, *Unchosen*; Davidman, *Becoming Unorthodox*; Fader, *Hidden Heretics*; and Newfield, *Degree of Separation.*
41 The difference between the professional and the semiprofessional lies in the artist's priorities. The professional artist is exclusively invested in her artistic career and has been recognized by her peers within and beyond her community; the semiprofessional, in contrast, often works in another field as well and, though recognized by her community, is not necessarily known beyond it.
42 About Jewish women ethnographers doing work with ultra-Orthodox Jews discussing the issue of *kiruv*, see: Fader, *Mitzvah Girls*; Davidman, *Tradition in a Rootless World*; El-Or, *Educated and Ignorant*; Kaufman, *Rachel's Daughters*; Levine and Gilligan, *Mystics, Mavericks, and Merrymakers*; Morris, *Lubavitcher Women in America.*
43 Throughout the writing process, I also adopted a collaborative approach: I sent my writing to the women I collaborated with and asked for feedback. They never asked for changes, but simply to rectify or specify details. For the artists who are publicly known on social media, I use their full names. For the private performers, I consulted each of them on their preferred way to be identified; sometimes I use their first names, while at others I change names to protect their privacy.
44 Taragin-Zeller, "Modesty for Heaven's Sake"; Taragin-Zeller, "Between Modesty and Beauty."
45 El-Or, *Educated and Ignorant*; Berger-Sofer, *Pious Women.*
46 Mahmood, *Politics of Piety*; Abu-Lughod, *Remaking Women.*
47 Consult the bibliography under the heading "Modesty and Ultra-Orthodoxy" to learn more.
48 Waldoks, "Religious Feminism(s) and Beyond."
49 Dána-Ain Davis and Christa Craven present the various understanding of "feminist ethnography," drawing upon the work of scholars from various waves and movements of feminism(s). See: Davis and Craven, *Feminist Ethnography.*
50 See: Mohanty, *Feminism without Borders*, 43–84; Khader, *Decolonizing Universalism.*
51 Strathern, "An Awkward Relationship."
52 Here I echo Erica Lehrer, whose ethnography of the Jewish-Polish relationship outlined conflicting yet coexisting memories and narratives of the past, and a method-

ological approach she called the "ethnography of possibility." Lehrer, *Jewish Poland Revisited*, 1–24.

53 I use the term "conservative" to label communities with less contact with the outside world, those that have strict rules regarding interaction with people who are not from the same community and that often define themselves as "enclaves." Among them are Hasidic groups such as Satmar, Belz, Bobov, Vishnitz, and Skver, with Satmar considered the most conservative. Liberal spaces, on the other hand, are fully connected to secular society, with individuals working beyond ultra-Orthodox circles and serving the broader society.

CHAPTER 2. THE *FRUM* FEMALE ARTIST

1 I use the term "artist" to describe the women presented in this book, but the term was claimed only by the women presented in chapters 3, 4, and 5. In conservative spaces such as the one described in chapter 2, women often refer instead to the artistic work they are engaged in (e.g., "painting," "singing"), or prefer the terms "performer," "educator," "composer," "singer," or "dancer."

2 Ferziger, "Feminism and Heresy"; Hartman, *Feminism Encounters Traditional Judaism.*

3 Fader, *Mitzvah Girls*, chapter 2.

4 I am using the term "female" to refer to the biological category that dictates the way gender is defined, embodied, and taught within ultra-Orthodox Judaism, which does not differentiate gender from biological sex. It is a term used by my interlocutors that encompasses both young girls and married women.

5 My invocation of the discursive aspect of Orthodoxy echoes Talal Assad's description of Islam as a "discursive tradition" underlying the diverse local manifestations of Islam.

6 *Hashkafa* refers to the philosophy that Orthodox Jews adopt to interpret Jewish texts. It plays a crucial role in the way they interact with the world and guides practical decisions such as at which school to register children, which synagogue to attend, and what community to live in.

7 Within Orthodox Judaism, the transmission of Jewishness is matrilineal, and the transmission of the *minhag* (tradition) is patrilineal. Thus, a woman becomes Jewish through the mother, and will be affiliated with and follow the tradition of the community of her father, then of her husband.

8 Harris, "Dignity in an Oversharing World."

9 I use the term "performance" to characterize the performative aspect of these art worlds. More importantly, this is Orthodoxy that I envisage as a performative gendered act, existing beyond the passing down of knowledge and rules, as Judith Butler suggested. Orthodoxy takes all its meaning in the performances of the woman, changing according to the age and the status of the gendered individual. Corporeal performances sustain and reflect their identities as ultra-Orthodox women. By performing Orthodox womanhood through the arts, women create and reinforce the group's narrative in an ongoing, systematic way. See: Davidman, *Becoming Un-Orthodox*. In this book, Orthodoxy is understood as a performance in which the bodily and aural expression of the self is relevant not only to the performance but also to its audience.

10 See: Butler, *Gender Trouble*; Butler, "Performative Acts and Gender Constitution."

11 The distinction between women and girls is made according to their marital status and their age. Girls are unmarried and attend schools or seminaries, while women are married, divorced, or widowed.

12 See: Cherney, "Kol Isha"; Koskoff, "Miriam Sings Her Song."

13 Translation by Sefaria, www.sefaria.org (original in Hebrew: "יָוְתִּי בְּחַגְוֵי הַסֶּלַע בְּסֵתֶר
הַמַּדְרֵגָה הַרְאִינִי אֶת־מַרְאַיִךְ הַשְׁמִיעִנִי אֶת־קוֹלֵךְ כִּי־קוֹלֵךְ עָרֵב וּמַרְאֵיךְ נָאוֶה").

14 Cherney, "Kol Isha."

15 See Koskoff, "Miriam Sings Her Song."

16 It is important to note that these pragmatic applications of *halakhic* restrictions vary depending on local contexts. For instance, in North Africa and among Sephardic or Mizrahi communities, women who live according to Jewish laws and customs have historically been active in singing for communal celebrations and tragedies, performing publicly during Jewish holidays, weddings, and circumcisions. Following the migration of North African Jews to France, Canada, Israel, and the United States in the 1960s and 1970s, as well as the Lubavitcher *rebbe*'s visit to Morocco in the early 1960s, interactions with Orthodox and ultra-Orthodox European Jews inspired a stricter application of *halakhah* within many Sephardic and Mizrahi communities. See: Elbaz, "Kol B'Isha Erva."

17 About the development of the music industry see: Jonathan Sterne, *The Audible Past.*

18 Seidman, *A Revolution in the Name of Tradition.*

19 Manekin, *The Rebellion of the Daughters.*

20 Seidman, *A Revolution in the Name of Tradition*; Manekin, *The Rebellion of the Daughters.*

21 Seidman, *A Revolution in the Name of Tradition.*

22 Seidman, *A Revolution in the Name of Tradition*, 58.

23 Seidman, *A Revolution in the Name of Tradition*, 54.

24 Seidman, *A Revolution in the Name of Tradition*, 200.

25 Seidman, *A Revolution in the Name of Tradition*, 147.

26 Weissman, "Bais Ya'acov."

27 Seidman, *A Revolution in the Name of Tradition*, 147.

28 According to Joanna Lisek, Sarah Schenirer loved Polish theater and frequented it like many other Orthodox and Hasidic girls from Galicia. See: Lisek, "'I Feel So Crazy, like Flying the Coop.'"

29 Seidman, "Legitimizing the Revolution."

30 Seidman, "Legitimizing the Revolution."

31 About Hasidic music and how it constitutes a form of communication with God, see: Wood, "Stepping across the Divide"; Koskoff, *Music in Lubavitcher Life.*

32 To learn more about the development of the Bais Yaakov movement in North America see: Seidman, et al., *Rebbetzin Vichna Kaplan*, 286–97; Klein, "Defining Bais Yaakov."

33 About the way I define tradition, read: Roda, *Se réinventer au présent*; Roda, "Constructing Patrimony, Updating the Modern."

34 Fader, *Mitzvah Girls*, 1–33; Deutsch and Casper, *A Fortress in Brooklyn.*

35 Ginsparg Klein, "Defining Bais Yaakov," 140–41.

36 Ginsparg Klein, "Defining Bais Yaakov," 135–73.

37 About the link between Orthodox Jewish music and American popular music see: Kligman, "Contemporary Jewish Music in America"; Dale, "Music in Haredi Life"; Lockwood, "Hasidic Cantors 'Out of Context.'"

38 Vaisman, "'She Who Seeks Shall Find.'"

39 For more on the prohibition against non-Jewish sources and generational discrepancies in listening habits see: Vaisman, "'She Who Seeks Shall Find.'"

40 See appendix 1.

41 These gatherings, where singing is often accompanied by guitar, take place after *shabbes.*
42 Yiddish and Loshn Koydesh are the most frequently used languages among Hasidim, while English and modern Hebrew are the most frequent among Litvish/Yeshivish circles.
43 Kligman, "Contemporary Jewish Music in America."
44 To learn more about ultra-Orthodox male performances and popular culture see: Finkelman, *Strictly Kosher Reading*; Stolow, *Orthodox by Design.*
45 See: Biale, et al., *Hasidism.*
46 See: Epstein, "The Celebration of a Contemporary Purim in the Bobover Hasidic Community"; Epstein, "Josef Is Still Alive in Brooklyn"; Epstein, "Going Far Away in Order to Better Understand the Familiar"; Koskoff, "The Sound of a Woman's Voice"; Koskoff, *Music in Lubavitcher Life.*
47 Kahan-Newman, "Women's Badkhones."
48 Vaisman, "'She Who Seeks Shall Find'"; Vaisman, "Seamed Stockings and Ponytails."
49 See Waldman, "Women's Voices in Contemporary Hasidic Communities."
50 Gellerman, "(Not Just) *Az der rebbe tantst.*"
51 See Isaacs, "Creativity in Contemporary Hasidic Yiddish."
52 Consult the bibliography under the heading "Ultra-Orthodoxy, Women, and Performances."
53 See Friedman and Hakak, "Jewish Revenge."
54 About the way exiters are pathologized by ultra-Orthodox communities see Newfield, *Degrees of Separation*, 32–72.
55 Assaf, "'My Tiny, Ugly World.'"
56 Asad, *Genealogies of Religion*, 200–238.

CHAPTER 3. THE PRIVATE PERFORMER

1 Serene J. Khader argues that feminist questions are not resolved by concerns with agency, while she also recognizes that Western feminists often ignore "other" women's systems of value and reasons for choosing to do what they do, and that this ignorance and objectification are pernicious. Here I echo Khader's view that ultra-Orthodox women develop different strategies than merely displaying their names and faces to gain visibility. Nevertheless, I also acknowledge that other *frum* women, as we will discover later, feel oppressed and restricted by this type of visibility. See: Khader, *Decolonizing Universalism.*
2 Fader, *Hidden Heretics*, chapters 1 and 2.
3 In Satmar schools, after the age of twelve, girls continue to perform in plays, but they cannot do it in front of a female audience beyond the school. This norm is in place in other Hasidic schools, while others have decided to change it, allowing the girls from all the grades to perform in front of broader female audiences, including female guests outside of the school.
4 Personal interview with Toby, July 2021, Kiryas Joel.
5 In the 1990s and early 2000s, ethnomusicologists and anthropologists also suggested a rethinking of this paradigm in the other direction—i.e., looking at traditions through the lens of individuality. Scholars working on religion and rituals have been particularly lively in this process; see: Qureshi, "Musical Sound and Contextual Input"; Rasmussen, *Women, the Recited Qur'an, and Islamic Music in Indonesia.* By celebrating and recognizing the role of individuals in rituals, these scholars decentered the collective dimension of tradition that occupied the field for decades. More recently, scholars have

emphasized the social aspect of creativity as a collective praxis guided by historical and local context (see: Born, "On Musical Mediation"; Frith, *Musical Imaginations*; Toynbee, *Migrating Music*) dependent upon society's technological and political arrangements (see: Stokes, "Globalization and the Politics of World Music"). This scholarship underlines the various kinds and expressions of creativity in the process of composition and performance (see: Burnard, *Musical Creativities in Practice*).

6   Scholars who have investigated creativity by women in religious spaces have highlighted the level of agency women and girls gain due to their public performances. About the subject see: Downing, *Gamelan Girls*; Rasmussen, *Women, the Recited Qur'an, and Islamic Music in Indonesia*. When women perform in private or secluded spaces, as many do in conservative religious circles, their performances are perceived as simply educational, social, and collective (see Isaacs, "Creativity in Contemporary Hasidic Yiddish"; Vaisman, "'She Who Seeks Shall Find'" and "Seamed Stockings and Ponytails."

7   To reassess creativity outside these schisms, this chapter draws on Howard Becker's conception of art worlds as collective processes, Marnia Lazreg's decolonizing of feminism to expand our understandings of the term beyond Western categories, Anne Rasmussen's redefinition of religious women as creative players and adapters of global music discourse in Indonesia, and Martin Stokes's definition of creativity according to technological and political arrangement. See: Becker, *Art Worlds*; Lazreg, "Decolonizing Feminism"; Rasmussen, *Women, the Recited Qur'an, and Islamic Music in Indonesia*; Stokes, "Creativity, Globalization, and Music."

8   Isaacs is one of the authors arguing that ultra-Orthodox women's performances exclude the concepts of fame and of creativity for its own sake (see: Isaacs, "Creativity in Contemporary Hasidic Yiddish"). This idea of the arts for their own sake is anchored in European Romanticism, referring to the role of art to create beauty, which echoes the purity of the arts discussed by Kant. See: Allison, *Kant's Theory of Taste*.

9   Conversation with the producer of the play, May 2019, Montreal. This comment about the power of the choir for community formation addressed by Rivka is seconded by an extensive literature about the power of collective performances, and more specifically of group singing. Consult the bibliography under the heading "Power of Collective Performances" to learn more.

10 About the health benefits of group singing see Livesey, et al., "Benefits of Choral Singing for Social and Mental Wellbeing"; Williams, Dingle, and Clift, "A Systematic Review of Mental Health and Wellbeing Outcomes of Group Singing for Adults with a Mental Health Condition"; Bailey and Davidson. "Effects of Group Singing and Performance for Marginalized and Middle-Class Singers."

11 Ellen Koskoff observed in the 1990s and 2000s that women from more conservative communities typically do not perform or participate in plays after their marriage.

12 Roda, "Orthodox Women and the Musical Shekhinah."

13 Phone conversation with Toby, November 2021.

14 The type of hair covering often characterizes the level of religious observance maintained in families, but also social status, group adherence, cultural practice, and fashion. The presence of only *shpitzel*, short *sheytl*, and short *sheytl* with a band indicates that the audience is affiliated with more conservative circles within ultra-Orthodoxy. So-called cosmopolitan or modern ultra-Orthodox women will wear long *sheytl*. On hair coverings, see Vizel, "A List of Hasidic Female Headgear, with Illustrations"; Milligan, *Hair, Headwear, and Orthodox Jewish Women*; Tarlo, "Great Expectations"; Carrel, "Hasidic Women's Head Coverings."

15 Conversation with Freida, January 2019, Brooklyn, New York.
16 Fader, *Hidden Heretics*, 121–50.
17 For more information on fitness and well-being see: Burkhardt and Rhodes, "Commissioning Dance for Health and Wellbeing"; Gardner, et al., "Dancing beyond Exercise"; Keogh, et al., "Physical Benefits of Dancing for Healthy Older Adults"; O'Neill, et al., "Descriptive Epidemiology of Dance Participation in Adolescents."
18 Murcia, et al., "Shall We Dance?"; Fernández-Argüelles, et al., "Effects of Dancing on the Risk of Falling-Related Factors of Healthy Older Adults."
19 See: Widdows, *Perfect Me*; Brewis, et al., "Body Norms and Fat Stigma in Global Perspective."
20 Archambault, "In Pursuit of Fitness."
21 *Hashkafa* refers to the philosophy that Orthodox Jews adopt to interpret Jewish texts. It plays a crucial role in the way they interact with the world and guides practical decisions such as at which school to register children, which synagogue to attend, and what community to live in.
22 Her name has been changed in order to maintain her confidentiality.
23 *Hekhsher* certification refers to the confirmation that a product has been certified by a particular rabbi or group of rabbis to be kosher. The term is often used in reference to food, but it also refers to literature and entertainment.
24 Personal interview with Zalman, Montreal, January 2021.
25 Haim Zicherman and Lee Cahaner, חרדיות מודרנית מעמד ביניים חרדי בישראל (Modern ultra-orthodoxy: The emerging Haredi middle class in Israel) (Jerusalem: Israel Democracy Institute, 2012) [Hebrew].
26 Finkelman, *Strictly Kosher Reading*.
27 The importance of beauty and thinness among ultra-Orthodox women, and notably for arranged marriage (*Shiddukh*), has been documented particularly by psychologists in the last decade. See: P. Scot Richards, et al., "Religiousness and Spirituality in the Etiology and Treatment of Eating Disorders"; Ozick, "The Relationship between Religious Orientation, Superwoman Ideal, and Disordered Eating Pathology in Israeli Orthodox Adolescent Girls."
28 Fader, *Hidden Heretics*, chapter 5.
29 Dale, "Music in Haredi Jewish Life."
30 See Ratzon Program website: https://ratzonprogram.com/.
31 The concept of well-being is complex and subjective to its cultural context. In the context of creativity, fitness, and dance in ultra-Orthodox circles, it refers to mental, physical, and spiritual well-being, notably meaning the absence of illness and the pursuit of happiness in one's commitment to religious life.
32 A news line is a telephone service that serves as an important source of news in the ultra-Orthodox world. As many do not listen to the radio, and do not have access to the news, religious authorities created the news-line system to disseminate relevant news to their members. The system has expanded to transmit additional information. Some lines are transmitting rabbinical lectures, entertainment, and business advice, and women also developed their own lines to transmit information among themselves, including music, as I observed in the field.
33 For more information on creativity, well-being, and psychology see: Compton and Hoffman, *Positive Psychology*; Csikszentmihalyi and Seligman, "Positive Psychology"; Acar, et al., "Creativity and Well-Being"; Chavez-Eakle, et al., "Personality"; Peterson and Seligman, *Character Strengths and Virtues*; Wright and Walton, "Affect, Psychological Wellbeing, and Creativity."

34 Simonton, "Creativity."
35 Archambault, "In Pursuit of Fitness." Both as an observer and as a participant in Canada and the United States, I witnessed the increased popularity of dance and yoga classes offered by *baalei tshuva* but also women born in the community, such as Freida.
36 This use of the Internet was possible as some male and female figures of authority saw no threat in it, as long as filters are used, but rather saw new opportunities to consolidate religiosity and sisterhood.
37 For the music industry, the digital turn meant the transformation of analog information into a digital form, such as the use of digital audio recordings.
38 Carpo, *The Second Digital Turn*, 9–97.
39 About copyright and the digital see: McLeod, "MP3s Are Killing Home Taping"; McLeod and Striphas, "Strategic Improprieties"; Guillebaud, Stoichita, and Mallet, et al., "La musique n'a pas d'auteur."
40 About the role of the digital in increasing access to music production outside the mainstream music industry, see: Fournier, "Positioning the New Reggaetón Stars in Cuba"; McLeod, "MP3s Are Killing Home Taping."
41 Wolfe, *Women in the Studio*.
42 Lysloff and Gay, *Music and Technoculture*.
43 For filmmaking see: Malik, Chapain, and Comunian, *Community Filmmaking*. For music making see: Barnat, "Vers une ethnomusicologie du studio d'enregistrement."
44 Artistic knowledge is often transmitted from professionals outside the community or via online training; this fact is usually kept secret because it implies external interaction—in person or online—that is forbidden by religious authorities.
45 The production of instrumental playback depends on the studio owner's knowledge of programmed MIDI (Musical Instrument Digital Interface) tracks that create virtual instrument sounds. Some women and girls create their own tracks, playing instruments they have in the studio, while others, less knowledgeable in studio recording, download programmed MIDI tracks from websites specializing in Jewish Orthodox music, and edit them according to their needs.
46 Two examples of women who have built such studios are Rochel Leah and Chayala Neuhaus, whom I discuss in greater detail in the next chapter.
47 Such as illegal music in Cuba (see: Fournier, "Positioning the New Reggaetón Stars in Cuba"; Magowan and Neuenfeldt, *Landscapes of Indigenous Performance*), underground techno-hybrid music in Indonesia (Wallach, "Underground Rock Music and Democratization in Indonesia"), or pop music produced in home studios in Mali (see Andrieu and Olivier, eds., *Création artistique et imaginaires de la globalisation*).
48 Copyright is here understood in its broader sense, as a type of intellectual property that gives the right to make copies of or use a creative work that serves as an original expression of an idea, resulting in a product that is either tangible (book, artwork) or intangible (music, choreography).
49 Guillebaud, Stoichita, and Mallet, "La musique n'a pas d'auteur."
50 See: Chon, "The Romantic Collective Author"; and Arewa, "From J. C. Bach to Hip Hop"; Hennion, "Loving Music."
51 Indeed, very few ultra-Orthodox composers of melodies can read music. Velvet Pasternak is one of the few who transcribed Hasidic songs from the supposedly old tradition from Eastern Europe. Ben Zion Shenker, a composer and *hazzan* associated with the Modzitz Hasidic dynasty, transcribed prewar Modzitz songs, as well as his

own compositions. Shenker was a pioneer in Orthodox musical recording, making the first recording of Hasidic music in 1950 (*Modzitzer Melaveh Malka Melodies*). David Wedyger later followed his lead in the 1970s.

52 McLucas, *The Musical Ear*.

53 Guillebaud, Stoichita, and Mallet, *La musique n'a pas d'auteur*.

54 Leach and Stern observe a similar dynamic in Melanesia. See: Leach and Stern, "The Value of Music in Melanesia."

55 Chon, "The Romantic Collective Author," 430.

56 Johansson and Berge, "Who Owns an Interpretation?"

57 Arditi, *Getting Signed*.

58 Johansson and Berge, "Who Owns an Interpretation?"

59 About Kay Kaufman Shelemay's contribution to the debate about creativity in ethnomusicology, see: Shelemay, "Musical Communities"; Shelemay, *Sing and Sing On*.

60 Leach and Stern, "The Value of Music in Melanesia."

61 Rasmussen, *Women, the Recited Qur'an, and Islamic Music in Indonesia*.

62 In her article "Musical Communities," Kay Kaufman Shelemay suggested a tripartite model based on processes of descent, dissent, and affinity. See: Shelemay, "Musical Communities."

63 Lea Taragin-Zeller looked at modesty as a creative sphere informed by the adoption of modern patterns of behavior and religious innovation. See: Taragin-Zeller, "Modesty for Heaven's Sake."

64 Holm, *The Rise of Online Counterpublics?*

65 Seidman, *A Revolution in the Name of Tradition*, 54.

CHAPTER 4. THE CELEBRITY

1 Kaplan, "A Studio Grows in Brooklyn."

2 To learn about American capitalism, women, and religiosity read: Kieffer, "Manifesting Millions."

3 Barry, "Celebrity, Cultural Production, and Public Life."

4 About the scholarship on male cantorial music see: Slobin, *Chosen Voices*; Shandler, "Sanctification of the Brand Name"; Roda and Tara Schwartz. "Home beyond Borders and the Sound of Al-Andalus"; Lockwood, "Prayer and Crime"; Lockwood, *Golden Ages*.

5 While men do not have access to this market, in certain cases some collaborate in the production of these women's art, such as by providing technical support.

6 Dyer, *Heavenly Bodies*, 87, quoted in Barry, "Celebrity, Cultural Production, and Public Life," 251.

7 Furedi, "Celebrity Culture."

8 It has been suggested that the star should be understood as a subcategory of the celebrity, and celebrity studies, as an expansion of star studies (which had been primarily concerned with film stars), has widened the scope of analysis by including stardom in sport, TV, and music. I have decided to privilege "celebrity" instead of "star" in this chapter because it has been used by some of my interlocutors in my fieldwork, and it encompasses multiple aspects of fame. On the culture of celebrity and stardom, see: Dyer and McDonald, *Stars*; Schickel, *Intimate Strangers*; Turner, *Understanding Celebrity*; Loy, Rickwood, and Bennett, eds., *Popular Music, Stars, and Stardom*; Toynbee, *Making Popular Music*; Inglis, *A Short History of Celebrity*.

9 Marcus, *The Drama of Celebrity*.

10 See Friedman and Hakak, "Jewish Revenge."

11 On digital and amateur filmmaking, see: Hudson, *Thinking through Digital Media*; Salazkina and Fibla-Gutiérrez, *Global Perspectives on Amateur Film Histories and Cultures*; Elsaesser, *Film History as Media Archaeology*; Gaudreault and Marion, *La fin du cinéma?*

12 While community media emerged in the 1960s and 1970s in western Europe and North America, the digitalization of filmmaking in the decades around the turn of the century carried this movement beyond the West. Importantly, *frum* female cinema was facilitated by a local media infrastructure owned by ultra-Orthodox men. Filmmakers are embedded in specific local and regional creative ecosystems, which can enable but also inhibit their practices. On community filmmaking see: Chapain and Comunian, "Enabling and Inhibiting the Creative Economy."

13 About models of celebrity see: Barron, *Celebrity Cultures*; Cashmore, *Celebrity Culture*.

14 Hayward, *Cinema Studies*, 375.

15 Dyer and McDonald, *Stars*.

16 See the poster for the "Vzakeini" campaign included in the article "Bonei Olam Presents: Vezakeini, a Song for the Children," *Yeshiva World*, January 28, 2020, without a single female depicted: www.theyeshivaworld.com, accessed November 16, 2022.

17 Poster for the Vzakeini campaign with detailed information in "Bonei Olam Vzakeini: The Power of Every Individual," *Matzav.com*, March 22, 2020: https://matzav.com, accessed November 16, 2022.

18 Poster with women's faces in "The Women and Girls Event of the Year Is Officially Open for Registration," *Yeshiva World*, June 12, 2020: www.theyeshivaworld.com, accessed November 16, 2022; poster without women's faces in "The Women and Girls Event of the Year Open for Registration," *Lakewood Scoop*, June 11, 2020: https://thelakewoodscoop.com, accessed November 16, 2022.

19 Poster promoted on the Orthodox Jewish newspaper website *Matzav*, in the article "Women and Girls Event of the Year Is Officially Open for Registration!" June 10, 2020: https://matzav.com, accessed November 16, 2022; poster promoted in the online Orthodox Jewish newspaper *Yeshiva World*, "Tonight! 9 pm: Woman's and Girls Event of the Year," June 16, 2020: www.theyeshivaworld.com, accessed November 16, 2022.

20 On celebrity stories helping to sell other commodities, see Deflem, *Lady Gaga and the Sociology of Fame*; Marcus, *The Drama of Celebrity*.

21 Franciska produced *Lekha Dodi* in 2012, and Nechama Cohen produced *Inside Out* in October 2014. Franciska is one of the only *frum* female singers to have self-produced music videos on a regular basis for several years. In them, she explores a mix of different musical genres, visual aesthetics, and narratives.

22 For women in the arts, it has been the norm to perform almost for free, or for a small honorarium to collect money for a social organization, instead of performing for personal economic growth.

23 Dobby Baum created the first online independent concert for women and girls in October 2020 for *Khol Hamoed*, but the concert received far less press coverage than Devorah Schwartz's "Chanukah Spectacular."

24 It is important to note that in North America, professional training takes the form of private lessons, while in Israel, the government has funded formal educational programs for Orthodox women in film and music, something that does not yet exist in the Americas or Europe.

25 Music video of "Ein Od Milvado: The COVID Cover," by Devorah Schwartz: www.youtube.com/watch?v=cVgX7CKOFas, accessed November 16, 2022.

26 Dance tutorial by Devorah Schwartz, released on March 13, 2021: www.youtube.com /watch?v=XEDp6AnTILY, accessed November 16, 2022.

27 Arts training by professionals from outside the community or via online classes often takes place but is not advertised and is even kept secret as it implies external interaction forbidden by religious authorities.

28 Interview with Chayala Neuhaus in 2019 on *The Franciska Show*, a podcast about Orthodox women in the arts with thousands of followers: https://thefranciskashow .libsyn.com. Chayala reinforced this idea during my own Zoom interview with her in February 2021.

29 Hasidic cantor David Werdyger founded Aderet in 1950, after his arrival in the United States following World War II. Today his son Mendel Werdyger owns the label, and he has expanded the business into a distribution company called Mostly Music.

30 Music Video "This One," released September 2, 2021: www.youtube.com/watch?v =kuP4YlUuuOg, accessed November 28, 2022.

31 Poster of the event Fire Works 2.0 on TicketTailor: www.tickettailor.com, accessed November 18, 2022.

32 Music video of the cover "A Yid" by Dobby Baum and Frimi, released on Instagram on May 15, 2021: www.youtube.com/watch?v=Jm2Gb9KcbuA, accessed November 18, 2022; music video of the cover "A Yid" by Devorah Schwartz and Esther Sara Zuskind, released June 13, 2021: www.youtube.com/watch?v=8ZDyYnH8Se8, accessed November 18, 2022.

33 Instagram post with the poster of the event: https://www.instagram.com/p /ChpX8tkuJP7/, accessed November 18, 2022.

34 Friedman and Hakak, "Jewish Revenge."

35 Malky Weingarten, personal conversation in Borough Park, November 2020.

36 In the video, titled "What Hasidic Women Have to Say (eye-opening experience!)," Santenello promotes Weingarten's films and social media, providing links to her work on nigunmusic.com and to her Instagram page, adding "women only please": www .youtube.com/watch?v=jUDFpt6lcew, accessed November 28, 2022.

37 On stigmas regarding neurodiversity, disabilities, and mental health in ultra-Orthodoxy, see: Orr, Unger, and Finkelstein, "Localization of Human Rights of People with Disabilities."

38 Instagram link to access the advertisement of the weekly show: www.instagram.com/p /CkrsaSbgqRH/, accessed on November 18, 2022.

39 Other renowned North American *frum* female filmmakers include Israeli Ronit Polin, Tobi Einhorn, and Robin Garbose. The literature on ultra-Orthodox cinema is essentially based on the Israeli scene. Consult the bibliography under the heading "Ultra-Orthodox Cinema" to learn more.

40 "*Emuna*" can be translated as "trust in God," "faith," or "belief." In ultra-Orthodox circles it is a very important concept related to the innate conviction of the presence of God in everyday life and one's physical commitment to the faith. For more on the interpretation of *Emuna* in Orthodox Judaism read: "The State of Orthodox Belief," summer 2019 issue of *Jewish Action*: https://jewishaction.com.

41 On independent filmmaking, see: Erickson and Baltruschat, eds., *Independent Filmmaking around the Globe*.

42 Information on Project Menucha may be found at www.projectmenucha.org/. The video in *Hush Hush* is for the organization Chazkeinu, offering support for women coping with mental health issues: https://chazkeinu.org/about/.

43 In her book *The Drama of Celebrity*, Sharon Marcus explains how celebrities do more than simply display unconventionality; they model an attitude of indifference to non-conformity's potential consequences. Marcus, "Introduction," 25.

44 Alease Annan, "BRIC's Two Community Media TV Networks—BRIC TV and Brooklyn Free Speech—Nominated for Eight 2019 Emmy Awards," *BRIC*, February 27, 2020: www.bricartsmedia.org; 2020 New York Emmy Awards, "2020 Nominees Press Release": www.nyemmys.org/.

45 Marcus, *The Drama of Celebrity*.

46 While mainstream media are not typically theorized in cultural studies as secular versus religious, as we will observe in chapter 5, both North American media coverage and mainstream media often portray religiosity and religious bodies as repressed and marginal. Winston, *Unchosen*.

47 Personal conversation, November 2020, Borough Park, Brooklyn.

48 Sabrina Qions Yu suggests that stardom has always functioned as a masquerade and that stars have always actively participated in the making of their own image, mobilizing ethnicity, aging, appearance, acting, and camp. See: Yu, "Introduction: Performing Stardom."

49 An example of such influence wielded by celebrities is the social media campaign, discussed in the introduction of chapter 4, launched by singer Dalia Oziel to defend *agunot*—a campaign that ultimately mobilized not only other *frum* female artists but also women and men from across North America.

50 About spiritual women's use of capitalism read: Kieffer, "Manifesting Millions."

51 Bowler, *The Preacher's Wife*.

52 My use of the term "translation" is inspired by the work of scholars analyzing the localization of human rights: Orr, Unger, and Finkelstein, "Localization of Human Rights of People with Disabilities"; Zwingel, "How Do Norms Travel?" It implies that different norms may be translated into another realm—for example, from global to national, or from local to national. The term also sees heavy use and discussion in anthropology to reflect on the emic/etic points of view, with the anthropologist as cultural translator. See: Chambers, "Anthropology as Cultural Translation"; Rossman and Rubel, *Translating*. The idea of translating ideas and concepts from broader North American society into ultra-Orthodox women's circles has been documented by Ayala Fader (*Mitzvah Girls*) and Lea Taragin-Zeller ("Between Modesty and Beauty"). Fader utilizes the term "Hasidification" in the context of North American fashion to demonstrate how Hasidic women maintain ultra-Orthodox standards of modesty and beauty in conjunction with this fashion, and Taragin-Zeller argues that Israeli Haredi women reinterpret female piety to construct a positive, religiously motivated ideology of materialism, beauty, and consumption.

53 Celebrity culture has its roots in nineteenth-century democratization, individualism, and the birth of the middle class, as people began to have more spare time (Marcus, *The Drama of Celebrity*). While the middle class has been shrinking over the last half-century, and in recent decades, dramatically so, in ultra-Orthodox circles, an opposite process occurs, as the middle class did not exist when ultra-Orthodox Jews settled in North America in the 1950s.

54 See: Stern, "Unpacking Adaptation."

55 In 1994, after a year of intense activism by indigenous women and their urban supporters, indigenous women in the New Territories of Hong Kong were legally allowed to inherit land for the first time.

56 Indraganti, "Song Taxonomies."
57 See Indraganti, "Song Taxonomies"; and Will Straw, "Scenes and Sensibilities," *Public* 22–23 (2001): 245–57.
58 Turner, *Understanding Celebrity*.
59 Bowler, *The Preacher's Wife*.

CHAPTER 5. THE INFLUENCER

1 All the number of views and followers presented in this chapter reflect data collected in December 2022.
2 The increased presence of women on social media, notably on Instagram, has been documented by various journalists. See: Gutenmacher, "The Orthodox Women of Instagram"; Chizhik-Goldschmidt, "Is Social Media Fueling a Women's Rights Revolution in the Orthodox Jewish Community"; Chizhik-Goldschmidt, "Orthodox Jewish Women Can't Sing in Front of Men"; Brown, "On Instagram, Orthodox Women Find a Voice—and Power"; Chizhik-Goldschmidt, "'They're Out to Get Us.'"
3 The Chesed fund is a global collaborative platform to raise funds for all Orthodox Jewish– related causes. See the page created to support Chava: Dalia Ozel, "#freechava," Chesed Fund, n.d.: https://thechesedfund.com, accessed March 31, 2023.
4 Instagram, @leahforster, posted on March 16, 2021.
5 The ultra-Orthodox press has various positions regarding the publication of women's and girls' faces, which depend on the intended audience, as well as the opinions of religious leadership within different communities. For instance, in magazines, pamphlets, or any publications within the Chabad-Lubavitch community, female faces will be published if they respect the codes of *tsnius*. For other Hasidim and Litvish, positions on this topic vary greatly. Some Hasidim will not even publish drawings of girls in schoolbooks, while others have no issue doing so. The idea is that women and girls should remain in the private sphere. For female artistic publications that are "for women and girls only," it has become more acceptable to publish a photo of the artist within a book or CD/DVD booklet, but not on the front or back covers. However, when it comes to most of the publications available for both genders, there is a general rule against publishing the faces of women and girls. The two most popular magazines, *Ami Magazine* (aligned with Hasidic leadership) and *Mishpahah Magazine* (more aligned with Litvish leadership) do not publish female faces. However, *Mishpahah* has started to include some female faces in the version of the magazine published online.
6 Fader, *Hidden Heretics*, chapters 1, 2, and 3.
7 Zion-Waldoks, "Birth of a Movement."
8 Mohanty, *Feminism without Borders*.
9 The concept of counterpublics emerged from Habermas's work on the public sphere, followed by Fraser and Warner, who contributed to the understanding of the publics as plural. The first anthropologist to use the concept in his work was Charles Hirschkind in his analysis of cassette recordings of Islamic sermons in Egypt. In the Jewish context, Ayala Fader uses the term "counterpublic" to discuss the blogosphere made by ultra-Orthodox Jews who are double-lifers, which she describes as a heretical counterpublic.
10 About cyberfeminism see: Batmanghelichi and Mouri, "Cyberfeminism, Iranian Style"; Radhika and Mamidipudi, "Cyberfeminism, Technology, and International 'Development.'"
11 Weinblatt and Livio, "Discursive Legitimation of a Controversial Technology."

12 To learn more about comparative work on the subject, see: Campbell, *Digital Religion*.

13 About the role of social media and its decentralization of religious leadership see: Eckert and Chadha, "Muslim Bloggers in Germany"; Harris and Roose, "DIY Citizenship amongst Young Muslims"; Kavakci and Kraeplin, "Religious Beings in Fashionable Bodies"; Mosemghvdlishvili and Jansz, "Framing and Praising Allah on YouTube"; Frissen, et al., "#Muslim?"

14 Personal interview, New York, August 2020.

15 Kieffer, "Manifesting Millions."

16 Fader, *Hidden Heretics*, chapters 2 and 3.

17 Allard, "Partages créatifs"; Laestadius, "Instagram."

18 Heilman, *Who Will Lead Us?*

19 I determine their popularity by the number of followers they have, a number that usually surpasses five thousand followers.

20 About the transformation of Instagram see: Perez, "Instagram's Big Redesign Goes Live with a Colorful New Icon, Black-and-White App, and More."

21 Constine, "Instagram Launches 'Stories,' a Snapchatty Feature for Imperfect Sharing."

22 An unlisted video is a type of private video that viewers must have a specific link to access. Such a video will not appear in any of YouTube's public search results.

23 Carrel, "Hasidic Women's Head Coverings."

24 Carrel, "Hasidic Women's Head Coverings."

25 Carrel, "Hasidic Women's Head Coverings."

26 The song is also available on Spotify, iTunes, and Deezer, and on YouTube as a video with only the audio and an image of the single's album cover, but viewers could access the unlisted music video only by visiting her personal website and, for a few weeks, by clicking the link available on her public Instagram account.

27 Malky's Instagram post, @malkys_media, April 5, 2019, www.instagram/com.

28 About gender as performance see: Butler, *Gender Trouble*.

29 Scholars of "digital religion" have investigated how new media facilitate the expansion of religious communities and how they strengthen existing communal bonds.

30 Interestingly, the concept of *tikkun olam* is often mobilized by the liberal Jewish community.

31 This site may be consulted at www.keepwomeninthepicture.com (formerly www.frumwomenhavefaces.com), accessed February 19, 2023.

32 Adina Miles-Sash has been drastically criticized for her critical position on the status of women within Orthodoxy. On her Instagram account she talks about the backlash her position has provoked, but I was also able to perceive the negative judgment via informal discussions during my fieldwork and in Orthodox publications: Tzippy Stimler, "Mailbag: An Open Letter to My Fellow Mothers in Flatbush," *Yeshiva World*, May 13, 2019: www.theyeshivaworld.com; "'People Say, the Longer It Is, the Sluttier It Is': Orthodox Jewish Woman Reveals the Hate She's Received from Her Own Community for Wearing Long Wigs," *Daily Mail*, September 9, 2018: www.dailymail.co.uk; Rebecca Schischa, "Meet Flatbush Girl: Frum, Funny, Feminist," *Jewish Chronicle*, December 20, 2018: www.thejc.com.

33 The video, titled "Judge Your Fellow Jew," currently has more than twenty thousand views: www.youtube.com/watch?v=CmuCPuXaQYA, accessed February 19, 2023.

34 BRIC TV is one arm of the arts and media institution BRIC, which is based in downtown Brooklyn and focuses on "contemporary visual and performing arts, media, and civic action." See www.bricartsmedia.org/about-bric.

35 Adina Miles-Sash, "Tech and Orthodox Jewish Women with Adina Miles, a.k.a. Flat-bush Girl & an RBG Bio," BRIC TV: https://www.youtube.com/watch?v=2uioMY98 -tQ, accessed February 19, 2023.

36 Personal exchange, Montreal, 2021.

37 Kieffer, "Manifesting Millions."

38 Daniels, "Rethinking Cyberfeminism(s)"; Gajjala, *Cyber Selves.*

39 The book was published in January 2017 by Menucha Publishers, an Orthodox pub-lishing company.

40 According to several Orthodox women experts in the field of girls' education, the concept of choice is an essential part of Judaism but has not been promoted since the rebuilding of the Orthodox world in North America after the Holocaust.

41 Chany Rosengarten Instagram post (July 10, 2017), @chany_rosengarten_: www .instagram.com (accessed July 4, 2023).

42 Chany Rosengarten Instagram post (November 5, 2017), @chany_rosengarten_: www .instagram.com (accessed July 4, 2023).

43 Chany Rosengarten Instagram video (January 29, 2020), @chany_rosengarten_: www .instagram.com (accessed July 4, 2023).

44 Chany Rosengarten Instagram reels (October 6, 2020), @chany_rosengarten_: www .instagram.com (accessed July 4, 2023).

45 Goldblatt, "Rockland Jewish Women's Chany Rosengarten."

46 Chany Rosengarten Instagram Post (March 12, 2020), @chany_rosengarten_: www .instagram.com (accessed July 4, 2023).

47 A summary of the book and blurbs for the authors can be found at "About the Au-thors," Saving Lives While Fighting for Mine: https://savinglivesbook.wordpress.com (accessed July 26, 2023).

48 Kymlicka, *Multicultural Citizenship*; Khader, *Decolonizing Universalism.*

49 Dobby Baum Instagram story (March 8, 2020), @dobbybaum: www.instagram.com.

50 Flowmotion Studios is located in Crown Heights and was established in 2000 as Jew-ish Films by Yankee Teitelbaum, joined in 2012 by Bracha Torenheim as chief editor and producer. Both are part of the Chabad-Lubavitch Hasidic community. See www .flowmotion.tv/about.

51 This video announcement is available at www.youtube.com/watch?v=4YdDUErB6lo, accessed December 13, 2020.

52 Dobby Baum Instagram (October 9, 2023), @dobbybaum: www.instagram.com (accessed July 4, 2023).

53 Khader, *Decolonizing Universalism*, 122–23.

54 Khader, *Decolonizing Universalism*, 122–23.

55 Shani Orgad, "The Transformative Potential of Online Communication," *Feminist Media Studies* 5, no. 2 (2005): 141–61.

56 Golan and Martini, "The Making of Contemporary Papacy."

57 See: Friedman, "Periodizing Modernism"; Meyers, "Feminism and Women's Auton-omy"; Christman, "Relational Autonomy, Liberal Individualism, and the Social Consti-tution of Selves"; Christman, "Autonomy and Deeply Embedded Cultural Identities."

58 Mishol-Shauli and Golan, "Mediatizing the Holy Community."

59 Gajjala, "Studying Feminist E-Spaces."

60 Messina-Dysert, Ruether, and Coleman, *Feminism and Religion in the 21st Century.*

61 Gifford, "Religious Authority."

62 For a summary of the studies on online communities and religious societies, see: Mishol-Shauli and Golan, "Smartphone Religious Networking."

63 Campbell, *Digital Religion*.
64 Golan and Fehl, "Legitimizing Academic Knowledge in Religious Bounded Communities."
65 Hoover and Echchaibi, "Media Theory and the 'Third Spaces of Digital Religion.'"

CHAPTER 6. THE PUBLIC ARTIST

1 I decided to use only the first name, "Malky," in this context to highlight my reciprocity with her. On the play *God of Vengeance*, see David Mazower, "10 Things You Need to Know about *God of Vengeance*," Digital Yiddish Theatre Project, University of Wisconsin–Milwaukee, February 2017: https://web.uwm.edu, accessed March 31, 2023; Caplan, "Sholem Asch's 'God of Vengeance.'"
2 Kilgannon, "An Incisive Play about Hasidisim, with Actors Who Lived It."
3 Roda, "Representation, Recognition, and Institutionalization of a New Community."
4 Rosilio, *Declining the Stereotype*.
5 The gallery's website is www.shtetlartgallery.com/. See also Chizhik-Golschmidt, "The Unorthodox Art of an Ultra-Orthodox Community."
6 Herzfield, *Cultural Intimacy*.
7 Herrera, "'But Do We Have the Actors for That?'"
8 About former ultra-Orthodox Jews and their process of re-creating themselves see: Davidman, *Becoming Un-Orthodox*; Newfield, *Degrees of Separation*.
9 Shryock, ed., *Off Stage/On Display*.
10 In his book *Acting Jewish*, film studies scholar Henry Bial addresses and explains criticisms of the casting of Alfred Molina, a non-Jewish actor, to play Tevye, an Orthodox Jew, in *Fiddler on the Roof*; here, the debate about legitimacy is about Jewishness, a positionality that does not necessarily guarantee the knowledge and experience of Orthodox Judaism. See: Bial, *Acting Jewish*.
11 Abrams, *The New Jew in Film*, 135.
12 Wiegman, "Race, Ethnicity, and Film."
13 Rocha, "Jewish Cinematic Self-Representations in Contemporary Argentine and Brazilian Films"; Abrams, *The New Jew in Film*, 134.
14 Abrams, *The New Jew in Film*, 134.
15 About white-passing Jews, see: Wiegman, "Race, Ethnicity, and Film," 159; Abrams, *The New Jew in Film*, 134; Goldstein, *The Price of Whiteness*.
16 Hammerman, *Silver Screen, Hasidic Jews*, xxi.
17 Hammerman, *Silver Screen, Hasidic Jews*, xxii.
18 Abrams. *The New Jew in Film*, 144–46.
19 Wright, "Judaism."
20 Hammerman, *Silver Screen, Hasidic Jews*, xxii.
21 Barrios, *Screened Out*; Diawara, *Black American Cinema*.
22 About *Fiddler on the Roof* see: Bial, *Acting Jewish*; Solomon, *Wonder of Wonders*.
23 See: Feldman, *Unorthodox*; Deen, *All Who Go Do Not Return*.
24 Skinazi, *Women of Valor*; Roda, "Rethinking Orthodoxy from Its Margins."
25 Solano, *Religion and Film*, 2.
26 According to a June 2021 report from Nielsen, 64 percent of time spent on television was on network and cable TV, while 26 percent was spent on streaming services such as Netflix and Hulu. See: "The Gauge Shows Streaming Is Taking a Seat at the Table," *Nielsen*, June 17, 2021: www.nielsen.com. Streaming companies have continued to gain dominance, especially during the pandemic, as consumers move away from traditional

pay television. On this topic, see: Jessica Bursztynsky, "About One-Quarter of U.S. TV Time Is Spent Watching Streaming Services, says Nielsen," *CNBC*, June 17, 2021, www.cnbc.com; Aaron Pressman, "Cord Cutting Is Speeding Up as the Coronavirus Pandemic Squeezes Consumers," *Fortune*, May 5, 2020, https://fortune.com; "One Foot in the Metaverse: As Young Generations Embrace Gaming and Social Media, Can Streaming Video Keep Up?" Press Release, *Deloitte*, March 29, 2015, www2.deloitte .com. About the role of Netflix in the shaping of images, read: McDonald and Smith-Rowsey, *The Netflix Effect*.

27 Ramji, "Examining the Critical Role American Popular Film Continues to Play in Maintaining the Muslim Terrorist Image, Post 9/11."

28 Motyl, "No Longer a Promised Land"; Ramji, "From Navy Seals to *The Siege*."

29 Semmerling, *"Evil" Arabs in American Popular Film*; Ramji, "From Navy Seals to *The Siege*"; Hussain, "Islam."

30 Bayraktaroglu, "The Muslim Male Character Typology in American Cinema Post-9/11."

31 Bayraktaroglu, "The Muslim Male Character Typology in American Cinema Post-9/11."

32 Stephens, *A History of News*; Gabriele, ed., *Sensationalism and the Genealogy of Modernity*.

33 About the Thursday Night Chulent and Isaac Schoenfeld, see: Bleyer, "'City of Refuge'"; Scott, *Leaving the Fold*; Boyarin, "Chulent"; Roda, "Rethinking Orthodoxy from Its Margins."

34 Since the time of my initial interview with Melissa Weisz, there have been controversies regarding recollecting the exact data about the seminude scene, and who asked whom to participate in the movie.

35 Yeğenoğlu, *Colonial Fantasies*.

36 "Ex-Hasidic Woman Embraces Her Jewish Identity," *NBC News*, July 27, 2016: interview with Melissa Weisz, available on YouTube: www.youtube.com/watch?v =O5Z9XoLspmo.

37 "Ex-Hasidic Woman Embraces Her Jewish Identity."

38 For an interview with Melissa Weisz, see Barcella, "Why I Left My Religion—Arranged Marriage & All—Behind."

39 For the interview with Giroux see: Miller, "Interview."

40 Homi Bhabha suggests that the stereotype is characterized by a "productive ambivalence" between "pleasure and desire" and "power and domination," echoing the sentiments of fascination, romanticization, and superiority that we see here. Babha, *The Location of Culture*, 96.

41 Melissa Weisz, January 2022, interview in New York City.

42 The film received awards in various categories at the Torino Film Festival, the Whistler Film Festival, the Quebec Cinema Awards, the Festival du nouveau cinéma, and the Haifa International Film Festival.

43 About the critique of the film consult: Debruge, "Film Review"; interview with Luzer Twersky: Elkon, "'Felix and Meira'"; interview with Maxime Giroux: Miller, "Interview."

44 O'Sullivan, "'Félix and Meira' Review."

45 Jeannette Catsoulis—writer and reviewer of film for the *New York Times*, see: Catsoulis, "Review."

46 Taylor, "Two Unmoored Souls Too Gloomily Drawn in 'Felix and Meira.'"

47 About the media coverage that Melissa Weisz received see: Barcella, "Why I Left My Religion—Arranged Marriage & All—Behind"; Satenstein, "*Off the Beaten Path*";

Kuruvilla, "Meet the Queer Ex-Hasidic Woman Embracing Life outside Her Faith";
Lipman, "Melissa Weisz."

48 Savitz, "Ex-Hasidic Woman Embraces Her Queer Identity."

49 Call for Artists: Miléna Kartowski-Aïach, "Experimental Theater between Ultraorthodox and Secular Worlds Is Looking for OTD Artists in New York City," Facebook, last edited March 13, 2021: www.facebook.com.

50 The play was presented as follows: "In English and Yiddish (followed by a Q&A session with the team); directed by: Miléna Kartowski-Aïach; with: M. Blip, Goldie Hoffman, Eli R., Luzer Twersky, Melissa Weisz; Suggested donation: $10 (to cover theater rental)." "Fray mit an Emes: Experimental Theater Lab": www.facebook.com/events/.

51 Personal exchange with Keith Thomas, Toronto International Film Festival, September 2019, Toronto.

52 Some former Hasidic women criticized the novel publicly. Frieda Vizel, who met Deborah's ex-husband and son, wrote a review about the book in 2020, after the adaptation of the autobiography to a miniseries, stating that Feldman's perception of her exit was influenced by her anger, and that she misrepresented her husband and the general situation. Vizel, "Book Review." Frimet Goldberger wrote an article in the *Forward* discussing her relationship with Feldman, how Feldman cut off ties with everyone, and how Feldman ultimately wrote a sensationalistic memoir with many untruths. See Goldberg, "Deborah Feldman Isn't Telling You the Whole Story."

53 Genest, "J'ai quitté la communauté juive ultra-orthodoxe dans laquelle j'ai grandi."

54 See Facebook page for Malky Squared Productions (previously website of Malkysquaredproductions): www.facebook.com.

55 On December 31, 2021, Hasidic journalist Meyer Labin posted a photo on Twitter about ultra-Orthodox Jewish mothers printing and distributing 350,000 flyers to Charedi households with the message that "we support, and listen to, victims, and we believe them"; Meyer Labin (@MeyerLabin), Twitter post, December 31, 2021, 12:42 a.m.: https://twitter.com/MeyerLabin/status/1476790760368451623/photo/3, accessed February 6, 2022.

56 Rabbi Ron Yitzchok Eisenman recorded a video about the need and responsibility to support victims that was disseminated on the website of Amudim, an organization offering support to victims of abuse in Orthodox circles. Ron Yitzchok Eisenman, "Rabbi Ron Yitzchok Eisenman on Supporting Victims," Amudim: https://amudim .org, accessed February 7, 2022.

57 Solomon, "When Weeping Is Not Enough."

58 The concept of the public culture dilemma has been inspired by the work of Ronnie Olesker, a political scientist specializing in security studies, who wrote her book *Israel's Securitization Dilemma* (New York: Routledge, 2021) on the treatment of BDS (the Boycott, Divest, and Sanctions movement) and the battle for the legitimacy of the Jewish state.

59 Roda and Stankovich, "Netflix's 'My Unorthodox Life' Spurred Ultra-Orthodox Jewish Women to Talk Publicly about Their Lives."

POSTLUDE. ARRIVAL

1 Bateson, *Steps to an Ecology of Mind*.

2 I would like to acknowledge the work of ethnomusicologists mobilizing the concept of ecosystem in relation to soundscape and sustainability. Nevertheless, here, ecology is used in a different way to discuss the interaction between the various spaces within Orthodoxy. See: Schippers and Grant, eds., *Sustainable Futures for Music Cultures*;

Farzaneh Hemmasi, "Tending the Urban 'Music Ecosystem': Cultural, Economic, and Scholarly Cultivation in Policy and on the Ground," Sound and Music in Kensington Market, 2020, https://kensingtonmarket.music.utoronto.ca, accessed April 1, 2023.

3 To learn about the use of Howard Becker's concept of art worlds, see chapter 2.

4 Francis, *When Art Disrupts Religion.*

5 For the controversy about Jewish male singers and cantors navigating multiple venues see: Dale, *Music in Haredi Jewish Life*; Slobin, *Chosen Voices*; Shandler, "Sanctification of the Brand Name"; Lockwood, "Prayer and Crime"; Lockwood, *Golden Ages.*

6 On the challenges faced by Jewish singers navigating between secular and religious stages, see Roda and Schwartz, "Home beyond Borders and the Sound of Al-Andalus."

7 Fader, *Mitzvah Girls.*

8 The ethnomusicologist Monique Desroches suggests discussing the ethics of research according to three dimensions: fieldwork, analysis, and diffusion. See Desroches, "L'éthique au-delà du protocole déontologique."

9 In 1996, Steven Feld discussed the role field recordings play in the public life of ethnomusicologists. See Feld, "Pygmy Pop." A few years after, Kay Kaufman Shelemay discussed extensively the impact of her musical scholarship in her two decades of research among Ethiopian Jews, shaking up the field of ethnomusicology on the topic of the role that our scholarship plays beyond the academy. See: Shelemay, "The Impact and Ethics of Musical Scholarship."

10 About this phenomenon see: Roda and Stankovich, "Netflix's 'My Unorthodox Life' Spurred Ultra-Orthodox Jewish Women to Talk Publicly about Their Lives."

11 About collaborative research and how it changes through time in anthropology and ethnomusicology see: Boyer and Marcus, eds., *Collaborative Anthropology Today*; Lassiter, "Collaborative Ethnography"; Slobin, "COVID-Era Online Collective Research Initiatives in Yiddish Traditional Music."

12 The phrasing "Assembly of Emissaries for Women of the Jewish People" is a translation from the Hebrew "Kinus N'Shei Klal Israel."

13 Website of TAG, the sponsor of the *asifa* gathering: https://tag.org.

SELECTED BIBLIOGRAPHY

PUBLIC, PRIVATE, AND THE COUNTERPUBLIC

Campbell, Heidi A. *Digital Religion: Understanding Religious Practice in New Media Worlds.* Abingdon, UK: Routledge, 2013.

Cody, Francis. "Publics and Politics." *Annual Review of Anthropology* 40, no. 1 (2011): 37–52.

Engelke, Matthew. "Religion and the Media Turn: A Review Essay." *American Ethnologist* 37, no. 2 (2010): 371–79.

———. "Angels in Swindon: Public Religion and Ambient Faith in England." *American Ethnologist* 39, no. 1 (2012): 155–70.

Fader, Ayala. "Ultra-Orthodox Jewish Interiority, the Internet, and the Crisis of Faith." *HAU: Journal of Ethnographic Theory* 7, no. 1 (March 2017): 185–206.

———. *Hidden Heretics: Jewish Doubt in the Digital Age.* Princeton Series in Culture and Technology. Princeton, NJ: Princeton University Press, 2020.

Fraser, Nancy. "Rethinking the Public Sphere: A Contribution to the Critique of Actually Existing Democracy." *Social Text*, no. 25/26 (1990): 56–80.

Golan, Oren, and Michele Martini. "Religious Live-Streaming: Constructing the Authentic in Real Time." *Information, Communication & Society* 22, no. 3 (2019): 437–54.

———. "The Making of Contemporary Papacy: Manufactured Charisma and Instagram." *Information, Communication & Society* 23, no. 9 (2020): 1368–85.

Golan, Oren, and Nakhi Mishol-Shauli. "Fundamentalist Web Journalism: Walking a Fine Line between Religious Ultra-Orthodoxy and the New Media Ethos." *European Journal of Communication* 33, no. 3 (2018): 304–20.

Golan, Oren, and Nurit Stadler. "Building the Sacred Community Online: The Dual Use of the Internet by Chabad." *Media, Culture & Society* 38, no. 1 (2016): 71–88.

Habermas, Jürgen. *The Structural Transformation of the Public Sphere: An Inquiry into a Category of Bourgeois Society.* 5th or later edition. Cambridge, MA: MIT Press, 1991.

Hirschkind, Charles. *The Ethical Soundscape: Cassette Sermons and Islamic Counterpublics.* New York: Columbia University Press, 2006.

Lieber, Andrea. "A Virtual *Veibershul*: Blogging and the Blurring of Public and Private among Orthodox Jewish Women." *College English* 72, no. 6 (2010): 621–37.

Mendieta, Eduardo, and Jonathan VanAntwerpen, eds. *The Power of Religion in the Public Sphere.* New York: Columbia University Press, 2011.

Meyer, Birgit, and Annelies Moors, eds. *Religion, Media, and the Public Sphere.* Illustrated edition. Bloomington: Indiana University Press, 2005.

Mishol-Shauli, Nakhi, and Oren Golan. "Mediatizing the Holy Community: Ultra-Orthodoxy Negotiation and Presentation on Public Social-Media." *Religions* 10, no. 7 (July 2019): 438.

Negt, Oskar, Alexander Kluge, and Peter Labanyi. "'The Public Sphere and Experience': Selections." *October* 46 (1988): 60–82.

Stolow, Jeremy, ed. *Deus in Machina: Religion, Technology, and the Things in Between*. Illustrated edition. New York: Fordham University Press, 2012.

Wagner, Rachel. *Godwired: Religion, Ritual, and Virtual Reality*. New York: Routledge, 2011.

Warner, Michael. "Publics and Counterpublics." *Public Culture* 14, no. 1 (2002): 49–90.

ULTRA-ORTHODOXY IN NORTH AMERICA

Biale, David, et al. *Hasidism: A New History*. Princeton, NJ: Princeton University Press, 2017.

Boyarin, Jonathan. *Yeshiva Days: Learning on the Lower East Side*. Princeton, NJ: Princeton University Press, 2020.

Deutsch, Nathaniel, and Michael Casper. *A Fortress in Brooklyn: Race, Real Estate, and the Making of Hasidic Williamsburg*. New Haven, CT: Yale University Press, 2021.

Fader, Ayala. *Mitzvah Girls: Bringing Up the Next Generation of Hasidic Jews in Brooklyn*. Princeton, NJ: Princeton University Press, 2009.

Goldschmidt, Henry. *Race and Religion among the Chosen People of Crown Heights*. New Brunswick, NJ: Rutgers University Press, 2006.

Heilman, Samuel C. *Sliding to the Right: The Contest for the Future of American Jewish Orthodoxy*. Berkeley: University of California Press, 2006.

———. *Who Will Lead Us? The Story of Five Hasidic Dynasties in America*, 1st edition. Oakland: University of California Press, 2017.

Kranzler, George. *Hasidic Williamsburg: A Contemporary American Hasidic Community*, 1st edition. Northvale, NJ: Jason Aronson, 1995.

Mintz, Jerome R. *Legends of the Hasidim: An Introduction to Hasidic Culture and Oral Tradition in the New World*. Chicago: University of Chicago Press, 1968.

Poll, Solomon. *The Hasidic Community of Williamsburg: A Study in the Sociology of Religion*. Abingdon, UK: Routledge, 2017.

Rosman, Moshe. *Founder of Hasidism: A Quest for the Historical Ba'al Shem Tov*. Berkeley: University of California Press, 1996.

Stolzenberg, Nomi M., and David N. Myers. *American Shtetl: The Making of Kiryas Joel, a Hasidic Village in Upstate New York*. Princeton, NJ: Princeton University Press, 2022.

Wodziński, Marcin. *Historical Atlas of Hasidism*. Princeton, NJ: Princeton University Press, 2018.

ULTRA-ORTHODOXY, WOMEN, AND PERFORMANCES

Avishai, Orit. "Imagining 'the Orthodox' in Emuna Elon's 'Heaven Rejoices': Voyeuristic, Reformist, and Pedagogical Orthodox Artistic Expression." *Israel Studies* 12, no. 2 (2007): 48–73.

Munro, Heather. "Navigating Change: Agency, Identity, and Embodiment in Haredi Women's Dance and Theater." *Shofar* 38, no. 2 (2020): 93–124.

Rutlinger-Reine, Reina. "'Drowning in the Marsh': Israeli Orthodox Theatrical Representations of the Singles Scene." *Israel Studies* 16, no. 3 (2011): 73–96.

———. "Crises in Orthodox Israeli Family Life Onstage." *Israel Studies Review* 28, no. 2 (2013): 83–101.

Schupak, Esther B. "Ultra-Orthodox Jewish Women Performing Gender in *Julius Caesar*." *Research in Drama Education: The Journal of Applied Theatre and Performance* 24, no. 2 (2019): 155–72.

Suskin, Gail, and Michal Al-Yagon, "Culturally Sensitive Dance Movement Therapy for Ultra-Orthodox Women: Group Protocol Targeting Bodily and Psychological Self-Perceptions." *Arts in Psychotherapy* 71 (2020): 1–10.

Taragin-Zeller, Lea. "Modesty for Heaven's Sake: Authority and Creativity among Female Ultra-Orthodox Teenagers in Israel." *Nashim: A Journal of Jewish Women's Studies and Gender Issues*, no. 26 (2014): 75–96.

———. "Between Modesty and Beauty: Reinterpreting Female Piety in the Israeli Haredi Community." In *Love, Marriage, and Jewish Families: Paradoxes of a Social Revolution*, edited by Sylvia Barack Fishman. Waltham, MA: Brandeis University Press, 2015.

WOMEN AND RELIGION

Abu-Lughod, Lila. *Do Muslim Women Need Saving?* Reprint edition. Cambridge, MA: Harvard University Press, 2015.

Avishai, Orit. "'Doing Religion' in a Secular World: Women in Conservative Religions and the Question of Agency." *Gender and Society* 22, no. 4 (2008): 409–33.

Brusco, Elizabeth E. *The Reformation of Machismo: Evangelical Conversion and Gender in Columbia*. Austin: University of Texas Press, 1995.

Fader, Ayala. *Mitzvah Girls: Bringing Up the Next Generation of Hasidic Jews in Brooklyn*. Princeton, NJ: Princeton University Press, 2009.

Khader, Serene J. *Decolonizing Universalism: A Transnational Feminist Ethic*. Oxford: Oxford University Press, 2018.

Mahmood, Saba. *Politics of Piety: The Islamic Revival and the Feminist Subject*. Princeton, NJ: Princeton University Press, 2011.

Raucher, Michal S. *Conceiving Agency: Reproductive Authority among Haredi Women*. Bloomington: Indiana University Press, 2020.

———. "Jewish Pronatalism: Policy and Praxis." *Religion Compass* 15, no. 7 (2021): 1–13.

Stacey, Judith, and Susan E. Gerard. "'We Are Not Doormats': The Influence of Feminism on Contemporary Evangelicals in the United States." In *Uncertain Terms: Negotiating Gender in American Culture*, edited by F. Ginsberg and A. L. Tsing. Boston: Beacon Press, 1990.

Taragin-Zeller, Lea. "Between Modesty and Beauty: Reinterpreting Female Piety in the Israeli Haredi Community." In *Love, Marriage, and Jewish Families: Paradoxes of a Social Revolution*, edited by Sylvia Barack Fishman. Waltham, MA: Brandeis University Press, 2015.

Zion Waldoks, Tanya. "Religious Feminism(s) and Beyond: Reflections on Politics of Change and Knowledge Production." *Religion and Gender* 11 (June 23, 2021): 137–43.

———. "Birth of a Movement: Narratives of the Haredi Feminist Emergence in Israel." *Israel Studies* 28, no. 1 (2023): 70–89.

TRANSNATIONAL AND TRANSLOCAL ETHNOGRAPHY

Capone, Stefania, and Monika Salzbrunn. "À l'écoute des transnationalisations religieuses: Introduction." *Civilisations* 67, no. 67 (2018): 11–22.

Capone, Stefania, et al. "Transnational Religions." *Civilisations* 51, no. 1–2 (2004) : 9–223.

Dankworth, Linda E., and Ann R. David. *Dance Ethnography and Global Perspectives: Identity, Embodiment, and Culture*. Basingstoke, UK: Palgrave Macmillan, 2014.

Greiner, Clemens, and Patrick Sakdapolrak. "Translocality: Concepts, Applications, and Emerging Research Perspectives." *Geography Compass* 7, no. 5 (2013): 373–84.

Guest, Kenneth J. *Cultural Anthropology: A Toolkit for a Global Age*. 2nd ed. New York: Norton, 2017.

Juris, Jeffrey S., and Alex Khasnabish. *Insurgent Encounters: Transnational Activism, Ethnography, and the Political*. Durham, NC: Duke University Press, 2013.

Kien, Grant. *Global Technography: Ethnography in the Age of Mobility*. Intersections in Communications and Culture, vol. 24. New York: Peter Lang, 2009.

Oakes, Tim, and Louisa Schein, eds. *Translocal China: Linkages, Identities, and the Reimagining of Space*. 1st edition. London: Routledge, 2006.

Tsing, Anna Lowenhaupt. *Friction: An Ethnography of Global Connection*. Princeton, NJ: Princeton University Press, 2005.

MODESTY AND ULTRA-ORTHODOXY

Block, Sima Zalcberg. "Shouldering the Burden of Redemption: How the 'Fashion' of Wearing Capes Developed in Ultra-Orthodox Society." *Nashim: A Journal of Jewish Women's Studies & Gender Issues*, no. 22 (2011): 32–55.

Goldman Carrel, Barbara. "Hasidic Women's Head Coverings: A Feminized System of Hasidic Distinction." Pp. 163–80 in *Religion, Dress, and the Body*. Oxford: Berg Fashion Library, 1999.

Harris, Rachel Sylvia, and Karen E. H. Skinazi, eds. "The Feminism and Art of Jewish Orthodox and Haredi Women." *Shofar: An Interdisciplinary Journal of Jewish Studies* 38 (2020).

Munro, Heather L. "Navigating Change: Agency, Identity, and Embodiment in Haredi Women's Dance and Theater." *Shofar: An Interdisciplinary Journal of Jewish Studies* 38, no. 2 (2020): 93–124.

Taragin-Zeller, Lea. "Modesty for Heaven's Sake: Authority and Creativity among Female Ultra-Orthodox Teenagers in Israel." *Nashim: A Journal of Jewish Women's Studies & Gender Issues*, no. 26 (2014): 75–96.

———. "Between Modesty and Beauty. Reinterpreting Female Piety in the Israeli Haredi Community." In *Love, Marriage, and Jewish Families: Paradoxes of a Social Revolution*, edited by Sylvia Barack Fishman. Waltham, MA: Brandeis University Press, 2015.

Yafeh, Orit. "The Time in the Body: Cultural Construction of Femininity in Ultraorthodox Kindergartens for Girls." *Ethos* 35, no. 4 (2007): 516–53.

POWER OF COLLECTIVE PERFORMANCES

Bailey, Betty A., and Jane W. Davidson. "Effects of Group Singing and Performance for Marginalized and Middle-Class Singers." *Psychology of Music* 33, no. 3 (2005): 269–303.

Bartleet, Brydie-Leigh, and Lee Higgins. *The Oxford Handbook of Community Music*. Oxford: Oxford University Press, 2018.

Bartleet, Brydie-Leigh, et al. "Enhancing Intercultural Engagement through Service Learning and Music Making with Indigenous Communities in Australia." *Research Studies in Music Education* 38, no. 2 (October 2016): 173–91.

Belfiore, Eleonora, and Oliver Bennett. *The Social Impact of the Arts: An Intellectual History*. London: Palgrave Macmillan, 2008.

Bithell, Caroline, and Juniper Hill. Chapter 7 in *The Oxford Handbook of Music Revival*. Oxford: Oxford University Press, 2014.

Buglass, Glen, and Mark Webster. *Finding Voices, Making Choices: Creativity for Social Change*. Shrewsbury, UK: Educational Heretics Press.

Camlin, David A., et al. "Group Singing as a Resource for the Development of a Healthy Public: A Study of Adult Group Singing." *Humanities and Social Sciences Communications* 7, no. 1 (2020): 1–15.

Clift, Stephen. "Optimism in the Field of Arts and Health." *Perspectives in Public Health* 133, no. 1 (January 2013): 18.

Coulton, Simon, et al. "Effectiveness and Cost-Effectiveness of Community Singing on Mental Health–Related Quality of Life of Older People: Randomized Controlled Trial." *BJ Psychiatry* 207, no. 3 (September 2015): 250–55.

DeNora, Tia. *Music Asylums: Wellbeing through Music in Everyday Life*. London: Routledge, 2013.

Dingle, Genevieve A., et al. "An Agenda for Best Practice Research on Group Singing, Health, and Well-Being." *Music & Science* 2 (2019): 1–15.

Elliott, David J., et al. *Artistic Citizenship: Artistry, Social Responsibility, and Ethical Praxis*. New York: Oxford University Press, 2016.

Fancourt, Daisy, et al. "Effects of Group Drumming Interventions on Anxiety, Depression, Social Resilience, and Inflammatory Immune Response among Mental Health Service Users." *PloS One* 11, no. 3 (March 2016): e0151136.

Hallam, Susan. *The Power of Music: A Research Synthesis of the Impact of Actively Making Music on the Intellectual, Social, and Personal Development of Children and Young People*. London: Institute of Education University College, 2015.

Livesey, Laetitia, et al. "Benefits of Choral Singing for Social and Mental Wellbeing: Qualitative Findings from a Cross-National Survey of Choir Members." *Journal of Public Mental Health* 11, no. 1 (2012): 10–26.

Skingley, Ann, and Hillary Bungay. "The Silver Song Club Project: A Sense of Well-Being through Participatory Singing." *Journal of Applied Arts and Health* 1, no. 2 (2010): 165–78.

Turino, Thomas. *Music as Social Life: The Politics of Participation*. Chicago: University of Chicago Press, 2008.

Williams, Elyse J., et al. "A Systematic Review of Mental Health and Wellbeing Outcomes of Group Singing for Adults with a Mental Health Condition." *European Journal of Public Health* 28, no. 6 (2018): 1035–42.

ULTRA-ORTHODOX CINEMA

Aharoni, Matan. "Eliciting 'Kosher Emotions' in Ultra-Orthodox Jewish Women's Film." Pp. 95–116 in *The Emotions Industry*, edited by Mira Moshe. New York: Nova Publishers, 2014.

Casey, Nikki. "These *Frum* Filmmakers Are Revolutionizing Orthodox Cinema." *Forward*, July 11, 2016.

Friedman, Yael, and Yohai Hakak. "Jewish Revenge: Haredi Action in the Zionist Sphere." *Jewish Film & New Media: An International Journal* 3, no. 1 (Spring 2015): 48–76.

Jacobson, David C. "The Ma'aleh School: Catalyst for the Entrance of Religious Zionists into the World of Media Production." *Israel Studies* 9, no. 1 (2004): 31–60.

Seigelshifer, Valeria, and Tova Hartman. "The Emergence of Israeli Orthodox Women Filmmakers." *Shofar: An Interdisciplinary Journal of Jewish Studies* 38, no. 2 (Summer 2020): 125–61.

Trappler Spielman, Sara. "Orthodox Women Are Making Films for Female Audiences: Are They Good Enough for the Secular World?" *Tablet Magazine*, May 30, 2012.

Vinig, Marlyn. *Haredi Cinema*. Tel Aviv: Resling, 2011. [Hebrew]

WORKS CITED

Abrams, Nathan. *The New Jew in Film: Exploring Jewishness and Judaism in Contemporary Cinema*. New Brunswick, NJ: Rutgers University Press, 2012.

Abu-Lughod, Lila. *Remaking Women: Feminism and Modernity in the Middle East*. Cairo: American University in Cairo Press, 1998.

Acar, Selcuk, et al. "Creativity and Well-Being: A Meta-Analysis." *Journal of Creative Behavior* 55, no. 3 (2020): 738–51.

Aharoni, Matan. "Eliciting 'Kosher Emotions' in Ultra-Orthodox Jewish Women's Film." Pp. 95–116 in *The Emotions Industry*, edited by Mira Moshe. New York: Nova Publishers, 2014.

Allard, Laurence. "Partages créatifs. Stylisation de soi et appsperimentation artistique." *Communication languages* 194, no. 4 (2017): 29–39.

Allison, Henry E. *Kant's Theory of Taste: A Reading of the Critique of Aesthetic Judgment*. Cambridge: Cambridge University Press, 2001.

Andrieu, Sarah, and Emmanuelle Olivier, eds. *Création artistique et imaginaires de la globalization*. Paris: Hermann, 2017.

Appadurai, Arjun, ed. *The Social Life of Things: Commodities in Cultural Perspective*. Cambridge: Cambridge University Press, 1986.

Archambault, Julie Soleil. "In Pursuit of Fitness: Bodywork, Temporality, and Self-Improvement in Mozambique." *Journal of Southern African Studies* 47, no. 4 (2021): 521–39.

Arditi, David. *Getting Signed: Record Contracts, Musicians, and Power in Society*. London: Palgrave Macmillan, 2020.

Arewa, Olufunmilayo B. "From J. C. Bach to Hip Hop: Musical Borrowing, Copyright, and Cultural Context." *North Carolina Law Review* 84, no. 2 (2006): 550–52.

Asad, Talal. *Genealogies of Religion: Discipline and Reasons of Power in Christianity and Islam*, 1st edition. Baltimore, MD: Johns Hopkins University Press, 1993.

———. *Formations of the Secular: Christianity, Islam, Modernity*. Stanford, CA: Stanford University Press, 2003.

Assaf, David. "'My Tiny, Ugly World': The Confession of Rabbi Yitzhak Nahum Twersky of Shpikov." *Contemporary Jewry* 26, no. 1 (October 1, 2006): 1–34.

Avishai, Orit. "Imagining 'the Orthodox' in Emuna Elon's 'Heaven Rejoices': Voyeuristic, Reformist, and Pedagogical Orthodox Artistic Expression." *Israel Studies* 12, no. 2 (2007): 48–73.

———. "'Doing Religion' in a Secular World: Women in Conservative Religions and the Question of Agency." *Gender and Society* 22, no. 4 (2008): 409–33.

Babha, Homi K. *The Location of Culture*. New York: Routledge, 1994.

Bailey, Betty A., and Jane W. Davidson. "Effects of Group Singing and Performance for Marginalized and Middle-Class Singers." *Psychology of Music* 33, no. 3 (July 1, 2005): 269–303.

Barcella, Laura. "Why I Left My Religion—Arranged Marriage & All—Behind." *Refinery29*, April 17, 2015: www.refinery29.com.

Barnat, Ons. "Vers une ethnomusicologie du studio d'enregistrement. Stonetree Records et la *paranda* garifuna en Amérique centrale." *Cahiers d'ethnomusicologie* 30 (2017): 121–35.

Barrios, Richard. *Screened Out: Playing Gay in Hollywood from Edison to Stonewall*. New York: Routledge, 2002

Barron, Lee. *Celebrity Cultures: An Introduction*, 1st edition. Los Angeles: Sage Publications, 2014.

Barry, Elizabeth. "Celebrity, Cultural Production, and Public Life." *International Journal of Culture Studies* 11, no. 3 (2008): 251.

Bartleet, Brydie-Leigh, and Lee Higgins. *The Oxford Handbook of Community Music*. Oxford: Oxford University Press, 2018.

Bartleet, Brydie-Leigh, et al. "Enhancing Intercultural Engagement through Service Learning and Music Making with Indigenous Communities in Australia." *Research Studies in Music Education* 38, no. 2 (October 2016): 173–91.

Bateson, Gregory. *Steps to an Ecology of Mind: Collected Essays in Anthropology, Psychiatry, Evolution, and Epistemology*. Chicago: University of Chicago Press, 2000 (first published 1972).

Batmanghelichi, Soraya Kristin, and Leila Mouri. "Cyberfeminism, Iranian Style: Online Feminism in Post-2009 Iran." *Feminist Media Histories* 3, no. 1 (2017): 50–80.

Batnitzky, Leora. *How Judaism Became a Religion: An Introduction to Modern Jewish Thought*, Book Collections on Project MUSE. Princeton, NJ: Princeton University Press, 2011.

Baumel-Schwartz, Judith. "*Frum* Surfing: Orthodox Jewish Women's Internet Forums as a Historical and Cultural Phenomenon." *Journal of Jewish Identities* 2 (January 1, 2009): 1–30.

Bayraktaroglu, Kerem. "The Muslim Male Character Typology in American Cinema Post-9/11." *Digest of Middle East Studies* 23, no. 2 (2014): 346.

Becker, Howard S. *Art Worlds*. Berkeley: University of California Press, 1982.

Belfiore, Eleonora, and Oliver Bennett. *The Social Impact of the Arts: An Intellectual History*. London: Palgrave Macmillan, 2008.

Berger-Sofer, Rhonda. *Pious Women: A Study of the Women's Roles in a Hasidic and Pious Community, Meah She'arim*. New Brunswick, NJ: Rutgers University Press, 1980.

Bial, Henry. *Acting Jewish: Negotiating Ethnicity on the American Stage and Screen*. Ann Arbor: University of Michigan Press, 2005.

Biale, David, et al. *Hasidism: A New History*. Princeton, NJ: Princeton University Press, 2017.

Bilge, Sirma. "Beyond Subordination vs. Resistance: An Intersectional Approach to the Agency of Veiled Muslim Women." *Journal of Intercultural Studies* 31, no. 1 (February 1, 2010): 9–28.

Bithell, Caroline, and Juniper Hill. Chapter 7 in *The Oxford Handbook of Music Revival*. Oxford: Oxford University Press, 2014.

Bleyer, Jennifer. "'City of Refuge.'" *New York Times*, March 18, 2007: www.nytimes.com.

Block, Sima Zalcberg. "Shouldering the Burden of Redemption: How the 'Fashion' of Wearing Capes Developed in Ultra-Orthodox Society." *Nashim: A Journal of Jewish Women's Studies & Gender Issues*, no. 22 (2011): 32–55.

Blutinger, Jeffrey C. "So-Called Orthodoxy: The History of an Unwanted Label." *Modern Judaism* 27, no. 3 (2007): 310–28.

Boellstorff, Tom. *Coming of Age in Second Life: An Anthropologist Explores the Virtually Human*. Revised edition. Princeton, NJ: Princeton University Press, 2015.

Born, Georgina. "On Musical Mediation: Ontology, Technology, and Creativity." *Twentieth-Century Music* 2, no. 1 (2005).

Bowler, Kate. *The Preacher's Wife: The Precarious Power of Evangelical Women Celebrities.* Princeton, NJ: Princeton University Press, 2019.

Boyarin, Daniel. *Judaism: The Genealogy of a Modern Notion.* Key Words in Jewish Studies. New Brunswick, NJ: Rutgers University Press, 2018.

Boyarin, Jonah Sampson. "Chulent: Post-Hasidic Explorations and Jewish Modernities." B.A. thesis, Wesleyan University, Middletown, CT, 2008.

Boyarin, Jonathan. *Yeshiva Days: Learning on the Lower East Side.* Princeton, NJ: Princeton University Press, 2020.

Boyer, Dominic, and George E. Marcus, eds. *Collaborative Anthropology Today: A Collection of Exceptions.* Ithaca, NY: Cornell University Press, 2021.

Brewis, Alexandra A., et al. "Body Norms and Fat Stigma in Global Perspective." *Current Anthropology* 52, no. 2 (2011): 269–76.

Brown, Rivkah. "On Instagram, Orthodox Women Find a Voice—and Power." *Haaretz*, October 21, 2019: www.haaretz.com, accessed December 10, 2022.

Brusco, Elizabeth E. *The Reformation of Machismo: Evangelical Conversion and Gender in Columbia.* Austin: University of Texas Press, 1995.

Buglass, Glen, and Mark Webster. *Finding Voices, Making Choices: Creativity for Social Change.* Shrewsbury, UK: Educational Heretics Press.

Burkhardt, Jan, and Jo Rhodes. "Commissioning Dance for Health and Wellbeing: Guidance and Resources for Commissioners." Pavilion Dance Southwest, 2012.

Burnard, Pamela. *Musical Creativities in Practice.* Oxford: Oxford University Press, 2012.

Butler, Judith. "Performative Acts and Gender Constitution: An Essay in Phenomenology and Feminist Theory." *Theatre Journal* 40, no. 4 (1988): 519–31.

———. *Gender Trouble: Feminism and the Subversion of Identity.* London: Routledge, 1990.

Camlin, David A., et al. "Group Singing as a Resource for the Development of a Healthy Public: A Study of Adult Group Singing." *Humanities and Social Sciences Communications* 7, no. 1 (2020): 1–15.

Campbell, Heidi A. *Digital Religion: Understanding Religious Practice in New Media Worlds.* London: Routledge, 2013.

Caplan, Debra. "Sholem Asch's 'God of Vengeance.'" The Yiddish Book Center's Great Jewish Books Teacher Resources: http://teachgreatjewishbooks.org, accessed March 31, 2023.

Capone, Stefania, and Monika Salzbrunn. "À l'écoute des transnationalisations religieuses: Introduction." *Civilisations* 67, no. 67 (2018): 11–22.

Capone, Stefania, et al. "Transnational Religions." *Civilisations* 51, no. 1–2 (2004) : 9–223.

Cappell, Ezra, and Jessica Lang, eds. *Off the Derech: Leaving Orthodox Judaism.* Albany: State University of New York Press, 2020.

Carpo, Mario. *The Second Digital Turn: Design beyond Intelligence.* Cambridge, MA: MIT Press, 2017.

Carrel, Barbara Goldman. "Hasidic Women's Head Coverings: A Feminized System of Hasidic Distinction." Pp. 63–80 in *Religion, Dress, and the Body*, edited by Linda B. Arthur. Oxford: Berg Fashion Library, 1999.

Casey, Nikki. "These *Frum* Filmmakers Are Revolutionizing Orthodox Cinema." *Forward*, July 11, 2016.

Cashmore, Ellis. *Celebrity Culture*, 1st edition. Abingdon, UK: Routledge, 2006.

Catsoulis, Jeannette. "Review: 'Felix and Meira,' a Portrait of a Tempted Hasidic Wife." *New York Times*, April 17, 2015: www.nytimes.com.

Chambers, Claire. "Anthropology as Cultural Translation: Amitav Ghosh's *In an Antique Land.*" *Postcolonial Text* 2, no. 1 (2006).

Chapain, Caroline, and Roberta Comunian. "Enabling and Inhibiting the Creative Economy: The Role of the Local and Regional Dimensions in England." *Regional Studies* 44, no. 6 (2010): 717–34.

Chavez-Eakle, Rosa Aurora, et al. "Personality: A Possible Bridge between Creativity and Psychopathology?" *Creativity Research Journal* 18, no. 1 (2006): 27–38.

Cherney, Ben. "Kol Isha." *Journal of Halacha and Contemporary Society* 10 (1985): 57–75.

Chizhik-Goldschmidt, Avital. "'They're Out to Get Us': Social Media Campaigns Reflect Tensions between Orthodox and Local Authorities." *Forward*, October 1, 2020: https://forward.com, accessed December 10, 2022.

———. "Is Social Media Fueling a Women's Rights Revolution in the Orthodox Jewish Community?" *Religion & Politics*, March 30, 2021: https://religionandpolitics.org.

———. "Orthodox Jewish Women Can't Sing in Front of Men: Instagram Is Giving Them a Voice." *Glamour*, April 12, 2021: www.glamour.com, accessed December 10, 2022.

———. "The Unorthodox Art of an Ultra-Orthodox Community." *Atlantic*, September 2021: www.theatlantic.com.

Chon, Margaret. "The Romantic Collective Author." *Vanderbilt Journal of Entertainment & Technology Law* 14, no. 4 (2012): 830.

Christman, John. "Relational Autonomy, Liberal Individualism, and the Social Constitution of Selves." *Philosophical Studies* 117, no. 1/2 (2004): 143–64.

———. "Autonomy and Deeply Embedded Cultural Identities." In *Personal Autonomy in Plural Societies*, edited by Marie-Claire Foblets, Michele Graziadei, and Alison Renteln. London: Routledge, 2017.

Clift, Stephen. "Optimism in the Field of Arts and Health." *Perspectives in Public Health* 133, no. 1 (January 2013): 18.

Cody, Francis. "Publics and Politics." *Annual Review of Anthropology* 40, no. 1 (2011): 37–52.

Compton, William C., and Edward Hoffman. *Positive Psychology: The Science of Happiness and Flourishing*. Newbury Park, CA: Sage Publications, 2019.

Constine, Josh. "Instagram Launches 'Stories,' a Snapchatty Feature for Imperfect Sharing." *TechCrunch*, August 2, 2016: https://techcrunch.com, accessed March 31, 2023.

Coulton, Simon, et al. "Effectiveness and Cost-Effectiveness of Community Singing on Mental Health–Related Quality of Life of Older People: Randomized Controlled Trial." *BJ Psychiatry* 207, no. 3 (September 2015): 250–55.

Csikszentmihalyi, Mihaly, and Martin E. P. Seligman. "Positive Psychology: An Introduction." *American Psychologist* 55, no. 1 (2000): 5–14.

Dale, Gordon A. "Music in Haredi Jewish Life: Liquid Modernity and the Negotiation of Boundaries in Greater New York." PhD thesis Graduate Center, City University of New York, 2017.

Daniels, Jessie. "Rethinking Cyberfeminism(s): Race, Gender, and Embodiment." *Women's Studies Quarterly* 37, no. 1/2 (2009): 101–24.

Dankworth, Linda E., and Ann R. David. *Dance Ethnography and Global Perspectives: Identity, Embodiment, and Culture*. Basingstoke, UK: Palgrave Macmillan, 2014.

Davidman, Lynn. *Tradition in a Rootless World: Women Turn to Orthodox Judaism*. Los Angeles: University of California Press, 1993.

———. *Becoming Un-Orthodox: Stories of Ex-Hasidic Jews*. New York: Oxford University Press, 2015.

Davis, Dána-Ain, and Christa Craven. *Feminist Ethnography: Thinking through Methodologies, Challenges, and Possibilities*. Lanham, MD: Rowman & Littlefield, 2016.

Debruge, Peter. "Film Review: 'Felix and Meira.'" *Variety*, September 26, 2014: https://variety.com, accessed July 22, 2023.

Deen, Shulem. *All Who Go Do Not Return*. Minneapolis, MN: Graywolf Press, 2015.

Deflem, Mathieu. *Lady Gaga and the Sociology of Fame: The Rise of a Pop Star in an Age of Celebrity*. New York: Palgrave Macmillan, 2017.

DeNora, Tia. *Music Asylums: Wellbeing through Music in Everyday Life*. London: Routledge, 2013.

Desroches, Monique. "L'éthique au-delà du protocole déontologique. À chaque terrain, son éthique?" *Les Cahiers de la Société québécoise de recherche en musique* 11, no. 1–2 (2010): 81–88.

Deutsch, Nathaniel, and Michael Casper. *A Fortress in Brooklyn: Race, Real Estate, and the Making of Hasidic Williamsburg*. New Haven, CT: Yale University Press, 2021.

Diawara, Manthia. *Black American Cinema*. New York: Routledge, 1993.

Dingle, Genevieve A., et al. "An Agenda for Best Practice Research on Group Singing, Health, and Well-Being." *Music & Science* 2 (2019): 1–15.

Downing, Sonja Lynn. *Gamelan Girls: Gender, Childhood, and Politics in Balinese Music Ensembles*. Urbana: University of Illinois Press, 2019.

Dyer, Richard. *Heavenly Bodies: Film Stars and Society*, 2nd edition. London: Routledge, 1987.

Dyer, Richard, and Paul McDonald. *Stars*, 2nd edition. London: Bloomsbury, 2019.

Eckert, Stine, and Kalyani Chadha. "Muslim Bloggers in Germany: An Emerging Counterpublic." *Media, Culture, and Society* 35, no. 8 (November 2013): 926–42.

Elbaz, Vanessa. "Kol B'Isha Erva: The Silencing of Jewish Women's Oral Traditions in Morocco." Pp. 263–88 in *Women and Social Change in North Africa: What Counts as Revolutionary?*, edited by Doris Gray and Nadia Sonneveld. Cambridge: Cambridge University Press, 2017.

Elkon, Gali. "'Felix and Meira': Interview with Luzer Twersky." *Selig Film News*, May 19, 2015: https://seligfilmnews.com.

Elliott, David J., et al. *Artistic Citizenship: Artistry, Social Responsibility, and Ethical Praxis*. New York: Oxford University Press, 2016.

El-Or, Tamar. *Educated and Ignorant: Ultraorthodox Jewish Women and Their World*, trans. Haim Watzman. Boulder, CO: Lynne Rienner, 1994.

Elsaesser, Thomas. *Film History as Media Archaeology: Tracking Digital Cinema*. Film Culture in Transition 50. Amsterdam, Netherlands: Amsterdam University Press, 2016.

Engelke, Matthew. "Religion and the Media Turn: A Review Essay." *American Ethnologist* 37, no. 2 (2010): 371–79.

———. "Angels in Swindon: Public Religion and Ambient Faith in England." *American Ethnologist* 39, no. 1 (2012): 155–70.

Epstein, Shifra. "The Celebration of a Contemporary Purim in the Bobover Hasidic Community." PhD thesis University of Texas at Austin, 1979.

———. "Josef Is Still Alive in Brooklyn: Tradition and Modernity in the Performance of a Musical in Yiddish by Hasidic Women." In *Di Froyen: Women and Yiddish, Tribute to the Past, Directions for the Future*. New York: National Council of Jewish Women, 1997.

———. "Going Far Away in Order to Better Understand the Familiar: Odyssey of a Jewish Folklorist into the Bobover Hasidic Community." *Journal of American Folklore* 112, no. 444 (1999): 200–212.

Erickson, Mary, and Doris Baltruschat, eds. *Independent Filmmaking around the Globe*. Toronto: University of Toronto Press, 2015.

Fader, Ayala. *Mitzvah Girls: Bringing Up the Next Generation of Hasidic Jews in Brooklyn*. Princeton, NJ: Princeton University Press, 2009.

———. "Ultra-Orthodox Jewish Interiority, the Internet, and the Crisis of Faith." *HAU: Journal of Ethnographic Theory* 7, no. 1 (March 2017): 185–206.

————. *Hidden Heretics: Jewish Doubt in the Digital Age.* Princeton Series in Culture and Technology. Princeton, NJ: Princeton University Press, 2020.

Falzon, Mark-Anthony. *Cosmopolitan Connections: The Sindhi Diaspora, 1860–2000.* International Comparative Social Studies, vol. 9. Leiden: Brill, 2004.

Fancourt, Daisy, et al. "Effects of Group Drumming Interventions on Anxiety, Depression, Social Resilience, and Inflammatory Immune Response among Mental Health Service Users." *PloS One* 11, no. 3 (March 2016): e0151136.

Feld, Steven. "Pygmy Pop: A Genealogy of Schizophonic Mimesis." *Yearbook for Traditional Music* 28 (1996): 1–35.

Feldman, Deborah. *Unorthodox: The Scandalous Rejection of My Hasidic Roots.* New York: Simon & Schuster, 2012.

Fernández-Argüelles, Esther López, et al. "Effects of Dancing on the Risk of Falling-Related Factors of Healthy Older Adults: A Systematic Review." *Archives of Gerontology and Geriatrics* 60, no. 1 (January–February 2015): 1–8.

Ferziger, Adam S. "Feminism and Heresy: The Construction of a Jewish Metanarrative." *Journal of the American Academy of Religion* 77, no. 3 (2009): 494–546.

Finkelman, Yoel. *Strictly Kosher Reading: Popular Literature and the Condition of Contemporary Orthodoxy.* Jewish Identities in Post-Modern Society. Boston: Academic Studies Press, 2011.

Fournier, Alexandrine Boudreault. "Positioning the New Reggaetón Stars in Cuba: From Home-Based Recording Studios to Alternative Narratives." *Journal of Latin American and Caribbean Anthropology* 13, no. 2 (2008): 336–60.

Francis, Philip Salim. *When Art Disrupts Religion: Aesthetic Experience and the Evangelical Mind.* Oxford: Oxford University Press, 2017.

Fraser, Nancy. "Rethinking the Public Sphere: A Contribution to the Critique of Actually Existing Democracy." *Social Text*, no. 25/26 (1990): 56–80.

Friedman, Susan Stanford. "Periodizing Modernism: Postcolonial Modernities and the Space/Time Borders of Modernist Studies." *Modernism/Modernity* 13, no. 3 (September 2006): 425–43.

Friedman, Yael, and Yohai Hakak. "Jewish Revenge: Haredi Action in the Zionist Sphere." *Jewish Film & New Media: An International Journal* 3, no. 1 (2015): 48–76.

Frissen, Thomas, et al. "#Muslim? Instagram, Visual Culture, and the Mediatization of Muslim Religiosity." In *European Muslims and New Media*, edited by Merve Kayikci and Leen d'Haenens. Leuven, Belgium: Leuven University Press, 2017.

Frith, Simon. *Musical Imaginations.* Oxford: Oxford University Press, 2011.

Furedi, Frank. "Celebrity Culture." *Society* 47, no. 6 (November 2010): 493–97.

Gabriele, Alberto, ed. *Sensationalism and the Genealogy of Modernity: A Global Nineteenth-Century Perspective.* New York: Palgrave Macmillan, 2016.

Gajjala, Radhika *Cyber Selves: Feminist Ethnographies of South Asian Women.* Walnut Creek, CA: AltaMira Press, 2001.

————. "Studying Feminist E-Spaces: Introducing Transnational/Post-Colonial Concerns." Pp. 113–25 in *Technospaces: Inside the New Media*, edited by Sally Munt. London: Continuum, 2001.

Gardner, Sally May, et al. "Dancing beyond Exercise: Young People's Experiences in Dance Classes." *Journal of Youth Studies* 11, no. 6 (2008).

Gaudreault, André, and Philippe Marion. *La fin du cinéma? Un média en crise à l'ère du numérique.* Paris: Armand Colin, 2013.

Gellerman, Jill. "(Not Just) *Az der rebbe tantst*: Toward an Inclusive History of Hasidic Dance." In *The Oxford Handbook of Jewishness and Dance*, edited by Naomi

Jackson, Rebecca Pappas, and Toni Shapiro-Phim. Oxford: Oxford University Press, 2022.

Genest, Catherine. "J'ai quitté la communauté juive ultra-orthodoxe dans laquelle j'ai grandi." *Elle Quebec*, May 20, 2020: www.ellequebec.com.

Gifford, Paul. "Religious Authority: Scripture, Tradition, Charisma." Pp. 379–410 in *The Routledge Companion to the Study of Religion*, edited by John Hinnells. London: Routledge, 2010.

Ginsparg Klein, Leslie M., "Defining Bais Yaakov: A Historical Study of Yeshivish Orthodox Girls' High School Education in America, 1963–1984." PhD thesis, New York University, 2009.

Golan, Oren, and Eldar Fehl. "Legitimizing Academic Knowledge in Religious Bounded Communities: Jewish Ultra-Orthodox Students in Israeli Higher Education." *International Journal of Educational Research* 102, no. 2 (2020): 101609.

Golan, Oren, and Michele Martini. "Religious Live-Streaming: Constructing the Authentic in Real Time." *Information, Communication & Society* 22, no. 3 (2019): 437–54.

———. "The Making of Contemporary Papacy: Manufactured Charisma and Instagram." *Information, Communication & Society* 23, no. 9 (2020): 1368–85.

Golan, Oren, and Nurit Stadler. "Building the Sacred Community Online: The Dual Use of the Internet by Chabad." *Media, Culture & Society* 38, no. 1 (2016): 71–88.

Goldberg, Frimet. "Deborah Feldman Isn't Telling You the Whole Story." *Forward*, April 2, 2014: https://forward.com.

Goldblatt, Rochel Leah. "Rockland Jewish Women's Chany Rosengarten: Author, Hasid, Feminist." *Rockland/Westchester Journal News*, May 24, 2018: www.lohud.com, accessed February 9, 2021.

Goldman Carrel, Barbara. "Hasidic Women's Head Coverings: A Feminized System of Hasidic Distinction." Pp. 163–80 in *Religion, Dress, and the Body*. Oxford: Berg Fashion Library, 1999.

Goldschmidt, Henry. *Race and Religion among the Chosen People of Crown Heights*. New Brunswick, NJ: Rutgers University Press, 2006.

Goldstein, Eric L. *The Price of Whiteness: Jews, Race, and American Identity*. Princeton, NJ: Princeton University Press, 2008.

Greiner, Clemens, and Patrick Sakdapolrak. "Translocality: Concepts, Applications, and Emerging Research Perspectives." *Geography Compass* 7, no. 5 (2013): 373–84.

Guest, Kenneth J. *Cultural Anthropology: A Toolkit for a Global Age*. 2nd ed. New York: Norton, 2017.

Guillebaud, Christine, Victor A. Stoichita, and Julien Mallet. "La musique n'a pas d'auteur. Ethnographies du copyright." *Gradhiva: Revue d'histoire et d'archives de l'anthropologie* 12 (2010): 5–19.

Gutenmacher, Yoni. "The Orthodox Women of Instagram." *Tablet Magazine*, December 6, 2022: https://www.tabletmag.com.

Habermas, Jürgen. *The Structural Transformation of the Public Sphere: An Inquiry into a Category of Bourgeois Society*. 5th or later edition. Cambridge, MA: MIT Press, 1991.

Hallam, Susan. *The Power of Music: A Research Synthesis of the Impact of Actively Making Music on the Intellectual, Social, and Personal Development of Children and Young People*. London: Institute of Education University College, 2015.

Hammerman, Shaina. *Silver Screen, Hasidic Jews: The Story of an Image*. Bloomington: Indiana University Press, 2018.

Hannerz, Ulf. *Transnational Connections: Culture, People, Places*. Comedia series. London: Routledge, 1996.

———. "'Transnational Research.'" P. 247 in *Handbook of Methods in Cultural Anthropology*, edited by H. Russell Bernard. Walnut Creek, CA: AltaMira Press, 1998.

Harris, Anita, and Joshua Roose. "DIY Citizenship amongst Young Muslims: Experiences of the 'Ordinary.'" *Journal of Youth Studies* 17, no. 6 (2013): 794–813.

Harris, Rachel Sylvia, and Karen E. H. Skinazi, eds. "The Feminism and Art of Jewish Orthodox and Haredi Women." *Shofar: An Interdisciplinary Journal of Jewish Studies* 38 (2020).

Harris, Rifka Wein. "Dignity in an Oversharing World." *Jewish Action: The Magazine of the Orthodox Union*, Fall 2022.

Hartman, Tova. *Feminism Encounters Traditional Judaism: Resistance and Accommodation.* Waltham, MA: Brandeis University Press, 2007.

Hayward, Susan. *Cinema Studies: Key Concepts*, 5th edition. London: Routledge, 2018.

Heilman, Samuel C. *Sliding to the Right: The Contest for the Future of American Jewish Orthodoxy.* Berkeley: University of California Press, 2006.

———. *Who Will Lead Us? The Story of Five Hasidic Dynasties in America.* Berkeley: University of California Press, 2017.

Hemmasi, Farzaneh. "Tending the Urban 'Music Ecosystem': Cultural, Economic, and Scholarly Cultivation in Policy and on the Ground." Sound and Music in Kensington Market, 2020: https://kensingtonmarket.music.utoronto.ca, accessed April 1, 2023.

Hennion, Antoine. "Loving Music: From a Sociology of Mediation to a Pragmatics of Taste." *Scientific Journal of Media Education* 34, no. 17 (2010): 25–33.

Herrera, Brian Eugenio. "'But Do We Have the Actors for That?': Some Principles of Practice for Staging Latinx Plays in a University Theatre Context." *Theatre Topics* 27, no. 1 (2017).

Herzfeld, Michael. *Cultural Intimacy: Social Poetics in the Nation-State.* London: Routledge, 1997.

Hirschkind, Charles. *The Ethical Soundscape: Cassette Sermons and Islamic Counterpublics.* Cultures of History. New York: Columbia University Press, 2006.

Holm, Malin. "The Rise of Online Counterpublics? The Limits of Inclusion in a Digital Age." PhD thesis, Uppsala: Uppsala University, 2019.

Hoover, Stewart M. and Nabil Echchaibi, "Media Theory and the 'Third Spaces of Digital Religion.'" *Research Methods and Theories in Digital Religion Studies* 3 (2014): 1–35.

Hudson, Dale. *Thinking through Digital Media: Transnational Environments and Locative Places*, 1st edition. New York: Palgrave Macmillan, 2015.

Hussain, Amir. "Islam." In *The Routledge Companion to Religion and Film*, edited by John Lyden. New York: Routledge, 2009.

Indraganti, Kiranmayi. "Song Taxonomies: Indian Popular Cinema's Territories of Stardom." Pp. 84–102 in *Revisiting Star Studies: Cultures, Themes, and Methods*, edited by Sabrina Qiong Yu and Guy Austin. Edinburgh: Edinburgh University Press, 2017.

Inglis, Fred. *A Short History of Celebrity.* Course Book. Princeton, NJ: Princeton University Press, 2010.

Isaacs, Miriam. "Creativity in Contemporary Hasidic Yiddish." Pp. 165–88 in *Yiddish Language and Culture, Then and Now: Proceedings of the Ninth Annual Symposium*, edited by Leonard J. Greenspoon. Omaha, NE: Creighton University Press, 1998.

Jacobson, David C. "The Ma'aleh School: Catalyst for the Entrance of Religious Zionists into the World of Media Production." *Israel Studies* 9, no. 1 (2004): 31–60.

Johansson, Mats, and Ola K. Berge. "Who Owns an Interpretation? Legal and Symbolic Ownership of Norwegian Folk Music." *Ethnomusicology* 58, no. 1 (Winter 2014): 30–53.

Juris, Jeffrey S., and Alex Khasnabish. *Insurgent Encounters: Transnational Activism, Ethnography, and the Political*. Durham, NC: Duke University Press, 2013.

Kahan-Newman, Zelda. "Women's Badkhones: The Satmar Poem Sung to a Bride." *International Journal of the Sociology of Language* 138 (1999): 81–99.

Kaplan, Musia. "A Studio Grows in Brooklyn." *Ami Living*, January 13, 2021.

Kaufman, Debra Renee. *Rachel's Daughters: Newly Orthodox Jewish Women*. New Brunswick, NJ: Rutgers University Press, 1991.

Kavakci, Elif, and Camille R. Kraeplin. "Religious Beings in Fashionable Bodies: The Online Identity Construction of Hijabi Social Media Personalities." *Media, Culture & Society* 39, no. 6 (2016): 850–68.

Keogh, Justin W. L., et al. "Physical Benefits of Dancing for Healthy Older Adults: A Review." *Journal of Aging and Physical Activity* 17, no. 4 (2009): 479–500.

Khader, Serene J. *Decolonizing Universalism: A Transnational Feminist Ethic*. Studies in Feminist Philosophy. New York: Oxford University Press, 2019.

Kieffer, Kira Ganga. "Manifesting Millions: How Women's Spiritual Entrepreneurship Genders Capitalism." *Nova Religio* 24, no. 2 (October 20, 2020): 80–104.

Kien, Grant. *Global Technography: Ethnography in the Age of Mobility*. Intersections in Communications and Culture, vol. 24. New York: Peter Lang, 2009.

Kilgannon, Corey. "An Incisive Play about Hasidisim, with Actors Who Lived It." *New York Times*, March 12, 2017: www.nytimes.com.

Kligman, Mark. "Contemporary Jewish Music in America." *American Jewish Year Book* 10 (2001): 88–141.

Koskoff, Ellen. "The Sound of a Woman's Voice: Gender and Music in a New York Hasidic Community." In *Women and Music in Cross-Cultural Perspective*, edited by Ellen Koskoff. Westport, CT: Greenwood Press, 1987.

———. "Miriam Sings Her Song: The Self and Other in Anthropological Discourse." Pp. 149–63 in *Musicology and Difference*, edited by Ruth Solie. Berkeley: University of California Press, 1993.

———. *Music in Lubavitcher Life*. Urbana: University of Illinois Press, 2000.

Kranzler, George. *Hasidic Williamsburg: A Contemporary American Hasidic Community*, 1st edition. Northvale, NJ: Jason Aronson, 1995.

Kuruvilla, Carol. "Meet the Queer Ex-Hasidic Woman Embracing Life outside Her Faith." *Huffington Post*, August 5, 2016: www.huffpost.com.

Kymlicka, Will. *Multicultural Citizenship*. Oxford: Oxford University Press, 1995.

Laestadius, Linnea. "Instagram." Pp. 573–92 in *The Sage Handbook of Social Media Research Methods*, edited by Luke Sloan and Anabel Quan-Haase. London: Sage Publications, 2016.

Lassiter, Luke Eric. "Collaborative Ethnography: Trends, Developments, and Opportunities." In *Transforming Ethnomusicology*, volume 1 of *Methodologies, Institutional Structures, and Policies*, edited by Beverly Diamond and Salwa El-Shawan Castelo-Branco. Oxford: Oxford University Press, 2021.

Lazreg, Marnia. "Decolonizing Feminism." Pp. 67–80 in *African Gender Studies: A Reader*, edited by Oyèrónké Oyěwùmí. New York: Palgrave Macmillan, 2005.

Leach, James, and Monika Stern. "The Value of Music in Melanesia: Creation, Circulation, and Transmission under Changing Economic and Intellectual Property Conditions." *HAL Open Science* (2020).

Lehrer, Erica. *Jewish Poland Revisited: Heritage Tourism in Unquiet Places*. Bloomington: Indiana University Press, 2013.

Leite, Naomi. *Unorthodox Kin: Portuguese Marranos and the Global Search for Belonging*. Los Angeles: University of California Press, 2017.

Levine, Stephanie Wellen, and Carol Gilligan. *Mystics, Mavericks, and Merrymakers: An Intimate Journey among Hasidic Girls*. New York: New York University Press, 2003.

Lieber, Andrea. "A Virtual *Veibershul*: Blogging and the Blurring of Public and Private among Orthodox Jewish Women." *College English* 72, no. 6 (2010): 621–37.

Lipman, Steve. "Melissa Weisz." *NY Jewish Week*, May 25, 2017: https://jewishweek.timesofisrael.com.

Lisek, Joanna. "'I Feel So Crazy, like Flying the Coop': The Lesser-Known Sarah Schenirer; Side Reflections on Naomi Seidman's Book." *Shofar* 38, no. 1 (2020): 272–90.

Livesey, Laetitia, et al. "Benefits of Choral Singing for Social and Mental Wellbeing: Qualitative Findings from a Cross-National Survey of Choir Members." *Journal of Public Mental Health* 11 (March 16, 2012): 10–26.

Lockwood, Jeremiah. "Prayer and Crime: Cantor Elias Zaludkovsky's Concert Performance Season in 1924 Poland." *In geveb*, May 22, 2022: https://ingeveb.org.

———. *Golden Ages: Hasidic Singers and Cantorial Revival in the Digital Era*. Berkeley: University of California Press, 2023.

———. "Hasidic Cantors 'out of Context': Venues of Contemporary Cantorial Performance." In *Handbook of Jewish Music*, edited by Tina Frühauf. Oxford: Oxford University Press, 2023.

Loy, Stephen, Julie Rickwood, and Samantha Bennett, eds. *Popular Music, Stars, and Stardom*. Canberra: Australian National University Press, 2018.

Lysloff, René T. A., and Leslie C. Gay Jr. *Music and Technoculture*. Middletown, CT: Wesleyan University Press, 2003.

Magowan, Fiona, and Karl Neuenfeldt. *Landscapes of Indigenous Performance: Music, Song, and Dance of the Torres Strait and Arnhem Land*. Canberra: Aboriginal Studies Press, 2005.

Mahmood, Saba. *Politics of Piety: The Islamic Revival and the Feminist Subject*. Revised edition. Princeton, NJ: Princeton University Press, 2011.

Malik, Sarita, Caroline Chapain, and Roberta Comunian. *Community Filmmaking: Diversity, Practices, and Places*. New York: Routledge, 2017.

Manekin, Rachel. *The Rebellion of the Daughters: Jewish Women Runaways in Habsburg Galicia*. Princeton, NJ: Princeton University Press, 2020.

Marcus, George E. "Ethnography in/of the World System: The Emergence of Multi-Sited Ethnography." *Annual Review of Anthropology* 24 (1995): 95–117.

Marcus, Sharon. *The Drama of Celebrity*. Princeton, NJ: Princeton University Press, 2019.

McDonald, Kevin, and Daniel Smith-Rowsey. *The Netflix Effect: Technology and Entertainment in the 21st Century*. New York: Bloomsbury Academic & Professional, 2016.

McLeod, Kembrew. "MP3s Are Killing Home Taping: The Rise of Internet Distribution and Its Challenge to the Major Label Music Monopoly." *Popular Music and Society* 28, no. 4 (2005).

McLeod, Kembrew, and Ted Striphas. "Strategic Improprieties: Cultural Studies, the Everyday, and the Politics of Intellectual Properties." *Cultural Studies* 20, no. 2 (March 2006).

McLucas, Anne Dhu. *The Musical Ear: Oral Tradition in the USA*. SEMPRE Studies in the Psychology of Music. Farnham, UK: Ashgate, 2010.

Mendieta, Eduardo, and Jonathan VanAntwerpen, eds. *The Power of Religion in the Public Sphere*. New York: Columbia University Press, 2011.

Messina-Dysert, Gina, Rosemary Radford Ruether, and Monica Coleman. *Feminism and Religion in the 21ˢᵗ Century: Technology, Dialogue, and Expanding Borders*. New York: Routledge, 2014.

Meyer, Birgit, and Annelies Moors, eds. *Religion, Media, and the Public Sphere.* Illustrated edition. Bloomington: Indiana University Press, 2005.

Meyers, Diana Tietjens. "Feminism and Women's Autonomy: The Challenge of Female Genital Cutting." *Metaphilosophy* 31, no. 5 (2000): 469–91.

Miller, Danny. "Interview: Writer/Director Maxime Giroux Explores Montreal's Hasidic Community in 'Félix and Meira.'" *Cinephiled*, 2015: www.cinephiled.com.

Milligan, Amy K. *Hair, Headwear, and Orthodox Jewish Women: Kallah's Choice.* London: Lexington Books, 2014.

Mintz, Jerome R. *Legends of the Hasidim: An Introduction to Hasidic Culture and Oral Tradition in the New World.* Chicago: University of Chicago Press, 1968.

Mishol-Shauli, Nakhi, and Oren Golan. "Mediatizing the Holy Community: Ultra-Orthodoxy Negotiation and Presentation on Public Social-Media." *Religions* 10, no. 7 (July 2019): 438–58.

———. "Smartphone Religious Networking: Negotiating Contested Identities within a Pious Community over WhatsApp." *Religions* 13, no. 11 (November 2022): 1034.

Mohanty, Chandra Talpade. *Feminism without Borders: Decolonizing Theory, Practicing Solidarity.* Durham, NC: Duke University Press, 2003.

Morris, Bonnie J. *Lubavitcher Women in America: Identity and Activism in the Postwar Era.* Albany: State University of New York Press, 1998.

Mosemghvdlishvili, Lela, and Jeroen Jansz. "Framing and Praising Allah on YouTube: Exploring User-Created Videos about Islam and the Motivations for Producing Them." *New Media & Society* 15, no. 4 (2012): 482–500.

Motyl, Katharina. "No Longer a Promised Land: The Arab and Muslim Experience in the U.S. after 9/11." Pp. 217–35 in *REAL: Yearbook of Research in English and American Literature*, vol. 27, edited by Winfried Fluck, Katharina Motyl, Donald E. Pease, and Christoph Raetzsch. Tuebingen, Germany: Narr Publisher, 2011.

Munro, Heather. "Navigating Change: Agency, Identity, and Embodiment in Haredi Women's Dance and Theater." *Shofar* 38, no. 2 (2020): 93–124.

Murcia, Cynthia Quiroga, et al. "Shall We Dance? An Exploration of the Perceived Benefits of Dancing on Well-Being." *Arts & Health* 2 (2010): 149–63.

Negt, Oskar, Alexander Kluge, and Peter Labanyi. "'The Public Sphere and Experience': Selections." *October* 46 (1988): 60–82.

Newfield, Schneur Zalman. *Degrees of Separation: Identity Formation while Leaving Ultra-Orthodox Judaism*, 1st edition. Philadelphia: Temple University Press, 2020.

Nongbri, Brent. *Before Religion: A History of a Modern Concept.* Reprint edition. New Haven, CT: Yale University Press, 2015.

Oakes, Tim, and Louisa Schein, eds. *Translocal China: Linkages, Identities, and the Reimagining of Space.* London: Routledge, 2006.

O'Neill, Jennifer R., et al. "Descriptive Epidemiology of Dance Participation in Adolescents." *Research Quarterly for Exercise and Sport* 82, no. 3 (2011): 373–80.

Orr, Zvika, Shifra Unger, and Adi Finkelstein. "Localization of Human Rights of People with Disabilities: The Case of Jewish Ultra-Orthodox People in Israel." *Human Rights Quarterly* 43, no. 1 (February 2021): 93–116.

O'Sullivan, Michael. "'Félix and Meira' Review: Two Lost Souls Seeking Love." *Washington Post*, May 21, 2015: www.washingtonpost.com.

Ozick, Rachel. "The Relationship between Religious Orientation, Superwoman Ideal, and Disordered Eating Pathology in Israeli Orthodox Adolescent Girls." Master's thesis, University of Haifa (Israel), 2012.

Perez, Sarah. "Instagram's Big Redesign Goes Live with a Colorful New Icon, Black-and-White App, and More." *TechCrunch,* May 11, 2016: https://techcrunch.com, accessed March 31, 2023.

Peterson, Christopher, and Martin E. P. Seligman. *Character Strengths and Virtues: A Handbook and Classification.* Oxford: Oxford University Press, 2004.

Poll, Solomon. *The Hasidic Community of Williamsburg: A Study in the Sociology of Religion.* Abingdon, UK: Routledge, 2017.

Qureshi, Regula Burkhardt. "Musical Sound and Contextual Input: A Performance Model for Musical Analysis." *Ethnomusicology* 31, no. 1 (Winter 1987): 56–86.

Radhika, Gajjala, and Annapurna Mamidipudi. "Cyberfeminism, Technology, and International 'Development.'" *Gender and Development* 7, no. 2 (1999): 8–16.

Ramji, Rubina. "From Navy Seals to *The Siege*: Getting to Know the Muslim Terrorist, Hollywood Style." *Journal of Religion and Film* 9, no. 2 (2005).

———. "Examining the Critical Role American Popular Film Continues to Play in Maintaining the Muslim Terrorist Image, Post 9/11." *Journal of Religion and Film* 20, no. 1 (2016).

Rasmussen, Anne. *Women, the Recited Qur'an, and Islamic Music in Indonesia.* Berkeley: University of California Press, 2010.

Raucher, Michal S. *Conceiving Agency: Reproductive Authority among Haredi Women.* Bloomington: Indiana University Press, 2020.

———. "Jewish Pronatalism: Policy and Praxis." *Religion Compass* 15, no. 7 (2021): 1–13.

Richards, P. Scott, et al. "Religiousness and Spirituality in the Etiology and Treatment of Eating Disorders." Pp. 319–33 in *APA Handbook of Psychology, Religion, and Spirituality,* vol. 2: *An Applied Psychology of Religion and Spirituality,* edited by K. I. Pargament, A. Mahoney, and E. P. Shafranske. Washington, DC: American Psychological Association, 2013.

Rocha, Carolina. "Jewish Cinematic Self-Representations in Contemporary Argentine and Brazilian Films." *Journal of Modern Jewish Studies* 9, no. 1 (March 1, 2010): 37–48.

Roda, Jessica. "Constructing Patrimony, Updating the Modern: Toward a Comprehensive Understanding of Sephardic Musical Experiences in France." Pp. 94–114 in *Music and Minorities: Research, Documentation, and Interdisciplinary Study of Minorities from around the World,* edited by Ursula Hemetek, Essica Marks, and Adelaida Reyes. Newcastle upon Tyne, UK: Cambridge Scholars Publishing, 2014.

———. *Se réinventer au présent. Les Judéo-espagnols de France; Famille, communauté et patrimoine musical.* Rennes, France: Presses universitaires de Rennes, 2018.

———. "Representation, Recognition, and Institutionalization of a New Community: Reflection on the Mediatization of the Ex-Ultra-Orthodox Jewish Life." In *Off the Derech: Orthodox Judaism in the Modern World,* edited by Ezra Cappell and Jessica Lang. Albany: State University of New York Press, 2020.

———. "Rethinking Orthodoxy from Its Margins: Growth, Functioning, and Challenges of an Underground Community of Ultra-Orthodox Jews." *Archives de sciences sociales des religions* 198, no. 2 (September 7, 2022): 52–82.

———. "Orthodox Women and the Musical Shekhinah: Performances, Technology, and the Artist in North America." In *Handbook of Jewish Music,* edited by Tina Fruhauf. Oxford: Oxford University Press, 2023.

Roda, Jessica, and Stephanie Tara Schwartz. "Home beyond Borders and the Sound of Al-Andalus: Jewishness in Arabic; The Odyssey of Samy Elmaghribi." *Religions* 11, no. 11 (November 2020): 609.

Roda, Jessica, and Alexandra Stankovich. "Netflix's 'My Unorthodox Life' Spurred Ultra-Orthodox Jewish Women to Talk Publicly about Their Lives." *Conversation,* September 7, 2021.

Rosilio, Mireille. *Declining the Stereotype: Ethnicity and Representation in French Cultures.* Lebanon, NH: Dartmouth College Press, 1998.

Rosman, Moshe. *Founder of Hasidism: A Quest for the Historical Ba'al Shem Tov.* Berkeley: University of California Press, 1996.

Rossman, Abraham, and Paula G. Rubel. *Translating Cultures: Perspectives on Translation and Anthropology.* Oxford: Berg, 2003.

Rutlinger-Reine, Reina. "'Drowning in the Marsh': Israeli Orthodox Theatrical Representations of the Singles Scene." *Israel Studies* 16, no. 3 (2011): 73–96.

———. "Crises in Orthodox Israeli Family Life Onstage." *Israel Studies Review* 28, no. 2 (2013): 83–101.

Salazkina, Masha, and Enrique Fibla-Gutiérrez. *Global Perspectives on Amateur Film Histories and Cultures.* Bloomington: Indiana University Press, 2020.

Satenstein, Liana. "*Off the Beaten Path*: After Leaving Orthodox Judaism, Women Forge a New Identity in the Secular World." *Vogue,* March 8, 2018: www.vogue.com.

Savitz, Jodie. "Ex-Hasidic Woman Embraces Her Queer Identity." Interview with Melissa "Malky" Weisz, *NBC News,* July 27, 2016: www.nbcnews.com.

Schickel, Richard. *Intimate Strangers: The Culture of Celebrity in America.* Chicago: Ivan R. Dee, 2000.

Schippers, Huib, and Catherine Grant, eds. *Sustainable Futures for Music Cultures: An Ecological Perspective.* New York: Oxford University Press, 2016.

Schupak, Esther B. "Ultra-Orthodox Jewish Women Performing Gender in *Julius Caesar.*" *Research in Drama Education: The Journal of Applied Theatre and Performance* 24, no. 2 (2019): 155–72.

Scott, Eric, writer and director, *Leaving the Fold,* Bunbury Films, 2008: www.bunburyfilms.com, accessed December 3, 2022.

Seidman, Naomi. "Legitimizing the Revolution: Sarah Schenirer and the Rhetoric of Torah Study for Girls." Pp. 356–65 in *New Directions in the History of the Jews in the Polish Lands,* edited by Antony Polonsky, Hanna Węgrzynek, and Andrzej Żbikowskip. Boston: Academic Studies Press, 2018.

———. *A Revolution in the Name of Tradition: Sarah Schenirer and Bais Yaakov.* Oxford: Oxford University Press, 2019.

Seidman, Naomi, Vichna Kaplan, Danielle S. Leibowitz, and Devora Gliksman. *Rebbetzin Vichna Kaplan: The Founder of the Bais Yaakov Movement in America.* New York: Feldheim Publishers, 2016.

Seigelshifer, Valeria, and Tova Hartman. "The Emergence of Israeli Orthodox Women Filmmakers." *Shofar: An Interdisciplinary Journal of Jewish Studies* 38, no. 2 (Summer 2020): 125–61.

Semmerling, Tim Jon. *"Evil" Arabs in American Popular Film: Orientalist Fear.* Chicago: University of Chicago Press, 2006.

Shandler, Jeffrey. "Sanctification of the Brand Name: The Marketing of Cantor Yossele Rosenblatt." Pp. 255–71 in *Chosen Capital: The Jewish Encounter with American Capitalism,* edited by Rebecca Kobrin. New Brunswick, NJ: Rutgers University Press, 2012.

Shelemay, Kay Kaufman. "The Impact and Ethics of Musical Scholarship." Pp. 531–44 in *Rethinking Music,* edited by Nicholas Cook and Mark Everist. Oxford: Oxford University Press, 1999.

———. "Musical Communities: Rethinking the Collective in Music." *Journal of the American Musicological Society* 64, no. 2 (2011): 349–90.

———. *Sing and Sing On: Sentinel Musicians and the Making of the Ethiopian American Diaspora.* Chicago: University of Chicago Press, 2022.

Shryock, Andrew, ed. *Off Stage/on Display: Intimacy and Ethnography in the Age of Public Culture*. Stanford, CA: Stanford University Press, 2004.

Shuman, Sam. "Cutting Out the Middleman: The Diamond Industry and the Politics of Displacement in a European Port City." PhD thesis University of Michigan, 2021.

Simonton, Dean Keith. "Creativity: Cognitive, Personal, Developmental, and Social Aspects." *American Psychologist* 55, no. 1 (2000): 151–58.

Skinazi, Karen E. H. *Women of Valor: Orthodox Jewish Troll Fighters, Crime Writers, and Rock Stars in Contemporary Literature and Culture*. New Brunswick, NJ: Rutgers University Press, 2018.

Skingley, Ann, and Hillary Bungay. "The Silver Song Club Project: A Sense of Well-Being through Participatory Singing." *Journal of Applied Arts and Health* 1, no. 2 (2010): 165–78.

Slobin, Mark. *Chosen Voices: The Story of the American Cantorate*. Urbana: University of Illinois Press, 1990.

———. "COVID-Era Online Collective Research Initiatives in Yiddish Traditional Music." *Ethnomusicology* 65, no. 3 (January 1, 2021): 630–33.

Smith, Michael Peter. "Translocality: A Critical Reflection." Pp. 181–98 in *Translocal Geographies: Spaces, Places*, edited by Katherine Brickell and Ayona Datta. Farnham, UK: Ashgate, 2011.

Solano, Jeanette Reedy. *Religion and Film: The Basics*. New York: Routledge, 2022.

Solomon, Alisa. *Wonder of Wonders: A Cultural History of "Fiddler on the Roof."* New York: Henry Holt, 2014.

Solomon, Rena. "When Weeping Is Not Enough." Letter included in "Powerful: Chaim Walder Abuse Victim Speaks Out in Open Letter to Community and Leaders." *Vos Iz Neias?*, January 31, 2022: https://vinnews.com, accessed February 7, 2022.

Stacey, Judith, and Susan E. Gerard. "'We Are Not Doormats': The Influence of Feminism on Contemporary Evangelicals in the United States." In *Uncertain Terms: Negotiating Gender in American Culture*, edited by F. Ginsberg and A. L. Tsing. Boston: Beacon Press, 1990.

Stadler, Nurit. *Yeshiva Fundamentalism: Piety, Gender, and Resistance in the Ultra-Orthodox World*. New York: New York University Press, 2009.

Stephens, Mitchell. *A History of News*. Oxford: Oxford University Press, 2006.

Stern, Rachel E. "Unpacking Adaptation: The Female Inheritance Movement in Hong Kong." *Mobilization* 10, no. 3 (October 1, 2005): 421–39.

Sterne, Jonathan. *The Audible Past: Cultural Origins of Sound Reproduction*. Durham, NC: Duke University Press, 2003.

Stokes, Martin. "Globalization and the Politics of World Music." Pp. 106–16 in *The Cultural Study of Music: A Critical Introduction*, edited by Trevor Herbert Clayton and Richard Middleton. New York: Routledge, 2012.

———. "Creativity, Globalization, and Music." *Volume! La Revue des Musiques Populaires* 10, no. 2 (June 10, 2014): 30–45.

Stolow, Jeremy. *Orthodox by Design: Judaism, Print Politics, and the ArtScroll Revolution*. Berkeley: University of California Press, 2010.

———, ed. *Deus in Machina: Religion, Technology, and the Things in Between*. Illustrated edition. New York: Fordham University Press, 2012.

Stolzenberg, Nomi M., and David N. Myers. *American Shtetl: The Making of Kiryas Joel, a Hasidic Village in Upstate New York*. Princeton, NJ: Princeton University Press, 2022.

Strathern, Marilyn. "An Awkward Relationship: The Case of Feminism and Anthropology." *Signs* 12, no. 2 (1987): 276–92.

Suskin, Gail, and Michal Al-Yagon, "Culturally Sensitive Dance Movement Therapy for Ultra-Orthodox Women: Group Protocol Targeting Bodily and Psychological Self-Perceptions." *Arts in Psychotherapy* 71 (2020): 1–10.

Taragin-Zeller, Lea. "Modesty for Heaven's Sake: Authority and Creativity among Female Ultra-Orthodox Teenagers in Israel." *Nashim: A Journal of Jewish Women's Studies & Gender Issues*, no. 26 (Spring 2014): 75–96.

———. "Between Modesty and Beauty: Reinterpreting Female Piety in the Israeli Haredi Community." In *Love, Marriage, and Jewish Families: Paradoxes of a Social Revolution*, edited by Sylvia Barack Fishman. Waltham, MA: Brandeis University Press, 2015.

Taragin-Zeller, Lea, and Ben Kasstan. "'I Didn't Know How to Be with My Husband': State-Religion Struggles over Sex Education in Israel and England." *Anthropology & Education Quarterly* 52, no. 1 (2021): 5–20.

Tarlo, Emma. "Great Expectations: The Role of the Wig Stylist (Sheitel Macher) in Orthodox Jewish Salons." *Fashion Theory* 22, no. 6 (November 2, 2018): 569–91.

Taylor, Ella. "Two Unmoored Souls Too Gloomily Drawn in 'Felix and Meira.'" *NPR*, April 16, 2015: www.npr.org.

Taylor, Jodie. "The Intimate Insider: Negotiating the Ethics of Friendship When Doing Insider Research." *Qualitative Research* 11, no. 1 (February 1, 2011): 3–22.

Tillmann-Healy, Lisa M. "Friendship as Method." *Qualitative Inquiry* 9, no. 5 (October 1, 2003): 729–49.

Todne, Thomas, Asiya Malik, and Rose Wellman, eds. *New Directions in Spiritual Kinship: Sacred Ties across the Abrahamic Religions*. Reprint edition. London: Palgrave Macmillan, 2018.

Toynbee, Jason. *Migrating Music*. London: Routledge, 2012.

———. *Making Popular Music: Musicians, Creativity, and Institution*. London: Arnold, 2000.

Trappler Spielman, Sara. "Orthodox Women Are Making Films for Female Audiences: Are They Good Enough for the Secular World?" *Tablet Magazine*, May 30, 2012.

Tsing, Anna Lowenhaupt. *Friction: An Ethnography of Global Connection*. Princeton, NJ: Princeton University Press, 2005.

Turino, Thomas. *Music as Social Life: The Politics of Participation*. Chicago: University of Chicago Press, 2008.

Turner, Graeme. *Understanding Celebrity*. London: Sage, 2004.

Vaisman, Esther-Basya (Asya). "'She Who Seeks Shall Find': The Role of Song in a Hasidic Woman's Life Cycle." *Journal of Synagogue Music* 35 (2010): 155–83.

———. "Seamed Stockings and Ponytails: Conducting Ethnographic Fieldwork in a Contemporary Hasidic Community." Pp. 282–99 in *Going to the People: Jews and the Ethnographic Impulse*, edited by Jeffrey Veidlinger. Bloomington: Indiana University Press, 2016.

Van der Geest, Sjaak. "Friendship and Fieldwork: A Retrospect as 'Foreword.'" *Curare* 38 (2015): 3–8.

Vinig, Marlyn. *Haredi Cinema*. Tel Aviv: Resling, 2011. [Hebrew]

Vizel, Frieda. "A List of Hasidic Female Headgear, with Illustrations." Tours by Frieda, May 27, 2014: https://friedavizel.com.

———. "Book Review: 'Unorthodox' by Deborah Feldman." Tours by Frieda, March 26, 2020: https://friedavizel.com.

Wagner, Rachel. *Godwired: Religion, Ritual, and Virtual Reality*. New York: Routledge, 2011.

Waldman, Rose. "Women's Voices in Contemporary Hasidic Communities." *Shofar: An Interdisciplinary Journal of Jewish Studies* 28, no. 2 (2020): 35–60.

Waldoks, Tanya Zion. "Religious Feminism(s) and Beyond: Reflections on Politics of Change and Knowledge Production." *Religion and Gender* 11 (June 23, 2021): 137–43.

Wallach, Jeremy. "Underground Rock Music and Democratization in Indonesia." *World Literature Today* 79, no. 3–4 (2005): 16–20.

Warner, Michael. "Publics and Counterpublics." *Public Culture* 14, no. 1 (2002): 49–90.

Weinblatt, Keren Tenenboim, and Oren Livio. "Discursive Legitimation of a Controversial Technology: Ultra-Orthodox Jewish Women in Israel and the Internet." *Communication Review* 10, no. 1 (2007): 29–56.

Weissman, Deborah. "Bais Ya'acov: A Historical Model for Jewish Feminists." In *The Jewish Woman: New Perspectives*, edited by Elizabeth Koltun. New York: Schocken Books, 1976.

Weston, Kath. *Families We Choose: Lesbians, Gays, Kinship*. Revised edition. New York: Columbia University Press, 1997.

Widdows, Heather. *Perfect Me: Beauty as an Ethical Ideal*. Princeton, NJ: Princeton University Press, 2018.

Wiegman, Robyn. "Race, Ethnicity, and Film." P. 134 in *The Oxford Guide to Film Studies*, edited by John Hill and Pamela Church Gibson. Oxford: Oxford University Press, 1998.

Williams, Elyse, Genevieve A. Dingle, and Stephen Clift. "A Systematic Review of Mental Health and Wellbeing Outcomes of Group Singing for Adults with a Mental Health Condition." *European Journal of Public Health* 28, no. 6 (December 1, 2018): 1035–42.

Winston, Hella. *Unchosen: The Hidden Lives of Hasidic Rebels*. Boston: Beacon Press, 2006.

Wodziński, Marcin. *Historical Atlas of Hasidism*. Princeton, NJ: Princeton University Press, 2018.

Wolfe, Paula. *Women in the Studio: Creativity, Control, and Gender in Popular Music Production*. Abingdon, UK: Routledge, 2020.

Wood, Abigail. "Stepping across the Divide: Hasidic Music in Today's Yiddish Canon." *Ethnomusicology* 51, no. 2 (2007): 205–37.

Wright, Melanie J. "Judaism." In *The Routledge Companion to Religion and Film*, edited by John Lyden. New York: Routledge, 2009.

Wright, Thomas A., and André P. Walton. "Affect, Psychological Wellbeing, and Creativity: Results of a Field Study." *Journal of Business and Management* 9, no. 1 (2003): 21–32.

Yafeh, Orit. "The Time in the Body: Cultural Construction of Femininity in Ultraorthodox Kindergartens for Girls." *Ethos* 35, no. 4 (2007): 516–53.

Yeğenoğlu, Meyda. *Colonial Fantasies: Toward a Feminist Reading of Orientalism*. Cambridge Cultural Social Studies. Cambridge: Cambridge University Press, 1998.

Yu, Sabrina Qiong. "Introduction: Performing Stardom; Star Studies in Transformation and Expansion." In *Revisiting Star Studies: Cultures, Themes, and Methods*, edited by Sabrina Qiong Yu and Guy Austin. Edinburgh: Edinburgh University Press, 2017.

Zion Waldoks, Tanya. "Religious Feminism(s) and Beyond: Reflections on Politics of Change and Knowledge Production." *Religion and Gender* 11 (June 23, 2021): 137–43.

———. "Birth of a Movement: Narratives of the Haredi Feminist Emergence in Israel." *Israel Studies* 28, no. 1 (2023): 70–89.

Zwingel, Susan. "How Do Norms Travel? Theorizing International Women's Rights in Transnational Perspective." *International Studies Quarterly* 56, no. 1 (2012): 115–29.

INDEX

Note: Page numbers in italic type indicate illustrations.

Abrams, Nathan, 190–91
Abu-Lughod, Lila, 35
abuse, 25, 55, 141, 194, 199, 216–18, 220
Aderet, 112, 120, 268n29
Adler, Amber, 143
Adler, Lea, 161
advertising: celebrities' use of, 101, 107, 112, 114, 123, 135, 139; Hasidism portrayed in mainstream, 218; images apparent in/absent from, 7, 9, 101, 107, 109, 123, 152, 159; influencers' use of, 152, 153, 156, 175; privacy balanced against desire for, 56, 62; private performers' use of, 78–79, 94; in ultra-Orthodox media, 7, 9, 70, 76, 79, 80, 109, 112, 132; "for women and girls only," 9, 12, 110
The Advocate (newspaper), 227
agency: the arts as source of, 6, 20, 73; feminist conceptions of, 61; of *frum* women, 5, 18, 20, 33–35, 37, 40, 178–79; of Hasidic public artists, 189; home studios and, 82–83; married women and, 73; of women, 40, 41. *See also* empowerment
agents of distribution, 86
agunot (women unable to get divorces from husbands), 140–43, 165
Aish, 223
Amazon Prime, 193
Ami Living (magazine), 98, 270n5
Anastasia (musical), 54
Ani Homa (play), 64
Anneberg, Eve, 197–98, 201, 204
Antelis, Shaindel, 10, 111, 251
anthropology. *See* ethnography
Archambault-Soleil, Julie, 74
Arditi, David, 92
arranged marriages. See *shiddukhim*
arts: agency cultivated through, 6, 20, 73; in the digital age, 6, 19; education in, 47, 49–50, 53, 58, 66–67, 116; for their own sake, 62, 95–96, 101, 118, 139, 223, 263n8; *frum* women and,

6, 9, 15, 46, 260n1; health and well-being benefits of, 71–74, 76–81; married women and, 49, 54; opportunities and possibilities offered by, 14, 19; OTD women and, 5–6; *parnasse* derived from, 36, 39, 42, 58, 61, 68, 70, 77, 80, 93; social and educational framing of, 43, 49–50, 53, 59, 62, 77–78, 87, 92, 95–96, 101, 223; *tsnius* and, 7--9, 53. *See also* creativity; dance; *frum* female art worlds; kosher entertainment industry; music; theater/performances
art worlds. *See frum* female art worlds
Asad, Talal, 21
Asch, Sholem, *Got Fun Nekome (God of Vengeance)*, 185–86, *186*, 205, 216
authenticity/legitimacy, of mainstream media's portrayals of ultra-Orthodoxy, 39, 188–90, 192–93, 195, 199, 202, 208, 210, 232, 273n10

baalei tshuva (non-Orthodox Jews who have become ultra-Orthodox), 21, 31, 32, 67, 71–72, 76, 104, 111, 134
Bachar, Shai, 111, 122
Bais Yaakov (House of Jacob) movement, 48–50
Balebusta (magazine), 57–58, 78, 81, 96, 98
bands, 68–70, *68*
Bateson, Gregory, 230
Baum, Dobby, 10, 54, 112, 122, 154–56, 159, 174–79, 182, 183, 250, 267n23; *The Dobby Show*, 155, 175, *176*; Instagram posts, *155*; *Rejuvenate*, 155
Baum, Frimi, 122
Becker, Howard, 13, 42, 60, 257n9
Bennett, Mirel, 114
Beresford, Bruce, 190
Berge, Ola, 92
Berlin Jewish Film Festival, 198
Bhabha, Homi, 274n40
Bial, Henry, 222, 273n10
binary distinctions, 14, 35, 61
Blatt, Mindy, 123

Kasstan, Ben, 23
Kessler, Mira, *186*
Khader, Serene J., 167, 177, 262n1
Khol Hamoed screenings, 129, 135
Kieffer, Kira Ganga, 149
Kinireth, 123
kinship. *See* sisterhood/kinship
Kirschner, Yehuda, 120
Kiryas Joel (KJ), New York, 57–59, 68–69, 78, 96, 136
Kluge, Alexander, 258n18
Kogan, Chaya, 113, 252
kol isha ("a woman's voice"): artistic activity governed by norms of, 53, 95, 102, 108, 119, 134–37, 150–51, 156; concept of, 45; home studios and, 82; informal market and, 62; interpretations of, 74, 112; kosher entertainment industry and, 99; restrictions on men and boys from, 25, 45–46, 100, 257n4, 261n16; transnational distribution of art and, 87. *See also* "for women and girls only"; gender segregation; *tsnius*
kol isha industry: accommodations, challenges, and transformations regarding ultra-Orthodox norms, 98–111, 118, 128–29, 134–39; and celebrity culture, 101–2, 118, 124; community building in, 137–39; controversies over, 100; features and goals of, 101; filmmakers in, 124–34; formation of, 96, 99–100, 103–5; and kosher entertainment industry, 102–6; publicity in, 101–2, 107, 109, 113–14, 123–24, 134–37; singers in, 111–16; studio owners in, 116–24
kosher arts, 58, 77
kosher entertainment industry, 12–13, 39, 77, 89, 99, 102–6, 118, 120, 137, 175
Koskoff, Ellen, 53
Kosman, Franciska, 10, 54, 111
kumzits (musical gatherings), 51, 74–75, 80

Labanyi, Peter, 258n18
Laferrière, Alexandre, 3–4, 199
Leah, Rochel, 118, 132
legitimacy, of *frum* female artists' activity, 9, 73, 75, 109, 129, 167, 182–83. *See also* authenticity/legitimacy, of mainstream media's portrayals of ultra-Orthodoxy
Lehrer, Erica, 222, 259n52
Lelio, Sebastian, 200
Lenchevsky, Esther, 161
Levine, Baruch, 107–8
LGBTQ individuals, 163, 164, 196, 199, 202, 225–27

Lincoln Center, New York, 198
Litvish/Yeshivish Judaism, 21–22, 52, 159, 200, 262n42
"Live Higher" rally, 236–37
Lohud (newspaper), 171
Loshn Koydesh, 52, 69, 262n42
love stories, 54
Lubavitch community, 42, 52, 53, 146, 151, 158, 159. *See also* Chabad-Lubavitch community
lyrics, 88–89

Ma'aleh School of Film and Television, 128
Mahmood, Saba, 18, 171
mainstream media, stereotypes in, 168, 191, 199–202, 212
Malkin, Rhonda, 111, 114
Malky Squared Productions, 202–10, 214
Mandelbaum David, 216, 218
Manekin, Rachel, 47
Marcus, Aaron, 48
Marcus, George E., 24
Margules, Raphael, 208
married women: agency of, 73; and the arts, 49, 54, 67, 70, 71. *See also* divorce; *get* refusal; *shiddukhim*
Martini, Michele, 178
Marty, M., 182
matchmaking. See *shiddukhim*
McAdams, Rachel, 200
McLucas, Anne Dhu, 89
media. *See* mainstream media; online media; ultra-Orthodox media
melodica, 123
melodies, 2, 51, 66, 88–89. *See also* composers
men: anti-Internet rally of, 147; *frum* female artists' work with or use of material by, 12, 52, 54, 89, 92, 99–100, 104, 108, 112, 116, 118–22, 124; *frum* girls' portrayal of, 65; in kosher entertainment industry, 13, 19, 32, 36, 41, 52, 54, 58, 77, 89–92, 137; responsibility of, to respect "for women and girls only," 9, 12, 46, 108, 113, 162, 235; roles of ultra-Orthodox, 6, 16, 36; singing practices of, 46–47, 66; support of women's artistic activity by, 18, 22, 83, 102, 112, 137, 176, 196, 233. *See also* gender inequality; gender segregation
Merry, Sally Engle, 24
Miami Boys Choir, 58, 119
middle class, 77, 136, 138, 269n53
Miles-Sash, Adina (FlatbushGirl), 140, 143, 161–67, *161*, *164*, 169–70, 178–79, 182, 271n32

ABOUT THE AUTHOR

JESSICA RODA is Assistant Professor of Jewish Civilization at the Edmund A. Walsh School of Foreign Service at Georgetown University. She is the author of *Se réinventer au present*, which was a finalist for the J.I. Segal Jewish Book Award in 2020.